Archaeological Perspectives on the
Battle of the Little Bighorn

ARCHAEOLOGICAL PERSPECTIVES ON THE BATTLE OF THE LITTLE BIGHORN

By
Douglas D. Scott
Richard A. Fox, Jr.
Melissa A. Connor
and
Dick Harmon

With Contributions by
John R. Bozell
John Fitzpatrick
C. Vance Haynes, Jr.
Ralph Heinz
Patrick Phillips
and
Clyde Collins Snow

UNIVERSITY OF OKLAHOMA PRESS : NORMAN AND LONDON

Also by Douglas D. Scott and Richard A. Fox, Jr. (with a Contribution by Dick Harmon)
Archaeological Insights into the Custer Battle: An Assessment of the 1984 Field Season

Library of Congress Cataloging-in-Publication Data

Archaeological perspectives on the battle of the Little
  Bighorn
  Bibliography: p.
  Includes index.
  1. Little Big Horn, Battle of the, 1876. 2. Custer
Battlefield National Monument (Mont.)—Antiquities.
3. Indians of North America—Montana—Antiquities.
4. Montana—Antiquities. I. Scott, Douglas D.
E83.876.A73 1989   973.8'2   88-40547
ISBN 0-8061-2179-3 (alk. paper)

Contents

Illustrations

Tables

Preface

Authors frequently express their sentiments and convictions in their books and articles, and few events have elicited such expressions as has the Battle of the Little Bighorn. Myth and legend, enigma and mystery, or tragedy and disaster are words common to the Custeriana lexicon, both in title and text. Indeed, what has come to be known as the Little Bighorn fight has entered the realm of American myth and legend. There is also little doubt that the fight highlights the tragic outcome of hostile relationships between two cultures. On June 25, 1876, the Seventh U.S. Cavalry led by Lieutenant Colonel George Armstrong Custer engaged the Sioux and their allies on the Little Bighorn River in what is now south-central Montana. The cavalry suffered a decisive loss. Heated debates over what happened began virtually as the gunsmoke wafted from the field, and they have raged ever since. Today, Custer Battlefield National Monument, which comprises only part of the field over which the battle was played out, commemorates the struggle. The monument is now a federal property administered by the National Park Service. Hundreds of thousands of people visit it each year, and their interest underscores the prominence of this episode in American history.

Some say that no other American battle has caused more ink to flow than the Little Bighorn fight; in fact, there are frequent observations that the literary obsession far exceeds the fight's historical import. Indeed, historians and Custer buffs have penned hundreds of volumes many of which contain provocative ideas that have helped to guide the battlefield's archaeological research strategies. The strategies and the results of their application to the Custer and Reno-Benteen battles are the subject of this study. But this is a new kind of story about the Little Bighorn fight. It is about history but it is not a history. Our centerpiece remains the celebrated fight, but our showcase is historical archaeology, a unique science that shares a common goal with history: understanding the past.

DOUGLAS D. SCOTT
RICHARD A. FOX, JR.
MELISSA A. CONNER
DICK HARMON

Lincoln, Nebraska

Acknowledgments

Every project involves many people. This project has had more than its fair share of those who have given their time, resources, and knowledge without thought of compensation. To all who have helped us we owe a debt of gratitude we can never repay.

We wish to thank everyone who has helped us, and we apologize if inadvertently we have overlooked anyone. Listed below are the primary organizations and people to whom we owe thanks.

The Custer Battlefield Historical and Museum Association provided most of the funds for the project. Shirley Coates, the association's business manager, deserves special thanks for patiently handling our requests and those of the volunteer crew. Former Superintendent Jim Court, former park Historian Neil Mangum, maintenance supervisors Cliff Arborgast and Bill Hartung, and the staff of the monument provided logistical support and were very patient with us while we disrupted their daily routine for ten weeks. All of the staff provided us with moral support during the project, and Dan Martinez and Caroline Bernaski volunteered on their days off.

White Metal Detectors and Fisher Metal Detectors provided us with equipment and personnel to guide us in the inventory phase of the project.

F. A. Calabrese, chief of the Midwest Archeological Center, National Park Service, provided logistical, financial, and moral support for the project, and many center staff members helped us in various ways. Carroll Moxham, Debbie McBride, Nancy Hartman, and Steve Baumann did the illustrations. Pat Phillips cleaned and sorted the artifacts before the analysis.

The 1985 fieldwork was conducted through a joint effort of the National Park Service and the University of Nebraska–Lincoln. Dr. Peter Bleed was most helpful in his role of UNL supervisor.

Dr. Warren Caldwell of the University of Nebraska and Charles Elias of Little Rock, Arkansas, shared their expansive knowledge of firearms and ammunition.

Ben Shaw of IBM, Lincoln, introduced us to the computer-assisted mapping program Fastdraft, and Larry Shaw and Dave Eberspacher of Southeast Community College in Milford, Nebraska, kindly allowed us access to the computer to produce the artifact-distribution map. Esley Kotschwar and Mark Bohaty of the Nebraska State Patrol Criminalistic Laboratory introduced us to the mysteries of firearms identification and taught us the intricacies of cartridge and bullet idendification.

Dr. Clyde Snow of Norman, Oklahoma, a consulting forensic anthropologist, volunteered to study the human remains recovered from the battlefield. Lanny Wisch of Lincoln volunteered to take the radiographs, and Dr. John Fitzpatrick of Cook County Hospital, Chicago, analyzed them. Rob Bozell of the Nebraska State Historical Society analyzed the nonhuman bone. Dr. C. Vance Haynes, Jr., of the University of Arizona conducted the geomorphological investigations of Deep Ravine, and Montana artist and Indian Wars cavalry-equipment collector Ralph Heinz identified and interpreted the horse-related equipment.

Walt Egged of Hardin, Montana, surveyed the battlefield in the 100-meter grid system. Without the grid and Walt's superb work, our task of accurately recording the locations of individual artifacts would have been extremely difficult.

The sketches that illustrate this report were made by Kris Harmon of Lincoln, Nebraska. Her contributions are gratefully acknowledged.

Drafts of the report were reviewed and commented on by several individuals: Dennis Dittmanson and Neil Mangum of Custer Battlefield National Monument, Adrienne Anderson and Ann Johnson of the Rocky Mountain Regional Office; and Paul Hedren, Richard Fike, Larry Babbits, Robert Bray, Edwin Bearss, Jerome A. Greene, Jim Hutchins, and Don Rickey. All of these historians and archaeologists provided us with very useful comments and criticisms, which we have incorporated into the report. Any remaining errors are, of course, our responsibility.

Last but not least, we wish to extend our most sincere thanks and appreciation to the ninety-four individuals, and the young ladies from the Sheridan Girls School, who volunteered to assist us in the fieldwork. These people volunteered more than five thousand hours of their time with no thought of recompense. We had the good fortune to work with many dedicated, enthusiastic, and knowledgeable people, and we gained much from the experience.

To all those who have aided us in this endeavor we extend our most sincere thanks and appreciation, but to those special "ninety-four" we respectfully dedicate this volume:

Bob Armao	Jack Columbus	J. C. Fleming
Warren Barnard	Joy Connor	Phil Frey
Derek Batten	John Craig	Dave Fouts
John Best	R. W. Davis	Val Gass
Don Bohna	Gene Dum	Lee Graves
Lucille Bowen	Kermit Edmonds	Bud Guthrie
Greg Brondos	Laura Fike	Ward Guthrie
Greg Brondos, Jr.	Opal Fike	Nancy Hamblin
Allan Burns	Rich Fike	Ken Harless
Dave Clements	Ronald Fike	Dick Harmon

Pat Harmon
Stanley Hart
Don Hefferman
Al Herem
Marlin Howe
John Husk
Ted Iverson
Donnie Sue Johnson
Robert Johnson
Jo Johnson-Ballard
Dean Kenney
Don King
Kermit Konzen
Mike Kloberdanz
Murray Kloberdanz
Jim Lafollette
Don Larson
Larry Larson
Irwin Lee
Riva Lee
Larry Lee
Dawn Lee

Fred Lillibridge
Otha Lines
Wilma Lines
Roye Lindsay
Cait Little
Lewis Malm
Dan Martinez
Farrell McCarthy
Wilma McCarthy
Milo McLeod
Kay Modgling
Tom Modgling
Buck Newbury
Ron Nichols
Dean O'Connor
Terry Osborn
Mike Parks
Pat Phillips
Brian Pohanka
John Pradere
Judith Pradere
Craig Repass

Lois Repass
Bill Sands
Jess Schwidde
Jay Scott
Ed Smyth
Don Sweet
Irene Switajewski
Tom Switajewski
Tom Switajewski, Jr.
Jim Thorpen
Georgia Thrower
Rex Thrower
Vernel Wagner
Betty Weeks
Juana Wilson
Colleen Winchell
Barbara Ulmanis
Ron Yuhas
Mike Zirpoli
Art Zody

Archaeological Perspectives on the
Battle of the Little Bighorn

PART ONE

BACKGROUND

Chapter 1

Introduction

If it can be said that history turns pages, then archaeology turns the ground. Historical archaeology, as the name implies, does both. Records and documents are essential ingredients in historical archaeology but no more so than the knowledge gleaned from artifacts left behind by historical personages. Thus historical archaeologists weave the strands of history with clues painstakingly sifted from the earth to form a fabric unlike that attainable through history or archaeology alone.

How is this fabric woven and what is the role of historical archaeology? An analogy may suffice. In solving a crime, police rely upon two disparate classes of evidence. Witness testimony is important but so are clues provided by the physical evidence of a crime. Detectives interview witnesses while other investigators gather fingerprints, blood samples and other physical evidence, the latter addressing different types of evidence by using unique methods. Working together the two types of investigators form a partnership that enhances the likelihood of solving the crime.

The records and documents that historical archaeologists utilize, especially firsthand accounts of historical events, are tantamount to eyewitness testimony. They provide the material for generating hypotheses that can be tested in the archaeological record. They also furnish the basis by which archaeologically observed patterns can be assigned historically meaningful identities. The archaeological record contains historical clues in the form of physical remains, including artifacts, and their contextual relationships. These relationships, which include distributions and spatial associations of various types of artifacts, can tell us a great deal about the activities that were carried out at a site. The historical archaeologist continually compares both sets of data as work progresses in order to explain better eventually the events under scrutiny. Sometimes history and archaeology may be at odds, necessitating, on occasion, significant revisions in current perceptions of historical events. Thus historical archaeology provides important mutual checks and balances between two data sets allowing more complete approaches to understanding historical events and the cultural milieu within which they transpired.

The basic tenet upon which anthropology and archaeology rest is straightforward. Human behavior is patterned. The residue of that behavior should also be patterned and reflect in varying degrees details of that behavior. Battlefields may seem an unlikely place to look for human behavioral patterns, since they represent the most violent expressions of human behavior, but it is precisely for that reason that behavioral patterns are likely to be evident. Warfare has special rules by which it is practiced. Within our own culture this may be seen in the preparation and training given members of the military. This training is given, and such was true in 1876, in order that those engaged in battle would perform their duties based on their training and respond to orders without dwelling on the consequences (Dyer 1985). That is patterned behavior. While the warriors of the Sioux and Cheyennes did not have the same training or respond to orders in the same manner as the soldiers, they nevertheless had a culturally established warfare behavior pattern.

The archaeological tenet argues that artifacts will occur in recognizable and interpretable patterns. Battlefields provide a unique opportunity to study the material by-products of human conflict. Gould (1983:105–7) argues that artifacts are signatures of particular kinds of behavior and that behavior can be identified if the signatures' relationships are studied. Gould (1983:105) further argues that these materials must be viewed as another form of documents to be understood and interpreted.

Beyond the ability of historical archaeology to provide additional details about historical events is its capability to "identify specific relationships between certain kinds of behavior under the stress of war and the characteristic material by-products of that behavior in their final (archaeological) context of discard" (Gould 1983:134). The means to understanding behavioral relationships in the archaeological record is pattern analysis.

Pattern analysis is almost as old as archaeology. Patterns are the way in which artifacts are found in the ground and the relationship of an artifact or a group of artifacts with other items—context and provenience. South (1977) and Lewis (1984) have brought these points out most forcefully. By way of example, a group of cut nails recovered in association with a structural foundation can provide the archaeologist and historical architect with an idea of what kind of structure once stood on the site. Certain sizes of nails were used by carpenters to erect framing, others for siding, lathing, and finish work. These nails provide clues as to how a building was constructed. Other artifacts are evidence of the location of doors and windows and even what type of doors and windows were in use. Even more important are the artifacts of daily life. Food refuse, food service, lighting, clothing, and personal items all reveal something of the personal habits of those who dwelled in the structure, the structure's function, the social and economic status of the inhabitants, and how those people viewed their own role and importance within their society. The analysis of the artifacts recovered in an archaeological investigation can take a myriad of forms. It can be simple inductive reasoning or it can be hypothetical and deductive. The process we follow is the deductive approach based on the development of research questions that guide the recovery of information and the analysis of the data. It is with these conceptual tools that we developed the archaeological investigations of Custer Battlefield National Monument.

Historical archaeology at the monument is not new, but by no means have such investigations been frequent. In the early 1940s, monument Superintendent Edward Luce (King 1980), recognizing the potential of historical archaeology, called for excavations at the Custer battlefield but world events and other management priorities took precedent. In 1958, archaeologist Robert Bray and Don Rickey, then Custer Battlefield National Monument historian, began work at the Reno-Benteen defense site (Bray 1958), where remaining elements of the Seventh Cavalry, having separated from Custer's command early in the fight, successfully defended their embattled position for nearly two days before relief arrived. Custer's subordinate officers, Major Marcus Reno and Captain Fredrick Benteen, commanded these units.

Bray and Rickey succeeded in locating defensive entrenchments, several soldier burials, and scatters of military hardware. Using these data and historical accounts, they were able to postulate the locations of defense perimeters and company positions within the Reno-Benteen defensive area. Their pioneering efforts were useful in developing our analysis of the Reno-Benteen battle.

The opportunity for our archaeological investigation of the battlefield occurred in 1983 after an accidental grass fire exposed the Custer battlefield surface, which for nearly three-quarters of a century had been obscured by thick vegetation. The fire laid bare the site on which Custer and his entire command died, exposing many artifacts from the fight. In 1983 the research was confined to the Custer battlefield area. The freshly exposed surface provided an opportunity to assess the kinds and numbers of extant battle-related artifacts and determine their potential for enhancing the knowledge of the Custer battle. Jim Court, then monument superintendent and Neil Mangum, monument historian, collaborated with one of the authors (Fox 1983) in formulating several research questions. These developed primarily from a desire on the part of monument officials to improve interpretive capabilities for the public. One of the most perplexing interpretive problems has long been the issue of where the battle participants took up positions and exactly how they moved about the field. Another centered on the mysterious disappearance of twenty-eight soldiers. Historical accounts indicate these men were found and buried in a rugged ravine on the battlefield, but they have never been fully accounted for. Shortly after the fight Custer's dead were buried on the field where each was found, and presumably where each fell. The marble markers were placed many years later at suspected burial sites. Today there are 252 markers on a field where about 210 army personnel died. This and other discrepancies, which are detailed later in the historical overview, have raised concerns that many markers are erroneously placed.

Therefore, in light of these questions we wished to know whether relevant data existed that could help in determining (1) the positions and movements of combatants, (2) the disposition of the twenty-eight missing soldiers, and (3) whether correlations between marble memorial markers, which now dot the battlefield and purportedly mark where soldiers fell in battle, and actual burial locations could be established.

Guided by these research questions, Fox conducted a reconnaissance survey of portions of the Custer battlefield after the August 1983 fire. He found a variety of artifact types, including human remains, cartridge cases, and buttons. Fox (1983, 1984) reported the likelihood that sufficient data remained at the site for detailed studies of the kind outlined above, and he provided recommendations for continuing research. From these reports and other documents, a comprehensive historical archaeology program was formulated and implemented in 1984 and 1985 (Scott 1984, 1985). The authors (Scott, Fox, and Connor) conceived the program and directed the investigation in 1984 and were joined by Harmon in 1985. The work was confined to the Custer battlefield in 1984, and in 1985 it concentrated on the Reno-Benteen defense site while work at the Custer site continued. This study integrates the results of the 1983–85 research. We were unable to study those portions of the battle which occurred on privately owned land, but, as we show later, our work at the two battlefields has important implications for research on the entire field of battle.

THE RESEARCH OBJECTIVES

For the past one hundred–plus years, Little Bighorn studies have taken nearly every twist and angle imaginable. Character flaws, personality conflicts, poor tactics, inadequate armament, disobedience, cowardly actions, alcohol, and glory have all figured in the debates over what happened. Sometimes these debates are reduced to minutiae, but the myriad of topics can be shuffled, as Utley (1980) has done, into four general categories: (1) Was Custer a fool or hero? (2) Did Custer disobey orders? (3) Were Major Reno's actions or inactions responsible for Custer's demise? and (4) What happened on the battlefield? The first three categories, in which arguments are so often tainted by blind allegiances, are mercifully beyond the realm of historical archaeology. However, the issues surrounding the nature of events during the Little Bighorn fight fall squarely into the analytical domain of historical archaeology. The goal is to investigate the events of the Little Bighorn fight as they are represented by the archaeological record at the Custer and Reno-Benteen battlefields.

The historical issues surrounding the events of the Little Bighorn fight have provided direction in the research. In this regard the major goal is to understand battle events. The specific research objectives, on the other hand, are shaped by the realization that there exists a behavioral relationship between historical events and the physical remains of events. Therefore, behavior on the battlefield can be understood by exposing these relationships and evaluating them in historical context. The research objectives are designed to do this and they are varied.

Armament, Weapon Types, and Numbers

The first objective is to analyze the nature of armaments used at the fight. History, of course, documents the weapons the troopers used. But the Indians may have been better equipped and could have had more firepower than supposed. Resolution of Indian firepower requires understanding the variety and number of weapons in the hands of the Indians. Modern firearm identification analysis, such as that used in crime labs, provides the key. Using these procedures, we identify firearm types by identifying ammunition calibers, distinguishing marks on cartridge cases and bullets, and firearm parts. Distinguishing marks, such as those left by firing pins, are indicative of individual firearms, as well as firearm type. By comparing these marks we are able to ascertain a minimum number of firearms per weapon type, thus providing important new information on the nature of Indian firearms.

Chronology of the Little Bighorn Fight

Second, we wish to trace deployments during the Custer and Reno-Benteen battles and account for these in behavioral terms. This issue has long been of interest to Custer historians, particularly as it applies to the Custer battle (cf. Kuhlman 1951; Greene 1979; Gray 1976). In our analysis, we recorded the precise locations of cartridge cases in order to trace combatant movements and assess the battle developments. Combatant positions can be evaluated on this basis also, but other criteria are relevant. We evaluate positioning by observing variations in artifact densities and associations. Also, we knew that burial locations could assist in establishing the final positions of troopers. We excavated at marble-marker locations in order to detect remains, such as clothing, equipment, or bones, that might indicate a soldier's final position. These excavations were necessary, of course, in correlating markers with trooper burials.

Analysis of Human Remains

Our third objective focuses on the analyses of skeletal remains of soldiers. In our excavations we recovered human remains, as expected, allowing us to address several concerns. One is the mutilation of corpses during the battle. Plains Indians often mutilated their victims to express ethnic identity or spiritual beliefs. If this type of behavior occurred, it should be evident in the mortal remains of soldiers. Bones contain not only evidence of trauma but also demographic data, such as disease, diet, stress, age at death, and stature (i.e., height and build). These data not only give us an idea of the physical conditions of cavalrymen in the 1870s but can help to identify particular individuals (or at least narrow the possibilities to a few individuals) through comparisons with vital statistics in enlistment records.

Campaign Equipment

The Seventh Cavalry brought with it to the Little Bighorn substantial variety in military hardware and personal belongings. Our fourth research objective was directed toward evaluating the equipment of the cavalryman on field campaign with respect to what might be expected from the fully and properly equipped soldier of the time (Hutchins 1976; Chappell 1972).

Deep Ravine

Finally, we maintained our interest in determining the whereabouts of the twenty-eight missing soldiers. Numerous historical accounts (Kuhlman 1951) agree that these soldiers were buried in a prominent coulee which is now called Deep Ravine. There is little agreement, however, on where in the ravine the bodies were interred. Research in Deep Ravine is important because ultimately any analysis of the progress of the Custer fight must consider the final whereabouts of these men. Only then may the circumstances of their presence in Deep Ravine be addressed. We first investigated Deep Ravine in 1984 but found no evidence of the soldiers, causing us to alter our strategies in 1985. These strategies and our research efforts are detailed in chapter 4.

A Research Framework

Concern with behavioral dynamics is not new in historical archaeology. We believe, however, that our research into the dynamics of the Little Bighorn fight is the first of its kind at an American battlefield. The ability to translate artifact patterning into behavioral dynamics, particularly through the use of modern firearm identification procedures, constitutes an important innovation in this regard. Accordingly, research into the Little Bighorn fight provides, in addition to new data bearing on the fight, a framework within which the behavioral aspects of many other battles can be studied. We offer this framework as our last objective. This approach to battlefield studies represents an improvement over the pessimism of Noel Hume (1969), who felt that "little can usefully be said about battlefield sites . . . [where] . . . the salvage of relics becomes the be all and end all." "Relics" can be "salvaged," but only when they are consigned to the fireplace mantel can little be usefully said about battles.

HISTORY AND HISTORICAL ARCHAEOLOGY

The accumulation of historical literature since the Little Bighorn fight is voluminous. Virtually every author who has dealt in depth with the fight has ultimately had to ask the same types of questions that occupy us (Utley 1980). How did the fight develop? How did the opposing forces deploy? Or, why did a number of men become trapped in Deep Ravine? What kind of weapons did the Indians use? It thus seems reasonable to ask why it is that we bring historical archaeology to bear on these questions. It is apparent to us that the very fact these questions continue to surface supplies the answer. Despite a plethora of theories for each of many issues, there is little or no resolution. Why is this?

Most of the uncertainties in historical perspectives of the Little Bighorn fight stem from limitations in the primary historical record. This primary record consists mostly of eyewitness accounts. In this respect, perhaps the most obvious limitation, particularly as it applies to the Custer battle, is the absence of testimony from white participants, all of whom were killed. The most basic of all questions, then, is the most difficult to answer. What happened and how? Indeed, behavioral patterning was of the utmost interest to Brigadier General Alfred Terry upon his arrival at the Little Bighorn River two days after the fight. Terry, the overall commander of the campaign, sent his officers over the field to observe the dispersal of bodies and hardware hoping to discern what happened. We have reasonably good accounts of these observations which aid us today in identifying army positions. Yet despite Terry's attempts the dynamics of the fight remained obscure. Facing this dilemma historians have usually turned to Indian accounts of the fight.

There is no dearth of available Indian testimony (Black Elk in Neihardt 1961;

Wooden Leg in Marquis 1976) regarding events during the battle. As might be expected, though, these accounts must be critically examined, and historians have long recognized this. Indeed, Graham (1953) found Indian accounts to be so ambiguous that he, as an extreme case, dismissed them as useless in Little Bighorn battle studies (Utley 1980:86). The major contribution to ambiguity in Indian testimony seems to lie in the nature of Indian warfare. Unencumbered by American Victorian standards of military obedience and duty, warriors were free to fight as individuals, and they rarely witnessed more than a few incidents in a fight. It is thus difficult to piece together various individual testimonies in order to form a coherent account in our own cultural terms of the fight's proceedings. As well, Indian informants, sometimes fearing retribution or expecting favors, often tailored their stories to conform with what they thought their white audience wished to hear. And even straightforward accounts could be subject to interpreter error.

There were, of course, white survivors of the Little Bighorn fight. About half of the Seventh Cavalry survived the Reno-Benteen defense. Accounts of their experiences are numerous (Hammer 1976) and provide invaluable assistance in analyzing the fight. But they, too, must be accepted critically, as historians know. One of the most immediate problems is the contradictory nature of much of the testimony. Contemporary accounts were often at odds. For example, some participants in the fight testified in a military court of inquiry that Reno's actions were justifiable; others were quite adamant that he was incompetent (Nichols 1983). The inconsistencies among accounts locating the bodies in Deep Ravine, which we briefly mentioned earlier, is another instance of confusion in the historical record (Hammer 1976). Also contributing was the tendency, in some instances, for testimonies to change over time as memories dimmed. Some accounts were not written down until thirty years after the fight (Hammer 1976). As well, an individual's statements might vary publicly and privately (Benteen in Carroll 1974). It is also probable that some aspects of public accounts were tainted, either through vagueness or omission, by a desire to protect the Seventh Cavalry image. Finally, eyewitnesses, who could not have anticipated the future, generally failed to comment on or were less than specific about details that are of interest today.

There is little doubt that vagaries punctuating the historical record have helped perpetuate the Little Bighorn mystery and have contributed to the obsession with the episode. We have outlined the importance of history in historical archaeology and the pages that follow should highlight our dependence on Little Bighorn histories. We also emphasize our belief that historical archaeology does not represent the last word in Little Bighorn studies. Each of us recalls the admonition of Graham (1953:iii): we do not "think that the Dis-solution of the Custer Myth is easy . . . [nor are we] . . . quite sure that we have Dis-solved it." On the contrary, we see our work as complementary to history and as a vehicle by which new data can be brought to bear on historical problems. We view the archaeological record only as a new set of data in the study of the battle. Thus we hope our contribution is a further stimulant in Little Bighorn studies.

Chapter 2

A Historical Overview

During the summer of 1874, Lieutenant Colonel George Custer led the Seventh Regiment of U.S. Cavalry into the Black Hills. These beautiful prairie mountains, in what is now South Dakota, were the sacred land of the Sioux and they lay in the heart of the vast Sioux reservation. Earlier treaties with the U.S. government had guaranteed the Sioux people that their reservation and sacred grounds would never pass from their possession. But the Seventh Cavalry expedition, dispatched primarily for scientific purposes, found gold. Despite attempts to suppress the discovery, word leaked rapidly and the rush was on. Eventually the great Sioux reservation was reduced drastically in size and the sacred Black Hills were lost. The complex political and legal machinery driven by manifest destiny had unilaterally decided the issue.

Beginning in the 1850s, government policy in the West was to confine Indian tribes to land areas, thereby opening vast tracts to white settlement. Frequent episodes of white encroachment on reservations, often tacitly condoned by high officialdom and in violation of solemn treaties, led to dissatisfaction on the part of dispossessed Indians. Disenchanted, many left their reservations, some committing depredations as they sought security in their old way of life. Few examples better illustrate these tragic episodes than the rush for Black Hills gold (Gray 1976). Ironically, the Little Bighorn fight was to be a repercussion of the 1874 confirmation of gold on the Sioux reservation. Many Sioux fled the reservation, often to join nontreaty brethren roaming unceded lands farther west. These Indians, allied with the Northern Cheyennes, were soon to meet Custer on the Little Bighorn River.

Government officials perceived the flight of the Sioux as hostile and as a threat, not only to Indian policies, but to the security of settlers pushing westward. So it was that in the spring of 1876 the Seventh U.S. Cavalry departed Fort Abraham Lincoln (located near Bismarck, North Dakota), as part of a campaign to force the Indians onto their reservations.

Based on the expectation that the Indians would be found in what is now southeastern

Montana, the plan called for the coordinated efforts of three units. Brigadier General George Crook with more than a thousand men left Wyoming Territory and moved north to block a possible southerly escape route. Colonel John Gibbon departed Fort Ellis (near present day Bozemen, Montana) and marched east down the Yellowstone River. In mid-June he joined with the third force, led by General Alfred Terry; this included the Seventh Cavalry. They met on the Yellowstone where Miles City, Montana, is now situated. It was from the mouth of Rosebud Creek that Custer would set out to find the Sioux and Cheyenne. On June 17, Crook's force would be checked at the Battle of the Rosebud. Eight days later, Sioux and Cheyenne warriors, many of whom had helped stalemate Crook, annihilated half of the Seventh Cavalry.

These were the circumstances that led the Seventh Cavalry to the banks of the Little Bighorn River on June 25, 1876. Major Marcus Reno, second in command, who began the Little Bighorn fight in the river valley, soon retreated and subsequently defended his precarious position for nearly two days during the hilltop fight. The Reno-Benteen defense site today encompasses the area where the soldiers entrenched on the bluffs. In a separate engagement, Custer, the officers, and men of five companies were killed to the man on what is now Custer Battlefield. The Custer fight evidently lasted only an hour or two, perhaps less. Reno with seven companies fought desperately until Terry and Gibbon arrived on June 27. In all, 268 of the nearly 600 man command died (262 died on the field and six later died of wounds). The Indians, some 10,000 people, of which perhaps 2,000 to 3,000 were warriors, escaped to the south, suffering an estimated loss of only 150 warriors

Within three weeks after the famous battle, concerned parties began laying plans for a memorial to commemorate Custer's fallen soldiers (Rickey 1967:27). Their efforts were realized on January 29, 1879, when the secretary of war authorized creation of Custer Battlefield National Cemetery. Six months later the national cemetery became a reality. Its boundaries coincided with what is today known as Custer Battlefield. Only a small portion of the battlefield was set aside for the cemetery. The remaining portion included the areas where Custer and his men had fallen.

Initially, veterans of many Indian Wars actions were laid to rest in the cemetery. Today, it serves as the final resting place for veterans of wars dating from the Indian campaigns to Vietnam. Of the entire Custer command killed June 25 and 26, only a few are buried in the cemetery. Those bodies that could be found, about 210 in all, were buried on the battlefield. Several, including Lieutenant John Crittenden, were later exhumed from their original resting places and reinterred in the cemetery. From time to time, exposed bones of unknown soldiers also have been buried here. A few who survived the Reno-Benteen battle, as well as Indian scouts, were later interred in the national cemetery. In 1967, Major Reno's remains were removed from a pauper's grave in Washington, D.C. and reinterred with military honors at the cemetery.

Custer Battlefield National Cemetery was initially administered by the War Department. Administration was provided first by the commanding officer of nearby Fort Custer, was established in 1877 at the confluence of the Little Bighorn and Big Horn rivers. Some ten miles from the battlefield, it was created as a direct response to the Little Bighorn fight. After Fort Custer was abandoned in the late 1890s, resident superintendents administered the national cemetery. It was not until 1940 that jurisdiction of the national cemetery was transferred to the Department of the Interior under the

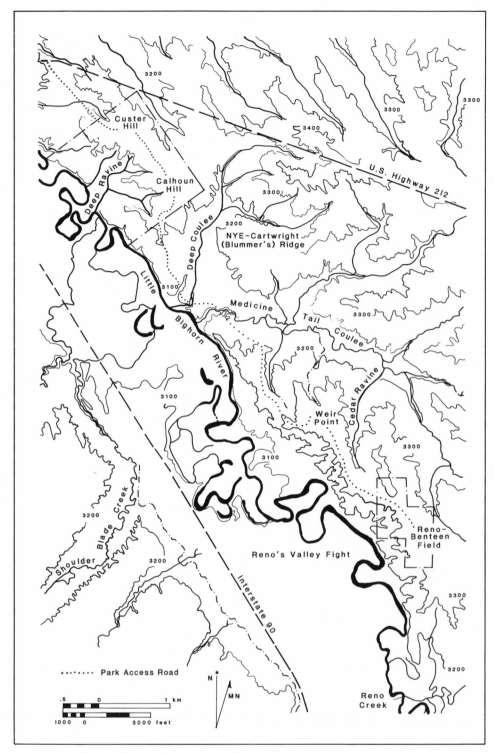

Fig. 1. Custer Battlefield National Monument and its local setting.

auspices of the National Park Service. The national cemetery included at this time 162 acres of the Reno-Benteen defense site which had been acquired some ten years earlier. Custer Battlefield National Cemetery was redesignated as Custer Battlefield National Monument in 1946. The National Park Service continues to administer the cemetery and the Custer and Reno-Benteen battlefields.

Under the War Department, management had focused on national-cemetery matters, but with the transfer to the National Park Service, emphasis shifted to Indian Wars history and to the historical interpretation of the Little Bighorn fight. The 1950s saw construction of an interpretive center for visitors, and archaeological work was done at the Reno-Benteen defense site (Bray 1958).

Though official policies belatedly emphasized the historical and interpretive aspects of the Little Bighorn fight, there was certainly no lack of interest in other sectors. Within months after the fight, controversies over what happened began to surface. It was in these controversies that the Custer myth emerged. Utley (1980) dissects the origin and development of the myth, fixing initial blame on an ill-informed and irresponsible press. While introducing most of the fallacies common to the myth, the press fed a receptive public caught in the patriotism of America's centennial celebration and polarized in political, moral, and philosophical debate of the Indian issue. Debates on what happened and who was responsible raged first in military circles and then among generations of historians. Many historians seemed to be influenced in their work by pro- or anti-Custer biases (cf. Brininstool 1952; Dustin 1936). For the most part these biases are absent today among serious scholars of the Little Bighorn fight.

Historians rely on primary sources and often these sources are eyewitness testimonies. In Little Bighorn studies, eyewitness accounts are numerous (Hammer 1976; Graham 1953), but one of the most important historical documents is the transcript of the Reno court of inquiry (Nichols 1983; Utley 1972). The military investigation was requested by Major Reno to rebut mounting criticism of his actions during the fight. Many, including Custer's sympathetic biographer (Whitaker 1876), had charged Reno with cowardice and blamed him for Custer's defeat. So in January 1879 the court convened in Chicago for the purpose of investigating Reno's conduct at the Little Bighorn fight. Coincidentally, the inquiry was in full session the moment Custer Battlefield National Cemetery was created. Pro-Custer sympathies must have run high, but the court's review of the evidence prompted a decision in favor of Reno. Reno was judged not as qualifying for a court martial, though it was found that his conduct had been less than exemplary. Of more immediate interest are the details of the transcript, which relate events from June 22 to June 29, 1876.

It was on June 22 that Custer left General Terry on the Yellowstone and began his march into history (fig. 1). Shortly thereafter, Terry and Gibbon marched west up the Yellowstone to the mouth of the Big Horn River, then up the Big Horn and Little Bighorn rivers, expecting to converge with Custer about June 26. Terry arrived on June 27 in time to relieve the beleaguered Reno but too late to help Custer. Crook, unbeknownst to Terry's command, was far to the south in Wyoming Territory.

The prelude to the Little Bighorn fight began late on June 24. Custer's column, after leaving the Yellowstone River and moving south up Rosebud Creek, camped near the present site of Busby, Montana. In late evening on the twenty-fourth, camp was broken and the column marched west in the dead of night to the divide between Rosebud Creek and the Little Bighorn River. Here it halted and waited until early morning on the twenty-fifth. The soldiers made coffee while atop the divide at a place called Crow's Nest. Here, Lieutenant Charles Varnum and his scouts peered down into the Little Bighorn Valley some fifteen miles distant. From Crow's Nest the scouts observed indications of the hostile encampment. The Indian camp was on the Little Bighorn River as suspected. Mitch Boyer, a mixed-blood Sioux employed as a scout-interpreter, a plainsman of considerable experience, ostensibly reported to Custer that the Indian village was the largest he had ever seen. According to him, to pitch into it invited certain death. Boyer died later that day with Custer.

Custer reportedly disputed Boyer's estimate of the number of Indians in the valley. Indeed, the nature of Custer's knowledge regarding the size of the force he would later meet has been a much-debated issue. Official reports indicated only about eight hundred Indians were missing from their reservations, but this figure was seriously deflated. Now Custer was on the divide and faced with a serious decision. The Indian trail the column had been following indicated a large body. Reno's scout of the Rosebud a few days earlier also suggested great numbers in the vicinity. Boyer's assessment, plus those of other scouts, also indicated a considerable gathering, contradicting official estimates. The Custer column left the divide and pushed forward to the Little Bighorn about midday on June 25.

Historians agree that Custer had planned to attack, using the element of surprise (Gray 1976). Several Indian sightings in the vicinity of the divide, however, evidently caused him to believe the cavalry had been detected. His decision to attack before his presence became known in the village was made immediately.

As the twelve companies of Seventh Cavalry, totaling nearly six hundred men, descended to the broken country east of the Little Bighorn River, Custer began the attack. Captain Frederick Benteen, the senior captain in the command, was ordered to feel to the southwest with three companies and block a possible southerly escape route. Captain Thomas McDougall with his company was to escort the ammunition pack train to the north, following Custer and Reno. Custer pressed on with the remaining eight companies, following what is now Reno Creek, a westerly flowing tributary of the Little Bighorn River. A few miles from the river, the command pulled up. Reno was ordered to take three companies and attack the Indians at their southern flank with the assurance that Custer would support him. With this, Reno's battalion continued west down Reno Creek, forded the Little Bighorn, and proceeded north to the attack. The Indian village lay in the floodplain on the west bank of the river.

Custer's battalion, now consisting of five companies, paralleled Reno on the opposite side of Reno Creek. At a point above the mouth of the creek, Custer, bearing to the right, left the creek valley. The battalion ascended the high bluffs lying immediately east of Little Bighorn River and proceeded in a northerly direction parallel to the river. Much of the Indian encampment lay hidden (timber and high ridges intervened) from Custer's view despite his vantage point. The immense size of the village had not yet become evident. Some in Custer's battalion, however, clearly saw Reno, who by this time had engaged the Indians. This engagement is known as the valley fight and it is here that the Battle of the Little Bighorn began.

The valley fight began at the southern extremity of the Indian village, which was later found to extend to the north for about three and a half miles (five and eight-tenths kilometers) and sheltered approximately ten thousand men, women and children. Custer was soon to confront terrible odds, perhaps ten to one, and in the final analysis these odds helped orchestrate his defeat.

Reno's approach to the south end of the village seems to have created confusion initially among the Sioux camped there. For the most part, mounted warriors rode furiously about but well out of range of the soldiers. Yet their number grew, perhaps to nine hundred, (Nichols 1983), and Reno elected to dismount and form a skirmish line a considerable distance away. The east-west line (near present Garryowen) extended in the open from the timber on the right to the valley bluffs on the left. While the troops were in skirmish order, the fighting evidently was light, but Indians soon began skirting the left end of the line. This development threatened the horses, which had been retired to the timber, as well as the command's rear. Though casualties to this point were light, Reno ordered the line redeployed in the timber. The redeployment was executed in good fashion and the horses were placed under protection.

Reno's command was now on the defensive. During the court of inquiry, Reno's subordinate officers differed in their opinion of the safety the timber provided. Some felt it was a good defensive position. Most, however, felt that it was poor and to maintain the position invited doom. In any case, Reno, within thirty minutes of his arrival in the timber, ordered the position abandoned. The expected support from Custer had not come, and it appeared that the command was slowly being encircled. A prolonged defense would not be possible without additional ammunition, and if the command were surrounded, access to McDougall's pack train would be impossible. The regiment retreated (Reno called it a charge) to the high bluffs across the river, where it dug in and successfully defended the position in the hilltop fight (fig. 2).

Custer had not informed Reno of his intent other than to promise support. The support came, not from the rear, as Reno apparently expected, but farther north near the center of the Indian camp. Custer departed the ridge near the point where Reno's command was observed. He proceeded in columns down a short draw (Cedar Coulee) that led to Medicine Tail Coulee, an ephemeral tributary of the Little Bighorn River. There he apparently bore left in a westerly direction down Medicine Tail Coulee, intent on fording the river to press the attack. It is at this point in the sequence of events that the consuming mystery of the Little Bighorn fight begins.

Custer must finally have realized the gravity of the situation as he swung into Medicine Tail Coulee. The northern half of the village came into full view and resistance began. Lieutenant William Cooke, Custer's adjutant, dispatched Trumpeter John Martin with a written order for Benteen. That order, is preserved today, reads simply: "Benteen, Come on. Big Village, be quick, bring packs. P.S. bring pacs [sic]. W. W. Cooke." Martin found Benteen still to the south near McDougall's pack train. These units came on as ordered, but they never reached Custer.

The progress of Custer's advance down Medicine Tail Coulee is a source of debate. Some argue that the cavalry attack was repulsed a considerable distance from the ford at the coulee's head; others maintain that the column reached a point near the river where elements perhaps crossed into the camp. The historical data are contradictory and on these data alone a case can be made for either argument. However, artifactual evidence (e.g., government cartridge cases, etc.) found over the years at the ford may suggest that Custer's battalion, or parts of it, progressed to the river intent on crossing

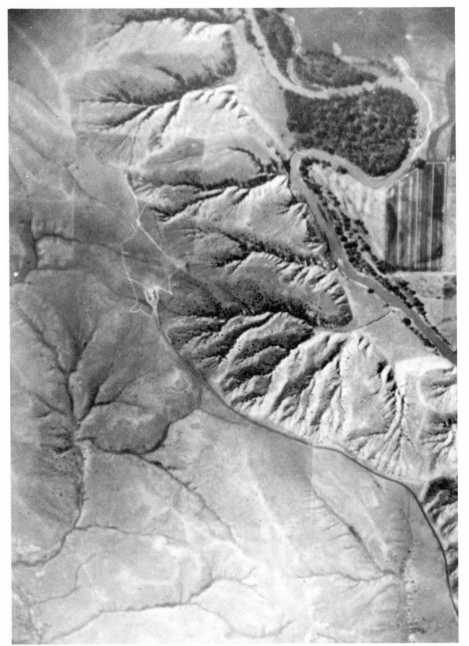

Fig. 2. The Reno–Benteen defense site in relation to the Little Bighorn River.

into the heart of the encampment (Greene 1979). On the other hand, Weibert (1986) has recently argued that these artifacts came from Indians celebrating their victory with cavalry weapons and that Custer never approached the river. Whatever the case, clearly the battalion was turned away in the vicinity of Medicine Tail Coulee. This development, coupled with Reno's predicament, thereby precluded any measure of mutual support.

Trumpeter Martin, riding to Benteen, turned and saw the doomed battalion for the last time as he reached the bluffs over which Custer had moments ago led his troops. Martin later recounted that it appeared the troopers were retreating (Hammer 1976). Certainly Custer was on the move, but the nature of his retirement is largely conjectural. At least a portion of his command, if not the entire battalion, either redeployed, retreated or was driven eastward to Nye-Cartwright Ridge. Some students conclude that Custer ordered two companies immediately to the north while the remaining three companies proceeded east to the ridge. There is presently little direct evidence for the separation of companies, but various Indian and government cartridges and bullets (Indians used a variety of weapons and ammunition; troopers carried a Colt pistol and a Springfield carbine) found in past years on Nye-Cartwright Ridge indicate action there. In any case, Custer's outfit ultimately moved north from Medicine Tail and Nye-Cartwright and made its way to the place where the memorial markers now stand, each declaring "U.S. Soldier, 7th Cavalry, fell here June 25, 1876."

Custer's northerly movement separated him farther from Reno's retreating battalion, which scrambled to the bluffs at a point some four and a half miles (seven and a half kilometers) from the ground on which Custer made his stand. By all accounts the retreat was far from orderly. Reno took the lead as the mounted cavalrymen dashed toward the river. Indians fired at close range from both flanks and some rode among the fleeing soldiers. Some wounded soldiers in the timber, unable to retreat without assistance, were left behind. Another sixteen able-bodied men either did not hear the order or could not mount their horses. They, too, were left in the timber where they hid, some for more than twenty-four hours, as hundreds of Indians passed—too close for comfort. Miraculously, some eventually made their way to the hilltop and relative safety.

As the troopers reached the river, it was apparent that safety lay only on the high bluffs immediately to the east. The battalion was left bunched and exposed as a crossing was gradually trampled into the high riverbank. Skirmishers were not thrown out to protect the crossing on either side of the river. Casualties mounted and confusion increased as the soldiers urged their mounts into the river. With great difficulty three-fourths of the command negotiated the crossing. The rest lay dead, dying, or hidden on both banks. Reno had lost thirty-three men, for which he was to suffer unceasing criticism.

The disorganized retreat continued up the very steep draws and ridges until the blufftop was reached. After the men attained it, Benteen rode up and joined his three companies with Reno's. McDougall's pack train arrived safely a short time later. So augmented, the defensive position selected by Reno proved satisfactory. The hilltop fight had begun. It was about 4:00 P.M. on June 25, 1876. Reno and Benteen held the position, now preserved as the Reno-Benteen defense site, until relief arrived on the morning of June 27.

Perhaps ninety minutes after the pack train arrived, Captain Thomas Weir mustered his company and set out to the north in an attempt to join Custer. Eventually each of Reno's and Benteen's companies struck out on the trail of Weir. McDougall's company straggled in the rear, burdened by the wounded. Weir reached a high hill some three miles from Custer battlefield, where he dimly saw figures dashing about and firing into the ground. Great clouds of dust and gunsmoke hampered vision, and as additional companies moved into Weir's position, a huge body of Indians began forming in the front. The halt at Weir Point, as it is now known, lasted about forty-five minutes before pressure from the Indians caused the column to turn back. The return to the original hilltop position was orderly and only one man was lost. Defensive lines were quickly formed about the hilltop and sustained pressure began, not to let up until nightfall. The Indians had surrounded the command, which consisted of some three hundred and fifty officers, men, and civilians.

Weir's movement was apparently undertaken on his own initiative, though he had conferred with Reno moments before. As Weir set out, the other company commanders followed assuming an order had been issued. But none in the command knew the location or disposition of Custer and his troops. Their observations from Weir Point apparently provided little information to resolve the matter. Indeed, throughout the hilltop fight the defenders suspected that Custer was either under siege as they were or, unable to rejoin Reno, had pushed north to link with Terry and Gibbon. Apparently none of the officers on the hilltop knew or even suspected that Custer had met a grim fate, or so they testified at the Reno court of inquiry.

The hilltop position was anything but secure. Throughout the siege, defenses were improved by piling hardtack boxes to form breastworks. Shallow trenches were scooped into the hard Montana prairie with cups, boards and a few shovels. Dead animals also served as protection. Men dared not show their heads to Indian marksmen. Despite great dangers, however, Captain Benteen strode about under heavy fire and took an active role in the two-day defense. On the twenty-sixth, Benteen found his position in danger of being overrun. The position was vital to the security of the command for it lay on high ground within the defense perimeter. With the help of Captain Thomas French's company, Benteen led a charge straight into the Indians and scattered them. The position was not seriously threatened thereafter. Later, Reno charged from his position at the suggestion of Benteen and successfully dispersed many encroaching warriors.

As night fell on the embattled group, the firing slackened. Many Indians returned to camp, but others remained to prevent the command from slipping away under cover of darkness. At sunup the deadly rain of bullets again began and continued well into the afternoon. By the second day, water became a critical factor. None was available on the stark hilltop. A sprinkle of rain that night had temporarily lifted spirits, but the hoped for deluge never came. Ninety-degree weather compounded the situation. Canteens were empty, and men on the line suffered a terrible thirst. The wounded cried for water, and at the surgeon's insistence, volunteers were called upon to go to the river. Sharpshooters several times covered their trips down a steep, rugged ravine to the Little Bighorn. Precious water was returned to slake the wounded's thirst. Later, nineteen men were decorated with the Medal of Honor for their bravery.

There was no lack of bravery among the Indians. Many got within a stone's throw of the defensive lines, probably intent on counting coup. Plains Indians placed much value on the act of touching or striking an enemy, alive or dead. Courage was a necessity for the warrior who counted coup on a live adversary. Sioux and Cheyenne continually crept among the ravines and through the tall grass, often hiding behind clumps of sagebrush. Their stealth made it difficult for the soldiers to find a target, yet the Indian fire was deadly. By late afternoon on the twenty-sixth the siege ended as the warriors slipped back to their village, warned of the advancing Gibbon and Terry columns. The Reno-Benteen command had lost 18 dead on the hilltop; many more were wounded. In all, 52 died in the valley and on the hilltop. Indian casualties, during both the Custer and Reno-Benteen battles, were never accurately recorded for it was the custom of the Plains Indians to remove their dead during and after a fight. The best estimates range from 30 to 150 warriors killed.

During the evening of June 26, the hilltop defenders watched as the massive body of Indians trailed south in the direction of the Big Horn Mountains. Many of these would elude the U.S. military for only a few more months before reluctantly settling on their reservations. Sitting Bull and his followers eventually escaped to Canada, where they lived for five years before returning to the reservation. But the soldiers found little comfort in the exodus, as it was generally believed that the siege would commence again early next morning. Most spent the night improving defenses and preparing for the next day's action.

The morning of June 27 brought a bright, clear day, but it little affected the men on the hill. The stench of dead horses and mules was overpowering and thirst still prevailed. To the northwest, in the vicinity of the Indian village, a large dust cloud gathered and the defenders prepared for the worst. But shortly come word that soldiers were approaching—probably Terry, Gibbon, and Custer. Reno sent two officers to meet the advancing column whereupon they found Terry and Gibbon near the abandoned village. Terry and the officer envoy asked of each other concerning the whereabouts of Custer. Neither knew. Lieutenant James Bradley (who commanded the Indian scouts under Gibbon) soon brought the grim news to Terry and Gibbon: Custer and many men lay dead on a ridge above the Little Bighorn River.

Bradley had counted 197 dead, and there was no indication of survivors. Later that day other officers tallied as many as 214 dead men. It became increasingly clear that, despite hopes that some had escaped, all in the battalion had died. Officers spent most of the day examining faint trails across the field, the positions of bodies and companies, and other telltale signs that might offer a glimpse into the course of events. Much of this information survives and can be used to portray a static picture of the final positions of Custer's soldiers (fig. 3).

That evening, the soldiers camped along the banks of the Little Bighorn. They made no attempt to pursue the fleeing Indians because a more somber task awaited the next day. The duty of burying Custer's dead fell to the men in Reno's outfit, though men from other units assisted. Burials were hasty and in most cases the dead merely had earth heaped over them. Custer's dead were buried where they were found; most of the dead from the valley fight were also buried on the spot. Those who died on the hilltop were buried in trenches or nearby. In 1958, remains of three men who fought with Reno were found in trenches during archaeological excavations at the Reno-Benteen battlefield (Bray 1958).

Often graves were not even dug into the ground; dirt was thrown over the body and

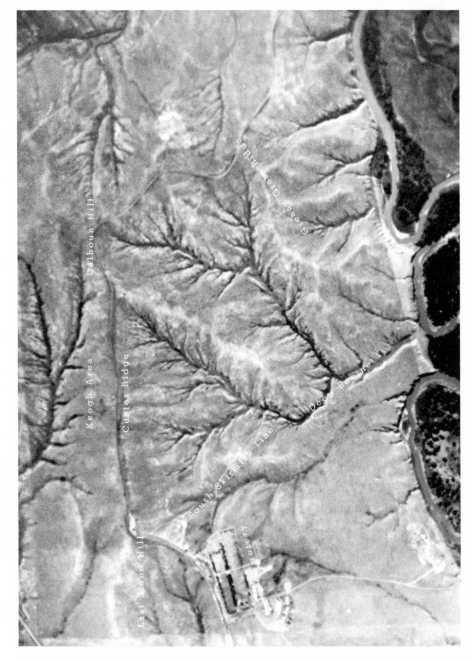

Fig. 3. The Custer battlefield in relation to the Little Bighorn River. North is to the top right corner of the photograph.

dirt or sagebrush was piled above. Officers were buried with some care, but grave pits did not exceed twelve to fourteen inches (thirty to thirty-five centimeters) in depth. The nature of these burials was to be a source of official embarrassment to the army for years to come. Several attempts were made in later years to rectify the situation, but the burial details in 1876 faced a most unpleasant task: the bodies had lain in the hot June sun for more than two days, and the stench was unbearable. The command had only a few shovels, and in any case the prairie was rock hard. Unpleasant emotions must have dictated expediency. But the most pressing problem was the need to get the wounded to proper medical facilities. So, before sunup on June 29, the column, burdened by the wounded, moved with great difficulty down the Little Bighorn to its mouth.

The steamboat *Far West*, captained by Grant Marsh, lay at the mouth of the Little Bighorn River. Reno's wounded were put aboard, and Marsh began an epic voyage that would end in Bismarck, Dakota Territory, within fifty-four hours. The injured had returned to Seventh Cavalry headquarters some seven hundred miles by river, first the Big Horn, then the Yellowstone, and finally the Missouri. It had been only forty-four days since Custer and Terry had, on May 17 and with spirits high, led their troops out of nearby Fort Abraham Lincoln and into immortality.

Today, marble markers resembling tombstones dot the landscape where Custer and his men died. They, more than anything, fix in the imaginations of visitors incalculable visions of the death struggle. And each says, in bold inscription, that a soldier or civilian fell here on a fateful day in June 1876.

Chapter 3

Gathering the Evidence

Historian Jerome A. Greene (1979:48sff.) recognized that Indian testimony provided essential information for understanding how the Custer battle evolved. He also recognized limitations much as we have, arguing that artifact patterning helped mitigate ambiguities in Indian accounts. Foreshadowing our work, Greene showed that concentrations of artifacts might signal whether combatants were stationary or fought on the move, that densities might indicate length of occupation at a position, and that distributions of artifacts could show the routes of adversaries. Greene was interested in behavioral patterning.

At the time Greene wrote, however, artifact locations were only generally known, as much of the information came from indirect reports of collectors. There had been no systematic, controlled investigations from which to draw detailed conclusions. We realized that only systematic examination of the Custer and Reno-Benteen battlefields and careful artifact provenience control could provide information necessary for detailed and precise studies of patterning. It was not enough to know generally that one or several artifacts came, for example, from Last Stand Hill. We needed to know the exact location of an artifact, as well as its depth and orientation in the ground, so that we could understand its contextual relationships with all other artifacts.

When conducting archaeological research it is important to know not only where artifacts are located but also where they are not found. It is not enough to concentrate on the "hot spots." Our first requirement, then, was to develop field procedures that were capable of examining the entire extent of both the battlefields. Faced with examining a large area (760 acres total) and assuming that most artifacts of war would either be metallic or associated with metal, we elected to employ metal detectors in our survey. We also knew that substantial numbers of artifacts would be buried, perhaps not deeply, but deep enough so they would not be visible. Ultimately, we found that the controlled use of metal detectors in the hands of skilled operators was highly successful in recovering artifacts. The procedure was also most effective in accomplishing our task within the ever-present time and financial constraints. In the end, metal detectors were used over the entire extent of Custer Battlefield National Monument, including the Reno-Benteen defense site. Moreover, this was accomplished in a systematic manner by spacing operators at five-meter or fifteen-foot intervals.

The value of systematic and controlled use of metal detectors was shown in England at Roman sites (Gregory and Rogerson 1984) and at historic sites in Canada (McLeod 1985). Bray (1958) used metal detectors in a controlled manner at the Reno-Benteen defense site during his pioneering work, but their effectiveness was hindered by technological limitations of the time. Many of the artifacts Greene (1979) examined were recovered by modern equipment, though unsystematically and by untrained people, many of whom were seeking relics rather than knowledge.

The use of metal detectors operated by knowledgeable people has overwhelmingly proved its value, in locating not only metallic objects but also non-metallic remains. Scores of nonmetallic items such as bone, leather, rubber articles, and shell buttons, were found when metal detectors sensed nearby metal objects. Our recovery methods, which meticulously uncovered artifacts without disturbance, were an integral part of the field procedures.

The metal-detector survey and our excavations located more than five thousand artifacts, many of which are battle related. We have repeatedly emphasized, though, that when taken out of context the scientific value of artifacts is seriously impaired. What we needed was a reference system by which the precise locations of all artifacts could be recorded. We accomplished this by establishing a permanent grid system that encompassed the Custer and Reno-Benteen battlefields. The intersections provide known reference points by which artifact locations can be determined. In our grid system, we placed the intersections at 100-meter intervals and recorded the distance and magnetic bearing of each artifact from a conveniently located intersection point. At the same time, each artifact was assigned a unique catalog number. This information allowed us to return to the laboratory and plot the exact location of every artifact. On this basis, we were able to discern the nature of artifact distributions and associations. In turn, this precise locational information allowed us to ask how and why these contextual relationships between artifacts came about. The how and why questions represent inquiry into the behavioral aspects of the Little Bighorn fight.

FIELD METHODS

The field investigations were conducted at Custer Battlefield in 1984 and on both the Custer battlefield and the Reno-Benteen defense site in 1985. The work was guided by work plans and research designs (Scott 1984; 1985) prepared as a part of the compliance procedures used by the National Park Service to meet legislative and regulatory requirements of the National Historic Preservation Act (as amended), the Secretary of Interior's Standards for Archeology and Historic Preservation, and the National Park Service's own internal cultural resource preservation guidelines.

The fieldwork consisted of four phases: the orientation phase, the inventory phase, the testing phase and the inventory evaluation phase. For the most part the last three phases were conducted concurrently. In the orientation phase a grid system was established by which precise artifact locations could be recorded. During the inventory phase we employed electronic metal detectors, visual survey methods, and piece-plot recording techniques. We conceived and executed the inventory-evaluation phase, using modified inventory-phase methods, to evaluate the effectiveness of the inventory. The testing phase consisted of three procedures: standard small-block excavation, shovel tests, and power-auger tests. Details of each phase are explained below. Procedures generally relevant to all phases follow.

General Procedures

Standard archaeological data-recording methods were used in each phase of the operation. Individual artifacts, spatially discrete clusters of identical specimens, or associated dissimilar specimens received unique field specimen (FS) numbers. We used field notes and a standardized Midwest Archeological Center excavation form to record the tests. Exposed excavations, selected in-place artifact specimens, and topography were photographed and recorded on black-and-white print and color-slide-film. Many crew activities, some excavations, and some artifact discoveries were recorded on videotape by a documentary-film maker who volunteered for the crew in 1984.

Artifact collection varied according to artifact class. We collected all artifacts except glass, nails, and bricks. Glass fragments were most often encountered in clusters; these were recorded and sampled. Not all nails found along the boundary fence line were collected since they were from an old fence line that is well documented. Other nails were recorded and collected. Bricks and mortar finds were recorded but not collected. We did not collect artifacts from several recent trash-dump areas; however, the dumps were recorded and the artifacts visible were noted. In every instance the decision to leave an object in place was made by a professional archaeologist.

In recording and collecting, we did not discriminate on the basis of period association. Prehistoric, battle-related, post-battle-related, and recent historic artifacts were considered equally.

Orientation Phase

A permanent grid or referencing system was surveyed and marked by a professional land surveyor using a transit. The grid was laid in 100-meter (328-foot) intervals over the Custer and Reno-Benteen battlefields. A permanent datum was placed at the intersection of each coordinate. The datum consisted of a piece of steel reinforcing bar set into the ground. A plastic head on each bar was inscribed with north and east coordinates. For convenience the grid was oriented at 90-degree angles from the eastern and southern boundaries and referenced to grid north. Grid north is 39 degrees west of magnetic north. The southeastern corner of the Custer battlefield was arbitrarily assigned grid coordinates 7,000N 3,000E (7,000 meters north and 3,000 meters east of 00N, 00E), and the grid was surveyed from this point. This procedure was designed to allow for future grid expansion to grid south and west while remaining in the same quadrant. Expansion to the south and west will encompass the site of the Indian village, the site of the valley fight, and the field of battle between the Reno-Benteen and Custer

battlefields. This will facilitate recording, mapping, description, comparisons, correlations, and computer applications should future investigations be conducted in these
important areas. The grid system was functional as we began the fieldwork.

Inventory Phase

The inventory phase included three sequential operations: survey, recovery, and recording. During survey we located and marked artifact finds. The recovery crew followed
and carefully uncovered subsurface finds, leaving them in place. The recording team
then plotted individual artifact locations, assigned field-specimen numbers, and collected the specimens.

Survey

Survey operations were designed primarily to locate subsurface metallic items with the
use of electronic metal detectors. Visual inspection of the surface was carried out concurrently with the metal-detector survey. The survey crew consisted of a crew chief,
metal-detector operators, and visual inspectors. An archaeologist directed survey operations and trained a volunteer. The volunteer then directed the crew for the remainder
of the field season, subject to regular checks by an archaeologist. We maintained conti-
nuity in survey operations by utilizing the same volunteer crew chief for each field
season.

We used various brands of metal detectors during the survey. Volunteer operators
furnished their own machines, and this contributed to the variety. We learned, however,
that standardization of machines (i.e., all one brand), though perhaps methodologically
desirable, was impractical. Like models operate on the same frequency, causing inter-
ference at close intervals. We therefore needed to alternate different brands of machines
on the line to ensure adequate survey coverage. Metal-detector operators were aligned
at approximately five-meter intervals. The operators walked transects oriented to grid
cardinal directions, maintaining, as closely as possible, the designated intervals. Orientation and interval spacing were maintained by direction from the crew chief. Deviations in spacing (not exceeding approximately eight meters (twenty-six and a half feet)
were unavoidable in rough terrain. The daily composition of the detector crew ranged
from four to six operators. This range was strictly adhered to. We found that fewer
than four operators were inefficient and more than six were unmanageable.

Detector operators proceeded in line, using a sweeping motion to examine the ground
(fig. 4). We estimate that each operator covered a sweep of 1.5 to 2 meters (5.8 to 6.6
feet), depending on individual height and technique. Another volunteer placed a pin
flag at each target located by an operator. As soon as the location was pinned, the operator continued along the transect. In some instances the location was excavated immediately to provide the operator with a check on machine performance. This was occasionally necessary because of the sophisticated nuances of interpreting machine functions,
such as depth readings, metallic and object type-differentiation functions, object size
interpretation, and pinpointing of subsurface objects. We also dug immediately when
we suspected a spurious detector reading. The usual procedure was to mark the location
and leave it intact for the recovery crew.

Fig. 4. A metal-detecting crew on a sweep across the Reno-Benteen defense site.

The visual inspectors walked behind the detector operators and served a dual function. They inspected the ground surface for artifacts and features while carrying pin flags. When an operator discovered a location, an inspector moved to pin that location. The number of visual inspectors largely depended on the number of people available each day, varying from two to as many as eight persons. Daily variation in numbers was great, thereby precluding any meaningful estimates of average crew composition. Visual inspectors were on the alert primarily for nonmetallic artifacts, such as bone, wood, glass, brick, and stone.

We recognize several problem areas in the metal-detector and visual surveys as presented above. Although each detector operator covered an area up to two meters wide, within each sweep it is unlikely that the entire subsurface was subjected to 100 percent electronic coverage. It is difficult to estimate exactly how much was surveyed. Detectors operate on the cone principle, by which electronic signals emanate from the coil and converge at the apex of a cone. Metal objects reflect the signals received by the coil and transmitted to the operator. The thoroughness of electronic coverage within the sweep depends on the distance between coil and ground surface, the diameter of the coil, and the closeness of the sweeps. Obviously, any given sweep coverage is better nearer the surface and dwindles toward the cone apex. The detectors that we used generally provided maximum depth readings of ten to fourteen inches.

The size of the object is also a factor in depth capabilities. These variables in metal detecting were largely uncontrollable; however, we endeavored to utilize only those operators with considerable experience. It was recognized that some areas between operators were not examined. The inventory-evaluation phase was designed to assess detector variables and interval coverage in toto.

A surface inspection, however unsystematic, helped us determine the variety of extant nonmetallic artifact classes. This was carried out largely in recognition of the biases inherent in metal detecting. Thus we conceived of the surface inspection as a secondary aspect of the metal-detector survey. Ultimately we were pleased with results despite its unsystematic nature. Surveyors found many artifacts, including prehistoric stone tools, various artifacts that metal detectors could not have identified, and some cartridges. Though not systematic, the results support an earlier study (Fox 1983) that recommended a surface survey of the battlefield. The Custer battlefield yielded several prehistoric projectile points, several aboriginal isolated finds, and aboriginal use areas. The Reno-Benteen defense site yielded no aboriginal materials not associated with the battle. The aboriginal materials are discussed in a report by Scott (1987).

Recovery

The recovery crew excavated artifact locations marked by pin flags and left the artifacts in place for recording (figs. 5–6). This team consisted of excavators and metal-detector operators. The number of operators and excavators varied from day to day depending on the workload.

Excavation procedure was based on the concept of artifact patterning, a central tenet in the research strategy. Thus provenience data, that is, the location in space and the

Fig. 5. An in-place picket pin as found by the recovery crew.

Fig. 6. A pin flag marks the location of a find. The recovery crew found a deformed bullet, seen below the flag, and an associated piece of horse bone.

position in the ground of each artifact, were considered of vital interest. We therefore excavated with great care so as to expose each artifact without disturbance. To this end, every recovery-crew member was thoroughly briefed on artifact patterning and the need for exposing artifacts in place. Techniques for doing so were demonstrated. The recovery crew was supervised by an archaeologist.

We used hand tools, such as trowels and dental picks, to expose subsurface artifacts. Excavators were assisted by metal-detector operators to ensure in-place exposure. Detector operators provided pinpointing and depth information to the excavator, thereby allowing a careful and accurate approach to the artifact. In a few instances accidental disturbance of the artifact occurred. Information to that effect was left at the artifact location to alert the recording crew.

Certain provisions were made for discontinuing excavation at an artifact location. Recovery-team members were briefed on these provisions. We required that excavation cease at any location where bone, leather, wood, or other sensitive or perishable artifacts were encountered when a metal object was being exposed. In such an event excavators were to alert an archaeologist. Usually the archaeologist elected to cease excavation, cover the exposure, and implement standard testing procedures at that location at a later date. Alternatively, the volunteer exposed the item immediately for proper handling.

After exposure the pin flag was left upright at the location to signal the recording crew. On some occasions the recording crew lagged behind the recovery team and it was impossible to record and collect the exposed artifacts before the end of the workday. In these instances we assigned a temporary alpha or numeric designation to the artifact and respective pin flag. We then recorded provenience, bagged the artifact, and placed it with the collection for security purposes. The following day the specimen was properly recorded.

Exposed artifacts near visitor locations presented minor security problems during working hours. In most instances the recovery crew worked in the immediate vicinity of exposed artifacts, and security was not a problem. When we anticipated leaving an area (for example at the lunch hour), either the procedure described above was implemented or a crew member was left in the area. Sites were closed to visitor traffic when necessary.

Recording

The recording crew assigned field-specimen numbers, recorded artifact proveniences, and collected specimens. Recorders backfilled artifact-location holes upon completion. The crew consisted of an instrument operator, a rodman, and two recorders. Artifacts were assigned sequential field-specimen numbers beginning at 0001. Records were kept in a field-specimen catalog. The catalog was transferred to computer storage while we were in the field to facilitate daily reference.

We maintained standardization by consistently designating the same person as one of the recorders. An archaeologist supervised the recording and operated the instrument with one exception: on May 22 and 23, 1984, two recording teams were utilized. The second included a volunteer experienced in surveying and an experienced recorder. This team recorded an area that contained primarily recent historic artifacts.

Each artifact marked by a pin flag was piece-plotted as follows. The instrument was set up at a selected grid coordinate marker (fig. 7). Distance and azimuth readings for each artifact location were recorded in reference to the known grid coordinates. Distance was read to the nearest ten centimeters (four inches); azimuth was read to the half-minute. The instrument operator transmitted this information to the recorders by portable two-way radio or by unaided voice. Recorders entered the information in the catalog and recorded the depth of the artifact and, when necessary, its orientation to the cardinal directions and declination from the horizontal. This information was used to determine bullet trajectories and fields of fire. Orientation and declination were not recorded for surface specimens. For certain types of artifacts this information either was not determinable or was considered superfluous to patterning studies. Examples were nails, buttons, spurs, suspender clips, coins, horse trappings, leather goods, most wood parts, cans, and amorphous metal fragments. In the main, orientation and declination were important considerations in recording projectiles (e.g., bullets and metal projectile points) and cartridge cases.

The marble markers were also recorded in reference to our grid. We instituted this procedure at the request of the superintendent, who noted that the marker locations had not been accurately mapped since 1891, when a U.S. Geological Survey team had undertaken the task. The superintendent also noted that there was no precise count of

Fig. 7. The recording crew utilized a transit to locate precisely and map each artifact. The transit was set up over a known grid point.

the number of markers actually on the battlefield. An accurate map of the markers was useful to the project, as well as in the artifact-pattern analysis. The association of battle-related artifacts and human remains with the markers provided insight into the relative accuracy of the original marker placement, as will be discussed. We found that there were 252 marble markers on the battlefield.

Testing Phase

We utilized three testing techniques during the fieldwork: standard small-block excavations, auger tests, and shovel tests. The shovel and auger tests were conducted exclusively in Deep Ravine; block excavations were conducted at marble marker locations and at locations not associated with marble markers on Custer Battlefield. No excavations were conducted on the Reno-Benteen defense site. All test units were referenced to the grid and backfilled upon completion of investigations. Crew members involved in excavations and other tests were supervised by an archaeologist at all times.

Block Excavation

Block excavations consisted of units 2 meters square (6.6 feet) and 1 by 2 meters (3.3 by 6.6 feet). Excavation units, without exception, were placed in areas of known or suspected battle activity. Six of the seven units excavated at Calhoun Hill were placed to assess the nature of subsurface-artifact patterning, if present. One unit was placed to discover the source of a surface concentration of small bone. Twenty-five additional units were excavated around selected marble markers to answer questions concerning marker-burial correlations.

Before excavations began at any unit, we inspected the surface visually and subjected the unit to metal detection. Each unit was excavated with hand tools after vegetation and sod had been removed with skimming shovels. All soil from the excavations was screened through quarter-inch-mesh hardware cloth as it was removed from the excavation unit. Artifacts were left in place as they were found, and the units were mapped at the completion of the excavation (see chapter 5 for more detail).

Calhoun Hill Excavations

In an attempt to learn to what degree, if any, the metal-detection inventory was missing nonmetallic items, excavations unassociated with marble markers were performed on Calhoun Hill. The selection of Calhoun Hill for these tests was based on the knowledge that this area had been noted by the first burial detail as having evidence of soldiers firing in skirmish order (Nichols 1983). That evidence consisted of cartridge cases found in groups spaced about five feet apart. It was reasoned that the markers would reflect only where men were buried, not necessarily where they had actually fought. Since the direct evidence for the fight at Calhoun Hill would be primarily cartridge cases and remains of equipment, we selected as test locales six localities identified by signals from the metal detectors.

These six areas were excavated in two meter square units. Three of the units (N6732 E2758, N6734 E2758, and N6736 E2758) were contiguous. Three noncontiguous units were designated N6732 E2750, N6654 E2760, and N6658 E2763. The artifacts were left in place as they were found, and all dirt removed from the excavations was screened through quarter-inch-mesh hardware cloth. In each of the six units excavated, only those artifacts which had been previously identified by the metal detectors were found. These items were recovered within three to six centimeters (one to four inches) of the present ground surface, essentially within the root zone of the native prairie soils.

These tests helped verify the value of the metal-detecting inventory technique and demonstrate that the inventory probably was not missing a sisnificant number of nonmetallic items at locations beyond the marble markers.

Shovel and Auger Tests

Shovel and auger tests were conducted in Deep Ravine in an attempt to locate the remains of soldiers reported buried there. The tests were unsuccessful in locating the remains (see chapters 4 and 8 for more detail).

Shovel tests resembled block excavations except that standard unit sizes were not adhered to. Most tests were conducted at moundlike anomalies, which varied in size and were suspected to contain burial remains. Some tests exceeded three meters (9.9 feet) in length and 1 meter (3.3 feet) in depth.

Auger tests were also utilized in the futile attempt to locate the missing remains. These were placed at regular intervals along both walls in the lower half of Deep Ravine. Some randomly placed units were placed in the ravine's upper half.

We used a five-horsepower two-man gasoline powered auger to drill the holes. The bit size was ten inches in diameter and four feet long. The bit length restricted the depth of the test holes to about 1 meter, or 3.3 feet. Each hole was inspected by an archaeologist after drilling, as was the dirt removed from the hole. All holes were backfilled.

Inventory Evaluation Phase

The evaluation phase was designed to test the validity of the metal-detecting procedure that we used throughout the project. The evaluation was a simple one. We selected seven 100-meter-square units that we had previously inventoried and reinventoried them, using a more detailed procedure. We selected the units to be reinventoried as representing areas that had yielded a large quantity of artifacts (square N6500 E3000), a moderate quantity (squares N7100 E2700 and N7500 E2400), a small quantity (squares N6600 E2200 and N7300 E2000), and two areas at Reno-Benteen defense site; one (square N2400 E2400) representing an Indian position and the other (square N2000 E2300) representing an army position. The relative quantity of artifacts was a subjective judgment of the archaeologists. The reinventory procedure divided the squares into a series of transects 2 meters wide. The metal-detector operators were lined up, and each walked the area very slowly, sweeping it with his or her detector in an arc 1.5 to 2 meters (4 to 6.6 feet) wide. When one transect was completed, the crew supervisor pivoted the group to the next set of transects and a new sweep began. The project procedures for pin flagging and artifact recording described above were used.

Each reinventoried 100-meter-square yielded about twice the number of artifacts that had been recovered during the initial detector sweeps. Statistically, this is a 30 to 35 percent sample of all the artifacts, far more than necessary to assess and interpret patterns and spatial distributions if the sample recovered is representative of the total variety of artifacts.

We cross-tabulated the artifacts, the quantity of artifact classes, and types of artifacts initially recovered against those found in the evaluation phase. In evaluating the data, we determined that the artifacts are truly representative of the artifact population and that we had a valid sample for interpreting the patterns of artifact distribution. The number of artifacts in the various classes and types are also representative of all the artifacts on the battlefield and are also a valid sample.

LABORATORY METHODS

The methods employed in cleaning the artifacts are the standard laboratory procedures of the Midwest Archeological Center. Essentially they consist of washing the accumulated dirt and mud from each artifact and then determining the condition of the artifact to see whether it requires further cleaning or conservation. Most metallic items required a treatment in dilute glycolic acid to remove oxides that had built up on them during the years they were in the ground. If the oxides were extremely heavy, some items were subjected to an electrolysis bath to remove them. After it was cleaned and stabilized, each artifact was rebagged in a self-sealing clear plastic bag with its appropriate field-specimen number on the bag. The artifacts were then identified, sorted, and analyzed.

The identification, sorting, and analysis consisted of dividing the artifacts into classes of like objects and then subsorting the artifacts into further identifiable discrete types. For example, all the cartridge cases were placed together and then subsorted into their respective types, such as .45/55-caliber Springfield carbine cases or .44-caliber Henry rimfire cartridge cases. Some artifacts were sorted to even more discrete levels if warranted, such as the .44-caliber Henry cases into long and short cases, headstamped and not headstamped, and double firing-pin marks, single firing-pin marks, and multiple firing-pin marks. Sorting and identification of the artifacts were undertaken by personnel experienced with artifacts of this period, who compared the artifacts with type collections and with standard reference materials. The pertinent reference material is cited in the discussion of the particular artifact in chapter 7.

Presently the artifacts and original supporting notes, records, and other documentation are held at the National Park Service's Midwest Archeological Center. Upon completion of the multiyear project the artifacts will be returned to Custer Battlefield National Monument for its collection and display and for use in further scientific research.

PART TWO

SYNTHESIS AND INTERPRETATION

Chapter 4

Mystery in the Deep Ravine

Mysteries, good ones at least, invariably yield their secrets grudgingly. That is part of the attraction to the Little Bighorn fight. And Deep Ravine is certainly a good mystery. A number of Custer's men were reportedly killed in the ravine, a rugged gully that dissects the sloping plain below Custer Ridge (fig. 3). The mystery begins with the question of how many men were killed there. Captain Frederick Benteen (Nichols 1983:474; Utley 1972:327) estimated twenty-two dead, while Myles Moylan (Utley 1972:224) thought there were "20 odd" bodies. Thirty-four seemed reasonable to Lieutenant Richard Thompson (Hammer 1976:248). The highest estimate is "some 40 or 50" (Gibbon 1877), but twenty-eight is the most frequently cited number (Bradley in Hardoff 1985:54; Godfrey 1892; Hare in Nichols 1983:34 and Utley 1972:262; Knipe in Hardoff 1985:55; Maguire in Nichols 1983:9; Maguire 1876; McClernand 1927:30). It is possible that twenty-eight somehow became erroneously fixed in the minds of men who moved about in military circles. But Good Voiced Elk (Hardoff 1985:59) and He Dog (Hammer 1976:207), both Indian participants in the Little Bighorn fight, agreed (Good Voiced Elk said twenty-five to thirty, He Dog corroborated twenty-eight), and it is doubtful that these men shared directly in the information that circulated among Little Bighorn army survivors. In terms of the number of dead in Deep Ravine, then, twenty-eight is a good starting point.

Whatever the number, and despite decades of speculation, the whereabouts of these men and the circumstances of their death remain obscure. Indeed, after considerable searching we, too, have failed to find the long-lost soldiers or any of the equipment they might have carried with them into the ravine. Nevertheless, the puzzle, after investigations during the years spanning 1983 to 1985, appears much less intractable today. A solution appears near, thanks largely to the recently acquired knowledge of the physical structure and natural history of Deep Ravine. Geomorphology, the study of the nature and origin of earth's topographic features, has provided the key. Through it Dr. Vance Haynes, Jr. (chapter 8) unearthed in Deep Ravine evidence of a deeply buried gully that matches nicely certain historical accounts which describe a narrow, steep-walled gully that trapped the luckless men. This gully is near the South Skirmish Line at the southerly end about where the battlefield's self-guided tour trail enters Deep Ravine. What lies buried here remains to be seen, but the potential is high. The concordance between the geomorphological finds and certain historical accounts bodes well for the prospect of eventually solving the mystery of Deep Ravine.

In chapter 1 we touched on the importance of Deep Ravine research, alluding to the potential for enhancing interpretation of the fight's progress. Nowhere is that potential greater than in exposing the relationships between the Deep Ravine dead and the action on the South Skirmish Line. We must then ask, were the Deep Ravine soldiers once part of the skirmish line? Sensing doom, did they flee the line, as some eyewitnesses have surmised, seeking escape or hiding in the ravine? Were they positioned in the ravine as part of an orderly defense along the line? Or was their presence there unrelated to the skirmish line action? Hardoff (1985:61) thinks so, arguing from Indian accounts that these men fled Custer Hill. There are many options and little resolution at the moment, but historical archaeology can provide answers or at the least provide some direction in resolving the issues.

What, then, are we looking for that might help in shedding light on the mystery of Deep Ravine? What can we expect? The answers seem straightforward. We can expect human remains such as bones and teeth. These undoubtedly will be useful in augmenting Seventh Cavalry demographic data. There is a reasonable chance that evidence of military hardware, bullets, and cartridge cases will be unearthed. Elsewhere on the battlefield were found horse trappings and personal accoutrements. These artifacts should also be in Deep Ravine, likely in direct association with the human bones. There is no reason why these and other artifact types from the ravine cannot be subjected to the various analytical methods that proved useful on other parts of the battlefield. For example, cartridge-case signatures can be compared to those found on the South Skirmish Line in an attempt to link the missing men to this episode in the battle. If the link is there, then with some confidence Company E can be placed on the skirmish line, for McDougall (Graham 1953:377; Hammer 1976:72; Nichols 1983:616; Utley 1972:379) said that it was men from this company that he found in the ravine. Others (Hare in Nichols 1983:341 and Utley 1972:262; Moylan in Utley 1972:224; Stanislas in Hammer 1976:116–17; Wallace in Nichols 1983:74) testified similarly and some (DeRudio in Hammer 1976:87; Goldin in Carroll 1974:19 and Hardoff 1985:58) identified E Company, otherwise called the Gray Horse Troop, on the basis of gray (or white) horses found nearby. Yet there are some (Hardoff 1985; Taunton 1980), using the same historical record, who argue that E Company was nowhere in the vicinity of Deep Ravine. Who is right?

Moreover, fixing the precise locations of the bodies can aid in describing the circumstances that led the men into the ravine. Once again, the historical record is far from clear in this regard. Some say the soldiers resisted in the ravine, quite likely in skirmish order (Wallace in Hammer 1976; Hare in Hammer 1976; McDougall in Hammer 1976; DeRudio in Hammer 1976). Others felt the troops fled into the ravine (Good Voiced Elk and He Dog in Hammer 1976; Maguire in Nichols 1983; McClernand 1927; Miles 1897) to hide (Black Elk in Neihardt 1961; Maguire 1876). Still others observed, contrary to those who "saw" a skirmish line, the bodies in a heap or pile

(Goldin in Graham 1953; Hardy in Hammer 1976; Martin in Hammer 1976). We feel that the escape theory will fare well if the bodies are found clustered. On the other hand, patterning at skirmish intervals or some semblance might point to either a coordinated defense, possibly as part of the skirmish line action, or at least, as Lieutenant Charles DeRudio (Hammer 1976) and Captain Myles Moylan (Utley 1972) deduced, an organized but unsuccessful retreat.

These are the issues that have been addressed and readdressed for years in the historical commentary of the Little Bighorn fight. While we recognize the value of historical accounts, particularly as they serve to focus our research, we also note the contradictions they contain. These contradictions are the source of the various theories about what happened in Deep Ravine and elsewhere. Some theories, of course, are stronger than others, but a theory well reasoned from an ambiguous historical record, no matter how plausible, is one thing. Confirmation based upon physical evidence is quite another. Contrary to those who feel they have the answers to Deep Ravine, we believe the questions remain open until the artifactual data are brought to bear on the issues. That is the value of historical archaeology in Deep Ravine.

There are other concerns as well. By all accounts the soldiers in Deep Ravine were hastily buried, as were men elsewhere on the field, without military pomp. Indeed, there were no graves; the bodies were merely covered with dirt (McDougall's and Goldin's accounts in Graham 1953:377; Carroll 1974:19, 27). Thus recovery of the missing troopers can ultimately lead to a belated but formal military interment.

The public interpretive aspect is also important. In recent years Deep Ravine has become a popular part of the interpretive program at Custer Battlefield. In answering the perplexing questions raised above we can provide a more meaningful program for thousands of yearly visitors. And what about matching bones with names? Hardoff (1985:57) identifies five men thought to have been slain in Deep Ravine. Though he is wrong about Mitch Boyer's presence there, it may be possible to identify the remains of some of these men.

Though Deep Ravine historical accounts are equivocal, first on one matter and then on the next, one thing is certain; soldiers died there and that is where they were buried (McDougall in Hammer 1976:72; Logan in Hammer 1976:140). There is not a single convincing account to the contrary. But marble memorial stones, like those elsewhere on the field that purport to mark where soldiers fell, are not now and apparently never have been in place. This has fueled speculation that the bodies are no longer there. Some early visitors to the battlefield, for example, reported seeing bones exposed by rainstorms. So is it possible that the evidence has been flushed from the ravine? As detailed later, that is not likely. The recent history of Deep Ravine has been characterized more by an accumulation of sediments than by severe erosion. Some remains may have been dislodged slightly but they almost certainly have not been eroded away. But what about the 1881 reburial party? Were they any more successful in locating and removing the skeletons in Deep Ravine than they were on the slopes and ridges above? That is not likely, either, given their lack of success elsewhere on the battlefield. In any case, there is no record that they even searched in the ravine, and even had they searched there, would they have removed all of the associated evidence? The answer, obviously, is no. They were not that efficient elsewhere. Nor can we lend credence to Kuhlman's (1951:237) suggestion that the 1877 burial detail removed the Deep Ravine bodies to positions on the South Skirmish Line. Finally, we might expect acidic soils to hasten decomposition of bones. But in Deep Ravine the soils are basic, or alkaline, and conducive to preservation of organics. Thus the evidence weighs heavily in favor of soldiers in Deep Ravine. They are undoubtedly still there.

Unfortunately, and despite several thorough visual and metal detector surveys in 1984 and 1985, the missing men of Deep Ravine were not located. Limited subsurface testing also proved negative (fig. 8). It was almost as if the naysayers were correct and the soldiers were actually no longer there. But the matter is considerably more involved than that. There is another and more reasonable possibility. Our predicament almost certainly resulted from the likelihood, as the geomorphology of Deep Ravine shows, that the artifacts, whether human bones or battle artifacts, are deeply buried, much beyond conventional testing and metal-detection capabilities.

Eyewitness accounts of the dead in Deep Ravine abound. We have assembled some fifty sources, but when it comes to fixing the soldiers, whereabouts, most pose the same problem. They are either vague or they do not deal with the matter at all. Time and again we are left with phrases, such as "they were in a ravine" or "we saw them in a deep gully" and nothing more. But where? Well, a few are more specific, and several of these are conspicuous in light of the 1984 fieldwork. The earthen mounds, so promising in 1983, turned out to be natural formations, and auger testing in the lower ravine produced nothing of import. Also, the metal detecting for the most part mirrored testing results (Scott and Fox 1987). The ravine, except in the upper reaches where detecting revealed some spent ammunition, showed absolutely no evidence of dead soldiers, bones or otherwise. More and more the archaeological evidence, though decidedly negative, tended to support historical accounts placing the soldiers in the upper ravine, nearer the headcut and South Skirmish Line.

In 1879 Captain C. K. Sanderson, the officer in charge of the burial improvement detail that year, erected a log memorial on Last Stand Hill. Later, in 1881, that site was used as the common grave for many of the Seventh Cavalry dead. With the logs removed, the grave was marked with a granite monument that still stands, and for a long time the hill and monument have provided good reference points. Today, measuring the straight-line distance from the monument to Deep Ravine's headcut a distance of about 2,000 feet (610 meters) is derived. Apparently there was not much difference in 1876 if some accounts of the Deep Ravine dead can be taken at face value. Sergeant Daniel Knipe combed the field a few days after the fight and later estimated (Hammer 1976:95) that the bodies in "the deep gully [were] about 2000 feet from where the monument now stands." W. R. Logan was there, too. He saw the bodies in a "coulee lying about six or seven hundred yards over the ridge from where the body of the General was found" (Hammer 1976:140). Though they did not say it, Knipe and Logan had remembered the bodies near the ravine headcut.

But others may have seen exactly this. Deep Ravine near the headcut, as described, is narrow, with high, steep walls; perhaps a similar configuration existed in 1876. Private Goldin, recollecting in 1928 and 1930, described the ravine that trapped the men as a cul-de-sac with high banks in front and on both sides (Carroll 1974:19, 27). Lieutenant James Bradley, the first officer to witness the fight's aftermath, also noticed a cul de sac (Hardoff 1985:59) where the bodies were found. Apparently the soldiers had unsuccessfully attempted to scramble out of the trap for Lieutenant Moylan (Nich-

Fig. 8. Excavations under way at one of the mounds in Deep Ravine.

ols 1983:264; Utley 1972:224) and William Hardy (Hardoff 1985:55) reported see-ing handprints halfway up the ravine walls. Captain Myles Moylan's and Trumpeter William Hardy's memories probably served them well for the cul de sac, though an imposing obstacle, must have been the only way out if Indians blocked the entrance. Indian informants told General Nelson Miles (1897:288–89) that the soldiers had fled, probably through the ravine, toward the river timber but were diverted to the head of a coulee. Once there, and with their only escape route sealed, the troopers were gunned down.

History was beginning to make a little more sense. DeRudio and Benteen remem-bered the bodies in a position very near the Little Bighorn River, but the archaeological investigations there diminished this possibility. Moylan (Nichols 1983:264; Utley 1972:224) used the river as a reference point, too, but he estimated the distance to be a "half or three-quarters of a mile." The headcut lies about a half-mile from the river. Still though, we had no idea where, in the headcut vicinity. Circumstantial evidence suggested the area below the South Skirmish Line. Lieutenant Edward McClernand (1927:30) said he saw the bodies at the lower end of the line, and so did McDougall (Nichols 1983:616; Utley 1972:339), reporting in 1879 that about half of E Company lay in the ravine while the other half were on a line outside. McDougall (Hammer 1976:62; Graham 1953:377) vacillated later in life (in the 1930s), stating that only a few bodies were found outside. Did memory fail him as the years passed? Probably, for all other aspects of his testimony remained consistent over the years. Nevertheless, the headcut vicinity near the skirmish line now seemed most promising. But we faced another problem. What did the ravine look like in 1876 and what processes had acted upon it since then?

To answer these questions, we had to understand the ravine's stratigraphic history, not only in the upper reaches but throughout. Until this was accomplished, future work on the problem would continue to be hit and miss. In 1985, Deep Ravine was investigated with several goals in mind. We wanted to identify the 1876 ground surface and pinpoint the physical configuration that best fit the historical record, a record now culled of the more unlikely accounts. If the soldiers were found in the process, so much the better.

At the outset it was quite apparent that to achieve these goals something besides picks and shovels was needed. Trenches were needed across the ravine to expose stratigraphic profiles. The profiles, in turn, would provide the information necessary to reconstruct the ravine's history, the processes by which the various strata were formed. It was hoped to secure organic remains to be used in dating the strata. To do this mechanized equipment, a backhoe, was the answer.

Of course the use of machinery at archaeological sites does not fit the common view of an archaeologist at work. Nonetheless, machinery is frequently employed, particularly at sites like Deep Ravine, where hand labor would be time consuming and costly. Graders, for example, are often used to remove overburden from deeply buried cultural deposits. And backhoes, in fact, are efficient tools for exposing stratigraphy. But their use is not undertaken haphazardly. The excavations were designed to minimize damage to the environment. When our work was finished each trench was restored, as nearly as possible, to its original contour, thereby allowing rapid revegetation of the exposed areas. It was possible that we might fortuitously expose soldiers' remains, so we made sure that a professional archaeologist monitored every excavation closely. And in one trench very near the modern headcut, artifacts were found. Though not related to the battle, they provide substantial new evidence bearing on the whereabouts of the missing soldiers. To grasp the importance of this discovery, it is necessary to understand the results of the geomorphological investigations, which are detailed in chapter 8.

By the end of the field season eleven trenches had been excavated in Deep Ravine. Nine lay in the upper ravine between the headcut and the junction at Calhoun Coulee; two lay below the coulee. The investigations emphasized the upper reaches on the strength of the historical evidence. The lower two trenches, though placed in areas with little historical potential, helped to reveal the complete stratigraphic history throughout the ravine.

Soil profiles in the eleven backhoe trenches revealed seven major geologic strata which form the structure of Deep Ravine. Although each stratum does not occur in every trench, they do provide the basis for a composite stratigraphic column. The lowest stratum is (K), bedrock shale dating from the Cretaceous geologic period, which ended about sixty million years ago. Decomposition and erosion of the shale, processes acting over millions of years, have produced the overlying sediments. Unit B, consisting of moderately sorted fluvial sand layers, was laid down on the bedrock by the Little Bighorn River, probably during the late Pleistocene. At that time, more than forty thousand years ago, the river channel was considerably farther east than it is now and above the present mouth of Deep Ravine. Unit B occurs only at the ravine mouth. Neither unit is of any consequence in our story of Deep Ravine.

Other stratigraphic units above bedrock are typical of alluvial strata deposited by water-discharge episodes in the ravine. Some very fine sediments are probably wind blown.

Unit F_2, nearly two feet (sixty centimeters) thick at its maximum, is the uppermost natural stratum in the column. It consists of light-yellowish-brown to olive-colored sand. The sand varies in places from clayey to silty in composition. The unit is located throughout most of the ravine. Unit F_2 is historic in age as radiocarbon samples from the carbonaceous lenses in the stratum show. The samples show that the unit can be no more than two hundred years old. The uppermost unit F carbon lenses could be from a range fire that swept the battlefield in 1908, the last before the fire of 1983. The radiocarbon dating is consistent with stratigraphic evidence that shows unit F to be historic in age.

Obviously the missing soldiers must be buried in unit F. The question is, where? Because unit F extends the entire length of the ravine the area must be narrowed further. It is possible to eliminate much of the ravine on the basis of structure alone. Unit F below trench 1 seems much too thin (the unit does not exceed two feet [sixty centimeters] in thickness) to bury twenty-eight skeletons deep enough to escape detection. After all, we inspected the ravine many times and test units were placed over much of the area, each time without success. Metallic items would have been detected if associated with the bodies in one of the thorough metal detector sweeps. Maximum depths of two feet (sixty centimeters) are just not sufficient to filter detector signals completely. It must also be realized that the stratum, which is quite consistent in profile below trench 1, does not physically resemble the steep, high bank structure predicted from historical accounts. Indeed, unit F deposits throughout are sufficiently thin below trench 1 to exclude the existence of a gully deep enough to trap more than two dozen men.

In historical archaeology it is just as important to know where things are not (or, in this case where they cannot be) as it is to know where they are. Exposing the geomorphology of the lower ravine, plus the earlier archaeological results, served to cull the historical record of bogus accounts. The descriptions of Benteen and DeRudio almost surely were inaccurate. Those of Hare, Knipe, and others were more likely correct. We now knew the missing men almost certainly had to be in the vicinity of the headcut.

The narrow ravine and soggy floor above trench 1 forced us to approach the trenching near the headcut from the banks above. This position allowed the excavation of three trenches: 9, 10 and 11.

The stratigraphy in trench 9 revealed two feet (sixty centimeters) of silt or fine sand that was presumed to be unit F, that is, a continuation of the historic-age stratum prevalent downstream. Immediately below we found a stratum (three feet or about one meter thick) consisting of stream-rounded cobblestones, and below the stones an unanticipated discovery was made. Here, nearly six feet (two meters) below the present ravine floor, a lens of historic trash that dates to the 1930s was found. The trash, including glass, crockery, cast iron pipe, rotten wood, and the river cobbles (designated as unit G), is inset against unit C, the prehistoric stratum that forms the south bank of Deep Ravine.

The trash lens may continue deeper, but we could not check this possibility. The backhoe arm would not extend farther, and for safety reasons we could not enter the trench to conduct hand excavations. But it was clear that unit G had not occurred naturally. Someone threw the trash into the ravine and the stream-rounded cobbles had to have come from a watery environment powerful enough to abrade and round the stones. The stones must have been carried into the ravine from the Little Bighorn River, likely to serve as riprap to prevent erosion in this area. Indeed, the ravine's south bank below the present headcut is also covered with stone riprap that is clearly visible today. And downstream, a small north-bank tributary also has been riprapped. The tributary riprap appears in a 1937 photograph taken by Charles Kuhlman, but not in the Walter Camp pre-1915 photographs of the same area, so the riprap was placed between 1915 and 1937.

Unfortunately we have found no record of bank stabilization, so we cannot say precisely why the riprap was placed. The ravine here was much deeper before it was filled with trash and stone riprap than it is today. The riprap was probably placed to prevent further erosion of what must have been an old headcut between trench 9 and the modern headcut. This is evident because trench 10, which was placed fifteen feet (five meters) above (upstream) trench 9, revealed only natural deposits identified as units C and F. Apparently the modern headcut formed after unit G was placed and it has subsequently migrated upstream furnishing the sediments that buried the riprap and trash. The historic deposits (unit G) appear to be even more deeply buried in the vicinity of trench 11, located twenty-five feet (eight meters) below (downstream) trench 9, because the backhoe arm could not reach the presumed extension of unit G downstream. We were able to expose only unit F, which was inset against sediments presumed to be unit C.

What does all this mean in terms of solving the Deep Ravine mystery? Very simply, it means that Deep Ravine in the vicinity of the South Skirmish Line was once substantially deeper than it is now. The cultural deposits (unit G) revealed in trench 9 fill a gully that is at least 6 feet (2 meters) deeper than the present floor of Deep Ravine. The steep south bank rises another 7½ feet (2.3 meters) above the ravine floor and the north bank, at nearly 9 feet (2.7 meters), is even higher. The north wall has slumped recently, apparently after 1937 for the slump is not visible in the Kuhlman photo, and this slumping has probably doubled the ravine width near the headcut. But before slumping the ravine was probably only 15 to 20 feet (5 to 6½ meters) wide here. Thus from these indications it is possible, if not probable, that this part of Deep Ravine was at least 15 feet (5 meters) deep and no more than 20 feet (6½ meters) wide in 1876. With a headcut height of perhaps 10 feet (3.2 meters), Deep Ravine did indeed form a cul-de-sac from which there was no chance for escape. We can expect the missing soldiers to be here, buried 6 feet (2 meters) or more below Deep Ravine's floor.

As Dr. Haynes (chapter 8) has noted the burials themselves may have helped to bury deeply the soldiers' remains. The corpses and the earth covering them could have created a low check dam on the ravine floor. This dam, particularly if the bodies were heaped in one or a few piles, may have promoted sedimentation and partial filling of the ravine above (upstream) the obstruction. In this scenario, sedimentation would have eventually reached and partially filled the old headcut as well. With the deepest portion of the ravine mostly filled, the modern headcut continued to migrate upstream. Possibly the renewed cutting reached intense proportions in the 1930s when infrequent but violent storms cut away at the parched earth. If so, emplacement of the trash and riprap at the headcut has apparently been effective. Except for bank slumping, this portion of Deep Ravine is not now severely eroded.

With the historical evidence and the recently acquired geomorphological data in hand, we believe that the missing troopers will be found somewhere between one hundred and two hundred feet (thirty to sixty meters) below (downstream) the modern headcut. The depth information from trench 11 suggests they are covered with well over six feet (two meters) of sediments, a depth that would place them below the water table. Bones, cloth, metal and other materials preserve well in water as long as they are not allowed to dry out periodically. The water table here probably has not receded substantially over time. But in order for excavations to get at the soldiers' remains, the water table would have to be lowered by pumping from a well placed above the area to be excavated. And to prevent deterioration, the remains would have to be preserved immediately once exposed to the air.

A DEEP RAVINE POSTSCRIPT

Though the missing soldiers have not yet been found, the investigations in Deep Ravine have accomplished two important tasks. First, through the use of geomorphology and historical archaeology, it has been shown where the troopers cannot be. They cannot be far below the modern headcut because the natural stratum formed in historic times is much too thin. The testing and metal detecting agrees with this. And they cannot be deeper because the next-lower stratum is prehistoric in age. This knowledge, which might appear redundant to those who have all along favored the upper ravine on historical grounds alone, is important because it complements the second contribution. We are reasonably sure where the bodies are not, and this enhances our ability to predict where they are. Thus geomorphology has shown, despite the lack of artifactual data, that in 1876 the ravine structure near the South Skirmish Line formed a cul-de-sac. People who shortly after the fight observed the cul de sac saw that it contained bodies and they saw it exactly where we found it, some 2,000 feet (610 meters) from the monument on Last Stand Hill. Future investigations must be concentrated here. The likelihood of finding the soldiers is even greater than before.

We have not yet found the soldiers but we can engage in some informed speculation based upon what we now know. If Dr. Haynes (chapter 8) is correct in surmising that the bodies were so tightly clustered that they formed a dam which helped fill the ravine with sediments, then what of Lieutenant George Wallace's (Hammer 1976) and Lieutenant Luther Hare's (Hammer 1976) observations. Twenty-eight men at skirmish order would be, assuming 15-foot intervals, spread over some 420 feet (128 meters). This is hardly a cluster pattern that prompted some to recall bodies piled in a heap. So far the geomorphological evidence, though circumstantial, argues against Wallace and Hare. We believe the bodies are contained in a much smaller area than skirmish intervals would allow. So perhaps the defense in Deep Ravine was not as organized as the two officers implied. It is known that men without leadership tend to cluster in panic situations, and perhaps that is what happened in Deep Ravine. Perhaps the men, sensing impending doom, fled in panic seeking cover in the ravine. This story fits at least some of the historical accounts, but we will never know until we bring the archaeological testimony from the depths.

Finally, there is one other matter that must be considered before consigning the Deep Ravine mystery to future archaeological investigations. Lieutenant Edward Maguire, a topographic engineer with General Terry's relief column, inspected the battlefield days after the fight, preparing sketches that were used for drawing official-report maps. Maguire's maps contain scale errors and topographic features are generally distorted. Despite this, one thing is certain: he clearly identified Deep Ravine. Furthermore, he placed X symbols in Deep Ravine (and Calhoun Coulee) that most researchers have interpreted as body locations. They have every right to do so because Maguire's X symbols elsewhere on the battlefield seem to place closely the bodies of other individuals, albeit the more prominent ones. The curious thing is that the symbols (twenty-two of them) in Deep Ravine are distributed in linear fashion from the headcut to Little Bighorn River. There are even seven symbols in Calhoun Coulee. Did Maguire actually see single bodies nicely, almost regularly, distributed throughout the ravine? Obviously, our investigations are entirely at odds with what Maguire portrayed, and we, of course, are inclined to place more faith in our results. So what is the answer? Well, we are not entirely sure, but the discrepancy is much more palatable if each X is seen as a symbolic representation. We think the symbols were meant to represent the ravine in which the dead men were found and not the precise location of each. This situation might have been reversed if important individuals, such as Custer, had been found in the ravine. But so far as we know they were not.

The circumstantial evidence is in and it is strong. The evidence is better than we have ever had before that the men were at one time buried near the head of the ravine.

Chapter 5

Markers and Maps

Custer Battlefield National Monument is unique among sites commemorating military actions because of the marble markers scattered about the field which denote where the men died in battle. But do the markers on the battlefield accurately reflect where Custer's men fell during the Battle of the Little Bighorn? This question was central to our research goals because the placement of these markers is integral to many reconstructions of the battle. However, their actual relation to the position of Custer's men is questionable—there are 252 markers for the 210 dead in Custer's command.

Since the battle there have been at least three episodes of burial and reburial of soldiers' remains. The first burial, or really the covering of the dead, was completed on June 28, 1876 by Major Reno's command and members of the relief column. In 1877 and again in 1879, details went to the field specifically to reinter remains exposed by the elements or by predators. In 1881 a detail of soldiers was sent to disinter all the soldiers' remains and rebury them in a mass grave. This mass grave is now located on the top of Last Stand Hill surrounding the granite memorial shaft (Charles Roe letter, Oct. 6, 1908 to W. M. Camp, Custer Battlefield National Monument files).

It was not until 1890 that the marble markers which now dot the battlefield were placed to commemorate locations where soldiers fell. The party to erect the headstones, under the command of Captain Owen Jay Sweet, arrived fourteen years after the battle, nine years after the soldiers' remains were reinterred in a mass grave:

A daily skirmish line searched over an area of about 2 square miles of the battlefield and the last of the 29 missing bodies were found and buried and the last headstone erected. During the search for [sic] bleaching skeletons of men were found and for some reason of neglect had remained unburied and with God's canopy alone to cover them for fourteen years. . . . On examination of the field it was found that the resting places of only 217 officers and men had been marked, exclusive of the places where Boston Custer and Arther [sic] (Autie) R. Reid fell, a difference of 29 graves. Lieut. Porter's not inclusive. This necessitated additional and trying work in an attempt, if possible, to discover and verify the resting places of the 29 missing bodies [official report of O. J. Sweet 1890, Custer Battlefield National Monument files].

Thus in 1890 there were 217 markers on the field, a number relatively consistent with the present estimate of approximately 210 men killed with Custer. It was Sweet's assumption that there should be 246 markers on the field that led the men to search for missing graves. The number 246 is approximately the number of men killed with both Custer and at the Reno-Benteen defense site. Sweet may well have confused the number of men who died in the battle with those who died under Custer's command and thereby added the Reno-Benteen dead to the number on the main battlefield. In fact, of the 249 headstones the party was given to erect, only two were placed on the Reno-Benteen defense site:

. . . making a total of 246 officers and men over whom headstones were erected on the Custer field. Two headstones, one for Lt. McIntosh and the other for Dr. DeWolf being erected on the Reno field, and that of Liet. Porter being returned to the post and turned over to the Post Quartermaster, accounts for 249 headstones [official report of O. J. Sweet 1890, Custer Battlefield National Monument files].

The extra markers, or at least the majority, we see today were probably first erected in 1890 under the mistaken assumption that 246 of the markers given the detail were for men who died on the main battlefield. Researchers today face the problem of ascertaining which markers represent the original 210 burials.

Sweet's report also documents another feature of the markers which students of the battle have discussed at length:

. . . all parts of the field show evidence of a large number of men who fell by two's or as comrades in battle . . . [official report of O. J. Sweet 1890, Custer Battlefield National Monument files].

There are indeed forty-three pairs of markers scattered over the main battlefield. Explanations like Sweet's have been proffered (i.e., the pairs represent places where "bunkies" [men who bunked together] fought and died together). An alternate explanation is that each pair represents only one soldier. In the original 1876 burials, dirt was scooped up from either side of the deceased and piled on top. This left a shallow indentation on either side of the burial. Later burial parties, seeing a scatter of human bone and two shallow indentations, may have assumed that each indentation represented a burial and may have placed two markers at that site.

These alternate explanations for the paired markers became the crux of the research questions that were tested through archaeological data-recovery means. If they represented a single soldier, remains consistent with those of a single individual would be found around the marker. If they represented the last stand of comrades, remains consistent with multiple individuals would be found at the marker.

MAPS OF THE CUSTER BATTLEFIELD

The first step in ascertaining which markers represented burials was to examine maps of the battlefield made both before and after the placement of the markers. It was hoped that discrepancies between the maps would help to locate and identify improperly placed markers.

In 1891 the United States Geological Survey sent topographer R. B. Marshall to map the main battlefield. Topographer Marshall also mapped the location of the marble markers set by Sweet. The 1891 map shows the location of 244 markers on the field, already a discrepancy of two markers in only one year.

Ever since this map was published, scholars have used it to visualize the last deployment of Custer's soldiers. Hammer (1976), Kuhlman (1951), and Hardorff (1985), among others, have used the map to argue where men died, lines of battle, and the validity of marker locations. Until the present archaeological project, the marker locations had been remapped only once, by Walter Camp, and then only informally for his research purposes (Taunton 1986).

Over the years, markers were moved or replaced by the battlefield's administrators; unfortunately, no accurate records of these activities were ever kept. The markers are numbered in an attempt to keep track of them, yet no precise count was ever made. Battlefield administrators estimated there were as many as 262 markers on the field. It was our task to remap the marker locations so as to make an accurate count of them.

In the process of recording the artifacts, the location and number of each marker was recorded, as were, abandoned brick and mortar marker bases and scattered brickbats. A map of these locations was also produced. From this data, we determined there are 252 markers on the field (fig. 9), a gain of eight markers over the 1891 map.

In order to determine where these eight markers are, a comparison was made between the current map and the 1891 map. The current map was electronically produced at a scale that matched that of the 1891 map. The two maps were then overlaid, using known marker locations as registration points. The marker locations on the two maps did not correlate well. We measured the distances between sets of markers on both maps to determine whether the mismatch was due to an error in scaling. The distances were not mathematically proportionate, so the error was not in scale.

A search of the USGS cartographic archives in Denver, Colorado, and the National Archives in Washington, D.C., failed to uncover the topographer's original notes, maps, or copies of the map. Les Porter of the USGS cartographic branch in Denver is familiar with early mapping techniques and pointed out that many topographic maps of that era contain inaccuracies not encountered in modern maps. The 1891 map was probably made using an alidade and plane table. Porter suggested that the topographer may have paced the distances between marker locations rather than measuring them. Pacing is not an accurate method of measurement, and could account for the differences between the two maps.

The lack of agreement between the current and 1891 maps required resolution, so the Walter Camp map of marker locations was also examined. A copy of this map is on file at Custer Battlefield National Monument and is published in Taunton (1986:20–21). It was obvious that the Camp topographic map features were scaled and drawn from the 1891 map, however, the marker locations do not match those on the earlier map. The marker locations on Camp's map compare well with those on our map. Camp's map has 246 markers, the current map 252. The Camp map's topographical features are not quite to scale, so there are small differences between the two, but there are no major discrepancies.

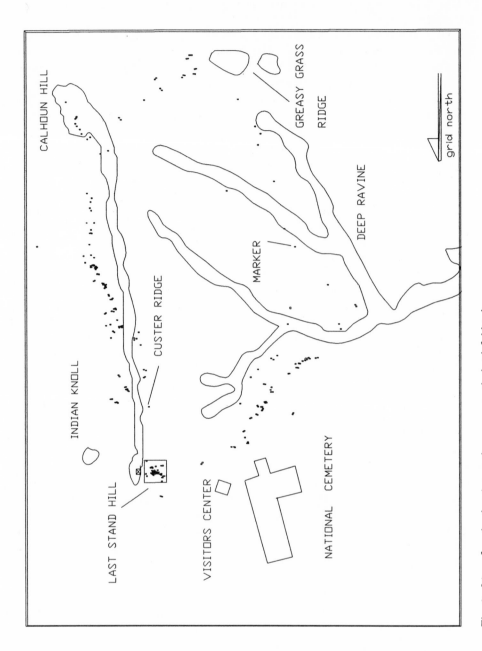

Fig. 9. Map of marker locations as they appear on the battlefield today.

Table 1 Markers with No Corollaries on the 1891 Map

	Archaeological Map	Camp Map
South Skirmish Line:	Marker Numbers: 20, 21, 24, 33, 40, 41, 48	Two markers between #'s 32, 35, 36, 39
		One marker east of #7
Last Stand Hill:	Marker Numbers: 70, 72, 82, 83, 86, 87, 88, 92, 108, 110	Three markers near #82 & #83
		Three markers west of #109
		Three markers east of #109
Keogh group:	Marker Numbers: 165, 171, 172, 173, 175, 176, 177, 184, 197, 198, 199, 221, 222, 223, 224, 225	One marker near #230
		One marker near #219
		Three markers near #191
		Four markers near #178
Calhoun Area:	None	Two markers east of #147
		One marker at #141 and #142
		One south of #138

Since precise correlations could not be made among the 1891 map and the later ones, we made relative correlations. A number of markers are depicted on all three maps in the same relative positions. These became the primary registration points for interpreting map differences. Independent verification of these points was made through analysis of the photographic documentation of marker placement available in the monument files. We found that thirty-three markers on the current map have no direct correlation with markers on the 1891 map (table 1).

On Last Stand Hill, Markers 82 to 89 have no correlation with any markers on the 1891 map. We have also been able to ascertain that Markers 57 and 58 are more than 330 feet (100 meters) south of their 1891 map location. Markers 92 and 93 have no correlation with locations on the earlier map. Indeed, Markers 93, 82, and 83 were placed some years after 1890 (Hardorff 1985). They represent Lieutenant Harrington, Armstrong Reed, and Boston Custer, respectively. Captain Sweet (Sweet to W. M. Camp, Jan. 13, 1913, Custer Battlefield National Monument files) indicated he also set these markers. The Sweet letter is not clear as to the date they were set, but it was probably in 1897. Interestingly, excavations on Last Stand Hill yielded human bone at Markers 86 and 87, which should not have had bone according to the 1891 map.

The markers in the Keogh area appear to have very little correlation with the locations shown on the 1891 map. However, all excavations in the Keogh area did recover human bone.

The markers around Calhoun Hill do not correlate with the 1891 map. The relative association between markers appears similar, but they seem to have been moved to be more visible to the motoring public. Excavations conducted at Marker 153, which is near the road, failed to reveal human remains or other battle-related artifacts. Excavations at Marker 131 also failed to reveal evidence of battle-related remains.

If the 1891 map is correct, Markers 3, 4, 5, and 6, along the South Skirmish Line, have been moved south, across Deep Ravine. Marker 257 also appears to have been

Fig. 10. A late 1890s or early 1900s photograph of Last Stand Hill. The brick and mortar marker bases are still visible.

Fig. 11. The markers on Last Stand Hill as seen in 1984. Note that the marker arrangement is identical to that seen in figure 10.

moved south, although excavations did yield human remains. In fact, a brick-and-mortar marker base was found north of the present Marker 252 location, and the current location shows no evidence of ever having a prepared base. However, excavations conducted at Markers 5, 6, and 252 yielded no battle-related remains. The excavations at Markers 5 and 6 found no artifactual material but revealed that the markers had been set on bedrock—not an area where it is likely men were buried.

As the preceding discussion illustrates, the lack of correlation between the 1891 map and the later maps serves to cloud further the issue of which markers are spurious. The excavation data are also inconsistent relative to the 1891 map. Battle-related remains were not always found where expected, and in areas the 1891 map suggested should be sterile, human bone was found. It appears that the 1891 map was incorrectly measured and the marker locations can only be considered as gross approximations of their actual locales.

Photographic documentation of markers was also examined. Special emphasis was placed on analysis of photographs taken of the battlefield before the markers were placed and in the three subsequent decades: 1890 to 1920. These photographs were compared with archaeological project photographs of the marker locations taken in 1984 and 1985.

The result of the comparisons is significant (figs. 10–11). The marker locations on the Camp map and our map show no major deviations between the maps and the photographs. A photograph of the Last Stand Hill locality dated 1894 (Custer Battlefield file photograph CB-G-52) shows that the markers are in the same relative locations on the ground as on the maps. The same can be said for a stereopticon photograph (copyright 1902 Universal Photo Art Company) of the same area. The correlation between the maps and a photograph of the Last Stand Hill and South Skirmish Line vicinities copyrighted in 1900 (Custer Battlefield file photograph CB-G-56) is also excellent. Correlations with the Camp map, Camp's pre-1915 battlefield photographs, and our map are also excellent.

Additional comparisons were made among the maps, the post-1890 photographic data, and the Stanley Morrow 1879 photographs of Last Stand Hill and the Keogh area. The locations of earth mounds, wooden markers, and wooden stakes shown in the 1879 photographs appear fairly well marked by marble markers today. The D. F. Barry photographs of the 1886 battle reenactment were also examined (Heski 1978). The wooden marker locations in these photographs also correlate very well with the current marker locations.

The correlations among the various photographs, the Camp map, and the current map are excellent. There is no evidence of large-scale or even moderate changes in the locations of the marble markers. Any changes in marker location have been on a very small scale. We conclude there is no doubt that the 1891 map is not an accurate representation of the marker locations and was not even in 1891. It should be discounted in any future analyses of marble-marker locations.

The differences of eight markers between the current map and the 1891 map and six between the Camp map and current map are less easily explained. It is possible that the differences may be attributed to a post-1915 but undocumented placement of additional markers. It is clear that the markers for the civilians (Boston Custer, Autie Reed, and Mark Kellogg) were placed by Sweet in either 1890 or 1897 (O. J. Sweet to W. M. Camp, Nov. 24, 1912 and Jan. 13, 1913, Custer Battlefield National Monument files). Sweet notes that the markers for the civilians were a different style from those of the soldiers, as they are today. In the January 13, 1913, letter Sweet states he placed Kellogg's marker at the spot where he found a board with Kellogg's name on it and on guidance offered by Major James Brisbin. Major Brisbin had helped bury the dead in 1876 and was with Sweet in 1890.

There are still forty-two more markers on the battlefield than there were soldiers killed in the fight. In order to determine where the soldiers fought and died, or at least were first interred, those extra forty-two markers need to be identified. It seems clear that examination of the historic documentation of the marker locations will not provide those answers. An examination of the battlefield itself is necessary.

ARCHAEOLOGICAL INVESTIGATIONS

Solving the mystery of the extra markers required a method to determine whether a body had ever been buried near the position of the marker. We also needed to test the paired markers to determine whether they represented one or two fallen soldiers. The archaeological team proposed that had a soldier been buried near a marker, the reburial party probably would not have managed to exhume all 206 bones in the body. In addition, they may have missed pieces of uniform or equipment. These remains and artifacts should be recoverable by archaeological excavation techniques. The 1984 excavations showed that that this was a valid argument (Scott and Fox 1987).

Field opportunities in 1984 resulted in the excavation of three sets of paired markers and five single markers. At each excavation, the remains of a single burial was located. We therefore hypothesized that paired markers represented only one interment. In that case, the majority of the extraneous markers can be identified as one of a pair of markers.

Selecting the Sample

Two five-week field seasons were not nearly enough to excavate around all the markers on the main battlefield. During the 1984 field season, 8 excavation units were completed. When planning the 1985 season, it seemed feasible to complete 18 more. This

Table 2 Locations of Archaeologically Excavated Markers

| | | Material Recovered | |
Location	Marker Number(s)	Human Remains	Battle-Related Artifacts
Last Stand Hill	63	—	—
	67–68	×	×
	78	×	×
	86–87	×	—
	105	×	×
Keogh	178	×	×
	194–195	×	×
	199	×	×
	200	×	×
	201–202	×	×
Calhoun Hill	131	—	—
	134–135	×	—
	148	×	—
	152–155	×	×
	153	—	—
South Skirmish Line	2	×	×
	7	×	×
	9–10	×	×
	33–34	×	×
	42	×	×
	52–53	×	×
Isolated	5–6	—	—
	112–113	×	×
	128	×	×
	252	—	—
	257	×	×
× = presence			

would bring the total number of units excavated to 26, and yield information from 37 of the 252 markers (14.7 percent) on the main battlefield.

During the various burial details it is probable that different work parties worked on different areas of the field. The differences in their treatment of partial remains, particularly after the remains had decayed to leave only bone, may mean that some work parties could have been more responsible for the erection of spurious markers than others. To ensure that markers from each area were tested and to help reduce variation caused by differences in how the remains in each area were originally treated, we divided the markers into five spatially discrete strata. The strata consisted of Last Stand Hill, the Keogh area, Calhoun Hill, the South Skirmish Line, and isolated markers. These groups are relatively discrete spatial clusters of markers around the field and are defined simply by natural breaks in the clusters as seen on the marker-distribution map.

Within each of these groups, the markers were substratified into paired and unpaired markers to ensure testing of both groups (21 percent of the paired and 4.10 percent of the single markers were tested). We decided to excavate equal numbers of markers within each group, resulting in a disproportionate sampling strategy. Disproportionate sampling prevents rare strata from being underrepresented in artifact samples and offers a fair chance of picking up variability in larger strata (Morris 1979). Table 2 shows the sampling fraction within each strata.

Within the substrata, selections of the markers were as random as possible. In some

Fig. 12. The excavations at Marker 200 revealed scattered human bone around the marker. This was typical of the majority of excavations undertaken in 1984 and 1985.

cases, the 1984 excavations had already selected the sample. In other cases, such as those where we knew markers had been moved during road construction, markers were eliminated from the sample. The selection process resulted in the excavation of the markers shown in table 2.

Excavation Techniques

Each of the excavation units laid out around a marker was two meters square (fig. 12). As the excavations proceeded, extensions were made to recover materials protruding from walls of the excavation units. Most of the work was done with the use of hand tools: trowels, spoons and even dental picks. All soil was screened through a quarter-inch-mesh hardware cloth and any artifacts not found in place were found in the screening and bagged as fill.

All material found in place was mapped before being removed from the ground. Photographs were taken before, during, and after excavation, to document the work. Each artifact or bone found in the excavation was given a unique field-specimen (FS) number by which it was mapped and bagged. Not only were artifacts and bone mapped and photographed, but so were cobbles, rocks, and pieces of wood—any item which may have resulted from combat or the subsequent burial and reburial activities.

The excavation units were placed with the markers in the center, so that if remains of a burial were within a meter of the marker, the excavation would uncover it. In the case of paired markers, the unit was placed to encompass both markers, placing them as near the center as possible.

THE EXCAVATIONS

The descriptions of the human remains are drawn from the detailed analysis of the human skeletal remains by Drs. Clyde Snow and John Fitzpatrick (chapter 9). More detailed nonbone artifact descriptions will be found in chapter 7 in the appropriate artifact description category.

Last Stand Hill

The horses were killed and scattered all over the hill, and at the point where Custer lay [it] showed to be the last stand. There was not hardly any horses around where he was lying when found. The soldiers lay thick at this point. Custer was lying across two or three soldiers, just a small portion of his back touching the ground. There is no such thing as them arrange to corral their horses, or make a fortification out of their horses, as there was nothing to show this. Custer had no clothing on whatever, nor none of the soldiers. There was nothing left but a foot of a boot. The leg of this being gone, on Custer. [Knipe to Camp 1908 in Hardoff 1984].

Marker 105

In 1984, a test excavation was made on Last Stand Hill adjacent to Marker 105, which is named for Lieutenant Algernon Smith. The excavation uncovered a complete and

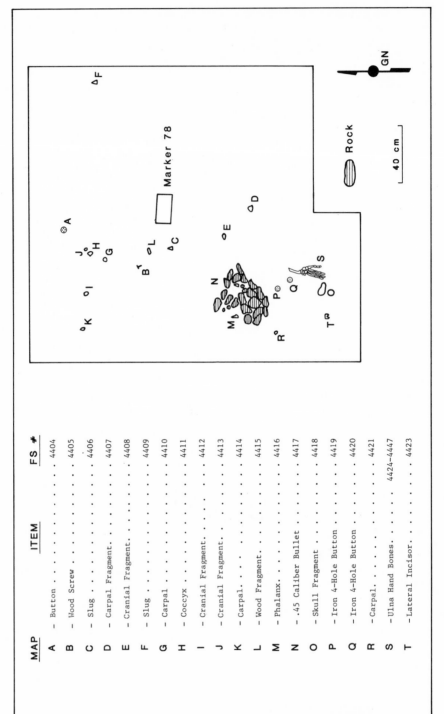

MAP	ITEM	FS #
A	– Button	4404
B	– Wood Screw	4405
C	– Slug	4406
D	– Carpal Fragment.	4407
E	– Cranial Fragment.	4408
F	– Slug	4409
G	– Carpal	4410
H	– Coccyx	4411
I	– Cranial Fragment.	4412
J	– Cranial Fragment.	4413
K	– Carpal.	4414
L	– Wood Fragment.	4415
M	– Phalanx.	4416
N	– .45 Caliber Bullet	4417
O	– Skull Fragment	4418
P	– Iron 4-Hole Button	4419
Q	– Iron 4-Hole Button	4420
R	– Carpal.	4421
S	– Ulna Hand Bones	4424–4447
T	– Lateral Incisor.	4423

Fig. 13. The plan map of the excavation at Marker 78 showing the finds uncovered.

mostly articulated left lower arm and hand and numerous other bones of the hand, back, and feet. The remains represent a single individual, an adult male between twenty and thirty-five years old and approximately five feet three inches tall. The foot bones showed that the individual had suffered a fracture, complicated by infection, sometime before the battle. There was a mark on one of the vertebrae made by a sharp edged instrument about the time of death. This can be interpreted as evidence of a wound made either by stabbing with a knife or by a metal-tipped arrow.

Associated with the bones were two trouser buttons of the type usually found on army pants for closing the fly and attaching suspenders. A .45/55 cartridge case was found lying under the arm and a .45/55 bullet was found near the center of the excavation unit. Five cobbles were found on either side of the articulated arm bones. The cobbles may have been placed there to help hold the dirt thrown over the body in place. The use of cobbles in such a way is recorded for officers in several period documents as cited by King (1980). Apparently cobbles were also used to support the wooden stakes placed at the original burial sites after the 1881 reinterment. Such cobble arrangements can be seen in an 1886 photograph of Last Stand Hill taken by D. F. Barry (Heski 1978:92).

Even though the marker is inscribed to Lieutenant Smith, the remains are not his. The individual interred at Marker 105 is not tall enough to be Lieutenant Smith.

Marker 78

This unit was chosen randomly from the single markers on Last Stand Hill. It contained a number of cobbles, four trouser buttons, a .45 Colt bullet, a wood screw, wood fragments, and human bone (fig. 13).

The human remains are consistent with those of a single individual, a male between eighteen and thirty years old at the time of death. The bone consisted of several skull fragments, almost all the bones of the left hand, a few of the right hand, three small bones of the foot, and the lower third of the left lower arm bone (fig. 14). The arm bone was shattered by a gunshot, and lead fragments are still embedded in the bone. The skull fragments suggest perimortem blunt-force trauma.

Marker 63

This marker was also chosen randomly from the single markers on Last Stand Hill. There was a large cobble concentration on the surface to the northeast of the unit, but whether it was associated with this marker or another is difficult to say. This unit yielded a few scattered river cobbles and eight pieces of a glass bottle. It was excavated to a depth of twenty centimeters below surface and no human bone or military accoutrements were found in this unit.

Markers 67 and 68

These markers are at the top of Last Stand Hill near the fence enclosing the area. The unit contained cobbles, bone, and wood (fig. 15). The cobbles were in a line south of Marker 68 and appear to be a scatter of rock rather than the circular concentrations found at Markers 105 and 78. During the first excavations at Custer Battlefield, we

Fig. 14. The bones of a human hand and part of an arm found at Marker 78.
The arm bone (ulna) was shattered by a gunshot.

assumed that wood found in the excavations was part of the wooden stakes erected by
the burial parties to mark the burials. However, this unit made it clear that there are
alternate explanations. Here wood was found in a disturbed area near the concrete foundation of the marker. It appears that the disturbed area is the hole excavated when a
concrete foundation was poured and the wood is part of the form.

This was the only unit enclosing paired markers where the bone found was consistent
with the remains of two individuals. In this case, one individual was human and the
other was a horse. Whether the horse remains were included fortuitously or whether
they were mistakenly identified as human, and buried, is not known.

The human remains are consistent with those of a single individual. The individual
was male and probably between thirty-five and forty-five years old. Parts of his face
were found, his back and ribs, and one hand bone. He had an old compressed fracture

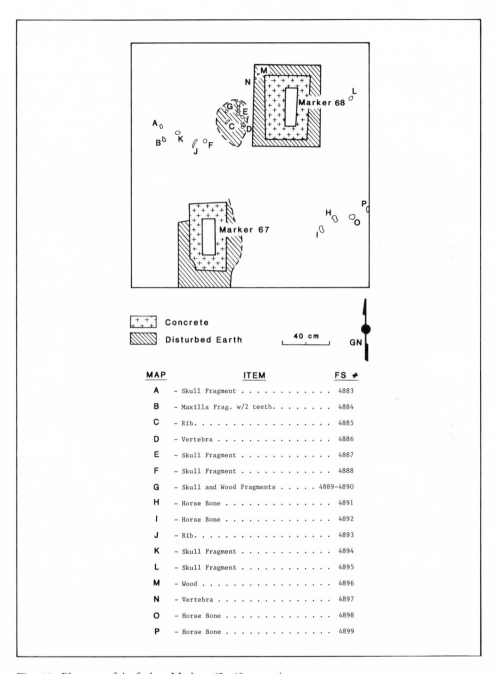

Fig. 15. Plan map of the finds at Markers 67−68 excavation.

on his lower lumbar vertebra. One of the ribs shows a slight defect, probably the result of a bullet entering or leaving the body. The facial bones are fragmented, and this appears to be the result of massive blunt-instrument trauma about the time of death.

That there are two markers associated with human and horse bone suggests that perhaps one of the later burial parties could not discriminate between human and horse bone and erected a marker for the horse. If this occurred in other areas also, such mistakes as this could account for some of the spurious markers.

Markers 86 and 88

These markers are at the bottom of the fenced area on Last Stand Hill and were also selected at random from the paired markers on the hill. The excavation uncovered three trouser buttons, a square nail, and a single human bone. The square nail is consistent with the period of the battle and may be associated with the construction of the wooden markers by one of the reburial parties.

The bone is a right kneecap from an adult. There is a slight defect on the upper side of the kneecap, suggesting an old injury or a congenital defect. Either way, it should not have caused the soldier much difficulty.

Keogh Area

We went over the battlefield pretty thoroughly and located the spot where Captain Keogh and several of his men of Company I had followed Custer. Here was a slight depression in the ground. Evidently at one time it had been a buffalo wallow and the wind had blown out the dirt, forming a semicircular depression covering several yards. The graves were around this depression. The men were buried where they fell, which clearly showed that their position had been taken for defense. [Wheeler 1923:185].

Marker 200

This unit was opened in 1984 when a metal detector signal was found to be nails in a leather boot. The excavation uncovered several human bones and a right cavalry boot with the upper cut away (fig. 12). The bones were scattered across the excavation, with several concentrated in the northwest corner of the area excavated. The bones represent a portion of the lower left arm, lower right leg, and small hand and foot bones. Other than the boot, no artifacts were found.

The bones are those of a young male between eighteen and twenty-two years old at the time of death. He was between five feet six inches and five feet eleven inches tall. The only evidence of a battle-related injury is a small cranial fragment, which suggests blunt force injury to the head.

Markers 201 and 202

These markers were picked at random from the paired markers in the Keogh area. This unit was west of the 1984 square surrounding Marker 200. Between these two markers and slightly to the east was a jumble of river cobbles. No material lay under the cobbles.

However, to the south of them, between Marker 201 and Marker 200, lay a thighbone, two wrist bones, a toe bone, a tooth, and a trouser button.

The bones are those of a young adult male who was between twenty and thirty-five years of age and was about five feet seven and a half inches tall. There are cut marks on the femur, which suggests some mutilation of the body.

It is possible that the remains found at Markers 200, 201, and 202 are from the same individual. The height and age range data derived from the bone from the adjacent excavation units overlap slightly. It is possible that these bones represent one individual and the three markers represent only one burial.

Marker 178

The inscription on Marker 178 says this is where Captain Myles Keogh fell. There are a number of markers in close proximity in this area, and in an attempt to isolate this marker for excavation, the unit was placed so that the marker fell in the southwest corner. Marker 181 was immediately outside the southwest corner of the square. Behind Marker 178 (to the southwest) there was a light scatter of cobbles which ran into the southern wall of the unit. In front of the marker (to the north and east) there was a scatter of small, disarticulated bone (fig. 16). Small fragments of deteriorated wood were also found in the unit.

The base of Marker 178 consisted of laid brick, so it is unlikely that the wood is part of a concrete form as at Last Stand Hill. The wood may be the remains of some of the stakes, or a wooden cross, originally used to mark Captain Keogh's grave. A disturbed area was found around the base of the marker, probably representing the area dug when the marker was reset in 1982. Researcher Brian Pohanka was able to confirm from photographic evidence (fig. 17) that Keogh's marker had been moved. After the original base was relocated, the marker was reset at that location (Taunton 1986:35).

The bone found includes a small piece of skull, one rib, a fragment of a wrist bone, a fragment of an ankle bone, and one toe bone. All bones are adult. The fracture lines on the skull indicate perimortem blunt-force trauma to the skull. The only battle-related artifact found in the unit was a trouser button. However, whether the site is where Captain Keogh was first interred is open to question. The individual cannot be identified from the bone recovered.

Marker 199

Marker 199 lies south of Marker 178. In an 1879 photograph (fig. 17) of Captain Keogh's marker taken by Stanley Morrow, some of the other markers to the south can be seen. By comparing the grouping of the markers in 1877 and in 1985, as well as looking at the distance between the markers and the coulee and lining up the outline of the horizon, Marker 199 appears to be in the approximate location of the 1877 wooden marker labeled "Wild I", perhaps to indicate Corporal John Wild's grave.

Most of the two-meter-square unit revealed little material (fig. 18). Small pieces of skull were found, as were several buttons. However, to the north of the marker, at the edge of the unit, an articulated arm was found (fig. 19). All the bones in the arm from the shoulder down were present. The arm was extended and the two lower arm bones

Brick

40 cm

GN

MAP	ITEM	FS #
A	– Capitate Fragment.	3563
B	– Bone Fragment	3564
C	– Bone Fragment	3565
D	– Rib	3566
E	– Cranial Vault Frag.	3567
F	– Bone Fragment	3568
G	– Wood Fragment	3569
H	– Wood Fragment	3570
I	– Tarsal.	3571
J	– Phalanges.	3572

were crossed, as when the palm faces behind the body. About thirty centimeters from the articulated arm lay a scatter of disarticulated bone representing most of the opposite hand. Found within and between these two concentrations of bone were a tailbone, four more buttons, and two five-cent pieces.

The bones found in this group did not have the epiphyses fused with the diaphyses. When bone grows, the ends (the epiphyses) are separate from the shaft (the diaphysis) until the individual has finished growing. That the epiphyses are unfused on this individual means that the soldier was probably fifteen to seventeen years old and no more than nineteen. Army enlistment records suggest that Corporal John Wild would have been around twenty-six or twenty-seven at the time of his last battle. Either Wild was passing himself off as much older than he was or this individual is not Wild.

Fig. 17. An 1879 photograph by S. J. Morrow of Captain Keogh's burial site. Note the wooden marker behind the officer.

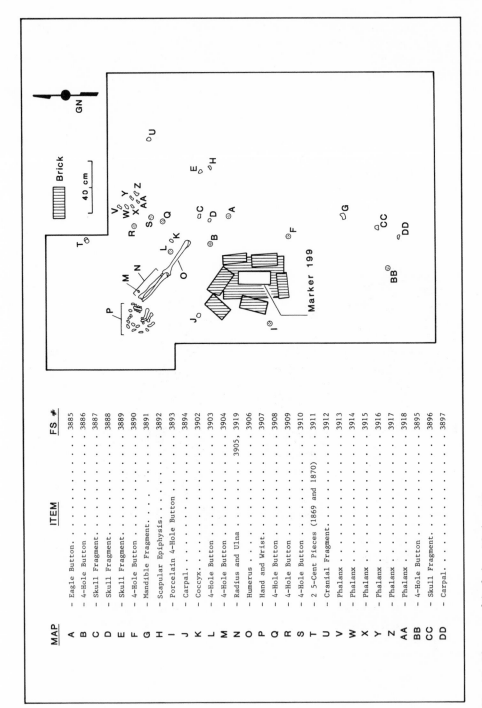

MAP	ITEM	FS #
A	– Eagle Button.	3885
B	– 4-Hole Button.	3886
C	– Skull Fragment.	3887
D	– Skull Fragment.	3888
E	– Skull Fragment.	3889
F	– 4-Hole Button.	3890
G	– Mandible Fragment.	3891
H	– Scapular Epiphysis.	3892
I	– Porcelain 4-Hole Button.	3893
J	– Carpal.	3894
K	– Coccyx.	3902
L	– 4-Hole Button.	3903
M	– 4-Hole Button.	3904
N	– Radius and Ulna	3905, 3919
O	– Humerus	3906
P	– Hand and Wrist.	3907
Q	– 4-Hole Button.	3908
R	– 4-Hole Button.	3909
S	– 4-Hole Button.	3910
T	– 2 5-Cent Pieces (1869 and 1870)	3911
U	– Cranial Fragment.	3912
V	– Phalanx	3913
W	– Phalanx	3914
X	– Phalanx	3915
Y	– Phalanx	3916
Z	– Phalanx	3917
AA	– Phalanx	3918
BB	– 4-Hole Button.	3895
CC	– Skull Fragment.	3896
DD	– Carpal.	3897

Fig. 18. Plan map of the finds at Marker 199.

Fig. 19. The articulated arm bones of a young soldier found at Marker 199.

The only individual who died with Custer's battalion who claimed to be about this age is Autie Reed, but historic accounts have his body firmly placed elsewhere. The official enlistment age during the 1870s was twenty-one, so the enlistment records show no soldiers under the age of twenty-one. Marker 199 seems to mark the remains of a young soldier who was so eager to go into service that he lied about his age when he enlisted.

The artifacts in the unit included eight trouser buttons, one white-glass button, and a general-service blouse button in addition to the two five-cent pieces. The artifacts are all consistent with a single regulation uniform.

The skull pieces found showed fracturing indicative of perimortem blunt-instrument trauma. No other trauma was found on the bone. The unit represents the place one soldier was originally buried. The soldier was probably about seventeen years old, about five feet seven and a half inches tall, wore a regulation uniform, and was carrying ten cents in cash. Sometime about the time of death, his skull was smashed; no other signs of wounds were found.

Markers 194 and 195

Like the excavation around Marker 178, this excavation uncovered a light scatter of bone throughout the area. The unit was extended a square meter on its southeast side so as to uncover a lower-arm bone that was found in the wall. The total excavations were then five square meters. The excavations uncovered two skull fragments, both of which showed indications of perimortem blunt-force trauma. Also found were a tooth, a lower-arm bone, and three right-hand bones. The only artifact found in the unit was a trouser button with thread attached.

Calhoun Hill and Greasy Grass Ridge

. . . Each soldier (was) lying just where he had fallen, each with a small amount of earth thrown over him, with his head protruding from one end of the grave and his feet from the other. One very noticeable feature presented itself to me, the boot tops had been cut from the dead. Their skulls in many instances had been crushed and shot with pistol bullets after being killed [Allen 1903: 67–68].

Marker 148

In 1984, excavation unit N6656 E2848 was placed near Marker 148 on Calhoun Hill. A few small fragments of extremely deteriorated bone were found in the excavation, as were two metal devices used to attach floral displays to their stands and bases. The bone fragments represent at least one individual, but they are too badly deteriorated for the part of the body represented to be positively identified. The fragments are probably ribs missed by the reburial party. The metal devices no doubt represent remains of floral displays which were placed on or near the Calhoun Hill markers from time to time during memorial occasions.

Marker 153

This unit is slightly northeast of the parking area on Calhoun Hill. It was excavated to a depth of twenty centimeters below ground surface and absolutely no historic material was unearthed.

Marker 131

This unit is on Greasy Grass Ridge. The unit was about ten meters (thirty-three feet) from the present park road. The unit was excavated to a depth of twenty centimeters below ground surface and no bone or historic artifacts were found. On the north edge of the unit, four river cobbles were found.

Markers 134 and 135

This excavation unit was meant to include paired Markers 134 and 135. However, the two markers were too far apart to be encompassed by a single two-meter unit, so we enclosed Marker 135 and the area between it and Marker 134. Indeed, all the material we found was between the two markers. In the southeast corner of the unit, a jumble of river cobbles was found extending into the southern wall.

   The bone found consisted of adult hand bones and a premolar tooth fragment. The meager remains are consistent with those of a single individual.

Markers 152 and 155

In the southeast corner of the unit was a pavement of river cobbles extending into both the south and east walls of the unit (figs. 20–21). The portion of the pavement uncovered measured sixty-five by sixty centimeters. Under this pavement lay a scatter of bone. The bones consisted of one finger bone, and ten foot bones. All of the foot bones are

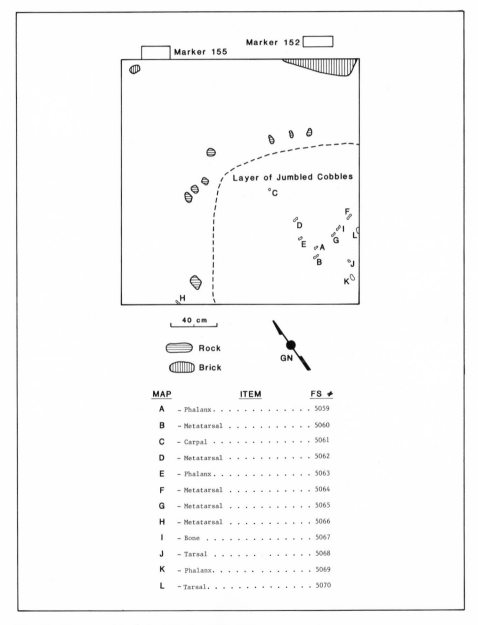

MAP	ITEM	FS #
A	– Phalanx	5059
B	– Metatarsal	5060
C	– Carpal	5061
D	– Metatarsal	5062
E	– Phalanx	5063
F	– Metatarsal	5064
G	– Metatarsal	5065
H	– Metatarsal	5066
I	– Bone	5067
J	– Tarsal	5068
K	– Phalanx	5069
L	– Tarsal	5070

Fig. 20. Plan map of the finds at Markers 152–155.

Fig. 21. The scattered cobbles found in many excavations always indicated that a soldier had once been buried at that location.

from the right foot except one, which is from the left. The remains are consistent with those of a single adult individual. The only artifact found was a gold watch chain. The chain is of a style available during the 1870s.

South Skirmish Line

. . . most of the soldiers, either singly or in groups, have a stake driven where they rest. They are not in graves, but lie with a sprinkling of earth upon each or in groups as they fell last year. More earth was heaped upon them. Some were found this year that were not last . . . Of course, where the remains were partly uncovered, an indescribable odor arose [*New York Herald*, July 18, 1877].

Marker 2

In 1984, excavation unit I was placed around Marker 2 on the southeast side of Deep Ravine. Marker 2 was excavated after six different types of bullets were found around the marker during the metal-detector inventory. The excavation recovered skull fragments and finger and toe bones as well as three trouser buttons. The bone remains are consistent with the presence of one individual. The individual was most likely between the ages of twenty-five and forty at the time of death. The only battle-related injury that could be determined was massive blunt-force trauma to the head.

This individual is one of the most interesting to speculate about because of the variety of weapons apparently used against him. Bullets from six different weapons were found around him. Possibly he was killed late in the battle, when fewer troopers were still resisting, and many Indians were shooting at him. He is slightly off the main skirmish line and may have been attempting to retreat back into Calhoun's or Keogh's areas—or possibly just away from the attacking Indians.

Marker 7

Excavation unit G was placed adjacent to Marker 7 at the end of the Deep Ravine trail where it enters the ravine proper. A horseshoe nail and a trouser button were recovered, but most finds here consisted of human bone.

The bone assemblage consisted of fourteen skull fragments, part of a neck vertebra, a nearly intact lumbar vertebra, a sternal body fragment, and two unidentified fragments. The assemblage is consistent with the remains of a single individual. Based on the cranial sutures and the condition of the bones, the individual was most likely between twenty and thirty-six years old at the time of death. The face and head bones showed evidence of extensive fracturing, suggesting massive blunt-force injury to the head.

The neck vertebra is probably from the lower portion of the neck. The right side of the bone is missing, having been separated from the rest by a single oblique cut extending transversely and inferiorly across the vertebral body and arch—exactly the injury that would occur if the trooper's head had been separated from his body in a single blow with a heavy, sharp-edged instrument, such as like an ax or a tomahawk.

Marker 42

Near Marker 42 a finger bone encircled by a ring was found in 1984. The 1985 excavations uncovered a jumble of river cobbles extending into the north and east walls. Other hand bones were located in the northeast quadrant of the unit. No artifacts were found.

The bone consisted of four adult hand bones. The base of one of the finger bones may have been severed, although it is badly weathered and this may account for its appearance.

Markers 33 and 34

In 1984, trench A, a two-meter by four-meter excavation unit, was placed adjacent to Markers 33 and 34 near the middle of the South Skirmish Line on the Deep Ravine trail. This area was selected for excavation because Fox (1983) had found human bones there during his initial inventory of the battlefield after the 1983 fire.

The 1984 excavations recovered a few river cobbles, a .50/70 bullet, a lead bullet fragment, lead shot, a bootheel and boot nails, a rubber button, three trouser buttons, and a shank-type mother-of-pearl shirt button. A deteriorated fragment of a cedar stake was also recovered and may represent one of the stakes or a portion of a lodgepole set into the ground by one of the burial parties to mark where the soldiers were buried (King 1980).

Bone found in the excavations included fragments of skull and a finger and the tailbone. All are consistent with the remains of one individual. The teeth on this individual are worn in a pattern resembling wear seen in pipe smokers. The bones suggest the individual was between thirty-five and forty-five years old at the time of death and that his racial heritage consisted of a Caucasian-Mongoloid admixture. The only injury evident on the remains was massive blunt-force trauma to the head.

The mother-of-pearl shirt button suggests this individual was not dressed in a regulation uniform, although he was attired in Euro-American clothing. His face bones suggest he may have been part Indian. He was shot at with weapons of the type used by the Indians, suggesting that he was with Custer's battalion. In all, the excavations suggest this marker represents the final location of a part-Indian civilian who fought with Custer's troops. The only person known to fit this description is scout Mitch Boyer.

Markers 9 and 10

In 1984, excavation unit H, adjacent to Markers 9 and 10, yielded a relatively complete grouping of human remains. Fragments of the skull, ribs, vertebrae, hands, right foot, both upper arms, and both lower arms were found in the excavation unit. While the remains were scattered across the unit, several of the skull fragments and both arms appeared to be in the approximately correct anatomical position. From the position of the arms it appears the individual buried at Markers 9 and 10 was covered over as he lay face down. The skull fragments suggest massive blunt-force trauma to the head. The breastbone has a cut mark across the front of it, indicating the soldier was cut across the chest and one arm was cut at the shoulder.

The artifacts recovered with the bone include a .44 caliber Henry bullet found in the lower chest or upper abdominal region, a .45-caliber Colt bullet found in the area of the head, eleven buttons, and an iron arrowhead. The buttons include several for trousers, three blouse buttons (two with cloth still attached), and three white glass shirt buttons. This excavation also found several cobbles which may have been used to hold a wooden marker in place after the initial burial.

Markers 52 and 53

In 1984, excavation unit J was placed at the head of the Deep Ravine trail about 150 meters (492 feet) from the Visitors Center around Markers 52 and 53. The excavations recovered a skull fragment, a trouser button, a Benét primer from a .45/55 cartridge, and a lead shot.

The bones found were consistent with those of a single individual, although they were too fragmented for any indication of age to be observed. There is a fracture through a portion of the mastoid process which appears to be from an obliquely directed blow from a heavy, edged instrument.

Isolated Markers

Marker 257

This marker is located between Deep Ravine and Greasy Grass Ridge. No artifacts were recovered from the excavation, but three bone fragments were. They were badly eroded bones from an adult hand and foot. The bones are too fragmentary for indications of stature or age determination more specific than adult. No signs of trauma or pathologies were found.

Marker 252

No historic artifacts or bone were recovered from this unit. However, the unit is at the top of a wash on the south side of the unit. It appears as though bricks have been thrown over the side of the wash. The original position of the marker may have been on the side of the wash, and erosion would have made the relocation of the marker to the top of the wash a necessity.

Marker 128

This unit, behind Greasy Grass Ridge, yielded an almost complete burial (fig 22). The lower right leg was articulated, the foot bones being encased in a boot (fig 23). The remainder of the bones had been gathered up and deposited in a pit extending about half a meter (nineteen inches) below ground surface (fig 24). The bones were jumbled and disarticulated, indicating reburial occurred after the flesh had completely decayed. When the marble marker was erected, the hole dug to set the marker intruded on the burial pit, scattering some of the bone. Rodents had also disturbed the burial, scattering small bones throughout the upper portions of the unit.

The individual represented by the burial was male, about twenty-two years old and roughly five feet six inches tall. Evidence of two gunshot wounds in the chest was found on the ribs. One shot entered from the right and one from the left side. A fragment of a bullet was found embedded in the left lower arm. This may be a third gunshot wound or a fragment of one of the other two bullets. Both thighbones showed three parallel cut marks near the proximal ends. Another cut mark was found on the collarbone.

The soldier suffered from a congenital defect of the spine: the lower-back vertebrae had not closed properly. While this had nothing to do with the battle, it is probable that the trooper suffered pains in his lower back frequently, particularly when riding for long periods.

The individual appears to have been buried originally in his clothes, as buttons from his blouse and trousers were found as were several fragments of army issue underwear cloth, and hooks and eyes, possibly from his campaign hat. When excavated, one leg was in correct anatomical position, indicating it probably had not been moved since the original burial. However, the remainder of the body was in a jumble that could have been achieved only after the flesh had decayed. He must, therefore, have been reburied in 1877 or 1879, before the mass grave was constructed. Immediately after the battle,

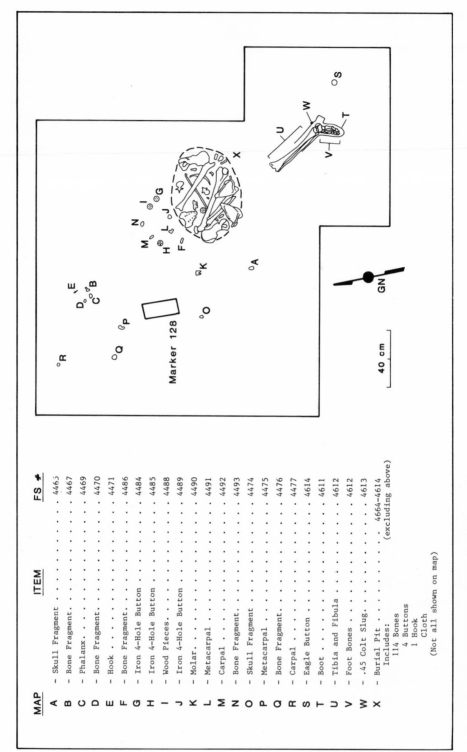

MAP	ITEM	FS #
A	– Skull Fragment	4465
B	– Bone Fragment.	4467
C	– Phalanx.	4469
D	– Bone Fragment.	4470
E	– Hook	4471
F	– Bone Fragment.	4486
G	– Iron 4-Hole Button	4484
H	– Iron 4-Hole Button	4485
I	– Wood Pieces.	4488
J	– Iron 4-Hole Button	4489
K	– Molar.	4490
L	– Metacarpal	4491
M	– Carpal	4492
N	– Bone Fragment.	4493
O	– Skull Fragment	4474
P	– Metacarpal	4475
Q	– Bone Fragment.	4476
R	– Carpal	4477
S	– Eagle Button	4614
T	– Boot	4611
U	– Tibia and Fibula	4612
V	– Foot Bones	4612
W	– .45 Colt Slug.	4613
X	– Burial Pit	4664–4614

(excluding above)

Includes:
114 Bones
4 Buttons
1 Hook
Cloth
(Not all shown on map)

Fig. 22. Plan map of the finds at the Marker 128 excavations.

the trooper was probably shallowly buried, but his lower right leg was buried slightly deeper than the remainder of the body. The parties later sent to clean up the battlefield found some of the trooper's bones exposed on the surface. Differential weathering of the bones indicates the left side was exposed. The reburial party found them and uncovered all the bones except the lower leg. They may have uncovered the head of the femur (thighbone) and pulled the rest out, never realizing that the remainder of the leg lay below the soil.

Markers 5 and 6

These markers are located on the Deep Ravine trail directly above the ravine itself. Bedrock was reached at five centimeters (two inches) below surface. The markers are on brick bases set on top of the rock. No artifacts or bone were found. If any soldiers had fallen in this area, it is unlikely that they could have been buried in this location. It is also unlikely that any wooden marker could have been set deeply enough into the earth to remain for any length of time. The excavation does not allow us to determine what could have been in this location that would lead the party to place marble markers here. It is possible these markers represent the burials in Deep Ravine.

Fig. 23. Excavations under way at Marker 128. Note the articulated lower leg and foot still encased in a cavalry boot in the foreground.

Fig. 24. The jumbled mass of human remains at Marker 128 that indicated a redeposited and later-overlooked burial.

Markers 112 and 113

These markers are on the west side of the park road southeast of Last Stand Hill. Marker 112 had been reset and not replaced on its brick foundation, which was also in the unit. Marker 113 had no base and was set into the native soil (fig. 25). Four trouser buttons, a white-glass button, and a .44- or .45-caliber ball were found in the unit. Most of the material was found between the two markers.

The bones found were from a male older than thirty-five. They consisted of a small portion of a tooth crown, the first segment of the tailbone, three finger bones, and a toe bone. There were no signs of disease or injury.

IDENTIFICATION OF THE REMAINS

Most of the human remains recovered are not conducive to individual identification. The historic record is very incomplete regarding the details of the soldiers' lives, such as records of old injuries or diseases, needed to associate an individual soldier with recovered bones. In most cases, the bone recovered represents those small and relatively nondiagnostic elements not collected by the reburial party. Only in a few cases is there a large-enough or unique assemblage which will allow speculation about identity.

All vital statistics utilized are from army records as assembled in Hammer (1973) and Carroll (1987). We emphasized that the suggested identifications are speculative. They are based on the available records, which are very incomplete. With one exception, no identifications can be considered as positive. We chose to include all individuals meeting the age and height criteria for a specific skeletal assemblage, regardless of conflicting historical information on where that individual's body was found.

Markers 9 and 10

The remains represent a white male between thirty and forty years old, about five feet ten and a half inches tall, with a possible range of five feet eight and three-quarters inches to six feet. There are eight possible candidates in the age and height range shown in table 3. Corporal William Teeman fits the criteria but was reportedly found elsewhere on the field (Taunton 1986:21) leaving only seven possible candidates. Without more information it is impossible to narrow the field further.

Markers 33 and 34

The remains here represent a racially admixed adult between thirty-five and forty-five years old. The only known white and Indian mixed-blood to have died with Custer's

Fig. 25. A marker (left) set forward of its brick and mortar base and a marker (right) with no base. The situation revealed here indicates some markers have been moved and some were placed after 1890, when the original markers and bases were erected.

Table 3   Possible Identities for an Individual at Markers 9–10

Company	Rank	Name	Age	Height
C	Pvt.	John Rauter	30	5′9″
C	Pvt.	L. St. John	32	5′9″
C	Pvt.	Alpheus Stuart	32	5′11½″
F	Pvt.	G. Warren	32	5′9½″
F	Cpl.	William Teeman	30	5′9″
I	Sgt.	F. Varden	30	5′10″
I	Pvt.	William Reed	32	5′9¾″
L	Sgt.	W. Cashan	30	5′9″

command is scout Mitch Boyer (fig. 26), who was about thirty-eight years old (Hammer 1976:167). In this particular case, we are fortunate to have facial fragments as a further aid to identification (fig. 27). The fragments consist of the left side of the cheek, a partial left eye orbit, and the front teeth and nasal cavity. Using a comparative technique (Dorion 1983; Klonpris 1980) to match the facial fragments with a photograph of Boyer, an identification can be posited (fig. 28). There is little doubt that the individual at Markers 33 and 34 is scout Mitch Boyer.

Marker 105

The individual at Marker 105 was a white male between thirty and forty years old and about five feet three and one-half inches tall, with a range of five feet one and three-quarters inches to five feet five and one-quarter inches. Nine possible candidates fit the criteria and are listed in table 4. No further identification is possible with the available evidence.

Marker 128

The individual interred here was a white male between nineteen and twenty-two years old and five feet six and three-quarters inches tall, with a range of five feet five and three-quarters inches to five feet seven and seven-eighths inches. Nine individuals are possible in this case and are listed in table 5. No other identification is possible without further data.

Marker 199

The individual at Marker 199 was a white male between the ages of fifteen and nineteen and five feet seven and one-half inches tall, with a range of five feet five and one-half inches to five feet nine and one-half inches. There are only two individuals known to have died with Custer's command in this age and height range. They are Autie Reed and Private Willis Wright of Company C. Reed is believed to have been found near his uncle, Boston Custer, near Last Stand Hill. Wright, who was seventeen and five feet six and one-half inches tall, fits the criteria well. Wright lied about his age to enlist in the army and this was probably not a unique occurrence. However, he is the only

Fig. 26. Mitch Boyer, the mixed-blood scout with the Custer battalion.

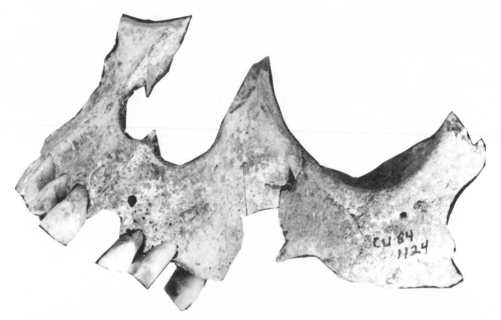

Fig. 27. The facial bones found at the excavations at Markers 33–34. The bones indicate the individual was a male, 35–45, of racially admixed heritage, and a pipe smoker.

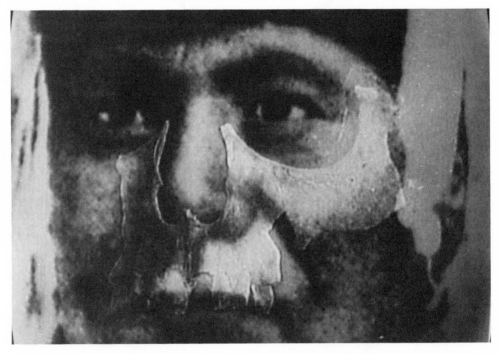

Fig. 28. A video overlay of the facial bones from Markers 33–34 and the photograph of Mitch Boyer. The match is exact, indicating that the bones are those of Boyer.

Table 4   Possible Identities for an Individual at Marker 105

Company	Rank	Name	Age	Height
E	Pvt.	B. Stafford	30	5'5¼"
F	Pvt.	J. Carney	32	5'4¼"
F	Pvt.	W. Liemann	33	5'5"
F	Pvt.	S. Omling	37	5'5¼"
F	Pvt.	T. Atcheson	41	5'5¼"
I	Pvt.	P. Kelly	35	5'5"
I	Pvt.	H. Lehmann	36	5'4"
I	Trumpeter	J. McCucker	39	5'5"
L	Pvt.	A. Assadaly	34	5'3"

Table 5   Possible Identities for an Individual at Marker 128

Company	Rank	Name	Age	Height
C	Pvt.	F. Meier	22	5'6½"
C	Pvt.	J. Shea	22	5'6¼"
C	Pvt.	J. Thadus	22	5'6¾"
C	Pvt.	N. Short	22	5'7"
E	Trumpeter	G. Moonie	21	5'6⅜"
E	Pvt.	W. Huber	22	5'7"
F	Pvt.	T. Donnelly	22	5'6"
L	Pvt.	E. Babcock	22	5'6½"
L	Pvt.	F. Hughes	22	5'7¾"

Table 6   Possible Identities for an Individual at Marker 200

Company	Rank	Name	Age	Height
C	Pvt.	F. Meier	22	5'6"
C	Pvt.	J. Shea	22	5'6¼"
C	Pvt.	J. Thadus	22	5'6¾"
C	Pvt.	N. Short	22	5'7"
E	Trumpeter	G. Moonie	21	5'6⅜"
E	Pvt.	W. Huber	22	5'7"
F	Pvt.	T. Donnelly	22	5'6"
L	Pvt.	W. Harrington	21	5'8"
L	Pvt.	F. Hughes	22	5'7"

one known to be younger than twenty-one who fits the criteria. Without further data, the identification must remain speculative.

Marker Marker 200

The individual found at Marker 200 was a white male between eighteen and twenty-two years old and five feet eight and one-quarter inches tall, with a range of five feet six inches to five feet eleven inches. There are ten possible candidates, listed in table 6. The candidate who best fits the description is Private Weston Harrington. Without further corroborating data, this must remain a speculative identification.

Marker 257

The last marker to have information applicable to identifying an individual is Marker 257. The bones indicate only that an adult male was interred at this location. The Camp interviews (Taunton 1986:) suggest that Corporal John Briody of Company F was found at this site. The only correlation between the Camp interview data and the archaeological evidence is that the foot bones were not found in their correct anatomical position. Camp's data indicate that Briody's leg had been amputated by the Indians and was found under his head. The bones found can be interpreted as being in that relative relationship. This evidence cannot be used to make a positive identification, but it does remain an intriguing possibility.

Summary

One positive and two possible identifications have been made from the few bones recovered and from the limited descriptions available in the historic record. While by no means an overwhelming number, they are significant, given the limited data available. Particularly significant is Mitch Boyer's identification. Controversy has revolved around the argument about the location of his body. Private Peter Thompson (Magnussen 1974:257) says he found the body on the left side of the river, and Sergeant Daniel Knipe (Hammer 1976:95) noted that Boyer was buried in Deep Ravine. Whereas Colonel John Gibbon (1899:621) says "the body of our poor guide Mitch Boyer was found lying in the midst of the troopers slain, as the Sioux had several times reported they had slain him in battle." And finally, White-Man-Runs-Him (Magnussen 1974:259 footnote) says Boyer was found on a ridge.

These recollections suggest that either Boyer's body was mistakenly identified by the various sources or their memory was dim after so many years. Boyer was found at Markers 33 and 34 (fig. 9) just below the crest of a ridge that forms the north side of the primary drainage area of Deep Ravine. If the area was considered a part of Deep Ravine by the burial details, then this has important ramifications in reinterpreting the locations of those killed in or near Deep Ravine. However, it is possible that because of the crushed skull and the poor condition of the body, it was not properly identified. On the other hand, Boyer was one of few present not dressed in military attire, so his remains would stand out from those of the soldiers. The identification of Mitch Boyer on the South Skirmish Line agrees more with Gibbon's (1899) account that Boyer was found among the slain troopers. The importance of the findings, however, is that the archaeological data flatly contradict some common interpretations of the historical accounts. Either the accounts or the common interpretations are inaccurate. In either case, the documentary records should be reassessed in light of the archaeological evidence.

MUTILATION

The human remains examined by Drs. Snow and Fitzpatrick (chapter 9) exhibited substantial evidence of perimortem trauma. The osteological data clearly demonstrate that some of the men were mutilated about the time of death. To what extent the bodies were mutilated cannot be precisely determined, but a relative impression of the type and extent of the injuries can be suggested on the basis of the osteological material. The marker excavations yielded partial remains of twenty-one individuals, a 10 percent sample of those killed during the battle.

In addition to the excavated remains, surface material found by the archaeological crew, by visitors, and by park staff yielded partial remains of another thirteen individuals. This provides a group of partial remains representing thirty-four of the soldiers who died at the Little Bighorn (roughly a 16 percent sample).

Many contemporary accounts of the June 27, 1876 burials note that mutilation was prevalent among the dead. The most common type of mutilation mentioned was the crushed skull. Lieutenant James Bradley (Brininstool 1952:258–60) claims to have seen most of the dead and he says he noted little mutilation, mainly an occasional scalping. He further states he believed most of the disfigurement seen on the dead resulted from a blow with a hatchet or war club to kill a wounded man. William White (Wagner 1972:236), Second Cavalry, helped bury the dead and states that "a few (bodies) were hacked or pounded with tomahawk or war club but not mutilated the way folks have said. It looked to us as though the Indians took that way to finish off the wounded." Graham's (1953:221, 243, 250, 254, 260) compilation of eyewitness accounts of the burials is also in this vein. Most accounts note the bashed heads. Occasionally they also discuss other forms of mutilation, such as scalping, arrow and knife wounds, decapitation, or dismemberment.

Contemporary Indian accounts (Marquis 1931:224, 238–39, 240, 263) also mention skull crushing, most often followed by arrow and knife wounds, decapitation, and dismemberment. Black Elk and Iron Hawk (Neihardt 1961:127–31) recall seeing soldiers stabbed, slashed, and struck in the head by war clubs. They also state they participated in shooting arrows into some bodies and scalping the dead. White Necklace (Powell 1969:117) recalled decapitating one soldier as an act of revenge. Probably the most graphic account of mutilation is the series of pictographs by Red Horse (Mallery 1893) showing most of the varieties of mutilation mentioned.

The archaeological evidence for incised wounds—those made by knives, arrows, and hatchets—occurs in about 21 percent of the remains. Wounds related to knives or arrows are seen in 11 percent of the individuals, and hatchet-related injuries were noted in 10 percent of the sample. It must be remembered that not all injuries are likely to have affected the bone, thus the sample reflects only those injuries that cut to the bone. Nevertheless, it appears that a significant percentage of the soldiers killed must have been shot with arrows, cut with knives, or struck with hatchets about the time of death.

Blunt-instrument trauma to the skull appears as the most prevalent perimortem feature in the contemporary accounts, and the archaeological evidence supports this. There are fourteen cases in the archaeological record where skull fragments are present. All cases exhibit blunt-instrument trauma. This group accounts for 41 percent of the individuals represented archaeologically and all of those cases where skull fragments were present. This direct physical evidence suggests that blunt-force trauma to the skull was common.

The incomplete nature of the skeletal remains recovered limits the quantification of the amount of mutilation at the battlefield. Qualitatively, it is obvious from the archaeological evidence, that mutilation was common. This is in concert with the historical record.

An interesting sidelight to the mutilation question involves the 1877 reburial party and a possible misinterpretation of the physical evidence seen by that group. P. W. Norris reported in the *New York Herald* on July 18, 1877, that the reburial party found the human bones disfigured by coyotes and savages. He noted most skulls were smashed to fragments and mangled or missing. He attributed this to animal and human predation. The smashed skulls can also be attributed to perimortem trauma during or immediately after the battle. In fact, this is a better explanation for the large number of smashed skulls than postmortem predation.

That mutilation of the dead occurred is clearly evident in the historic and archaeologic records. But the cause of mutilation must be placed in a cultural context. Most of our perspective of mutilation is derived from the Victorian view that mutilation is barbaric. That viewpoint has been perpetuated in much of the literature about Indian "atrocities" (Hans 1907).

However, it is more appropriate to view mutilation from the cultural context of the Sioux and Cheyennes rather than the Victorians. One of the most common themes in Indian explanations of mutilation is one that pervades human nature: a sense of rage and revenge. Gall (Graham 1953:) said his "heart was bad" at the battle because of the loss of several members of his family during the fighting. That sense of rage and revenge also contributed to the mutilation of the dead. White Necklace, Wolf Chief's wife, had found her niece decapitated after the Sand Creek Massacre, and in revenge she decapitated a soldier at the Little Bighorn with her belt ax (Powell 1969:117). While revenge may have been the most obvious motive for mutilation, deeper cultural meanings also are ascribed to the practice. General Henry B. Carrington (1973) interviewed a member of Red Cloud's band concerning the reason for mutilation of the dead at the Fetterman fight. Carrington reported that the key to understanding the mutilation was an understanding of the Indians' own view of life after death. He noted:

Their idea of the spirit land is that it is a physical paradise; but we enter upon its mysteries just in the condition we hold when we die. In the Indian paradise every physical taste or longing is promptly met . . . In the light of this idea, those tortured bodies had a new significance. With the muscles of the arms cut out, the victim could not pull a bowstring or trigger; with other muscles gone, he could not put foot in a stirrup or stoop to drink; so that, while every sense was in agony for relief from hunger or thirst, there could be no relief at all.

In this context, mutilation, in the view of the Sioux and Cheyenne participants, was a part of their culture. It must be viewed as a normal cultural expression of victory over a vanquished foe. That expression has two levels. The first is the overt and obvious level of rage and revenge. The second is symbolic or religious, a level where mutilation is a means to ensure that an enemy cannot enjoy the afterlife in the fullness that the victor might anticipate. Thus the mutilated dead at the Little Bighorn become symbols of victory to the culture that defeated them.

THE LOCATIONS OF SPURIOUS MARKERS

The beginning of this chapter put forth the mystery of the extra markers, and indeed the extra markers were the primary reason for the excavations. The archaeological investigations have shown that the paired markers are a major source of spurious markers. Each excavated pair represented only one human interment or, in some cases, no interment at all. The investigators also learned that not all single markers represent interment sites. From this sample a projection of the spurious markers can be made.

Eleven sets of paired markers were examined. One set, two markers, had no human remains. One set, two markers, was surrounded by the remains of two individuals, one a human and one a horse. The remainder contained the remains of only a single individual. In several cases, the remains of the individual lay directly between the two markers. This left little doubt, in the excavators' minds, that the two markers commemorated the location where a single soldier fell. This is probably true of the majority of the paired markers. If so, the paired markers could account for up to thirty-seven of the extra forty-two markers. While the occurrence of the single pair that represented no burial is too rare an occurrence to from which extrapolate, it suggests that the paired markers might account for even more of the spurious markers.

Interestingly, other than the extra marker in a pair, no spurious markers were excavated at either the South Skirmish Line or the Keogh area. Every single marker excavated represented a fallen soldier, every pair represented a fallen soldier. Other than the second marker in each pair, the placement of markers in these areas appears accurate.

It is appropriate to point out that *accurate*, as used here in discussing the markers, means only that remains consistent with those of a single individual were found around the marker. Remains from a single individual could lie scattered around several markers, and our forensic analysis would have difficulty identifying the remains as belonging to the same person. On a subjective note, the excavations on the South Skirmish Line and the Keogh area produced the feeling that there may be much bone scattered throughout the area, that the original scatter of human bone in these areas was almost continuous, and that the markers, at best, may only pinpoint the areas of greatest density. However, only excavations not related to markers could test that hypothesis.

The isolated markers and the markers at Calhoun Hill appear equally inaccurate. In each case, 57 percent of the markers excavated did not represent a fallen soldier. This figure is comparable between the two areas because the sampling fraction for each is the same. In the isolates, there was a pair of markers that represented no fallen soldier and a single marker that represented no fallen soldier. At Calhoun Hill, the pairs of markers represented only a single fallen soldier, and only one of the three single markers excavated represented a fallen soldier. The markers at Calhoun have probably been significantly disturbed by construction of the road, which may mean that the original battle line was closer to the alignment of the road than to where the markers stand today.

The markers in the Last Stand Hill area appear more accurate than those in the Calhoun area or the isolates but slightly less accurate than the South Skirmish Line or the Keogh area. The paired markers excavated, as in most of the rest of the field, represented a single fallen soldier. Only one of the three single markers excavated was spurious.

Overall, the paired markers almost always represent a single soldier. In fact, a pair of markers is a more reliable indication of the location of a single soldier than is a single marker.

We began this work knowing that at least forty-two of the markers were incorrectly placed, mainly those extra markers set in 1890. We guessed that another twenty-eight might be spurious—markers sent for the dead in Deep Ravine but not placed in Deep Ravine. This would mean that as many as seventy markers on the field could be erroneous. Our projections suggest that about thirty-seven spurious markers are the second marker in a pair or the rare occasion when the pair represents no fallen soldier. Another projected thirty-five markers are single markers that are spurious. Projecting from the disproportionate sampling strategy employed, we suspect the marker population on the field could include seventy-two spurious markers.

That would be a nice, straightforward conclusion to this chapter, and it is very tempting to end with this. However, the identification of Mitch Boyer on the South Skirmish Line has added a new dimension. As discussed above, Boyer was one of the twenty-eight men supposed to be buried in Deep Ravine. Four explanations were presented: Mitch Boyer was misidentified, the South Skirmish Line was referred to as the ravine, the memories of the participants had dimmed by the time the account was taken by historians, or Gibbon's account is accurate. Because of Boyer's civilian attire, relatively unique in a field of dead soldiers, it is possible he was correctly identified. If the lower end of the South Skirmish line was referred to as part of the ravine, then some of the twenty-eight men could be buried along that portion of the line and may be correctly marked. This still means that the number of incorrectly placed markers is between forty-two and seventy. Our statistical projection of seventy-two incorrect markers on the field, based on our sample, remains the same, but the change in the population which we are sampling would suggest that not only are there incorrect markers, but there are locations of fallen soldiers which are not marked—that is, those in Deep Ravine.

The only reliable way to resolve the question of the extra markers is to conduct archaeological excavations at each marker and outside the marked areas, such as in Deep Ravine, which would be a time-consuming and expensive process.

Even with all these twists and nuances, we have achieved a certain measure of success. The excavations have clearly demonstrated that some markers are improperly located, do not identify the site of a fallen soldier, and potentially bias the interpretation of battle events. The excavations have also shown, however, that most markers do represent the location where a soldier was laid to rest, albeit temporarily. The results of the archaeological testing program demonstrate that the distribution of markers on the field conveys a relatively accurate impression of where a soldier fell on June 25 or 26, 1876.

Chapter 6

Interpreting the Evidence

It is here that we combine the historical documentary evidence with the data derived from the artifact analysis and begin to interpret the story. While it may seem odd to interpret the data before we have presented it, we chose to do so in order to avoid the interruption of a long descriptive section. The detailed artifact analysis can be found in chapter 7.

In reading these interpretations, it is best to keep in mind the crime-scene analogy we presented in chapter 1. The historical documentation is analogous to the witness testimony and the archaeological data are the event's new and unstudied physical evidence. With it we can brighten the dark glass through which we have come to study the Battle of the Little Bighorn.

Interpretation of the battle through archaeological evidence is subject to several biases. For one thing, relic collecting during the past one-hundred-plus years has reduced artifact quantity and has undoubtedly has disrupted some artifact distribution patterns. However, we studied the available documentation on past collection efforts and attempted to compensate for this bias. Another bias we considered is that the battle is not the only cultural event to have taken place at this location. Construction of fences, buildings, roads, and graves and even trash disposal have added to the battlefield's archaeological record through time. The pre- and postbattle activities were easily recognizable by datable artifact types. These biases were kept in mind as the interpretations were developed.

We do not presume that this presentation of the archaeological evidence is the last word in Little Bighorn studies. The archaeological evidence does fill in some gaps in the story and, in some cases, does clarify conflicting historical accounts, but it also raises new questions in its own right.

There are those who will dispute one point or another in our interpretations. We invite such criticism, as scholarly debate is the most effective means to achieve a better understanding of past events. It is precisely for these reasons that we have included, in subsequent chapters, the descriptive and analytical studies that were undertaken. It is our intent that the data we have collected and utilized to draw our conclusions be laid out and available for all concerned.

The interpretations offered here are based on analysis of the archaeological evidence; the artifacts. Artifacts are the physical evidence of human behavior. They are the material-culture remains of past activities. As such, they retain information regarding the nature of those activities. That information resides not only in the individual artifact but in the spatial and contextual relationships among artifacts. Whether the artifact is a bullet from the battle, a piece of equipment used by a soldier, or a nail used in boundary-fence construction, it helps to piece together the history of human use of Custer Battlefield National Monument.

THE EVIDENCE OF CLOTHING AND EQUIPMENT

The number of artifacts representing clothing and equipment used by the combatants is relatively small. This is not unexpected, given the nature of the battle and the historical accounts of scavenging the battlefield. Both army and Indian accounts (Nichols 1983; Graham 1953; Marquis 1931; Neihardt 1967) refer to the Custer battlefield dead as stripped of clothing and equipment. The victorious warriors apparently retrieved most useful items. Wooden Leg (Marquis 1931) and another Indian had to scrounge the battlefield a year later to find items they deemed worthy of salvage.

At the Reno-Benteen defense site the situation was different. Army personnel gathered broken and discarded equipment, placed it in piles, then burned or destroyed the items (Wagner 1972:182). However, the comments of later battlefield visitors and the subsequent artifactual finds at both sites suggest that not all items were collected. Lieutenant J. G. Bourke found cavalry bits during the process of reburying the dead in July 1877 (Hardorff 1985:68–69), and other equipment and clothing items have been found in recent years (Weibert 1986; Scott and Fox 1987).

Clothing

The clothing worn by the battle participants has been the subject of several studies (Hutchins 1976; Reedstrom 1977). Most previous discussions focused almost exclusively on the soldiers' attire. This discussion will be no exception. The archaeological project recovered only a few Indian associated personal items and no clothing items whatever, so the question of Indian attire cannot be addressed with the archaeological data. But army clothing and equipment-related artifacts were recovered in moderate quantity.

The command's attire has been the subject of exhaustive research by James Hutchins (1956; 1958; 1976), who consulted many contemporary records and accounts of battle survivors (cf. Godfrey 1892) to develop a comprehensive synthesis of the Seventh Cavalry's 1876 campaign clothing. Hutchins (1976:4–7) concluded that the enlisted personnel wore regulation sky-blue kersey trousers over canton-flannel underwears, a coarse pullover shirt in either prescribed gray or older Civil War–issue white, and some men possibly wore privately purchased shirts and military blouses. There are several possible blouse patterns, such as the 1874 fatigue blouse, the obsolete 1872 plaited blouse, the 1858-pattern long frock coat (possibly modified by cutting off the skirt), or the cavalry shell jacket, which became obsolete in 1872. The foot was covered by the issue cavalry boot and the head covered by either the unpopular 1872 campaign hat or one of private purchase. The other clothing item mentioned by Hutchins (1976:6) is the heavy wool overcoat, a sky-blue kersey double-breasted item with a long cape.

Hutchins (1976:13–19) indicates the officers had much more latitude in choosing their campaign clothing. The trousers resembled those of the enlisted men, and it appears officers favored the regulation boot and overcoat for campaign. Shirts tended to be private purchase, including the popular bib-front shirt. The officers wore either the regulation campaign blouse or, as did several officers, including George Custer, a buckskin coat. The officers' headgear was varied. Most wore a broadbrimmed hat. Some wore the regulation black felt campaign hat, others a whitish-gray hat, and still others a straw hat. Officers' clothing was privately purchased from commerical sources or from the quartermaster's stores. The same was true of small arms.

Archaeological evidence of clothing consists of buttons, cloth fragments, hooks and eyes, a chin-strap slide, a trouser buckle, a suspender grip, boots, and boot nails. The cloth fragments are of two types. One group of fragments found in the excavations at Marker 128, belong to a pair of canton flannel underdrawers. The other group of cloth fragments was found attached to regulation blouse buttons. These fragments, found in several different marker excavation units, consist of wool cloth and cotton thread. The cloth represents pieces of blouse preserved by the contact with the brass button. The thread was that used to attach the button to the blouse. The blouse pieces were too small to identify the specific blouse type.

Three types of buttons were found: general-service brass, trouser fly and suspender, and nonmilitary clothing. The brass general-service buttons were found in three sizes. The two smaller sizes are commonly worn on blouse cuffs and forage-cap chin straps. With one exception, all the smaller buttons are plain eagle-style general service buttons. The exception has an *I* in the eagle's shield. The *I* (infantry) button could have been on the blouse cuff or the forage cap of an infantry officer and was lost by one of the officers in Terry's command or a later visitor to the site. This button was found near the Company H position at the Reno-Benteen defense site. At least one 1858 pattern frock coat or 1872 pattern plaited blouse was present at the battle. This is suggested by the button arrangement found on a soldier burial excavated in 1958. Bray (1958) found the disturbed burial of a soldier near the hospital area. A row of nine large general-service buttons was found in place on the body's thorax. The nine-button arrangement occurred on the 1858-pattern frock coat and the 1872 plaited blouse.

The other general-service buttons are the large blouse type. Seventeen of these were found on the Custer battlefield in association with the marker excavations. While the specific blouse type cannot be ascertained, it is clear that some soldiers were wearing their blouse during the battle.

Ninety iron and white-metal trouser buttons were found on the two battlefields. Most were found on the Custer battlefield in the marker excavations. These buttons were used to close the fly and attach suspenders on trousers. The button types are common on nineteenth-century trousers and were the regulation buttons for army-issue trousers. The buttons suggest that the men were wearing regulation trousers.

Two porcelain buttons were found in marker excavations on the Custer battlefield. This button type was common on shirts and underdrawers. One mother-of-pearl shank-type button was found in association with the human remains recovered at the Markers 33–34 excavation. This button type was commonly seen on bib-front shirts and may represent one of the privately purchased shirts worn during the battle. One other button was found in this excavation. It was a hard-rubber button of the type used on rain slickers and ponchos. It may indicate that one or the other item was with this individual or that he was wrapped in a poncho at burial.

A few other clothing-related artifacts either corroborate the association of other finds or suggest that additional items of clothing were present. A trouser adjustment buckle adds to the trouser-button data base, as does the presence of a suspender grip. The grip is a private-purchase type. The army did not issue suspenders in 1876, so its association could be with either an officer or an enlisted man. A slide from a forage-cap chin strap suggests that at least one individual had a forage cap along on the campaign. Hooks and eyes were also recovered. Hooks and eyes were used to fasten the brim up on the issue campaign hat and to fasten the collar or skirt on the obsolete blouses and coats. These hooks and eyes are the large variety and were most likely used on the campaign hat. The blouse alternative cannot be completely dismissed, however.

The final piece of apparel represented is footwear. The boot nails and portions of three boots recovered suggest the 1872 cavalry boot was the most common footwear. Hutchins (1976:4) suggests the boot would have been of wooden-peg or brass-nail construction. The archaeological samples, which may represent at least thirty-six different boots, were all made with iron and brass nails. The battlefield museum also contains a number of 1872 issue boots. All exhibit the same construction as the archaeological sample. With one exception, the uppers from the more complete boots in the museum collection and from the archaeological sample have been removed. The uppers were probably cut away by the Indians to salvage the leather. Gall (Graham 1953:92) and Wooden Leg (Marquis 1931:266) recalled taking boot uppers from the dead, and Sergeant John Ryan (Graham 1953:345–47) remembered seeing boots with the uppers cut away. The exception was the boot in the burial at Marker 128. This boot encased an articulated right foot and lower human leg. The boot was poorly preserved, but enough remained to indicate it was not removed from the foot, nor was the upper cut away. Apparently, not all boots were salvaged for their leather.

The apparel artifacts support Hutchins' (1976) findings. Hutchins' analyses of contemporary and survivor accounts contain more detailed information on clothing than the archaeological data. Hutchins does not document the use of the forage cap, but the chin-strap slide found during the archaeological investigations does suggest the forage cap was present at the battle, perhaps stored in a saddlebag.

A few personal items were recovered. Four five-cent pieces, two dated 1869 and one each dated 1870 and 1876, were found. All four coins exhibit very little wear, which is consistent with their loss in 1876. Two of the five-cent pieces were found in one of the marker excavations in association with human bone. Their position suggests they were in a trouser pocket or a bag.

A gold watch chain from the Calhoun position on Custer battlefield and an almost complete imported Swiss gold-plated brass hunting-case watch from Reno-Benteen attest to the presence of timepieces.

Warriors recalled finding several watches after the battle (Graham 1953; Marquis 1931), along with field glasses, a compass, and other personal items. Lieutenant John Crittenden's watch was recovered from the Indians about 1880 and returned to his family (Hutchins 1976:16). The watch recovered at Reno is representative of the type of timepieces used during the battle.

While no field glasses or compasses were recovered archaeologically, the eyepiece to a telescope was found at the Reno-Benteen defense site. The eyepiece is very similar to that of French telescopes of the era. The artifact was found near an Indian position at the north end of the Reno-Benteen defense site and on the approximate line of the command's retreat from Weir Point. The item may have been lost by either a soldier or an Indian.

Tobacco was definitely present at the battle. The historic record documents that some Indian warriors recovered tobacco from the dead soldiers at both the Reno-Benteen and Custer battlefields. Wooden Leg (Marquis 1931:225, 260) recalled that he found tobacco in the pocket of a dead soldier from the valley fight. *New York Herald* correspondent Mark Kellogg's grip, which was with the pack train and is now in the North Dakota State Historical Society's collections, contained a twist of tobacco and a large bag of Bull Durham tobacco. The presence of tobacco is also documented in the archaeological record. Three tobacco tags were found, two at Custer and one at Reno-Benteen. Tobacco tags were devices attached to plug tobacco to identify it by brand name. This indicates plug tobacco was present at the battle, but whether for smoking or chewing is not clear. No pipes were found on the battlefield. Pipe smoking was popular in this era. One might not expect briar pipes to be preserved, but clay pipes, if present, should have been recovered. Perhaps the absence of pipes reflects the practice of chewing tobacco on campaign. A pipe is cumbersome to use on horseback, and clay pipes would probably have been subject to a high breakage rate in field service. However, indirect evidence for pipe smoking is present in one set of human remains recovered. The teeth of the individual (fig. 20) found at the Marker 33–34 excavation exhibited extensive wear. The pattern of wear indicates he was a longtime pipe smoker. Whether he carried a pipe on this campaign is not known. There is no archaeological evidence for cigar or cigarette smoking.

Perhaps the most poignant personal item recovered was a silver-plated brass wedding band. The ring was found on the South Skirmish Line still encircling a joint of the left third finger. Over the years, other rings, such as Lieutenant William Van W. Reily's, were recovered and returned to the family (Hutchins 1976:17). This particular artifact is a sad reminder that the Battle of the Little Bighorn left not only dead combatants, but twenty-one widows as well (Stewart 1972).

Three artifacts can be ascribed to the Indian combatants. One is a Hudson's Bay–style trade fire steel. It was found near the Indian position named Henryville. Two ornaments were also recovered. One from the Reno-Benteen defense site is a brass bracelet found in an Indian position and associated with a group of .44-caliber Henry cartridge cases. The other artifact is an ornament made from two cartridge cases and a piece of lead. Its purpose has not been determined.

Soldiers' Equipment

The average soldier carried a variety of equipment during a campaign. He carried weapons, of course, but he also had a cartridge belt with a buckle, a holster for his revolver, and a carbine sling. He wore spurs and would have had a canteen, mess gear, and a haversack. Hutchins (1976:33–55) addresses the equipment carried by the Seventh Cavalry trooper in excellent detail.

The archaeological evidence for equipment is limited in number but diverse. Only six firearm parts were found. Three screws (fig. 29) are associated with the carbines used by the command, and a backstrap and a ejector-rod button (fig. 30) are from two of the command's Colt revolvers. The other two parts represent Indian firearms. One is the loading lever (fig. 31) from a Model 1858 New Model Army Remington percussion revolver, and the other is a trigger from a shotgun.

Two army-issue brass 1859-pattern spurs were recovered, as were three iron spur-strap buckles. The iron buckles suggest that the 1859 or Civil War–period spur and strap were used in the campaign. A single brass private-purchase spur was found at the Reno-Benteen defense site. Another equipment item recovered was the carbine-sling snap swivel (fig. 29). Two were found, one each at Custer and Reno-Benteen. Wooden Leg (Marquis 1931) recalled how he had pulled a soldier from his horse during the Reno retreat by his carbine sling. The historical and archaeological evidence indicate the carbine sling was in use at the battle.

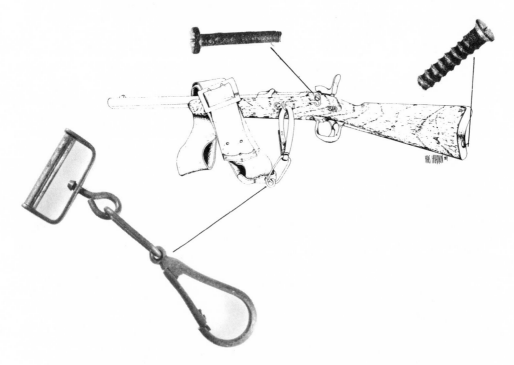

Fig. 29. Springfield Model 1873 carbine parts with their relative placement on the gun. The parts are a lock retaining screw, a butt-plate screw, and a carbine sling swivel and snap.

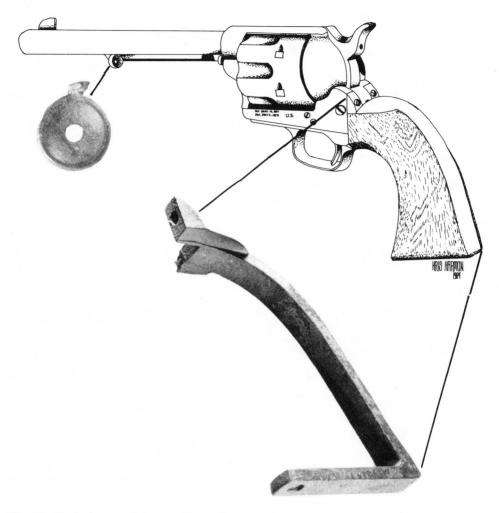

Fig. 30. The backstrap and ejector rod button from a Model 1873 Colt revolver. The lines indicate where the artifacts fitted on the revolver.

There is direct and possibly some indirect evidence of the use of belts. An adjustment hook for a Model 1855 waist belt was recovered on the Custer battlefield. A small fragment of black buff leather was also found. The leather is the style that was used in manufacturing the Model 1855 waist belt. The fragment is too small to be positively identified, however. The Model 1855 waist belt was not a issue item at the time of the battle but could have been used by a soldier as a campaign item, modified for use as a cartridge belt. Older army-issue waist belts were converted by company saddlers to cartridge, or thimble, belts by adding leather loops to hold the cartridges. The adjustment hook and possible belt fragment may represent such a use at the battle. Indirect evidence for a thimble belt may also exist. Two unusual .45/55 Springfield carbine rounds (fig. 32) were found on Last Stand Hill. Both rounds were unfired but each had

Fig. 31. The loading lever for a Model 1858 Remington revolver. The line indicates the lever's position on the gun.

been damaged when struck by a bullet. The rounds were found near each other on the ground, suggesting they may have been in the same cartridge box or thimble belt when struck.

A few mess items were recovered at the Reno-Benteen defense site. An iron-handled three-tine mess fork was found in the June 27 camp area, as was a fragment of a nonissue three-legged cast-iron cooking pot. One nearly complete, and one fragmentary issue tin cup were also found. The nearly complete cup (fig. 33) was crushed flat and appears to be the 1874-pattern cup, although no U.S. stamp was present on the handle. Three crudely scratched block letters (KKK) were noted on the cup's bottom. The letters' association has not been determined. A canteen stopper ring (fig. 34) found on the Custer battlefield was the only canteen artifact recovered. The ring could have come from either the Model 1858 canteen or the Model 1874 canteen. The later model was nothing more than a reconditioned version of the earlier canteen with new hangers, a new cover, and a new suspension strap (Sylvia and O'Donnell 1983).

As with the clothing artifacts, the soldiers' equipment items confirm the available historical documentation. Most of that documentation has been ably assembled by Hutchins (1976).

Miscellaneous Equipment

A few other equipment items were recovered from the battlefield. A sectional-tent-pole ferrule was found at the Reno-Benteen defense site. Other tent-related artifacts, also found at Reno-Benteen, are grommet stiffeners. These stiffeners, small iron rings, were stitched into canvas tent grommets to give them more strength. The presence of these items confirms the use of tents during the battle. Tents were known to have been with the column as it took the field (Godfrey 1892:4), and Lieutenant Thomas McGuire (Hammer 1976:124) noted the Reno-Benteen wounded were placed under a tent fly in

Fig. 32. Two .45/55-caliber cartridges struck by bullets.

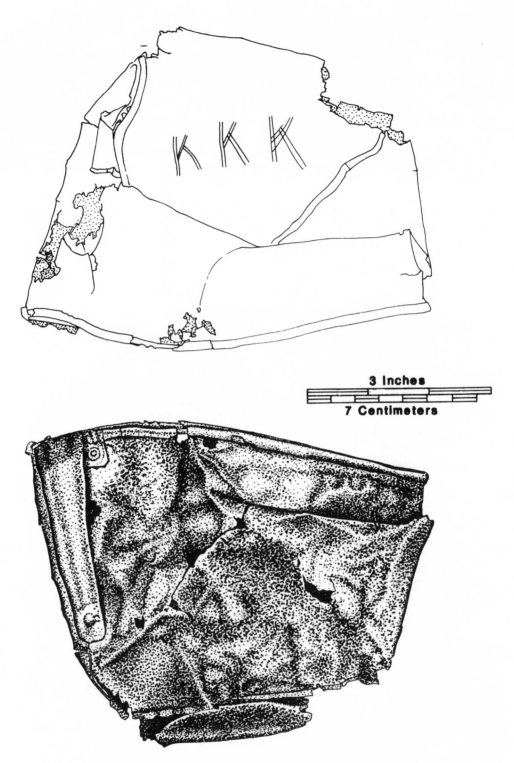

3 Inches

7 Centimeters

Fig. 33. An artist's rendering of the Model 1874 tin cup and the location of the block initials on the bottom.

Fig. 34. A canteen stopper ring in relation to a canteen of the type carried by the Seventh Cavalry.

the field hospital. Lieutenant Charles Varnum (Carroll 1982:74) recalled that Dr. Henry Porter used a shelter tent as a ground cover and operating table to amputate Private Michael Madden's leg. The items could be related to the hospital site of June 26–27, or they could represent other tenting carried in the pack train.

Another group of items found exclusivly at Reno-Benteen are the ammunition-box nails and screws and ration-box nails. These artifacts were recovered in large quantities near the barricade area and in the camp of June 26–27. The nails and screws indicate where boxes were discarded or broken up for fuel. Their presence helps to define the barricade and camp areas more precisely than has been possible in the past, even with the available survivor accounts.

Horse-Related Equipment

Artifacts related to horses, saddles, bridles, and other equipment were found in larger quantities than the soldier-related equipment. A poorly preserved Model 1859 carbine socket (fig. 35) was found at the Reno-Benteen defense site. Several buckles of the size found on carbine sockets were also recovered. This buckle size was also found on other horse-related equipment, as will be noted.

Other horse-related equipment found at Reno-Benteen includes a hand-forged hoof pick and several Model 1859 picket pins or parts. Horseshoes and horseshoe nails were found on both battlefields. The context and association of all but one horseshoe fragment suggest they are battle related. Since horseshoes and nails changed very little with time, unlike most other artifact categories, the relation of the shoes and nails must remain speculative. A number of saddle parts were recovered from Reno-Benteen, although none was found at the Custer battlefield. The brass saddle plates, foot-rings, and foot ring staples (fig. 35) are from Model 1859 McClellan saddles or the 1872 modification. Halter and bridle buckles were found on both battlefields, as were other buckles in sizes used on harness and other equipment as well. Several sizes of girth rings were recovered at Reno-Benteen. The context of recovery suggests they were associated with the pack animals' saddles and harness.

A few tack items were recovered that indicate some of the command's horse-related tack met the specifications of 1874. A brass staple was found at the Reno-Benteen defense site, as was a iron girth ring for the near side. Two side-line (hobble) snap hooks were also found at Reno-Benteen. This indicates that the new model items had reached Custer or that the company saddlers were making up items to meet the new specifications.

Some nonmilitary but battle-associated horse-related materials were found. A nickled or tinned buckle may indicate an officer's private-purchase bridle or possibly an army experimental buckle. A large iron girth ring may also represent an officer's private purchase or a company saddler's modification of an issue saddle to accept a horsehair cinch. Finally, a small iron ring from the Custer battlefield may represent either a civilian's saddle rigging or the rigging from an Indian pony.

Summary of Clothing and Equipment

The small quantity of clothing- and equipment-related artifacts adds new information to the historical documentation but does not prove exceptionally enlightening. The primary value of the archaeological data, in this case, is that they strongly support the battle's historical information and oral traditions. There is no conflict with the archaeological and historical evidence as to the clothing or equipment types utilized by the battle participants. The agreement between the two data sources is important in that it strengthens the validity of archaeological interpretations where the historical record is either in conflict with itself or is silent on a subject.

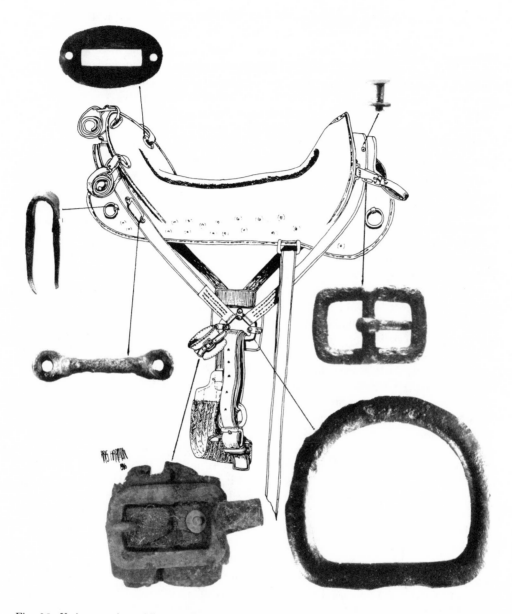

Fig. 35. Various cavalry saddle parts found at Reno-Benteen and their placement on a saddle. The parts are a saddle guard plate, a skirt-ring staple, a foot staple, a girth D-ring, a bar buckle, and a harness rivet.

WEAPONS AT THE BATTLE OF THE LITTLE BIGHORN

Bullets, cartridges, cartridge cases, arrowheads, and knives are the direct evidence of the weapons used during the battle. Combining the direct physical evidence with the available historical documentation allows, in expanded detail, examination of the role of weaponry in the battle.

Nonfirearms Weapons

Weapons, other than firearms, used at the Battle of the Little Bighorn are limited to cutting and crushing implements. These include knives, arrows, spears or lances, tomahawks or belt axes, and war clubs. The archaeological evidence for the use of such items is present as both indirect and direct evidence. Nonfirearm artifacts are few, particularly from the direct evidence, but the indirect evidence conclusively supports their use and corroborates the historical accounts.

Historical accounts indicate the bow and arrow played a large role in the fight. Wooden Leg (Marquis 1931:230) recalled that the Indian participants had more bows than guns. Standing Bear and Iron Hawk both recalled using bows and arrows during the battle (Neihardt 1967:117, 125), and Graham's (1953:250) compilation of Indian battle accounts notes that many soldiers' bodies were shot full of arrows after the battle. The archaeological evidence for the use of the bow is limited to nine arrowheads, all from the Custer battlefield. Indirect evidence of bow-and-arrow use is present on the human remains. At least two, and possibly three, bones from different bodies exhibit cut marks that could have been made by arrows (see chapter 9 for more discussion of wound-trauma evidence on human remains).

Knives, spears or lances, tomahawks or belt axes, and war clubs are also mentioned in the warriors' recollections (Marquis 1931:238, 263, 284−5; Neihardt 1967:127−28). Iron Hawk, one of the few participating warriors to recall specific mutilation incidents, remembered seeing Brings Plenty kill a soldier with a war club (Neihardt 1967:127), and Private Peter Thompson (Magnussen 1974:254) recalled finding "mallets" (war clubs) matted with blood in the Indian village after the battle. In addition to the weapons used by the warriors, Wooden Leg (Marquis 1931:260, 284) recalled taking folding knives and a sheath knife from the dead soldiers.

The archaeological evidence for the use of tomahawks and war clubs is indirect. The human remains bear the marks of crushing by heavy blunt instruments, such as war clubs, and at least one soldier was decapitated by a blow to the neck with a heavy edged instrument, such as a belt ax. There is direct archaeological evidence of knives. Three blade fragments and three complete folding knives are the archaeological examples that demonstrate the use of knives by the soldiers. There is also some indirect evidence. Several .45/55-caliber cartridge cases retain evidence of having been pried from a carbine chamber with pointed instruments (see **The Question of Extractor Failure** for more detail). Only one sheath-knife fragment attests to the Indian use of knives in the battle. The blade fragment (fig. 36), found in an Indian position at Reno-Benteen, is a large butcher-knife style. It is painted gold and closely resembles a Green River Russell trade knife. Blades of this type are also known to have been set into Sioux war clubs of this period. While this evidence is not striking, it does confirm the recollections

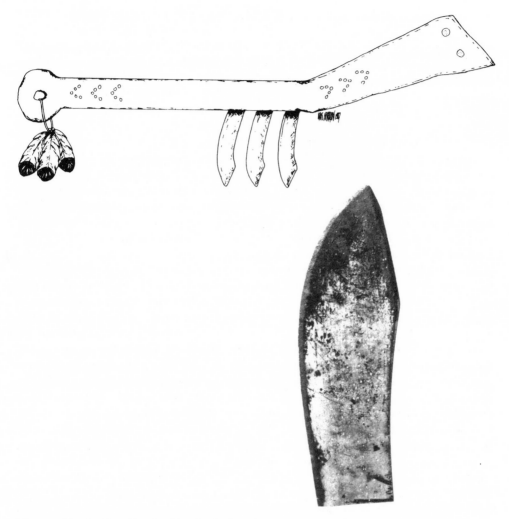

Fig. 36. The tip of a gold-painted butcher knife and a conjectural use of the blade in a war club.

of the battle participants. That more evidence was not found cannot be considered too surprising, as knives, arrows, spears, and tomahawks are reusable resources and would have been collected after the battle by the warriors for reuse and later by the soldiers and visitors as souvenirs.

Firearm Types

The different firearm types and their quantity, particularly those used by the Indian participants, has intrigued Little Bighorn enthusiasts for years (DuMont 1974). Most authors have relied on battle survivor accounts to document the use of firearms. These accounts are interesting remembrances, but, unfortunately, they lack the specificity required to assess and quantify reliably the firearm types used in the battle.

Recollections of Indian participants illustrate this point. Black Elk (Neihardt 1961) and Wooden Leg (Marquis 1931) both recall having had six-shooters (revolvers), but neither discusses the specific type. He Dog (Hammer 1976:208) recalls that the warriors had many Winchesters but notes that many other kinds of firearms were also used during the battle. Graham's (1953:52) and Marquis' (1931:134–35) summaries of Indian battle accounts note the use of a variety of guns, including Winchesters. Again, neither discusses quantity.

The army has no better documentation of the weapons used against it. Graham (1953:341) quotes Lieutenant Thomas French as saying the Indians all had Winchesters and pistols. Other accounts appear in the *Army and Navy Journal* of May 12, 1877, and May 19, 1877, referring to the surrender of Crazy Horse's band and noting 117 guns and pistols turned in at that time. The May 12 article notes in addition that Crazy Horse and Little Hawk turned in five Winchesters between them. Lieutenants Charles Varnum and Charles De Rudio both offered the opinion at the Reno Court of Inquiry in 1879, that the Indians were armed with Winchesters. Major Marcus Reno testified at the court that the Indians were armed with Winchesters.

These same accounts also mention army carbines used by Indians during the battle. Presumably they were captured from Custer's command by the Indians and were eventually surrendered when the Indians returned to the reservation. Wooden Leg (Marquis 1931:305–6) recalled surrendering the carbine he captured but said other warriors did not surrender theirs.

There is no doubt that Indians used firearms against the Custer and Reno-Benteen commands during the battle. The predominant opinion among the army participants was that substantial numbers of repeating firearms were used against the command. The types and quantities are still unknown. The only viable means to assess this question is through examination of the physical evidence, the artifacts. One of the first to attempt such an assessment was B. William Henry, a former monument historian. He evaluated and described the variety of bullets and cartridge cases from Indian positions around the Reno-Benteen defense site and the Custer battlefield. Henry's (DuMont 1974:55–56) analysis of 1,672 artifacts identified thirteen different types of cases and bullets representing thirteen different battle-related firearm types.

Using Henry's study as baseline data and applying modern firearm-identification procedures, we evaluated the archaeologically derived sample. The ability to identify firearm types and determine the minimum number of individual guns used in the battle is a powerful interpretive tool that has been adapted from the realm of the criminal investigator. The technique of firearms identification has been discussed in Scott and Fox (1987), and there is a summary in chapter 7.

The bullets and cartridges recovered during the archaeological investigations form the core of data on which the analyses were based. Between the Custer battlefield and the Reno-Benteen defense site, 2,361 cartridges, cartridge cases, and bullets were recovered. There are 141 cartridges of various calibers, 767 cartridge cases, and 1,453 bullets. The .44-caliber rimfire Henry and Model 1873 Winchester cases represent 27 percent of the total, and .45/55 Model 1873 Springfield cases account for another 54 percent. Corresponding bullets were found in similar quantities with 17.3 percent and 46.8 percent, respectively. The Custer Battlefield museum collection also has similar quantities of .45/55 cases (1069) and .44 rimfire cases (222). The sheer number of these cases indicates the Model 1873 Springfield and the Winchester-manufactured repeating firearms played a prominent role in the battle.

The firearm-identification analysis has found evidence for at least 371 individual guns among the forty-two firearm types used in the battle (tables 7, 8). The archaeological data provide the direct physical evidence of the guns used on the battlefield site. As demonstrated in chapter 7, it was relatively easy to differentiate between the bullets and cartridge cases used during the battle and those deposited later. In most cases, the post-battle firearm artifacts were distinctly different from the battle associated remains. The manufacturing technology was different, and the items are easily deleted from the study of battle-related artifacts. The degree to which cases and bullets had oxidized was also a factor in assessing the length of deposition. A few artifacts, such as cartridge cases or bullets that could have been fired before the battle or within a few years after the battle, were not so easily identified. For military bullets, different weights or alloy ratios were aids, but the most important factor in identification was artifact association and distribution. This extremely important sorting criterion would not have been possible without the precise contextual relationship of each artifact. The cartridges, cases, and bullets that are discussed here are those that can be reliably associated with the events of the Battle of the Little Bighorn.

The firearm-identification analysis indicated that at least forty-two firearm types were used in the battle (table 7). Three other types—.44-caliber rimfire used in the Frank Wesson guns, the .44-caliber center-fire Colt, and .58-caliber muzzle-loaders—were identified by Henry from one artifact each, but these types were not seen in the archaeological collections. These additions bring the total to forty-five types. The cavalry utilized the .45-caliber Model 1873 Springfield carbine and the .45-caliber Model 1873 Colt revolver. Some army participants are also known to have utilized personal firearms during the battle. Even taking these into account, the Indian warriors had at least forty-three firearm types at their disposal at the battle's beginning. As the battle progressed, the warriors took carbines and revolvers from the dead soldiers, so they eventually utilized all forty-five types against the cavalry.

Among the ammunition identified are shot from shotguns or weapons firing shot, eleven types of nonmetallic-cartridge firearm types, with the remaining types being metallic cartridge firearms. The nonmetallic-cartridge and muzzle-loading firearms include at least three types of revolvers, five types of long guns, and three unidentified types. The five long guns include at least three military types: Maynard, Starr, and Smith carbines. The other two types are the .58-caliber balls and the .577-caliber Enfield that could have been fired in either a military musket or a commercial weapon, such as a trade musket. The three unidentified types are the .44- .45- and .50-caliber balls. The rifling marks on these balls have not been identified.

The thirty-three types of metallic-cartridge weapons are represented by eight revolver types, thirteen single-shot long-gun types, four repeating long-gun types, and eight unidentified cartridge-bullet types (table 8). The firearms are an impressive array of weaponry. This archaeologically identified group can be compared with the list of weapons turned over to the army in 1877 when some Sioux and Cheyenne Indian bands returned to the reservation. These bands surrendered 410 guns (War Department 1879), including 160 muzzle-loading guns. The rest were cartridge guns. While these guns may not have been used at the Battle of the Little Bighorn, they do represent the

Table 7 Cartridge Cases Representing the Number of Individual Firearms Identified by Caliber

Firearm, FS Numbers	Firearm, FS Numbers	Firearm, FS Numbers	Firearm, FS Numbers
Spencer .56/.56:	**.50/70:**	**.44 Henry:**	**.45/55:**
Custer	*Custer*	*Custer*	*Custer*
1. 006, 1056, 1290	1. 94, 185	1. 48, 79, 637, 1601, 1799	1. 2
2. 1295, 1297, 1298	2. 73, 229	2. 57, 58, 60	2. 72
	3. 348, 769, 1279, 1407	3. 63, 352, 1296, 1300	3. 74, 133, 226, 232
Spencer .56/.50:	4. 1258, 1447	4. 81	4. 80
Custer	5. 1299, 1732	5. 82, 564, 638, 639	5. 92
1. 1257	6. 1273, 1334, 1337	6. 84, 1752, 1758	6. 99
2. 1277	7. 1557, 1610	7. 90	7. 135, 136, 148
	8. 59, 222	8. 95	8. 150
Unidentified .50	9. 1602, 1607	9. 178, 1808	9. 175, 240, 244
Custer	10. 1308, 1755	10. 184, 1630	10. 196, 199, 200
1. 644	11. 311	11. 375	11. 238
	12. 378	12. 379, 1333	12. 239, 334
Smith & Wesson American .44:	13. 566	13. 556, 1545, 1778	13. 241
Custer	14. 599	14. 640	14. 242, 243
1. 23, 49	15. 647	15. 648, 1030, 1031	15. 253
2. 645	16. 1067	16. 959, 1700, 1704, 1705	16. 264
3. 1815	17. 1272	17. 984	17. 272
	18. 1281	18. 1035	18. 273
Model 1873 Winchester .44/40:	19. 1285	19. 1150, 1151, 1777	19. 282
Custer	20. 1289	20. 1267	20. 309
1. 109, 1527	21. 1546	21. 1274	21. 326
2. 646, 1710	22. 1556	22. 1278b	22. 403, 447
3. 1335, 1621, 1771	23. 1568	23. 1283	23. 523
4. 1749, 1821	24. 1595	24. 1292, 1757	24. 533
5. 1770, 1776	25. 1599	25. 1294	25. 539
6. 1763	26. 1717	26. 1309, 1330, 1332, 1338, 1339, 1750	26. 560
Reno-Benteen	27. 1772	27. 1310, 1331	27. 561
7. 4654, 4655	28. 1792	28. 1435, 1436	28. 562
Both Battlefields	29. 1809	29. 1531, 1533, 1534	29. 563
8. 108, 634, 2240, 2258, 2259, 2267, 4983	30. 1845		30. 626
	31. 5051		31. 637
			32. 643

Evans Old Model .44:

Custer

1. 1392

.32 Forehand and Wadsworth

Custer

1. 34

.44 Rimfire Colt, Remington, and
 Balland

Custer

1. 93
2. 115, 1276
3. 1289a, b
4. 1529
5. 1793, 1794, 1795, 1796
6. 5021

Reno-Benteen

7. 2199
8. 2204
9. 2265
10. 2355

Colt .45:

Custer

1. 147
2. 269
3. 381
4. 577
5. 578
6. 829
7. 1149
8. 1379
9. 1605
10. 4977
11. 4978
12. 4979

32. 5054
33. 5058

Reno-Benteen

34. 2005
35. 2025
36. 2027, 2070
37. 2060
38. 2081
39. 2207
40. 2260
41. 2361
42. 2550, 2551
43. 2796
44. 2880
45. 3201
46. 4814a
47. 4844
48. 5064

30. 1536
31. 1543, 1547, 1761
32. 1543, 1544
33. 1553, 1554
34. 1596, 1597, 1609
35. 1598
36. 1608, 1611
37. 1612, 1613
38. 1615, 1616
39. 1706
40. 1707
41. 1708
42. 1722
43. 1751
44. 1753, 1754
45. 1756, 1759
46. 1760
47. 1766, 1767, 1768
48. 1769
49. 1774, 1775
50. 1786
51. 1814
52. 1820
53. 1877, 1878
54. 2211, 2565
55. 5053
56. 5055
57. 5056
58. 5057

Reno-Benteen

59. 2002
60. 2004
61. 2018
62. 2036, 2039
63. 2037
64. 2041, 2079, 2093
65. 2044
66. 2047

33. 687
34. 700
35. 707
36. 712
37. 771
38. 870
39. 923
40. 948
41. 1046
42. 1112
43. 1271, 1701
44. 1291
45. 1345
46. 1377
47. 1380, 1381
48. 1390
49. 1530, 1532, 1535, 1555,
 1582, 5049
50. 1537
51. 1538
52. 1539
53. 1540
54. 1541
55. 1548
56. 1549
57. 1550
58. 1551
59. 1552
60. 1583, 1584
61. 1603, 1604
62. 1614
63. 1651
64. 1730
65. 1764
66. 1765
67. 1813
68. 1819
69. 2580

Table 7 *continued*

Firearm, FS Numbers	*Firearm, FS Numbers*	*Firearm, FS Numbers*
Colt .45:	.44 Henry:	.45/.55:

Reno-Benteen	*Reno-Benteen*	*Reno-Benteen*
13. 2094	67. 2048	70. 2019, 2020, 2056, 2062,
14. 2315	68. 2049	2083, 2205, 2206, 2208,
15. 2353	69. 2050	2237, 2330, 2367, 2369,
16. 2616	70. 2053	2847, 3607, 3747
17. 2625	71. 2057	71. 2066
18. 2660	72. 2069	72. 2067, 2243, 2248, 2281,
19. 2798	73. 2072	2283, 2287, 2291, 2303,
20. 2800	74. 2074	2304, 2633, 2765, 3000,
21. 3063	75. 2075	3003, 3008, 3012, 3056,
22. 3099, 3101	76. 2080	4752, 4790, 4800, 4816,
23. 3139	77. 2094	4818
24. 3146	78. 2098	73. 2082, 2121, 2279, 2289,
25. 3960, 4023, 4035,	79. 2221	2290, 2295, 2311, 2312,
4037, 4038	80. 2238	2585, 2655, 2657, 2739,
26. 4148	81. 2241	2786, 2787, 2925, 3137,
27. 4325	82. 2257	3138, 3206, 3207, 3208,
28. 4758	83. 2263, 2264, 2308	3722, 4746, 4794
29. 4830	84. 2266, 5004	74. 2084, 2120, 2298, 2669,
30. 4988	85. 2268	2744, 2792, 2923, 3725
31. 4990, 4991	86. 2273, 2274, 2275,	75. 2095, 2293, 2305, 2307,
	2276, 2277, 2278,	2309, 2310, 2434, 2435,
	2280	2437, 2438, 2653, 2654,
	87. 2282, 4998, 4999,	3190, 4104
	5000, 5001	76. 2096, 2100, 2329, 2374,
	88. 2288	2461, 2462, 2465, 2466,
	89. 2296	2468, 2482a, b, c, d, e, f,
	90. 2357, 2359, 2363	g, 2486, 2813
	91. 2365	77. 2023, 2026, 2051, 2052,
	92. 2582, 4229	2071, 2076, 2097, 2099,
	93. 3837	2101, 2197, 2328, 2412,

2433, 2696, 2866, 2867, 3950, 4674
78. 2242, 2247, 2261, 2294, 3004, 3163a, b, c, d, e, f, g, h, i, j, k, 4306, 4312, 4313, 4319, 4320, 4321, 4322, 4364
79. 2584, 3050
80. 2628, 2646, 3192
81. 2656, 4009, 4024, 4041, 4042, 4046, 4048, 4049, 4050, 4052, 4054, 4057, 4058, 4066, 4070, 4090
82. 2779, 2791, 2793, 2794, 2799
83. 2910, 2995, 2997, 3317, 3324, 3343, 3344, 3346, 3347, 4147, 4150, 4155, 5002
84. 2918, 2920, 2926, 2929, 2999, 3202, 3203, 3211, 3213, 3215, 3216, 3217, 3220, 3222, 3228, 3244
85. 2924, 2928, 2941, 2998, 4367
86. 2927, 2939, 3011, 3016
87. 2940, 3834
88. 2948, 3001, 3005, 3009a, 3025, 4308, 4309, 4632
89. 2994, 4025, 4053, 4093
90. 2996, 3191, 3824, 4403
91. 3057, 4103
92. 3193
93. 3194, 3944, 4032, 4064
94. 3200, 3205, 3214, 3231, 3232, 3247

94. 4036
95. 4145
96. 4146
97. 4149
98. 4232
99. 4335
100. 4338
101. 4339
102. 4984
103. 4997
104. 5003

Both Battlefields
105. 471, 1293, 1343, 2000
106. 1259, 1280, 1288, 2055
107. 1278a, 2017
108. 2068, 5022

Table 7 *continued*

Firearm, FS Numbers

.45/55 Henry:

Reno-Benteen

95. 3204, 3219
96. 3328, 3340, 3341
97. 3329
98. 3577, 4941, 4958
99. 3667, 3672, 3673, 3677,
    3681, 3684, 3685, 3686,
    3687
100. 3669, 4935
101. 3724
102. 3726
103. 3742, 3753
104. 3863, 3864
105. 3971
106. 3990, 3991, 3992, 3995,
    3997, 3998, 4850
107. 4000, 4001, 4002, 4003,
    4005, 4006, 4007, 4014,
    4017, 4019, 4021, 4027,
    4056, 4063, 4068, 4151
108. 4047
109. 4051

110. 4055
111. 4152
112. 4217
113. 4225
114. 4226
115. 4227, 4284, 4292a, 4295
116. 4230, 4270, 4271, 4287,
     4289
117. 4283
118. 4288, 4296
119. 4362
120. 4625, 4636, 4683
121. 4651
122. 4742a, b, c, 4745
123. 4778
124. 4840, 4851
125. 4940
126. 4968
127. 4982, 4992
128. 4987
129. 4989
130. 4996
131. 5061

Note: Field-specimen number groups represent cases matched during firearms identification analysis.

Table 8 Firearm Types, Quantities, and Distribution

Firearm Type	Cartridge Cases	Bullets	Guns Represented Total	Custer	Reno
Forehand and					
Wadsworth .32	1	1	1	1	0
Colt .36	—	2	1	1	1*
Colt .38	—	2	1	—	1
Sharps .40	—	18	1	1	1
Unknown .40a	—	2	1	1	1
" .40b	—	1	1	1	—
" .40c	—	1	1	1	—
" .40d	—	1	1	1	—
" .40e	—	2	1	—	1
Forehand and					
Wadsworth .42	—	2	1	—	1
Smith and Wesson .44	4	9	3	3	—
Evans .44	1	—	1	1	—
Henry .44	202	252	108	62	50
Winchester M1873	21	—	8	7	2
Colt conv. .44	4	—	4	1	3
Colt M1860 .44	—	1	1	1	—
Colt M1871 .44	4	—	2	1	1
Colt M1872 .44	—	4	1	—	1
Remington M1858 .44	—	1	1	1	—
conversion .44	4	—	4	1	3
Ballard .44	2	—	2	1	1
Colt M1873 .45	37	66	31	12	19
Springfield M1873 .45	715	680	130	69	62
Sharps Sporting Rifle .45	—	1	1	—	1
Sharps .45	—	4	1	1	1
Unknown .45	—	2	1	1	—
Unidentified .50	1	—	1	1	—
Maynard .50	—	1	1	1	—
Sharps .50	44	35	35	27	9
Springfield .50	19	286	13	6	7
Smith .50	—	3	1	—	1
Unknown .50a	—	2	1	—	1
" .50b	—	2	1	—	1
Starr .54	—	1	1	1	—
Spencer .56/56	6	5	2	2	1
" .56/50	2	—	2	2	—
Enfield .577	—	1	1	1	—
Unknown					
ball .44−.45a	—	13	1	1	1
ball .44−.45b	—	2	1	1	—
ball .50	—	40	1	1	1
shotgun	—	9	1	1	1
Total	767	1453	371	215	171

*Where no cases were present, bullets were assumed to represent only one firearm for that type. If bullets were present on each battlefield, one gun was noted for each.

variety of firearms available to the Indians of the Northern Plains. The archaeological sample does not correspond to the surrendered guns one for one, but the comparability is excellent.

The bullets and cartridge cases found on the field are the definitive evidence of firearms used by the combatants. The analysis has shown at least forty-five firearm types were used in the battle. Several other questions have intrigued Little Bighorn enthusiasts (cf. DuMont 1974). One of the most controversial is, how extensive was extractor failure among the soldiers' carbines? Coupled with that question is how much of an effect extractor failure had on the outcome of the battle. Other firearm questions include these: What personal firearms were actually used at the battle? What was the quantity or how many individual firearms were used by the Indian warriors? This study, utilizing modern firearm-identification techniques, can, at least in part, answer some of these questions.

The Question of Extraction Failure

Some Indian accounts of the battle (Marquis 1976), as well as comments by Major Reno (Hedren 1973: 66), have suggested many of the soldiers' carbines jammed as they tried to extract the spent case. Some authors have even gone so far as to speculate the cause of Custer's defeat was, in part, due to the extraction failure (Graham 1953: 146–147). There is no doubt that some carbines failed to extract cases properly, as the historical and archaeological evidence clearly indicate.

Major Reno (1876) noted that of 380 carbines in his command 6 were rendered unserviceable owing to cartridge extraction failure. He does not, however, identify the total number of carbines that had problems with case extraction. As Private John Newell (Everett 1930) has noted, carbines in Captain Thomas French's company were successfully put back into operation after removal of the stuck case, either by prying with a knife or by using French's .50/70 rifle ramrod. Newell is not explicit about the number of carbines that failed, although he says most in the company were affected.

Captain C. E. Dutton (1876) questioned thirty-seven officers about the 1876 campaign, not just the Battle of the Little Bighorn, and found that all had seen at least one example of extraction failure. Some indicated they had seen six or seven extraction failure situations. At least one carbine from the Reno-Benteen defense site was examined by Captain O. E. Michaelis, an ordnance officer. Captain Michaelis (1876) reported he had examined a carbine in which was stuck the body of a cartridge. He notes the carbine was turned in by Captain Myles Moylan. Michaelis extracted the case and noted the carbine had been carelessly handled and the cartridge was dirty. Presumably this carbine is one of the six referred to by Reno.

The Indian accounts of extraction problems are generally less specific; however, several are known. One of the more specific comes from Wooden Leg (Marquis 1971: 266) when he states that he found a carbine on the Custer battlefield with a cartridge stuck in the chamber. He recovered the weapon but, finding it unservicable, threw it in the river.

Clearly the historical evidence indicates that carbine cartridge-case extraction failure was a factor in the battle. To what extent it was a factor is not clear. The archaeological data provide more direct evidence to clarify further the role of extraction failure. We are not the first to examine the physical evidence of extraction failure. Hedren (1973) examined all of the available .45/55 carbine cases from the park and private collections in 1972. He found 3 cases out of 1,625 he examined had evidence of extraction problems.

Evidence of case-extraction problems is present in the archaeological sample. The microscopic examination of the cases from the Custer battlefield identified two cases (FS1537, 1539) with scratch marks on the head. These could have been caused by prying the case from the carbine chamber with a knife. A third case (FS734) has two gouges present in the rim, which could have been the result of prying the case from the chamber. All three cases were fired in different weapons. Six cases from the Reno-Benteen defense site exhibited extraction problems. Four cases (FS2290, 2787, 2923, 4651) exhibit scratch marks on the case rim and head. One case (FS4651) exhibits marks which could only have been made if someone was prying the case from the left side of the receiver. The other two Reno-Benteen cases (FS2584, 2669) have had the rim and head ripped in the process of extraction. Four different guns are represented by the Reno-Benteen cases, with two different ones exhibiting extraction failure at least twice each.

The number of cases exhibiting extraction failure amounts to 2 percent of the total number of archaeologically recovered specimens (1.8 percent at Reno-Benteen and 3.3 percent at the Custer battlefield). Taken with Hedren's data, the extraction failure rate amounts to 6 percent of all examined examples of .45/55 cases. The archaeological cases represent 69 different guns from the Custer battlefield and 62 different guns from the Reno-Benteen defense site. The extraction problems represent 4.3 percent and 5.6 percent failure rates for the two battlefields, respectively. This yields an average of 5 percent as an overall failure rate. Since the cartridge cases represent 131 guns, or about 22 percent of the carbines used by the army in the battle, then a 5 percent failure rate would mean about 30 of the total battle carbines would have been involved (10 on the Custer battlefield and 20 at Reno-Benteen).

The archaeological sample has identified more carbines with extraction problems than are specifically historically documented. Obviously, two factors that archaeology cannot control for are those carbines where the case could not be removed after firing or the cases where the cartridge was removed by using Captain French's rifle ramrod. The latter situation would not leave any clear physical change in the case. The absence of the guns from the record biases the sample, but from the Reno account of only six guns being rendered unserviceable it is unlikely the bias is significant. Even with these biases considered, the number of guns involved is not statistically significant.

If the army had extraction-failure problems, then the question arises as to whether the Indian warriors faced a similar problem. In 1872 the army formed a board of officers to assess the quality and reliability of various types of firearms in an effort to select a breech-loading system for general service (Report of the Chief of Ordnance 1873). Major Reno was a member of that board. The field trials compared the Sharps, Remington, and Springfield firearms. In those trials 76,628 rounds were fired in the Sharps with 2,699 (3.52 percent) cartridge failures. The Remington had 89,828 rounds fired and experienced 2,595 cartridge failures (2.86 percent), and the Springfield had 96,628 rounds fired with 1,882 failures (1.96 percent). The results of the field trials showed a clear preference for the Springfield, which was later adopted as the service arm. The lower Springfield cartridge-failure rate was a factor in its selection. Some of the warriors who fought Custer were using some of the same weapon types examined by the board, and on the basis of the army's field-trial results, they should have experienced cartridge failures.

Two historical accounts suggest that the Indians did indeed have extraction problems with which to contend. George Herendeen (Hammer 1976:225) commented on finding a dead Sioux warrior during his attempt to rejoin the Reno command. Near the warrior's body he found a gun with a cartridge stuck fast in the chamber. Captain Michaelis (1876) reported he had in his possession a cut-down .50/70 musket used by the Indians during the battle. It is possible the gun referred to is the same one Herendeen noted. In any event, at least one Indian gun had an extraction problem.

The archaeological record contains further information. About 8 percent of the .50/70 and Spencer cases have pry or scratch marks on them. Forty-six .50/70 and Spencer firearms are represented by the cases; 9 percent exhibit extraction problems (6.6 percent at the Custer battlefield and 11 percent at Reno-Benteen). These figures exclude the .45/55-caliber army cases that were fired in .50-caliber arms. Those cases all exhibit extraction failure, as might be expected with a ruptured case. From the archaeological data, the case-extraction failure rate during the battle was about the same on both sides. This information on Indian extraction failure further reinforces the argument that extraction failures did occur, but not in large numbers. That extraction failure did occur is not debatable but it was not significant to the outcome of the battle.

Evidence of Personal Firearms

Captain Thomas French used a .50/70-caliber infantry rifle at the Reno-Benteen defense site. Sergeant John Ryan (Graham 1953:244) recalled French cut a notch in the stock of his "Springfield rifle, caliber .50, breechloader, . . . whenever he shot an Indian." Private Dan Newell also remembered Captain French's rifle, but in connection with using its ramrod to remove stuck cartridges from Company M's carbines (Everett 1930:2). Several .50/70 cartridges and cases were found in the defense perimeter during the archaeological investigations. These seven cases indicate that six different guns firing the .50/70 cartridge were used within the Reno-Benteen defense perimeter. Two Benét-primed and one bar-primed cases, representing three different Springfield .50/70s and four unfired cartridges were found in the barricade area occupied by Company D. One Benét and one bar-primed cases fired from different Springfields were found on the northwest portion of the perimeter in the area occupied by Company M the first day and Company B the second day. Two brass UMC-primed cases fired in the same Springfield were found on the eastern perimeter edge in the area occupied by Company B the first day of the battle and Company M the second day.

The presence of cases fired in six different Springfields in the defense perimeter suggests that Captain French was not the only person to have a .50/70-caliber gun. Other officers or enlisted personnel may have favored that caliber over the Model 1873 carbine. However, it is more likely that the civilian packers and Indian scouts were issued these older-model guns. The presence of brass cases raises an interesting question which is addressed in the next section.

Sergeant John Ryan also carried and used a personal firearm during the battle (Graham 1953:239–47). It was a Sharps sporting rifle chambered for the government carbine round. He was one of several individuals at the Reno-Benteen defense site to return long-range fire at a warrior on Sharpshooter Ridge, or Wooden Leg Hill, located at the north end of the current monument boundary.

During the day of June 26, Captain Thomas French asked Ryan to help silence Indian fire from the vicinity of Wooden Leg Hill. Ryan used his Sharps sporting rifle and as he recalled, "I fired a couple of shots until I got range of that group of Indians. Then I put in a half a dozen shots in rapid succession, and those Indians scampered away from that point of the bluff, and that ended the firing on the part of the Indians in that memorable engagement, and the boys set up quite a cheer" (Graham 1953:245). Indirect evidence of Ryan's use of his Sharps may be a bullet found embedded in the south face of the ridge. This bullet is a standard .45-caliber 405-grain government bullet, but the land and groove impressions on its surface indicate it was fired in a Sharps sporting rifle. While it is possible that this round may be attributed to a Sharps other than Ryan's, the location certainly favors the interpretation that this bullet represents Ryan's efforts to silence the Indian sharpshooter.

No direct evidence for George Custer's personal firearms (a Remington sporting rifle and Royal Irish Constabulary pistols) was located on the Custer battlefield. However, a single .50-caliber bullet fired from a Remington sporting rifle was found at the Reno-Benteen defense site. The bullet was found embedded in the hospital area, and its orientation suggests it was fired from an Indian position east of the defense site. The bullet is not definitive evidence of Custer's Remington in Indian hands, but it shows that at least one .50-caliber Remington sporting rifle was used in the battle.

Brass Cases and George Custer's Guns

For many years some people have assumed George Custer was the only person to have used a .50-caliber brass cartridge during the battle. This unfortunate notion has crept into the literature on the battle and has been used to reconstruct Custer's personal movements (Weibert 1986). George Custer is known to have used a .50/70 Remington sporting rifle that may have utilized a brass case (DuMont 1974). He also may have used one or a brace of Royal Irish Constabulary pistols that used a brass case (DuMont 1974; Palmer 1975). Corporal Daniel Ryan, who helped bury Custer (DuMont 1974:67), recalled finding brass cartridge cases under Custer's body. He also noted the cases were collected for souvenirs. It has since been assumed that the presence of brass .50/70 cases is indicative of Custer's location during the battle. Weibert (1986) has been the most forceful proponent of this viewpoint.

Brass cartridge cases began to come into use in the 1870s and were commercially produced. In fact, the government bought several million rounds for its .50/70 military models in 1874 and 1875 (Lewis 1972:19). Commerical brass cartridge cases were also produced for a number of different weapons, such as the Model 1873 Winchester and the Evans Old Model.

Several dozen brass archaeological cases were recovered on both battlefields, and this was no surprise, given the quantity on the civilian market and in government hands. The case types include the .44-caliber Evans and the .44/40-caliber cases for the Model 1873 Winchester. The only other brass cases found were in the .50/70-caliber.

The Winchester-Millbank primed cases are brass and were found on the Custer battle-field and at the Reno-Benteen defense site. Twenty-one brass .50/70 cases were recovered. Firearm-identification analysis indicates they were fired in fourteen different Springfield and Sharps or Remington manufactured guns.

The distribution and context of the brass cases suggests an Indian association for those on the Custer battlefield and both Indian and soldier use at the Reno-Benteen defense site. Clearly these brass cases cannot be associated with George Custer's Remington sporting rifle. Neither can the presence of brass cases in other contexts be the primary evidence to support the reconstruction of George Custer's personal movements.

Firearms Quantities

The question of how many individual firearms were used by the Indians at the battle has intrigued Custer buffs and historians for years (cf. DuMont 1974). Until this inventory and study of the salient artifacts, using the most up-to-date firearm-identification techniques, that question could not be reliably addressed. Our study has at least a partial answer regarding the minimum number of guns used during the battle. The firearm-identification analysis has identified 44 individual revolvers (31 Model 1873 Colts and 13 others, table 8), 119 repeating rifles and carbines (table 8), 188 single-shot rifles and carbines (131 Model 1873 Springfield carbines and 58 others, table 8), and 8 unidentified guns (table 8). This is a conservative estimate in that we have counted only those cartridges and bullets which can be sorted and identified with certainty. Groups of balls, such as the .44- and .45-caliber and the .50-caliber, as well as the shot, were counted as representing only 1 gun in each type. There is little question that if these round balls could have been sorted and identified further, the tally of individual firearms would have mounted considerably. We are well aware that our count of firearms represents only those cartridges and bullets found by the archaeological project within the formal monument boundary and by no means represents all of the possible firearms used. The figures represent only a minimum number of firearms that can be identified from the archaeological evidence. No doubt many more were used by the combatants.

The largest number of individual guns is represented by 131 Springfield Model 1873 .45/55-caliber carbines. (table 8). The cartridge cases indicate a minimum of 69 Springfield carbines were used on Custer battlefield and 62 on the Reno-Benteen defense site. These figures represent 34 percent and 16 percent, respectively, of the Springfield carbines known to have been used at Custer and Reno-Benteen. The second-largest group is the 108 Henry and Winchester Model 1866s (table 8). The cases indicate at least 62 guns were used at the Custer battlefield and 50 at the Reno-Benteen defense site. Four Henrys, or Winchesters, were used at both battlefields (table 7) and account for the discrepancy between the individual battlefield figures and the total. Thirty-five Sharps and 13 Springfield .50/70s were identified. Twenty-seven Sharps and 6 Springfields were associated with Custer battlefield and the rest with Reno-Benteen. Six of the Reno Springfields were utilized by combatants in the defense perimeter.

The Colt Model 1873 army-revolver cases indicated 12 were used at Custer and 19 at Reno-Benteen for a total of 31 guns. The Model 1873 Winchester .44/40 cases indicate 7 guns were used at Custer and 2 at Reno-Benteen. One of these guns was used at both battlefields thus the minimum number of Winchester Model 1873 firearms is

8. The remaining types account for as many as 4 guns and at a minimum 1 additional firearm each. The cartridge-case evidence totals 371 individual firearms, with 162 associated with either the Model 1873 Springfield army carbine or the Model 1873 Colt army revolver. The other 209 guns are probably Indian firearms. The evidence from the Custer battlefield indicates at least 215 guns were used there (81 army-related and 124 Indian-related). The Reno-Benteen defense site evidence indicates the use of a minimum of 171 guns (87 army-related and 84 Indian-related).

The army firearms account for 43.6 percent of all individually identified guns. The Henrys and Winchester Models 1866 and 1873 repeating firearms amount to 31.2 percent of all firearms and 55 percent of the nonarmy firearms.

The figure of 371 guns is derived from the firearm-identification analysis and is a minimum number since, as we have noted, we have not had the opportunity to examine every cartridge case and bullet used at the battle. However, this minimum figure can be used as a basis for extrapolating the level of Indian armament. The means to accomplish this is the application of statistical procedures.

During the 1984 and 1985 fieldwork a statistically valid sample of grids was reinventoried to determine the validity of the metal-detecting technique. This was the inventory-evaluation phase (Scott and Fox 1987). That effort indicated artifact recovery to be between 30 and 35 percent of all artifacts present on the battlefield. The sample grids also indicated that the artifact classes and quantities recovered through metal-detecting are representative of the total artifact universe found at the site (Scott and Fox 1987). Since the collection is representative, then statistical techniques can be applied to project, and with reasonable certainty the actual number of firearms employed in the battle can be estimated.

If the artifact sample, from which the 209 nonarmy individual-firearms number is derived, does represent 30 to 35 percent of the battlefield archaeological record, then a projected range of 597 to 697 individual firearms potentially used by the Indians can be derived. If the sample size is lower, the firearm numbers will go correspondingly higher.

For the Custer battlefield the number of Indian firearms is projected between 354 and 414. These figures suggest Custer's command was outgunned about two to one. These projections also suggest that 198 to 232 of the Indian guns were Henrys or Winchester Models 1866 or 1873. At the Reno-Benteen defense site the projected number of Indian guns ranges between 259 and 300, with the repeating guns ranging between 150 and 174.

If one projects the amount of ammunition with which the repeating guns at the Custer battlefield could be loaded, if each magazine was full at the beginning of the battle, the result is about 3,792 rounds. That means that when these guns were brought to bear on Custer's men, there were more than eighteen bullets for each of the men who died with Custer. And this only counts the repeating arms. We consider these figures conservative for two reasons. First, if we were able to discriminate among individual muzzle-loaders more finitely, this would have added to the minimum Indian-firearm figure. Second, many Indian firing positions lie outside the area investigated. Certainly additional individual firearm evidence exists in those areas, given the thousands of cartridge cases found outside the monument boundaries by collectors (cf. Weibert 1986).

Further corroboration of the firearm projection is available through examination of the troopers' firearms. Earlier it was concluded that the Custer battlefield .45/55 Springfield carbine cases represented rounds fired from 69 different guns, or 32.2 percent of the approximately 210 carbines Custer had in his command. This percentage is remarkably consistent with our sample size estimate of 30 to 35 percent, derived independently in the inventory-evaluation phase.

The Reno-Benteen .45/55-caliber cases represent only 62 individual soldier fire-arms. This is only 16 percent of the known Springfield carbines in use at the battlefield. This does not correlate with the 30 to 35 percent sample from Custer battlefield. There is a reason for this bias. The Reno-Benteen defense site was the subject of sporadic metal-detecting inventory from 1956 to 1969 and was the site of a formal archaeological investigation in 1958 (Bray 1958; Custer Battlefield administrative files). These inves-tigations collected a large quantity of artifacts, but the records are incomplete as to the precise artifact numbers and types. The monument's administrative files contain some information, and we have ascertained that at least 420 .45/55-caliber cartridges and cases were recovered during those investigations. The Custer battlefield was not subject to the same level of investigation. Our archaeological project recovered about 325 .45/55-caliber cartridges and cases from Reno-Benteen. The earlier investigations recov-ered 130 percent more cartridges and cases. Those cases create a bias that could account for the discrepancy between the two samples. The approximately 420 carbine cases previously recovered could not be subjected to firearm-identification analysis because the park staff wished to maintain them in their uncleaned condition for future interpretive purposes. Since they could not be analyzed this artifact group creates a bias in the Reno-Benteen sample. The bias is recognized but cannot be wholly controlled in this analysis. Until the collection can be analyzed and compared with our analysis, the 30 to 35 percent sample from Custer battlefield, must be assumed to be accurate, and that sample size ratio will be applied to the Reno-Benteen defense-site materials.

The validity of our statistical argument can be further assessed by analyzing Sergeant Charles Windolph's statement about Indian armaments:

It has been generally accepted that all the red warriors were armed with the latest model repeat-ing Winchester rifles and that they had a plentiful supply of ammunition. For my part, I believe that fully half the warriors carried only bows and arrows and lances, and that possibly half the remainder carried odds and ends of old muzzle-loaders and single shot rifles of various vintages. Probably not more than 25 or 30 per cent of the warriors carried modern repeating rifles [DuMont 1974:50].

If it is assumed that only 1,500 warriors, which is a generally accepted conservative estimate, took part in the battle, then about one-quarter, or 375 would have been armed with the "muzzle-loaders and single shot rifles" referred to by Windolph. He also suggested that 25 percent of the warriors may have carried the various models of the repeating rifles. If his speculations are accurate, then there should have been 375 re-peating rifles at the battle (based on an estimate of 1,500 warriors). The archaeologically derived minimum number of repeating firearms, Henrys, Winchester Model 1866s, and Model 1873s, is 116, with a statistical projection of 340 to 403 guns, based upon a 30 to 35 percent sample. These figures correlate well with the range of Windolph's estimate.

When all the firearm data are taken into account, it becomes readily apparent that

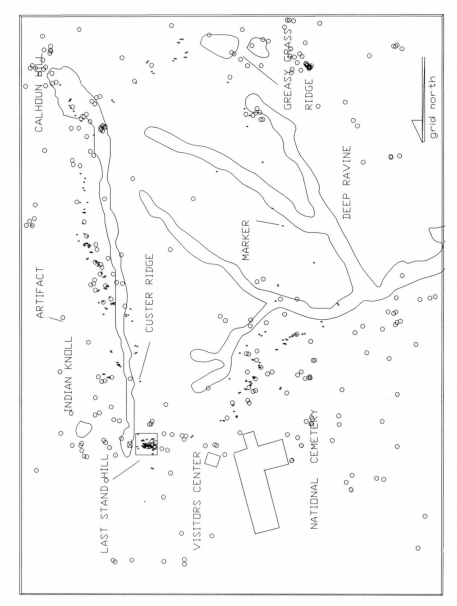

Fig. 37. The distribution of army-related artifacts on the Custer battlefield in relation to markers, major topographic features, and modern cultural features.

Custer and his men were outgunned, if not in range or stopping power, then certainly in firepower. U.S. Army ordnance reports (War Department 1879) comparing the Springfield carbine to a surrendered Sharps and a repeating rifle clearly demonstrate that the Springfield was superior in stopping power, range, and accuracy. However, the repeating rifles would have been very effective, perhaps even superior in firepower, to the single-shot Springfield carbines as the Indians drew progressively closer to the cavalry positions.

The ability to identify individual weapons is an important achievement in the study of the Battle of the Little Bighorn. It helps to address questions on the numbers and armament of the Indians. But, coupled with the piece-plotted data locating precisely where cartridges and bullets were found, this capability becomes even more important by allowing us to trace individual movements during the battle and to reinterpret the chronology of events of that short span of time.

CHRONOLOGY OF EVENTS ON THE CUSTER BATTLEFIELD

The analysis of spatial distributions of artifacts across the Custer battlefield adds to the battle's existing historical data base. The following interpretation of the chronology and sequence of the battle is derived from the study of the spatial distributions of artifacts taken in combination with firearm-identification analysis and historical documentation.

The gross distribution of army-related artifacts provides some idea of the combatant locations during the battle (fig. 37). First, it is clear that at least the final Seventh Cavalry position is in a V-shaped formation. The positions of army-related artifacts (cartridge cases, buttons, spurs, equipment, and human bone) indicate that this formation stretched along the east side of Custer Ridge and along the South Skirmish Line. Second, the clustering of army-related artifacts around Custer Ridge corresponds to Calhoun Hill, the Keogh position, and Last Stand Hill. The cluster is also evident at the northernmost extent of the South Skirmish Line. These troop positions are further corroborated by the presence of impacted bullets from Indian-associated weapons.

At least seven discrete Indian positions (fig. 38) can be discerned on the basis of the variety of cartridge-case types (representing the variety of weapons used by the Indians) and government bullets impacted around these positions. Two positions are on Greasy Grass Ridge, a previously known Indian position (cf. Greene 1979). The remaining Indian positions were previously unidentified. Two indicate rather close-in fighting. One is what we have named Henryville Ridge, where numerous .44 Henry cartridge cases were found, and the second is a knoll 200 meters (660 feet) northeast of Last Stand Hill. In addition to a variety of nongovernment cartridge cases found at the knoll, we also found split .45/55 government cases, which probably represent captured government ammunition fired from .50-caliber weapons.

The three additional Indian positions are on the lower end of Greasy Grass Ridge and on the flanks of the upper portion of Deep Ravine. Government cartridge cases are found at most of the seven Indian positions. It is remotely possible that troops passed through the localities before they were utilized by the Indians; however, the clear association of the government cases with the Indian cases suggests that the Indians were

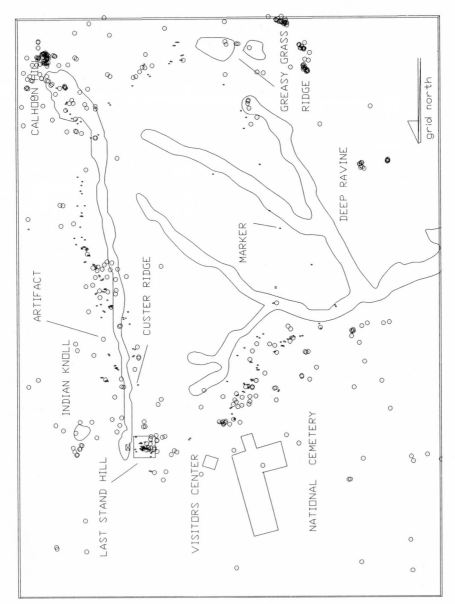

Fig. 38. The distribution of Indian-related artifacts on Custer battlefield in relation to the markers, major topographic features, and modern cultural features.

using captured Springfield carbines. If so, these most likely came from the Reno valley fight, from the earlier Rosebud fight, or from some of the soldier dead.

Battle-related artifacts occur in areas other than those just mentioned. These, however, are for the most part sporadic occurrences. It is difficult to interpret these relatively isolated finds. For example, what is the meaning of the three army cartridges near the northwest corner of the battlefield? Do they represent an isolated soldier's fight or an Indian firing a captured Colt revolver in celebration of a great victory? Or could they represent target practice by the troops from Fort Custer (established in 1877)? Without clearer artifact associations, we are reluctant to interpret many of the isolated occurrences. On the other hand, the scattered findings of army bullets within the western area of the battlefield suggest that soldiers, perhaps those on the South Skirmish Line, laid down fire at the Indians advancing from the encampment on the west side of the Little Bighorn River. In like manner, the virtual absence of battle-related artifacts from some areas suggests that the combatants found some topography inadequate and did not utilize those areas.

While acknowledging that artifact distributions in some areas preclude definitive statements on patterning and recognizing that the observations presented here are subject to alternative conclusions, we offer some clarification regarding the historical reality of the South Skirmish Line. This concept was introduced by Kuhlman (1951), who concluded, from the numerous marble markers along the line, that troopers skirmished there at near regular intervals. Taunton (1980:115) and Hardorff (1986) have rejected Kuhlman's thesis on two grounds (1) historical accounts (cf. McDougall in Hammer 1976:12; Thompson in Hammer 1976:248) suggest that no more than twelve bodies were found here, and (2) a mere dozen men could not have formed regular skirmish intervals over an area 500 meters (1,650 feet) long. Taunton and Hardorff state that the South Skirmish Line did not exist.

The thesis does not hold up when compared with the archaeological data. Indeed, the archaeological data demonstrate the contrary. Clearly the number and nature of the finds in this area (figs. 37, 38) support the idea that a fight took place there. Whether or not a line at skirmish intervals existed is yet open to debate; gross artifact patterning might suggest that South Defensive Area is a more appropriate appellation. Nevertheless, a distribution of combat-related artifacts is clearly discernible from just short of Last Stand Hill to Deep Ravine.

Further corroborating data on the existence of the line come from the discovery of human remains in the five areas excavated along the line. As noted in chapter 5, human remains were found in association with each marker location excavated. The human remains flanked the line and were also found in middle units as well. King (1980:11ff) has argued that roughly the southern half of the line was abandoned as the soldiers fled into Deep Ravine and were killed. He concludes that at least twenty-eight marble markers presently along the line do not mark where soldiers fell. Since human remains were found at Markers 7, 9 and 10, and 33 and 34 we suggest that many of the markers along the southern half of the line do indeed represent close approximations of locations where soldiers fought to the death. It is likely that some markers are spurious, but present evidence suggests that King, in stating that each of the markers in this area is spurious, is incorrect. The evidence at hand supports the concept that the South Skirmish Line was an integral part of the Seventh Cavalry defensive effort and formed one projection of the overall V-shaped formation.

Finally, the excavations have shown that at least some of the South Skirmish Line markers do indicate the location of interments, and, coupled with the recovered battle-related artifacts from this area, the data firmly establish the proposition that this area was, in reality, a zone of combat and that the South Skirmish Line is a valid historical concept.

Spatial Distribution and Firearms Signatures

Greene (1979) suggested, on the basis of his study of the Indian accounts relating to the battle and then-available data on relic finds, that Custer or elements of his command attempted to enter the Indian encampment by fording the Little Bighorn at Medicine Tail Coulee. Greene has further suggested that this attempt failed and that the soldiers were pushed back north and east and attempted to rejoin the rest of the command, which may have been on a ridge now known as Nye-Cartwright Ridge. The evidence from relic finds outside the monument boundary suggested to Greene that some elements of the command did move from Nye-Cartwright Ridge to Custer Ridge.

Subsequent to Greene's analysis, Henry Weibert (1986) tackled the subject by inter-preting relic finds he made over the many years he lived and worked around the monu-ment. Weibert (1986) argues, based on his evidence, that movement to the final posi-tions did not involve an attempt to cross the ford. He speculates that Custer's command moved directly from Nye-Cartwright to the final positions. His reconstruction of the battle before the command reached its final positions is based on findings of relic equip-ment and cartridge cases. He offers his opinion on the final troop disposition in the area now encompassed by the boundary fence, but he has no artifactual data to support his point of view. It is here that the archaeological data become important. First, the current archaeological data supersede those available to Greene for his interpretations; second, they enlarge upon Weibert's reconstructions.

By whatever route Custer and his men reached Custer Ridge, the last segment of the battle ensued. This is the segment that the current archaeological data can elucidate. The following interpretation of events is, we believe, logical and defensible. It is based on a careful analysis of the artifact patterns and a study of locations at which cartridge cases fired from the same weapons were recovered (table 7).

Upon gaining the ridge, Custer, or someone else in command, deployed a group of men on a line facing in a southerly direction (fig. 39). Traditionally, the men deployed are assumed to have been from Company L and possibly some from Company C, owing to the presence of identifiable remains of men of these two companies in this location after the battle. This includes ground at and surrounding the area traditionally known as Calhoun Hill. The soldiers on this line faced intense fire from Indians located south and east of their position. The deployment probably protected the southern end of Cus-ter Ridge. We found evidence of at least fifteen Springfield carbines and two Colt pistols in use in the Calhoun position. Historical and relic evidence presented by Greene and artifacts subsequently collected by Weibert (1986) and other amateurs suggest that the Sioux with Gall attacked from the south and southeast. These Indians found cover below the tops of ridges 100 to 800 yards (90 to 750 meters) away.

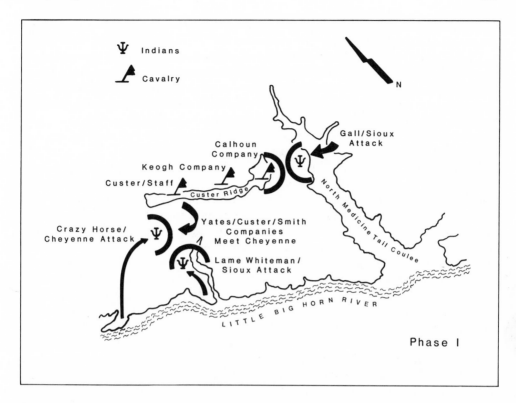

Fig. 39. The early part of the Custer battle as derived from the archaeological evidence.

As the men deployed along the southern end of the ridge, the rest of the command moved along the ridge to the north. The commander may have noticed another group of Indians moving on his position from the west and north, traditionally identified as Crazy Horse and Lame White Man with more Sioux and Cheyennes. To respond to this new threat, another deployment was made from below Last Stand Hill south to the head of Deep Ravine. Historians generally identify this group as the officers and men of Companies E and F and sometimes Company C. This is the South Skirmish Line.

In the meantime, a third element of the command, historically identified as Captain Myles Keogh and the men of Company I, deployed below the ridgetop on the east side of Custer Ridge. Perhaps they were being held in reserve, perhaps they were on their way to aid Calhoun, or perhaps they had been covering Calhoun's withdrawal. It is even conceivable that Keogh and his men were one group attempting a breakout during the last segment of the battle. In any event, they were not sent along the ridgetop. The archaeological data do not support the theory that Keogh and his men were pushed from the ridgetop to the base of the ridge, where they were killed. The spatial distribution of army-related artifacts clearly indicates very few battle-related artifacts on either side of the ridgetop above Keogh's position. Undoubtedly the construction of the road along the ridgetop has biased the data by destroying some information, but lack of artifactual evidence of any equipment, cartridge cases, or bullets from either side of the ridgetop suggests that it did not play an important role in the battle. Perhaps the ridgetop was too sharp to be utilized for deployment, as suggested by Hardorff (1984:54).

As the various deployments took place, the soldiers were formed into a broad V-shaped pattern (fig. 39), with Last Stand Hill at the apex to the north. Most of the cartridge cases associated with the soldiers (fig. 37) were found in the area of the broad V-shaped deployment. Today this area is dotted with marble markers, which are assumed to indicate where soldiers fell in battle. There is very little evidence of unit movement after the deployment. The fight may have been a running one until this final deployment, but after that the units apparently stood their ground.

The firing must have been intense from both sides. The finds of spent cartridge cases and bullets certainly suggest this. Bullets fired from the soldiers' guns were found embedded in the ground, often within or at the front of the areas where quantities of Indian cartridge cases were found. Bullets in the calibers corresponding to the cartridge cases found at Indian positions were discovered embedded in the army positions. A few were even found in direct association with human remains.

From their positions under cover, and initially at a distance from the soldiers, the Indians' fire began to take its toll. As the return fire from the soldiers began to slacken, the Indians moved in closer. From the south and east came Gall and the Sioux. They took positions close to Calhoun's line and poured intense fire into his men. The heaviest fire came from the southeast from a ridge about three hundred feet (one hundred meters) from Calhoun Hill. The number of .44-caliber lever-action weapons in use here was substantial, with at least twenty-three Henrys or Model 1866s and at least six Model 1873 Winchesters indicated by the cartridge case evidence. That same evidence also indicates at least one Smith and Wesson revolver and two .44-caliber rimfire revolvers, and seven .50/70-caliber guns were also in use here. This area, which we have called Henryville, may also have been used to fire at the Keogh positions.

More heavy Indian fire came from south and west of the Calhoun position on a lower portion of Greasy Grass Ridge. At least twenty-two .44 rimfire lever-action weapons, thirteen .50/70-caliber guns, two Spencers, an unidentified .50-caliber rimfire, and one Model 1873 Winchester were in use in this area. The heavy fire must have decimated Calhoun's men. From the cartridge-case distributions, it appears that Calhoun's position was overrun by the same Indians firing from Henryville and Greasy Grass Ridge. A few army survivors from the Calhoun position may have attempted to join their comrades in Keogh's command. Several .45/55 cartridge cases fired from two carbines were found in the Calhoun position, then scattered along a line toward the Keogh position, and finally intermixed with the Keogh group. It is also possible that these cases represent Springfield carbines recovered by the Indians and subsequently used against the soldiers. However, the casings were found in a coulee that could have provided some protection from the hostile fire from Henryville and Greasy Grass Ridge.

The cartridge-case evidence suggests that as the Calhoun position fell, some Indians broke off and moved northwest toward Deep Ravine and the South Skirmish Line (fig. 40). These Indian groups were firing at ranges up to 500 yards (476 meters) into the soldiers on the South Skirmish Line. They brought to bear at least seven .44-caliber repeating guns, eight .50/70 guns, one Model 1873 Winchester, and several captured

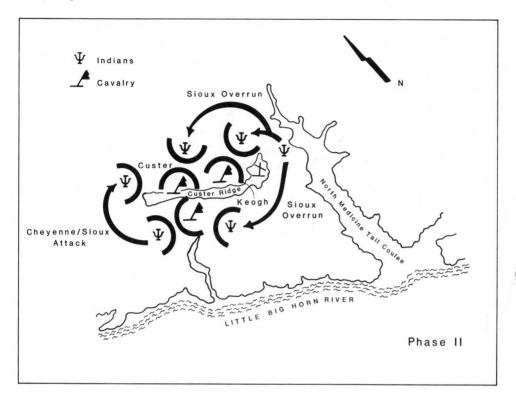

Fig. 40. The second phase of the Custer battle, illustrating the increasing concentration of Indian forces.

army Springfield carbines. As the Indians from the Calhoun fight moved toward Deep Ravine, they were joining a fight already in progress.

The Indian attackers coming from the north and west met the men deployed from Last Stand Hill to the head of Deep Ravine. These soldiers fired at and into the Indians, perhaps halting their advance. The relatively small number of Indian cartridge cases found to the north and west of the South Skirmish Line suggests that the Indians attacking from this quarter were not as well armed as those attacking Calhoun. We must take into consideration that our sample of artifacts from the Indian positions in this area is somewhat biased. This area now contains the national cemetery, the Visitors Center, and a road. The construction of these facilities probably destroyed some information, but how much will never be known.

Another data source may also be interpreted to support this point of view. Henry Weibert (1986) alludes to and Don Weibert (personal communication Nov. 12, 1986) confirmed that a ridgetop immediately north of the present north monument boundary fence yielded numerous .45/55-caliber cartridge cases in association with Indian cartridge cases. These data may be interpreted to mean that warriors from the Calhoun phase of the engagement, now equipped with captured army carbines and ammunition, fired into the South Skirmish Line while occupying the northern ridge.

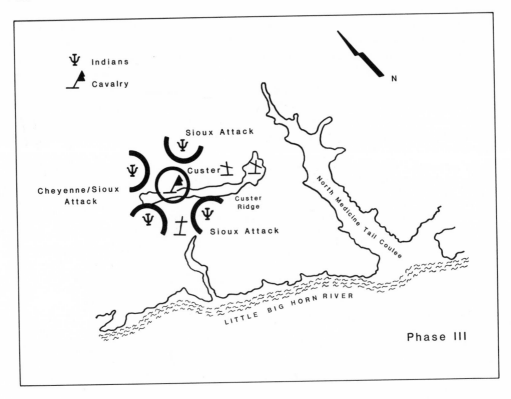

Fig. 41. The final phase of the Custer battle and the destruction of the command.

Perhaps the Indians joining the foray from the south after the Calhoun fight added the right combination of firepower and numbers to overwhelm the South Skirmish Line. There is very little evidence of fighting in or around Deep Ravine, with the exception of that immediately adjacent to the head of the ravine. The head of the ravine defined the south end of the South Skirmish Line. Most of the archaeologically recovered battle-related items found in or along the ravine suggest that Indian positions received only light fire from the soldiers. This interpretation is consistent with the accounts of battle participants Black Elk and Iron Hawk (Neihardt 1961:105–34).

Cartridge cases fired from some of the same Indian weapons that had been used at Calhoun Hill and near Deep Ravine are also found near Last Stand Hill. These include at least three of the .44-caliber repeating guns. One .44-caliber gun was used at Henryville and Calhoun Hill before coming into play at Last Stand Hill. The other repeating firearms were used against the South Skirmish Line and then Last Stand Hill. In addition, cartridge cases from other Indian weapons found at Calhoun Hill and the Keogh position were found on and around a small hill north and east of Last Stand Hill. This Indian position provided some cover to the attackers as they fired into the knot of men on Last Stand Hill (fig. 41).

We have suggested that Calhoun Hill survivors fled to the Keogh area; however, we cannot demonstrate from the firearm evidence that similar army movements occurred from either the Keogh position or the South Skirmish Line. Matching firearm signatures from these three areas have not been identified. We believe there are two alternatives to account for the absence of positive signature correlations. First, it is possible that the archaeological sample did not recover evidence of these movements and that such evidence exists in the unrecovered cartridge cases, or that earlier collecting may have biased the chances of recovering data to this effect. Second, it is possible that heavy fighting after the Calhoun position fell allowed the Indian advance as described above. These new pressures perhaps precluded the decimated Keogh and South Skirmish Line troopers from retiring en masse over exposed terrain to Last Stand Hill.

In summary, the cartridge-case data suggest Indian movements along two broad lines. One was from south to north, from Calhoun Hill to Last Stand Hill through the Keogh position; the second was from Calhoun Hill and Greasy Grass Ridge to the South Skirmish Line, joining with the Indian group attacking from the north and west. These two broad and probably opportunistic movements converged at Last Stand Hill, indicating that the hill was the last position occupied by remnants of the five companies of Seventh Cavalry that had ridden onto the ridge a very short time earlier. This last position was overwhelmed by the combined forces of Cheyennes and Sioux.

Additional Data Bearing on the Fight

In addition to the artifact distribution data and firearm interpretations that have been presented, some .45/55 carbine cases also aid the interpretations. It has been shown that split .45/55 cartridges were fired by Indians in .50-caliber weapons, but the locational data on these cases have not been interpreted. Some of the split cases were found in the Indian position north and east of Last Stand Hill. This suggests that these cases were probably collected by the Indian warriors from the dead soldiers on the field and were fired against Custer in the latter part of the battle. Other ruptured cases were found in the Indian positions on Greasy Grass Ridge opposite those of Calhoun. Since these Indian positions were utilized early in the battle, the .45/55 rounds were probably retrieved from the valley fight or possibly from the fight on the Rosebud eight days earlier (Stands in Timber and Liberty 1972).

The presence of .45/55 carbine cases at Indian positions near Deep Ravine and around the knoll near Last Stand Hill suggests that the Indians collected carbines and ammunition from the dead soldiers as the battle progressed. These weapons were likely turned against the surviving elements of the command. The discovery of these cases in positions which in all probability were used only by Indians supports some of the accounts by the surviving warriors, such as Wooden Leg (Marquis 1931) and Foolish Dog (Hammer 1976:139).

There are also army carbine rounds which were fired in .45/55 carbines in two of the other Indian positions. A number of army and Indian cases were found intermixed in the Indian positions on Greasy Grass Ridge and at Henryville, southeast of Calhoun Hill. Since these positions were utilized early in the battle, these data can be interpreted in two ways. One is that some army carbines and ammunition fell into Indian hands in the valley fight and at the Rosebud fight, as is known (Stands in Timber and Liberty 1972:181–90), and were subsequently used against Custer's command. Given the historical documentation, this is a credible interpretation, but there is an alternative. The finding of army cases in these areas may suggest that these artifacts mark a segment of Custer's line of retreat to the final battle scene. This alternative would suggest that Custer did not retire without some intermittent fighting. In fact, given the all too general but provocative patterning of relic finds at Nye-Cartwright Ridge (Weibert 1986), where at least some elements of Custer's command were engaged, the troop movement to Custer Ridge was probably under pressure.

The various Indian accounts (Graham 1953) suggest there was hand-to-hand fighting near the end of the battle. The Indians noted that near the end the soldiers began using their Colt pistols and that, after emptying them, they did not have time to reload before the Indians were upon them. The archaeological findings of Colt revolver cases and bullets support the statements in general. Relatively few Colt bullets (twenty-nine) or cases (eleven) were found during the recovery project. These were associated with the South Skirmish Line and the Keogh area.

While the paucity of Colt .45 cases somewhat confirms these Indian accounts, the small number of bullets found further suggests that not many soldiers had an opportunity to fire their revolvers. This also is consistent with Stands in Timber's account noted earlier. It suggests that many of the soldiers were already dead or wounded and out of action by the time the Colt came into play. The proportion of Colt bullets found among the soldier positions is about one-third of those found scattered around the entire battlefield. Perhaps these rounds were fired by the Indians into the bodies of the soldiers after the troop positions had been overrun. Indeed, many Colt bullets, as well as some .45/55 carbine bullets in troop positions, were found vertically impacted, or nearly so, into the ground. This could occur as Indians fired downward into the bodies. This evidence corresponds with Lieutenant Winfield Edgerly's observations (Nichols 1984:510) on June 25, 1876, from Weir Point. Gall (Stewart 1955:397) later confirmed that Indians administered the coup de grace in this manner.

The archaeological evidence we have presented on the fight at Custer Battlefield is supported more often than not by the testimony of the warriors who participated in the battle. While some historians have suggested that the Indian accounts be dismissed as poor historical references, we agree with others, such as Greene (1979), who have called for a reanalysis of the Indian accounts. The archaeological evidence suggests that the Indian battle accounts, taken as a whole, are more accurate than those of the soldiers who buried the dead. We suggest that a thorough reassessment of the Indian testimony is a valid historical study and that may well change some interpretations of the battle's progress.

THE SEQUENCE AND CHRONOLOGY OF EVENTS AT THE RENO-BENTEEN DEFENSE SITE

The historical sequence and chronology of events at the Reno-Benteen defense site are well documented in a variety of accounts. The voluminous detail available for this portion of the fight is due to the number of survivors and the testimony and recollections they gave during the ensuing years. With the eyewitness accounts available it might seem the archaeological data would be redundant or superfluous. The archaeological data base is important precisely for this reason. The recovery of archaeological information from the Reno-Benteen defense site can be correlated directly with the historical accounts. On the one hand, the correlation of archaeological data and interpretations to the historical accounts provides a means to assess the accuracy of the interpretations drawn from the archaeological record. In essence, if the interpretations of the archaeological record demonstrate positive correlations with the historical record of the Reno-Benteen fight, then the archaeological interpretations of the Custer fight are strengthened. A second point is that where the historical record is incomplete or even silent on individual movements, the archaeological data provide the opportunity to elucidate those levels of individual movements or participation.

Historical archaeological studies are often used in this confirmation role (Noel Hume 1969). Validation studies have been undertaken to determine the correlation levels of archaeological and historical data. The studies (Scott 1977; 1972) have shown the techniques of archaeology to be a valid means to reconstruct events of the past. They have also shown that no precise or one-to-one correlation between an event's historical documentation and the archaeological record is likely to exist. The level of correlation is often excellent, but each of the two data sources provides information not contained in the other. It is at this point that the value of historical archaeology becomes apparent.

It is with this in mind that the archaeological investigations at the Reno-Benteen defense site are discussed. First is presented a synopsis of the historic documentation of the fight. The synopsis focuses on that portion of the fight which took place on 160 acres of land investigated by the archaeological project. That land is a part of Custer Battlefield National Monument. The synopsis is drawn from a number of historical assessments of the fight (Nichols 1983; Gray 1976; Hammer 1976; Stewart 1955; Graham 1953; Everett 1930).

When Major Marcus Reno's command made its unorganized movement from the timber in the valley to the bluffs, the first area it traversed after crossing the river consisted of steep slopes and ravines. Reno's men were under fire during their movement up the slopes and a number of men were killed or wounded in their attempt to reach the heights. The available historical documentation notes the movement was somewhat random and perhaps on a broad front. The command does not appear to have used any one locale or trail to climb to the blufftop. The men appear to have scrambled up the slopes wherever they could. Dr. J. M. DeWolf and his orderly went up a slope which angles to the east-northeast and away from the defense site. They were warned by some members of the command that they were about to run into warriors above them. Before they could retrace their step, both were killed by warriors firing at them from above. White marble markers have since been placed on a the bench of the slope where they were believed killed.

When those of the command who survived the river crossing and the upslope climb to the blufftops gathered, little attention appears to have been given to organizing a defensive perimeter. Captain Frederick Benteen and his battalion arrived from the south about the time Reno's command gained the heights. Benteen was moving north to join Custer's command after receiving a communication from Custer via messenger. As Benteen joined Reno, the warriors commenced firing into the command's position. Company D threw out skirmishers under Captain Thomas Weir and returned fire. With this, the Indian fire slackened.

A discussion ensued among several of the officers concerning the appropriateness of attempting to join Custer's command. Major Reno apparently decided not to attempt to find Custer until the pack train, with the command's extra ammunition, could join his command; that train had been following the battalion. In the meantime Major Reno and several others attempted, unsuccessfully, to recover the body of Lieutenant Benjamin Hodgson, who had been killed trying to cross the river.

Captain Weir, demonstrating a great deal of impatience, mounted his horse and set out to the north to determine the whereabouts of Custer. Lieutenant Winfield Edgerly, assuming that Weir was under orders, mounted Company D and followed him. Captain Wier and Company D reached a high point about one mile to the north, where they stopped to observe the country. The point, now known as Wier Point, is about the farthest north any of the Reno command went. When the pack train reached Reno's position, Reno sent Lieutenant Luther Hare to tell Weir that the rest of the command was about to follow him. Companies H, K, and M under Benteen joined Weir as the rest of the command with the wounded began to move north.

At this time the Indians, began to move to the south from their victory over Custer. The soldiers at Weir Point saw this movement and began to withdraw to their first position. Companies M and D covered the rather unorganized withdrawal until a they were few hundred yards north of the first position. Here, probably near the northern boundary fence of the present-day monument, Company K dismounted and deployed in skirmish order to cover the retreat. Lieutenant Edward Godfrey and his men began to withdraw slowly, covering the other companies' retirement. The men's fire slackened and they bunched up, but Godfrey reestablished skirmish order and they continued the withdrawal in good order until they were within a few yards of the defensive position, when they were told to make a dash for the lines.

Within a short time the command was under fire from all sides as the warriors took cover on hilltops, in ravines, and wherever they could shoot into Reno's position. There was little protection from the Indian gunfire in the soldiers' position, so they used saddles, dead horses, and ration boxes as cover from which to return fire. The soldiers were deployed around the position, with Company M on the northwest, Company K on the northeast and east, Company D on the east (along the most open area and where the animals were picketed), Company A on the southeast, Company H along a ridge to the south and southwest, and Company B on the west. A field hospital was established by the surviving surgeon, Dr. Henry Porter, in a swale to the west of the area where the animals were picketed. The animals and a barricade of saddles and ration boxes provided the only protection from Indian fire coming from the east. This eastern area was the most exposed zone of the defense site. As night fell, Major Reno ordered the men to dig in and erect defenses. There were only a few tools with the command, and the defenses consisted of mounds of dirt thrown up to the front of the men. Most of these rifle pits were dug with mess plates, cups, sheath knives, and bare hands. The only company that failed to dig in was H, the most exposed unit.

Beginning at daybreak on June 26, the Indians began to pour a heavy fire into the cavalry position. The warriors appear to have positioned themselves so as to encircle the army's position. They fired into the army's exposed position from points as close as a few yards away to up to positions twelve hundred yards distant. No Indian mass attacks occurred, although individual warriors did attempt to distinguish themselves by rushing the army's positions.

Water, particularly for the wounded, became a critical need during the day. Captain Benteen cleared a ravine and adjacent ground to the west of his position with a charge in order to open an access corridor to the river. A number of volunteers then went down the ravine, today called Water Carriers Ravine, and successfully filled canteens, cups, and camp kettles. Benteen then detailed four of his best shots to fire on the Indians concealed in the timber on the west side of the river, while more men went down to the river for water. One man was killed and several wounded in this attempt, including Private Mike Madden, who was shot in the leg and suffered a double fracture. His leg was amputated in the field by Dr. Porter. Other unorganized efforts were made by some men to get water for themselves and the wounded.

As the gunfire slackened near noon, Captain Benteen obtained tools and had Company H dig in. During the day on June 26, Companies B and M exchanged places on the line. Company B under Captain Thomas McDougall and some elements of Company D charged a group of warriors to the north of the defense site. The warriors' return fire was heavy enough to compel the soldiers to retire after gaining about sixty yards. The Indian fire slackened in vigor and intensity for the rest of the afternoon. By late afternoon and into the evening, the soldiers noted a long column of Indians moving southward up the valley.

At dusk the horses and mules were led down to the river for a drink of water. The command's position was shifted that evening to a bench above the river and adjacent to Water Carriers Ravine so they could better protect their water supply. The move was also made to get away from the stench of the bodies on the hill. A small redoubt was dug on the bench and occupied. The cooks made fires and prepared a meal for the men.

Captain McDougall and two privates recovered Lieutenant Hodgson's body and, sewing it into a blanket, buried it above the camp. A number of missing men who had been left behind in the retreat of June 25 now rejoined the command. The wounded were moved to the new camp, and better provisions were made for their care. It may have been at this location that Dr. Porter amputated Madden's leg.

During the morning of June 27, General Alfred Terry and Colonel John Gibbon found the remains of Custer's command and joined Reno. June 27 and 28 were spent in preparing the wounded to travel, burying the dead, and destroying Indian and army property which could not be taken along. Reno's dead from the valley fight were buried where they fell. The dead from the hilltop fight were buried either in the rifle pits or were buried in a mass grave. Both accounts are noted in the historical record, and both probably occurred. A number of saddles and related equipment, as well as unserviceable weapons, were broken up and burned. The command left the battlefield that evening and moved to the Big Horn River at the mouth of the Little Bighorn, where the steamboat *Far West* took the wounded downriver.

The archaeological evidence for the Reno-Benteen fight is nearly the same as that of the Custer battlefield. Cartridges, cartridge cases, bullets, and miscellaneous equipment were found scattered over the area historically known to have been occupied by the opposing forces. The archaeological evidence supports the historical record in almost every case and adds a new and personal dimension to the historical record.

In interpreting the Reno-Benteen archaeological pattern data we must make clear that we recognize that the inventory area does not include all possible battle-related zones. As with the Custer battlefield, we were restricted in our investigations to the land within

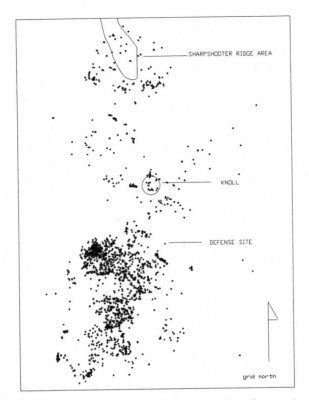

Fig. 42. The distribution of all classes of artifacts at the
Reno-Benteen defense site.

the National Park Service boundaries. At Reno-Benteen, the boundary fence excludes
many of the Indian warrior positions. This is clearly demonstrated by the studies of
former battlefield historians Don Rickey and B. William Henry (Custer Battlefield
administrative files) and the relic-collection efforts of others (Weibert 1986) on lands
outside the park boundary. The conclusions offered here are based on the information
garnered from the artifact-distribution pattern, coupled with the documentary record
and factoring in the relic-find evidence from outside the park boundary.

The gross artifact distribution correlates well with the historically known combatant
positions (fig. 42). The distribution of army-related artifacts concentrates in the defensive position, as was expected. Pieces of equipment and numerous tin fragments from
either cans or ration-box liners were found in the position. The equipment appears to
be randomly scattered except for two locations: in the hospital swale and on the bench
below the defensive position near the June 26–27 redoubt.

The tin fragments and horse-related equipment were concentrated on the eastern edge
of the hospital swale, with some horse-related material scattered around the swale's
flank, roughly encircling the hospital area (fig. 43). This correlates with the defensive
barricade established to protect the wounded. The artifact distribution also correlates
well with Lieutenant Charles Varnum's recollection that the horses were picketed in a

circle around the hospital (Carroll 1982:71). The recovery of horse equipment, horse bone, horseshoes, and a vertical in-place picket pin strongly correlates with historical description of the barricade and horse-picketing area. Further corroboration can be found by studying the distribution of horse skeletal material visible in the 1886 D. F. Barry photographs of the Reno-Benteen defense site. Clearly, most of the horse skeletal material is seen in the swale area.

Other miscellaneous equipment and material was concentrated on the bench below the defensive positions. The artifacts found there included some camp equipage, and this correlates with the location of the June 26–27 redoubt and camp. The very small quantity of combat-related artifacts provides added confirmation concerning the function of this artifact pattern.

There was also a line of army-related miscellaneous artifacts scattered to the northeast of the defensive position. This low density of material can be correlated with the northern movement and subsequent retreat of the command on June 25. The linear artifact scatter includes horse-related items and the eyepiece from a telescope. As an isolated artifact class, the distribution cannot be interpreted with accuracy, but when it is con-

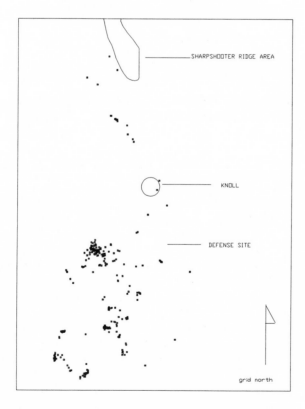

Fig. 43. The distribution of army-related equipment and nonfirearm debris at the Reno-Benteen defense site.

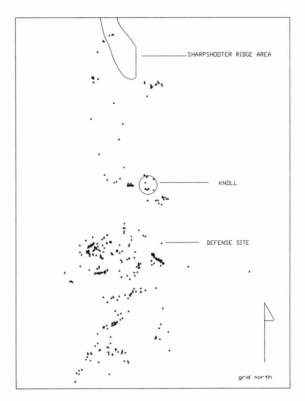

Fig. 44. The distribution of Colt and Springfield cartridge
cases at the Reno-Benteen defense site.

sidered in conjunction with other artifact classes' distributions, a more reliable association can be made with the historical record.

The primary evidence of the army's positions is the distribution of the .45/55
Springfield carbine and .45 Colt cartridges and cartridge cases (fig. 44). The majority
of cartridges and cases were found in the historically documented defensive perimeter.
Literally hundreds of cartridges and cases were found on the perimeter occupied by the
various companies. A few carbine cases were found in and along the retreat ravine and
are suggestive of fighting during the movement to the bluffs. A few other cases were
recovered to the west of the defensive area and may represent Indian-utilized Springfield
carbines captured from Custer's command.

There was also a moderate quantity of carbine cases north of the defensive perimeter.
The gross distribution allows for three possible interpretations. First is that the cases
represent the line of retreat and covering fire laid down by Company K. The east to
west linear distribution of the carbine cases found in the vicinity of the knoll located
north of the defense perimeter may be where Lieutenant Godfrey reorganized the skirmish line, fired the last volleys of the retreat, and told the men to make a dash for the
lines. The second explanation for the northern carbine case distribution is an Indian

association. The cases may also represent captured carbines used against the Reno-Benteen command. The case distribution would indicate scattered warriors firing into the defense perimeter from the vicinity of Wooden Leg Hill or Sharpshooter Ridge. Two areas of case concentration are noted: one on the northeastern side of the hill, the other at the knoll. The linear case concentration at the knoll would suggest the warriors utilized any available cover at that location. The third option is that the case distribution represents a combination of the previous two interpretations. The cases then represent a mixing of Indian and soldier positions as they moved across the same ground during the course of the fight.

There is only limited gross distributional evidence of the charges by Captain McDougall and Benteen. There is a small concentration of Springfield cases to the north of the Company B positions. These cases may represent the northern charge. A line of cases was found below and to the west of the Company H position. These may represent the Benteen charge to clear Water Carrier Ravine. This is also the vicinity of the camp debris, and that material may have obscured other evidence of the charge.

The distribution of .44-caliber rimfire cases (fig. 45) indicates there were at least

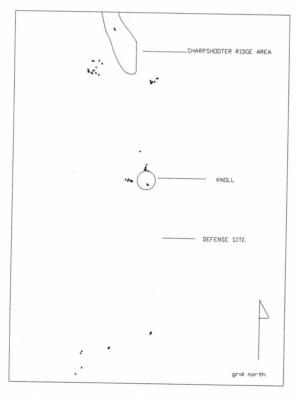

Fig. 45. The distribution of Indian-related .44-caliber cartridge cases at the Reno-Benteen defense site.

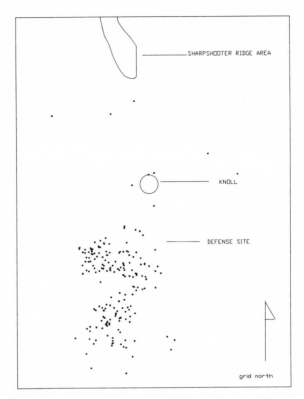

Fig. 46. The distribution of .44-caliber bullets at the Reno-
Benteen defense site. Compare this with fig. 45.

nine distinct concentrations. Two concentrations, representing different warrior groups, were found to the south and below the Company H position. Four Henry case concentrations were found around the knoll, and three Henry case concentrations were found on and adjacent to Wooden Leg Hill. The knoll and Wooden Leg Hill concentrations correspond to Springfield carbine-case concentrations in those same localities, suggesting an Indian affiliation or a reuse of the same positions may be the more likely interpretations.

The distribution of bullets provides further clarification of combatant positions. The .44-caliber bullets (fig. 46) are found almost exclusively in the defense perimeter. These bullets represent rounds fired by the warriors at the soldiers. The few scattered bullets not found in the defense perimeter were found to the north in the vicinity of the knoll. These bullets could represent rounds fired at the soldiers during their movement up to the bluffs, rounds fired during the soldiers' retreat from Weir Point, or rounds that over- or undershot their intended mark.

The distribution of .50-caliber bullets (fig. 47) nearly duplicates that of the .44-caliber bullets. The highest density occurs in the defense perimeter, and the quantity is nearly the same as the .44-caliber bullets as well. A small number of bullets were recovered in the vicinity of the knoll and Wooden Leg Hill. These may represent bullets fired by the civilian packers and Captain French during the battle, or they may indicate where the warriors fired at the command, either during its attempt to gain the bluffs or during the retreat from Weir Point.

The miscellaneous Indian bullets and other items (fig. 48) are distributed in a manner similar to those of the .44-caliber and .50-caliber bullets. Most concentrated in the defense perimeter, but a few were found near the knoll and Wooden Leg Hill. The items found near the knoll are the bracelet and the broken gold painted knife. The bullets found in the northern area can be interpreted in the same manner as the .44-caliber and .50-caliber bullets. The quantity of miscellaneous items is about half that of either the .44-caliber and .50-caliber bullets. Since many of the miscellaneous bullets represent muzzle-loading firearms, the preference for cartridge firearms demonstrated by the other bullets is apparent.

Bullets from the Springfield carbine (fig. 49) dominate the collection. The number recovered exceeds the total of all other bullet classes. The majority of Springfield carbine bullets were found in the defense perimeter—clear corroboration of the historical accounts of the warriors' turning captured carbines against the Reno-Benteen command.

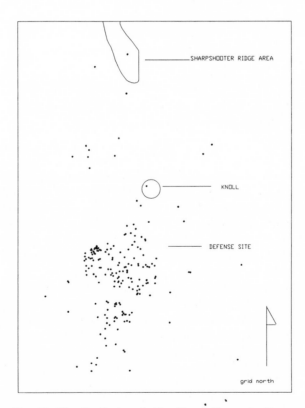

Fig. 47. The distribution of .50-caliber bullets at the Reno-Benteen defense site.

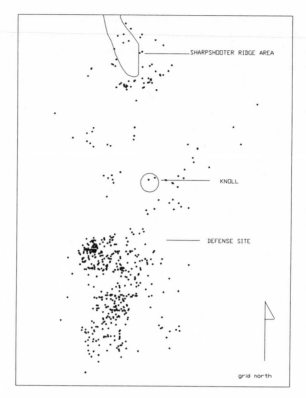

Fig. 48. The distribution of .45-caliber army-related bullets
at the Reno-Benteen defense site.

The number of bullets impacted in the defense perimeter strongly suggests that the incoming fire must have been heavy. About one-third of the carbine bullets were found impacted to the north and northwest of the army positions. These rounds are most likely those fired by the soldiers at the warriors.

Most of bullets found outside the defense perimeter were impacted in the vicinity of the knoll and Wooden Leg Hill. The interpretation posited is that these rounds represent those fired by the soldiers; however, they could also be associated with fire from the warriors during the retreat. The carbine-bullet gross distribution pattern strongly suggests a dichotomous depositional pattern. One area represents those rounds impacted in the defense perimeter and the other those impacted in warrior positions. The two depositional patterns are distinct and spatially separate.

Combining all artifact classes, the gross distribution pattern defines three main artifact concentrations. First is the area on and adjacent to Wooden Leg Hill. The mixture of army-related and Indian-related artifacts in this area demonstrates the use of this site by both sides during the fight, as is documented in the historical record. Second is the vicinity of the knoll. The same mixture of army-related and Indian-related itmes occurs here as well. The mixture of artifacts also correlates with the historical documentation.

The third area is the historically documented and interpreted army defensive perimeter. The largest concentration of artifacts occurs in this area. The artifacts exhibit a mixture of army-related and Indian-related items, but the class of artifacts recovered is distinctly different from those of the other two areas. Army cartridges, cartridge cases, equipment, and horse-related artifacts dominate the artifact assemblage. The other two areas do not have the same mixture of artifacts. The Indian-related artifacts are almost exclusively bullets. The Indian bullet density is higher here than anywhere else on the battlefield. The artifact density and classes again correlate with the historical documentation of the fight. The distribution of army cartridge case is generally linear, while that of the Indian cases is cluster or bunched. This distribution mirrors the fighting patterns of the two cultural entities engaged in the battle: regular intervals for the cavalry and loose individual associations for the Indian warriors.

The current defense-perimeter interpretive-trail system was designed on the basis of archaeological excavations (Bray 1958) and oral and documentary history of the Reno-Benteen fight. The new archaeological evidence indicates the trail is not quite accurate. The defense perimeter extended farther to the east than defined by the current trail. It

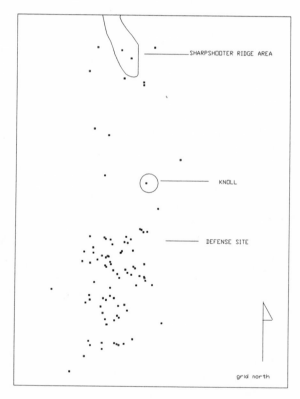

Fig. 49. The distribution of miscellaneous bullets and other artifacts attributed to the Indians at Reno-Benteen.

also extended farther north than the current trail would suggest. The barricade of dead horses, ration boxes, saddles, and other equipment, as well as the picket line, was about midway between the line of the eastern trail and the hospital marker. It extended across the swale bottom and up the slopes about fifty meters on either side of the swale bottom. As in the excavations by Bray (1958), no direct evidence of the hospital locale was found. The absence of artifacts in the hospital-marker vicinity indicates that it is probably accurate in its siting.

Bray's (1958) archaeological investigations identified nine rifle pits. The current investigations located two deeply buried cartridge-case concentrations that may be rifle-pit sites. One is on the eastern side near the bottom of the swale. It is situated between two previously identified rifle pits. The other site is on the Company B line on the northwest line of the defense perimeter. Other cartridge-case concentrations were found on the northeast defense-perimeter line, but they were not deeply buried. These concentrations were scattered on a line in the historically documented Company K positions and may represent the location of very shallow defense sites or at the very least a site where a soldier or soldiers fired at the warriors.

Spatial Distribution and Firearms Signatures at Reno-Benteen

As in the case of the Custer battlefield, the firearm-signature data add a significant amount of detail to the fight's story. They indicate, at a minimum, how many firearms were used in a specific position and where else they may have come into play. The advantage of the Reno-Benteen data over that of Custer is the abundant historical record available to us for comparative purposes.

The .50/70 cartridge cases indicate that fourteen guns were used at Reno. Six of them were Springfields and were used in the defense perimeter by either the scouts and civilian packers or perhaps some of the soldiers. Evidence for two Springfields was found in the Company K position near its juncture with the Company D position on the barricade. Two others were on the northwest portion of the perimeter in the Companies B and M area. One isolated cartridge case was south of the Company K position on the swale slope above the barricade. Two brass cases representing one Springfield were found on the perimeter's western edge in the Companies B and M position.

The nine cases representing eight Sharps or Remington guns were found several hundred meters north of the defense perimeter. These cases include seven .45/55 carbine cases which were fired in the larger caliber guns. These cases are ruptured and appear to have been extracted from their respective guns with difficulty. One .50/70 case was found near the north boundary fence on Wooden Leg Hill. The case head was missing, but it was found 250 meters (820 feet) to the south. The case has scratches on it, suggesting, with the blown head, that the weapon failed to extract the case properly.

Two ruptured .45/55-caliber cases were found on the west flank of Wooden Leg Hill, as was a .50/70 case. Each represented a separate gun. Two other ruptured .45/55-caliber cases were found east of the hill near the boundary fence. One case matched one of those found on the west side of the hill. The other three ruptured cases were located in two distinct areas. A single case was found near the monument road and above the steep bluffs leading to the river. Two cases were found about 300 meters (984 feet) northeast of the defense perimeter.

The .50/70-caliber guns were more widely dispersed than any others. The .44-caliber cases, representing at least fifty-eight guns, were clustered in five distinct areas. The first concentration was located on the west flank of Wooden Leg Hill and running down to the bluff edge. The matching-case evidence indicates at least sixteen .44-caliber lever-action guns were used here. The second cluster, which can be divided into two slightly spatially separated units, contained evidence of nine .44-caliber lever-action guns, one revolver, and a Ballard rifle. The third cluster was situated around the knoll between Wooden Leg Hill and the defense perimeter. The cluster can be subdivided into several units. Here eleven .44-caliber lever-action guns and at least one revolver were used. Among these three large clusters, there is evidence for the use of ten other .44-caliber guns. The cartridge cases were scattered and generally isolated from the clusters. Cartridge cases fired in two Model 1873 Winchesters were found intermixed with the rimfire cases on the flank of Wooden Leg Hill. One of those Model 1873 Winchesters was also used on the Custer battlefield at Henryville and Last Stand Hill.

Two additional .44-caliber clusters were noted south of the defense perimeter. One cluster contained evidence of eight lever-action guns, the other evidence of two lever-action guns and one revolver. No .44-caliber cases were found within the defense perimeter.

The .44-caliber and .50/70-caliber data indicate that the warriors utilized Wooden Leg Hill, the knoll, and the ravines south of the defense perimeter as firing positions. The cartridge-case concentrations in these areas suggest that the warriors tended to take advantage of the same general locales; perhaps it was the best cover available. The isolated cases also indicate that almost every area of the battlefield was used. The distribution of Indian-associated cartridge cases confirms the historical accounts that the warriors surrounded the command and poured a heavy fire into the defense perimeter. The cartridge-case concentrations also indicate that the survivors' accounts of directions of fire are also accurate.

The gross distribution of .45/55 Springfield carbine cases suggested several alternative explanations. The analysis of the firearm signatures focuses on one interpretation: the cases represent movements of and positions occupied by the soldiers.

The carbine-case distributional evidence is complicated, so perhaps it is best to begin with the least-complicated portion. This also happens to be, chronologically, the first part of the battle with which we are concerned. The ridges and bluffs surrounding Retreat Ravine contained a few Springfield cartridge cases. The cases indicate, along with Indian-associated bullets found impacted in the vicinity, that the retreat was under fire. The Springfield cases found along the ravine correlate with those found in the defense perimeter. The ravine cases match cases found in the B, D, K, and M Company positions. Only one case, with no corresponding match, was found near the DeWolf marker. It is intriguing to speculate that this round was fired by surgeon DeWolf's acting steward during their attempt to retrace their steps before being killed. But it is well to keep in mind that Captain Sweet (Sweet to W. M. Camp Jan. 13, 1913, Custer Battlefield National Monument files), who set DeWolf's marker, stated that he placed that marker at a convenient spot near where he thought DeWolf was killed. Nevertheless, someone did fire at least one shot on that ridgetop.

The gross distribution analysis identified four discrete areas of Springfield carbine-case concentrations north of the defense perimeter. These are located on the west flank of Wooden Leg Hill, between the hill and the knoll, and in the vicinity of the knoll. The carbine cases found on the flank of Wooden Leg Hill all match cases found in the other positions and in the defense perimeter. The cases in the two concentrations between the hill and knoll also match cases at the knoll and in the defense perimeter. All but four cases at the knoll match cases in the defense perimeter. This strongly suggests that the carbine cases found north of the defense perimeter are associated with the movement to and from Weir Point. Further corroboration is found by analyzing the specific defense-perimeter match locations.

The majority of the carbine cases found north of the perimeter match cases found in the northeast perimeter area. Those cases found around the knoll and some to its immediate north correlate with the historically documented Company K position. It was Company K, commanded by Lieutenant Godfrey, that formed a skirmish line to cover the latter part of the retreat from Weir Point. The cases found near Wooden Leg Hill match cases found on the northwest part of the perimeter. This area was occupied by Companies B and D during the fight. They also covered the early part of the Weir Point retreat. In this situation it is not just one or two case matches we are discussing, but evidence for the use of eight different guns moving from Wooden Leg Hill, then to the knoll, and finally to the Company K position in the perimeter. It is also interesting to note that one gun used in the Weir Point retreat was also used in Retreat Ravine.

Matching case evidence for one gun used at the knoll and in the Company K position was found on the bench above the river below the June 26 camp location. This evidence does not correlate with the known locations of sharpshooters who protected the water carriers. It may, however, represent one of the less well-noted attempts to retrieve water for the wounded. There also may be cartridge case evidence for the sharpshooters who covered the first water-carrier party. Several carbine cases were found in the vicinity of Medal of Honor Point, but unfortunately they did not match any cases found in the perimeter.

There is virtually no intermixing of matching cases in the perimeter among the historically known company positions. Case matches, with perhaps a half-dozen exceptions, are found in very close proximity to one another. The largest group was found in the Company K position on the northeast perimeter. Companies A and D on the southeast and east, respectively, also had several carbines represented. One of the few situations of intermixing was found with a carbine in the Company A position. A matching case was found northeast of the Company D position in context with several other cases that had no corresponding match with cases in the perimeter. These cases may very well represent Captain McDougall's Company B charge on June 26. Company D and possibly elements of Company K charged the Indians to their north at the same time. There are cases north of the perimeter in each of these areas that may indicate the extent of the charge. The cases suggest the movement was about 50 meters (164 feet). The historic accounts indicate a gain of about 60 yards was made before the men returned to the lines. The distances are certainly within tolerance of each other.

Another exceptional case is a carbine which was mentioned earlier. It was used in the retreat up the ravine after the river crossing, then on the Weir Point retreat line and in the perimeter in the A, B, and M Company lines. The dispersion of this gun's matching cases suggests an individual with enough authority to move about the lines. These cases may represent the weapon of one of the officers or senior noncommissioned officers as he moved about rallying the men.

The only other area of matching-case intermixing was along the B and M Company lines. This was no surprise, since the two units are known to have exchanged places on the line on June 26. The rest of the cases, although they indicate many carbines were fired many times, do not exhibit extensive movement. In fact, there are three instances where more than seven rounds were fired in the same carbines and the associated cases were found within fifty centimeters (sixteen and a half inches) of one another.

Most carbine cases were clustered in spatially discrete units that are easily defined. These discrete spatial patterns clearly correlate with the historically documented defense perimeter, and, more important, they correlate with specific units known to have occupied those positions.

Summary of the Reno-Benteen Data

On the gross level, the Reno-Benteen data correlate with historical documentation. There is evidence of combat at the site, and it appears to have been conducted between two different groups. The discrete spatial-distribution data, primarily drawn from the matching-cartridge-case evidence, add a tremendous amount of detail. The discrete spatial data correlate with the historical accounts on nearly every point. Evidence of the retreat up the bluff is clear, as is that for the retreat from Weir Point and the Company D charge. The cartridge-case data has allowed us to identify cartridge case groups that can be associated with historically known unit positions. Even if we had not had the historical documentation of unit locations, we would have been able to identify discrete unit assemblages and trace their movement. This is, in fact, what we have done with the Indian-associated firearm data.

In the case of the Reno-Benteen defense site, the archaeological data correlate with the historical data. There are no significant conflicts between the two data sets. The gross pattern analysis and the identification of unit patterns that can be ascribed to identified unit positions validates the archaeological record's ability to interpret historic events correctly. In the realm of validation studies, the degree of correlation between the Reno-Benteen archaeological data set and the historical documentation borders on the incredible. Perhaps the most important aspect of the high degree of correlation is the added strength it gives archaeological interpretation of the events at Custer Battlefield. This by no means implies that the interpretations we have given the data are inviolate, but, rather, that the data patterns and the ability to interpret them are given new strength.

DEFINING AN ARCHAEOLOGICAL POST–CIVIL WAR BATTLEFIELD PATTERN

The archaeological investigations at Custer Battlefield National Monument have provided a new perspective on the various elements of the Battle of the Little Bighorn. Combatant positions have been identified, firearms identified and quantified, and the sequence of events has been elucidated. History has been enhanced and in some areas revised. Undoubtedly, additional revisions will be forthcoming if similar investigations are carried out on the field of battle surrounding the areas of this investigation. Nevertheless, this study of the the Battle of the Little Bighorn highlights the value of battlefield archaeological studies as a valid means to study battle events of the past.

Archaeological investigations are a part of anthropology. The goal of anthropology is to define the culture of man and how man uses his environment, how he interacts with other social groups, and to define broad patterns or rules of culture. This study has focused on the historical reconstruction of battle events through the use of archaeological methods. In the field of historical archaeology, this is known as historical particularism. It is a valid goal of research, but it is not the only goal.

Up to this point, our study has attempted to reconstruct past events. Here the attention is focused on theoretical and methodological framework within which behavioral dynamics on the battlefield can be investigated: the Post–Civil War Battlefield Pattern.

Our definition of a Post–Civil War Battlefield Pattern is predicated on an axiom basic to archaeological investigation. Human behavior is patterned. Behavioral patterns are expressed through individual behaviors constrained by the norms, values, sanctions, and statuses governing the group within which the individual operates. Among standing armies, military groups are rigidly defined and hierarchically ordered; they are less well defined among guerrilla forces, and individual behavioral roles are structured accordingly. Thus in warfare, tactical operations, both defensive and offensive, precipitate individual behaviors that are carried out within and on behalf of the military unit to which the individual belongs. War tactics, which represent patterned behavior, include establishment of positions and the deployment and movement of combatants. The residues of tactics in warfare, artifacts, features, and their contextual relationships should also be patterned and reflect details of battlefield behavior.

The foundation of the Post–Civil War Battlefield Pattern is laid by recognizing individual behavioral patterns. Such recognition is tied to the identification of individual positions and movements about the battlefield. As noted above, however, individual patterns must be viewed in the aggregate as products of group operations (though in some cases isolated, aberrant behaviors may be identified). Individual behavioral patterns, which are themselves discrete, should also reflect group behavioral patterns. These groups, or military units, are varied but, for example, might include the regiment, company, or platoon. Thus when individual patterns are integrated, unit patterns emerge, and this patterning should be recognizable on the battlefield. Together, these patterns are vital in establishing the Post–Civil War Battlefield Pattern, which seeks to interpret behavior on the battlefield.

ESTABLISHING THE POST–CIVIL WAR BATTLEFIELD PATTERN

Resolution of the Post–Civil War Battlefield Pattern requires investigations at two inclusive levels of analysis. These are gross pattern and dynamic pattern analyses. Typically, gross patterning represents a composite of battle events exclusive of or poorly understood in time. Battle events are static representations of behavior by combatants at specific locations on the battlefield. These spatial and behavioral criteria, characteristic of gross patterning, are inferred from correlations among artifact densities, artifact class associations, and historical data. Dynamic patterning allows refinement, particularly within spatial parameters, of gross-pattern analysis. Moreover, dynamic-pattern analysis sorts in time the composite of battle events observed in gross patterning. This sorting, or chronological ordering of events, provides the basis on which behaviors that may account for a battle's progression can be hypothesized. These tasks are accomplished through firearm identification, the comparative analysis of unique signatures representative of discrete behavior.

Gross Patterning

Discerning gross patterning is reasonably straightforward, as has been shown in this study. It requires the archaeological identification of battle events, that is, combatant positions and the correlation, to the extent possible, of these phenomena with the historical record. Once this correlation has been established, we are left with a historically meaningful but static perception of battle events that provide a model for discerning behavioral dynamics.

Archaeological density information, such as clustering, clinal distributions or presence-absence criteria, provide the data necessary for locating battle events in space. Clustering of features (e.g., rifle pits) and/or military hardware, for example, tends to signal combatant positions. Behaviors are read from the nature and proportions of the artifact classes present. An individual combat event, by way of example, might be signaled by a discrete concentration of a few cartridge cases, or perhaps human remains. Such occurrences may or may not be isolated from identifiable unit patterns. Unit patterns might be distinguished spatially and behaviorally by sheer artifact volume and diversity at discrete locations or by patterning, such as evidence for lines at skirmish intervals, associated with clusters of individual positions.

Gross patterns cannot, however, be assigned historically meaningful identities on the basis of archaeological data alone. It is here that the importance of the historical record intervenes. History provides a means by which gross patterning can be differentiated. Certain combatant positions may be ascribed to one side, others to the opposing force, by using historical data. Accounts such as eyewitness testimony, maps, and battle reports may allow identification of archaeologically discrete data as the residues of known units, such as companies, comprising a regiment.

The task of imparting historical reality to that observed archaeologically may or may not be difficult. Recognizing opposing sides from the Indian Wars period, for example, is not usually fraught with difficulty. Indian military equipage, including weaponry, was substantially different from U.S. Army issue equipment. History informs us of this. Yet this degree of disparity cannot be expected routinely. When studying the residues of armies similarly equipped and trained, subtle equipment or artifact distribution variations might be recognized, but their meanings may be obscured.

Certainly each investigation poses its own peculiar obstacles to resolving gross patterning satisfactorily. The archaeological record might coincide nicely with historical accounts of a particular battle. On the other hand, history and archaeology may be partly or wholly at odds, thus demanding resolution of discrepancies before gross patterning can be satisfactorily established. Once resolved, however, dynamic-pattern analysis sets the historical actors and battle events into motion.

Dynamic Patterning

Dynamic-pattern analysis allows confirmation, modification, or refinement of the behavioral-spatial nature of battle events observed in gross patterning. Equally important, dynamic patterning provides the basis on which these events can be sorted in time. The key to dynamic patterning is based on modern firearm-identification methods that allow resolution of individual positions and movements across the battlefield. Individual patterns can then be integrated to form unit patterns, and the flow or progress of a battle can be discerned. Again this study of the Battle of the Little Bighorn becomes a pioneering example of dynamic-pattern analysis. The application of firearm identification and the subsequent determination of individual and unit patterns, especially at the Reno-Benteen defense site, is a prime example of the utility of the analysis.

Individual Patterns

Comparative signature data, coupled with precise artifact locational data obtained in the field, can be used to trace the positions and movements of individual weapons across the field of battle. A tight clustering of cartridge cases from the same weapon would likely indicate a single firing position. Cases from several discrete locations but with identical signatures would indicate that the weapon in which they were fired moved about the battlefield. With proper care, observed locations and movements of weapons may be correlated with individual combatants. Caution must be exercised, however, for certain variables confounding such correlations may need to be considered.

One variable that may be present at any site is the potential for severe soil disturbances to affect artifact proveniences. Undoubtedly there are numerous site-specific variables that also may affect correlations between weapons and individuals. Not all can be conjectured here, but the bias of captured weapons provides an example. Opposition weaponry might be perceived as superior, either in firepower or mechanical reliability, and captured weapons may be highly valued. This phenomenon is clear at Custer battlefield, where historical accounts suggest that government weapons were obtained by Indians either from dead soldiers during the battle or from a previous engagement with troopers. Indeed, we found government casings in association with other cases typical of the variety of firearms in the hands of Indians at the time. We identified their signatures and used these to reduce the possibility of interpreting their occurrence elsewhere as soldier positions.

The integration of individual patterns, as has been noted, provides the basis on which unit patterns can be constructed. This also involves tracing positions and movements, but at the unit-pattern level. In effect, we are following the deployments of combat units (or others, such as support units).

Unit Patterns

The dynamic-pattern analysis provides a check, either through confirmation, modification, or refinement, on battle events observed in gross patterning on a battlefield. This is particularly true as it applies to the spatial parameters represented by the event. That is, discrete occurrences of identical firearm signatures may confirm or refine notions of individual combat locations discerned in gross patterning. The same holds true for the locations of units identified through gross-pattern analysis. A spatially discrete occurrence of a set of firearm signatures dissimilar in composition to other sets elsewhere in space reflects in principle the unique composition of individuals as a discrete unit. It is likely that completely discrete firearm-signature sets will seldom be encountered, particularly if individuals moved during a fight from unit to unit, but, barring complete disorganization, discrete units ought to be evident on this basis, as we have seen in the case of the Reno-Benteen defense site. Thus firearms identification compliments gross patterning, and this complementary function is, in fact, a logical product of dynamic patterning. Having identified discrete units, and having ascribed to them historical identities, we can trace their movements and positioning about the battlefield much in the same manner as we trace individuals.

THE POST–CIVIL WAR BATTLEFIELD PATTERN

Two problems remain to be considered in establishing the Post–Civil War Battlefield Pattern. So far, we have shown that individuals and units comprised of individuals can be traced, given certain data, on a battlefield. However, the sequencing, or order of deployments, is not necessarily inherent in these data. For example, were the deployments from north to south or vice versa? We need to establish a starting point or points, and this may not always be an easy task.

Historical accounts will be valuable in determining where on the battlefield a fight began, and dynamic patterning may be structured from that starting point. Fortunately, this is possible for the Custer battle. But in the absence of historical accounts or where accounts are so vague that several possibilities may be entertained, other clues are required. It may be necessary to return to the archaeological record, and the nature of its clues may be as varied as the number of battles in history. So each investigation will likely pose its own circumstances. Some possibilities may, however, be considered.

The composition of artifactual data present at discrete locations representing battle events may vary. This composition may signal sequencing such that the location with one or a few artifact classes may represent the initial engagement and the adjacent locations with increasing artifact class variation subsequent encounters. Similar variation in artifact densities may also be considered. And finally, attrition in manpower may signal sequencing and a progressive reduction in unique firearm signatures and may be interpreted as attrition. In any case, establishing order in dynamic patterning is necessary before the remaining problem can be addressed. Once established, the Post–Civil War Battlefield Pattern can be explicated by proposing behaviors that can account for a battle's progression. In other words, we can not only discern the progress of a battle, we can explain how the battle came to be played out in the manner that it was.

The Battle of the Little Bighorn provides a relevant application of the Post–Civil War Battlefield Pattern for several reasons. The artifact inventory, including ammunition components, is readily amenable to the kind of analyses necessary to establish the pattern. Also, despite the vast literature spawned by the battle and notwithstanding the outcome, there is little resolution of the tactical details of the fight. Finally, the Custer battle furnishes a test of the Post–Civil War Battlefield Pattern as it applies to two types of military organization virtually at polar opposites: the rigid military structure of the cavalry and the comparatively unstructured, individually based tactics of the Plains Indians.

The Post–Civil War Battlefield Pattern is potentially informative within broader contexts other than battle reconstructions. Lewis (1981) anticipated this in proposing a Frontier Military Pattern. He briefly mentions the concept of a Battlefield Pattern but does not develop the concept. South (1977:160) was more specific in proposing that a Revolutionary War Military Battle Pattern might be defined. He thought the pattern could be explained "either in terms of a battle, supply lines, logistic base, military supply, types of arms, etc." South's proposal resembles the Battlefield Pattern posited here. The Custer Battlefield Model has been defined and explained but, whether it represents, for example, an Indian War Military Pattern or a broader Post–Civil War Battlefield Pattern as proposed needs to be determined.

Yet the Battle of the Little Bighorn case example remains valuable for two reasons. First, collectors of comparative data from other Indian Wars battle sites (which do not yet exist) will have a model on which to test their data. Second, and probably more important, these battles will, as does the Custer Battlefield Model now, provide patterns of actual behavior that may be compared with models of expected behavior. Relevant tactical manuals should provide the basis for conceiving models of expected behavior. Emory Upton's 1874 *Cavalry Tactics*, for example, should provide a basis on which the actual behavior observed in the Custer Battlefield Model can be compared with expected behavior under the circumstances. This comparison will provide a firmer basis for accounting for particular events at the Battle of the Little Bighorn and a basis on which an Indian Wars behavioral pattern can be established.

It is also important to reiterate that these data exist in a recognizable form in space on a field of battle, where organization is supposedly least likely to exist. In this case those organizations and culturally opposing forces are recognizable. This study then becomes another step in defining the archaeological aspect of the anthropology of war. It is an early step, but it is one on which we can build a base of solid theory and practice on cultures in conflict.

PART THREE

ARTIFACT DESCRIPTIONS AND SPECIALIST REPORTS

Chapter 7

Artifact Description and Analysis

The archaeological investigations at Custer Battlefield National Monument yielded a wide array of artifacts. The majority of the specimens recovered can definitely be attributed to the battle, while the remainder are mainly related to the postbattle era. These latter artifacts represent items lost or discarded by visitors to the field as well as items relating to the administration of the site by the army and the National Park Service. A few stone artifacts relating to aboriginal utilization of the area were also found.

This chapter consists of a description and an analysis of the artifacts from the archaeological inventory. The emphasis of these descriptions focuses on the battle-related artifacts, but the postbattle artifacts are also discussed. Most of the recovered artifacts are bullets and cartridge cases, and most of these are battle-related artifacts. Because of the large quantity of firearm-related artifacts recovered, the description and analysis emphasize that artifact type.

FIREARMS: GENERAL INFORMATION

Cartridges, cartridge cases, and bullets make up the majority of artifacts recovered from the battlefield, and through their signatures they have the potential to reveal the most artifactual information about the battle. The comparative study of ammunition components is known as firearm-identification analysis. Firearm signatures on cartridge cases are firing-pin and extractor marks; on bullets they are land-and-groove marks. These signatures allow the determination of the type of firearm (i.e., model or brand) in which a given casing or bullet was fired. This then allows determination of the number of different types of guns in use at the battle. Further, it allows the identification of individual weapons through comparison of the unique qualities of firearm signatures. For example, the number of individual Sharps rifles or Henry repeating rifles represented in the archaeological collection can be demonstrated. The latter capability is very important because, coupled with precise artifact locations, identical signatures can be used to trace the movement of individual weapons on the field of battle. This can be done with cartridge cases and bullets even though the actual weapons are not in hand. With this information, patterns of movement can be established and the battle sequence can be interpreted more precisely.

The means to this analytical end require some explanation. When a weapon is fired, the firing pin strikes the primer contained in the cartridge, leaving a distinctive imprint on the case. The primer ignites the powder, forcing the bullet down the barrel. The rifling in the barrel imprints the lands and grooves on the bullet in mirror image. So also does the extractor imprint the spent case as it is extracted from the gun's chamber. These imprints are called signatures. Microscopic examination of a signature allows determination of the weapon type. This is important because many types of ammunition can be fired in a variety of firearms. By way of example, the .44-caliber Henry cartridge could be fired not only in the Henry repeating rifle (for which the Henry cartridge was designed), but also in the Model 1866 Winchester, the .44 rimfire Colt pistol, and the .44 rimfire Remington revolver. The firing pin of each weapon type is distinctive, and it is thus possible to identify the weapon type in which a given .44 Henry cartridge was fired.

Police agencies have long used the investigative technique of firearm-identification as an aid in solving crimes. Two methods commonly used by police departments include comparisons of bullets and cartridge cases (Harris 1980; Hatcher, Jury, and Weller 1977) to identify the weapon types from which they were fired. Police are routinely successful in matching bullet and/or cartridge-case signatures to the crime weapon simply by demonstrating that the firing pin, extractor marks, or the land-and-groove marks could have been made only by a certain weapon. In the event that weapons used in a crime are not recovered, police can say with certainty, on the basis of signatures from recovered bullets and cases, that specific types and numbers of weapons were used. We have employed these procedures in this investigation.

Macroscopically, firing pins and their signatures often appear identical from weapon to weapon within a single type. However, minute variations unique to each firing pin allow the identification of individual weapons. Such variations are visible only via the microscope. These unique variations are caused by tolerances in tooling machinery and wear to cutting surfaces involved in the manufacture of the firearm. Thus the signatures left on most ammunition components from the Custer battlefield are amenable to firearm-identification procedures even after a century in the ground. In essence, the mark is a metallic fingerprint.

Extractor signatures are valuable metallic fingerprints. A fired cartridge case is removed or ejected from a firearm by a mechanical device called an extractor. Just like the firing pin, the extractor leaves its imprint on the case. Extractors installed in weapons of a given type, for example U.S. Arsenal breech-loading Springfields, leave a signature peculiar to the type. That is, the extractor signature on casings fired in the Springfield carbine is different from signatures left by other weapon types. Furthermore, and again like firing pins, each extractor has unique traits that distinguish it from all other extractors of the same type. Given these extractor signatures, it is possible to identify individual weapons within each type by microscopic examination. The ability to read extractor signatures provides strong corroborating data when used in conjunction with analysis of firing-pin signatures, for both occur together on most cartridge cases.

Bullets, of course, are also important in firearm-identification. The barrel of rifled guns has a series of lands and grooves that impart a spin to the bullet as it travels down the barrel. This spin gives the bullet more aerodynamic stability and accuracy in its trajectory. The bullet is lead and the barrel is steel. Since the bullet fits tightly in the barrel, the barrel leaves land-and-groove impressions, in reverse, on the softer bullet. As with a firing pin, each barrel manufactured for a certain weapon type has individually recognizable characteristics. The land-and-groove signatures left on the bullets can be used to determine weapon type and individual weapons within a type.

The thousands of bullets and cartridge cases from the archaeological investigations were subjected to comparative firearm-identification analyses to determine the minimum number of weapon types present and the minimum number of individual firearms within each weapon type. The analyses presented below are discussed by weapon type as identified through firearm signatures. The minimum number of weapons within each type is enumerated in each discussion. It is important to emphasize that these are *minimum* figures based on the artifact sample recovered during the archaeological work at Custer Battlefield National Monument.

In general, we found that most cartridge cases could be sorted as to type and individual guns, although a few were too corroded to identify beyond type. The bullets, on the other hand, were generally too corroded by lead oxides to sort beyond the weapon type except in a few instances. The process of microscopic comparison of each cartridge case to every other cartridge case of the same caliber, as well as each bullet, is very time consuming, but results are worth the effort, as will be seen in the discussion that follows.

ARMS AND AMMUNITION

Forehand and Wadsworth .32-Caliber

One .32-caliber long rimfire cartridge case (FS34) was recovered. In addition to the cartridge case, a single bullet belonging to a .32-caliber long rimfire was also recovered (FS1069). Both were found on the Custer battlefield. The .32 long rimfire cartridge (fig. 50g) was first introduced for the Smith and Wesson Model #2 revolver in 1861 and was chambered for a variety of other firearms. It was a moderately popular cartridge, but it was not considered effective beyond a range of fifty yards (Barnes 1969:277). This cartridge was fired in an Ethan Allen or Forehand and Wadsworth gun. The firearms are the same; the name was changed because Ethan Allen sold the company to Forehand and Wadsworth.

Colt .36-Caliber

One .36-caliber conical bullet (fig. 51g) and one .36-caliber round ball from the Reno-Benteen defense site (FS2299, 4945) were fired in a Colt-manufactured gun. Both are imprinted with the distinctive seven-land-and-groove, left-hand-twist Colt rifling.

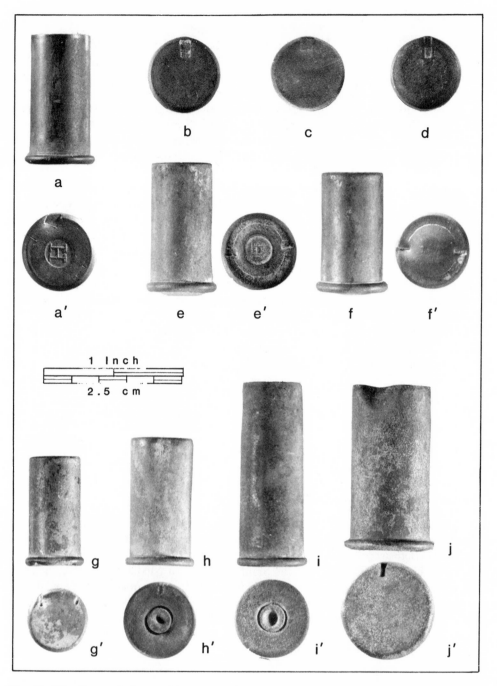

Fig. 50. Miscellaneous Indian cartridge cases. a, a′: A .44-caliber rimfire case fired in a Model 1872 Colt Open Top. b: A .44 Henry fired in a Colt revolver. c: A .44 Henry fired in a Ballard. d: A .44 Henry fired in a Remington revolver. e, e′: A .44 Henry long with H headstamp. f, f′: A .44 Henry short. g, g′: A .32 long fired in Forehand and Wadsworth. h, h′: A .44 Smith and Wesson center-fire. i, i′: A .44/40 Winchester center-fire. j, j′: A .56/50 Spencer.

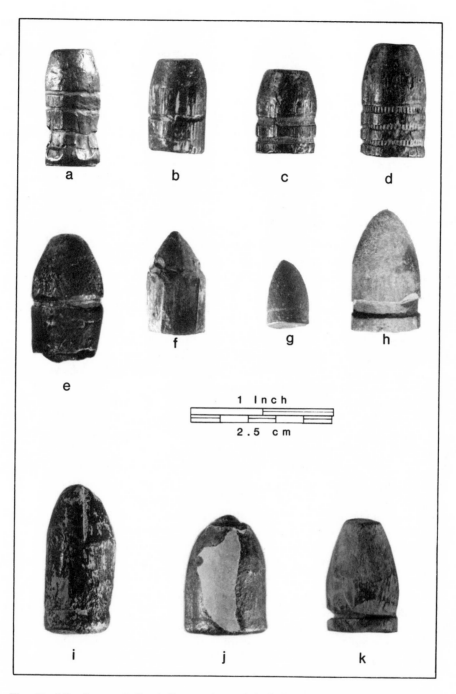

Fig. 51. Miscellaneous Indian bullets. a: A .38 Colt. b-d: variations of .44-caliber Henry bullets. e: A .50 Sharps f: A .40-caliber bullet with teeth marks. g: A .36 Colt h: A .42 Smith bullet. i: A .54 Starr. j: A .577 Enfield. k: A .54-caliber Maynard.

The gun could have been any one of eight different percussion models (Flayderman 1983:88–100)

Colt .38-Caliber

Two hollow-based two-cannelure .38-caliber bullets (FS2855, 4799) from the Reno-Benteen defense site have the seven-land-and-groove, left-hand-twist Colt rifling (fig. 51a). The bullets were probably fired from one of the nine different Colt model handguns chambered for the .38-caliber rimfire cartridge (Flayderman 1983: 88–110).

Sharps .40-, .45-, and .50-Caliber

The Sharps firearm was patented in 1852 and was a very popular military and commercial firearm for the next fifty years. It was produced in both percussion and cartridge styles. Its popularity was due to its accuracy and its reputation for having effective stopping power. Particularly in the larger calibers, it was the favored gun of big-game hunters on the Great Plains and in the West in general (Gluckman 1965:230, 268; Barnes 1969:139).

Weapons manufactured by Sharps fired thirty-three of the .50/70 cartridge cases recovered, and three types of distinctive Sharps bullets also were found (Sellers 1978). A number of other bullet types with Sharps land-and-groove impressions were present and are discussed in the appropriate section.

The first distinctive Sharps bullet is a round-nose smooth-body paper-patch type (fig. 52i) found in both .45- and .50-caliber. The .50-caliber smooth bullets are from the Custer battlefield (FS151, 217, 221, 5011, and 5043) and the Reno-Benteen defense site (FS2323, 2541, 2581, 3095, 3254, 3608, 3666, 4766, 4781, 4783, 4872, and 4953). All of these are cast bullets. Ten of them have been deformed by striking some object, and one (FS2581) has cloth impressions on its base. It is possible this bullet struck some object, but it is more likely that the fabric impression is from a linen cartridge used in one of the first models of Sharps guns. The .45-caliber smooth bullets are FS1068 and 1690, and both are from the Custer battlefield.

The second Sharps type has a flat nose and a single crimping groove. This bullet type (fig. 51e) is found in both .40- and .50-caliber sizes (.40-caliber FS852, 983, 1302, 1640 from Custer battlefield; 3293, 3718, 3862, 3928, 4118, 4119 from the Reno-Benteen defense site and .50-caliber FS42 from Custer battlefield; 3833, 4688 from the Reno-Benteen defense site). Five of these bullets were deformed by impact. The third type is also found in .40-, .45-, and .50-caliber and is a pointed-nose bullet with three cannelures and a raised base (.40-caliber FS286 and .50-caliber FS339, 406 are from Custer battlefield and .45-caliber FS2415, 3295 are from the Reno-Benteen defense site). FS339 is slightly deformed from striking an object. A groove on one side suggests it may have struck bone.

Miscellaneous and Unknown .40-Caliber Bullets

There are eight types of .40-caliber bullets in the collection. The first is flat nosed with a single crimping groove (FS33, 247, 544, 671, 731). These Custer battlefield bullets

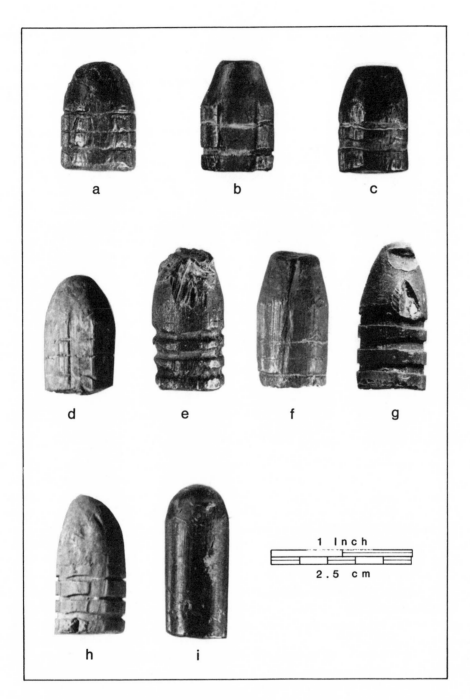

Fig. 52. Large-caliber Indian bullets. a: A .50 Spencer. b: A Dimick .50/70 experimental. c: A .50/70 Cadet. d: A .50 Remington sporting rifle. e-f: Variations of the .50/70 bullet. g: A .50/70 with bone embedded. h: A .50 Sharps sporting rifle. i: A Sharps .45-caliber bullet.

are imprinted with the Sharps sporting-rifle six-land-and-groove marks. A group of Reno-Benteen defense site bullets with four cannelures and a raised base are imprinted with an unidentified five-land-and-groove, right-hand-twist rifling (FS4076, 4311). Two bullets, one each from the Custer battlefield (FS 286) and the Reno-Benteen defense site (FS2612), are a three-cannelure pointed-nose type with imprints of an unidentified three-land-and-groove rifling. The other types are represented by one bullet each: round nose with three cannelures and five-land-and-groove, right-hand-twist rifling (FS318) from the Custer battlefield; flat nose with three knurled cannelures (FS793) from the Custer battlefield; flat nose with two cannelures bullet and five-land-and-groove, right-hand-twist marks (FS2389) from Reno-Benteen; a bullet with one crimping groove and Sharps sporting-rifle six-land-and-groove rifling (FS4378) from Reno-Benteen; and a smooth-side bullet with a slightly rounded nose with Sharps sporting-rifle six-land-and-groove marks (FS1681) from the Custer battlefield.

Nine bullets were deformed on impact, one appears hammered (FS2612), and one (FS4311) appears to have teeth marks (fig. 51f) on it. The teeth marks could have resulted from an attempt to remove the bullet from a cartridge.

Ethan Allen or Forehand and Wadsworth .42-Caliber

The Forehand and Wadsworth arms company and its predecessors, Allen and Wheelock and Ethan Allen and Company, manufactured a .42-caliber rimfire rifle (Fladyerman 1986:66). Two .42-caliber, three-cannelure, raised-base bullets (FS2987, 4768) for this rifle were recovered from the Reno-Benteen defense site. One was deformed on impact.

Smith and Wesson American .44-Caliber

Four brass cases (FS23, 49, 645, 1815) were recovered from the Custer battlefield that were fired from a .44-caliber Smith and Wesson American pistol (fig. 50h). All are center-fire with a Berdan primer. The .44-caliber Smith and Wesson American cartridge was introduced in 1869 or 1870 for the Smith and Wesson Model #3 or American-model pistol. The army used the round for a few years, but it was more popular as a commercial pistol round (Barnes 1969:167). At least three different firearms using this cartridge are represented in the collection, based on firing-pin and extractor-mark analysis (table 7).

Nine bullets with three cannelures and a raised base imprinted with the Smith and Wesson .44-caliber right-hand-twist, five-land-and-groove rifling were recovered. One bullet (FS19) was found on the Custer battlefield, and the other eight (FS3258, 3288, 3290, 3578, 3662, 3702, 4102, 4168) are associated with the Reno-Benteen defense site. Two Reno-Benteen bullets had been deformed on impact.

Evans Old Model .44-Caliber

One center-fire, Berdan-primed Evans Old Model .44-caliber brass cartridge case was found on the Custer battlefield (FS1392). The .44-caliber Evans Old Model, or short,

Table 9 Henry .44 Cartridges and Cartridge Cases by Field-Specimen Number

Fired in a Henry Rifle or Winchester Model 1866

Misfired cartridges (2 specimens):
  Custer Battlefield
1708, 1722

Cartridge cases (185 specimens):
  Custer Battlefield
48, 57, 58, 60, 63, 79, 81, 82, 84, 90, 95, 178, 184, 352, 375, 379, 471, 556, 564, 637, 638, 639, 640, 648, 959, 984, 1030, 1031, 1035, 1150, 1151, 1259, 1267, 1274, 1278a, 1278b, 1280, 1283, 1288, 1292, 1293, 1294, 1296, 1300, 1309, 1310, 1330, 1331, 1332, 1333, 1338, 1339, 1343, 1435, 1436, 1531, 1533, 1534, 1536, 1542, 1543, 1544, 1545, 1547, 1553, 1554, 1596, 1597, 1598, 1601, 1608, 1609, 1611, 1612, 1613, 1615, 1616, 1630, 1700, 1704, 1705, 1706, 1707, 1750, 1751, 1752, 1753, 1754, 1756, 1757, 1758, 1759, 1760, 1761, 1766, 1767, 1768, 1769, 1774, 1775, 1777, 1778, 1786, 1799, 1808, 1814, 1820, 1877, 1878, 2211, 2565, 5053, 5055, 5056, 5057, 5022

  Reno-Benteen Defense Site
2000, 2002, 2004, 2017, 2018, 2036, 2037, 2039, 2041, 2044, 2047, 2048, 2049, 2050, 2053, 2055, 2057, 2068, 2069, 2072, 2074, 2075, 2079, 2080, 2093, 2094, 2098, 2221, 2238, 2241, 2257, 2263, 2264, 2266, 2268, 2273, 2274, 2275, 2276, 2277, 2278, 2280, 2282, 2288, 2296, 2308, 2357, 2359, 2363, 2365, 2582, 3837, 4036, 4145, 4146, 4149, 4229, 4232, 4325, 4338, 4339, 4984, 4997, 4998, 4999, 5000, 5001, 5003, 5004

Fired from weapons other than the Henry and Winchester 66 (15 specimens):
  Custer Battlefield
93, 115, 1276, 1289a, 1289b, 1529, 1793, 1794, 1795, 1796, 5021

  Reno-Benteen Defense Site
2199, 2204, 2265, 2355

Cartridges and cases with more than one set of double-strike firing-pin marks from the Henry or Winchester 66 (57 specimens):

Two sets of double firing-pin marks:
  Custer Battlefield
81, 90, 184, 639, 1283, 1543, 1544, 1547, 1553, 1597, 1598, 1615, 1630, 1706, 1753, 1757, 1760, 1761, 1769, 1820, 5053, 5055

  Reno-Benteen Defense Site
2000, 2002, 2017, 2044, 2049, 2075, 2098, 2288, 2359, 2365, 3837, 4146, 4229, 4232, 5022

Three sets of double firing-pin marks:
  Custer Battlefield
178, 984, 1333, 1536, 1542, 1554, 1708

  Reno-Benteen Defense Site
2074, 2268, 2296, 2582, 4758

Four sets of double firing-pin marks:
  Custer Battlefield
82, 1609

  Reno-Benteen Defense Site
2069, 2363, 4338, 4991

Five sets of double firing-pin marks:
  Custer Battlefield
2565

cartridge was introduced just one year before the battle. The cartridge and a rifle chambered for it were originally designed for use by the military. The chief of ordnance rejected the design and the weapon was sold for sporting purposes (Barnes 1969:101).

Henry .44-Caliber

Two hundred two .44-caliber Henry rimfire cartridges and cartridge cases were recovered from the Custer battlefield and the Reno-Benteen defense site. Two hundred of the total are fired cases; the other two are loaded cartridges (table 9). The .44-caliber bullets relating to these cartridges and cases are described in the following section.

The .44-caliber Henry rimfire cartridge was developed in the late 1850s by B. Tyler Henry, the plant superintendent for Oliver Winchester at the New Haven Arms Company. The company's name was changed to Winchester Repeating Arms Company in the mid-1860s. Henry also developed the first successful repeating rifle that would fire this cartridge by improving the Smith and Wesson Volcanic repeating arms, which were a failure because of their small caliber and extraction problems. Henry's conception of a flexible claw-shaped extractor was probably the most important single improvement leading to the success of the Henry repeating rifle and its .44-caliber rimfire cartridge. This extractor principle is still in use today, being used in the Ingram submachine gun (Kinzer 1983:34–38).

The manufacture of the Henry cartridge is outlined in the 1984 report (Scott and Fox 1987). The 202 cartridges and cases in the collection fall into four variations. The majority are the long-case variety with a raised-H headstamp in a recessed depression (fig. 50a). The other varieties are long case with no headstamp, short case with H headstamp, and short case with no headstamp (fig. 50f).

The tendency for this rimfire ammunition to misfire was a serious problem in the early development of cartridge firearms. Henry designed for his repeating rifle a double firing pin that would strike the rim of the cartridge at points on opposite sides. The firing pins were wedge-shaped, each being located on one side of the breech-pin collar. The collar was threaded into the breech pin, which was designed to move a fraction of an inch forward and rearward during firing. Both the Henry rifle and its improved version, the Model 1866 Winchester, had firing pins that were exactly alike in shape and dimensions (Madis 1979:97). The firing pins were less pointed on some Model 1866s between serial numbers 24,000 and 26,000 but were changed back to their original shape because of misfire problems (Madis 1979:79).

Even with the double-strike firing pin used in the Henry and Winchester Model 1866 rifles, these weapons were still prone to misfire. If the breech pin was dirty or rusty, a very hard blow was required before the firing pins would penetrate the rim of the cartridge deeply enough to detonate the primer. This problem is very evident on the cartridges and cartridge cases listed in table 9. Fifty-seven cartridges and cases bear more than one set of the double-strike firing-pin marks, indicating misfires. One case, FS82, has four sets of firing-pin marks. Three sets were made by the same weapon, while the fourth set, which is deeper in the rim of the base than the other three and probably detonated the primer, was made by another weapon. Some of the cases show bulging of the head, which is commonly found on fired .44 Henry cases. This is the result of the failure of the breech bolt, in either the Henry or Model 1866, to fit snugly against the face of the chamber; it is not the result of being fired in one model or the other.

It would be safe to assume that most, if not all, of the .44-caliber Henry cartridges and cases in the collection were fired from Indian weapons during the battle. Most Indian firearms recovered after a battle were in need of repairs and cleaning. This helps explain the large number (28 percent) of misfired cases and cartridges recovered from the battlefield.

These misfires bring up some interesting facts. Spacing of the firing-pin marks on the cases and cartridges indicate they were rotated in the chamber slightly each time they were fired. This was not a easy task to perform with loaded cartridges in a Henry and Winchester Model 1866, as experimentation by one of us (Harmon) has shown. If the finger lever is gently thrown down when extracting the cartridge, the case will drop back onto the cartridge lifter and it can be inserted in the chamber manually. One must also look at the base of the case and rotate the misfire marks away from the firing pins. This all takes time, and it is doubtful that a warrior in the heat of battle would have bothered to worry about saving a misfired cartridge. It is conceivable this task would be somewhat more difficult on the back of a horse and was more often accomplished while fighting on foot. This leads to speculation that misfires were repeatedly chambered until they finally were fired at some point in the battle when warriors had plenty of time for single-shot reloading or they were running low on ammunition and tried the misfires until they detonated.

One case in the collection, FS2565, was fired five times before it went off, while another, FS2211, was fired only once, both cases being fired in the same weapon. Three cases (FS1542, 1547, 1761) fired from the same weapon all have multiple sets of firing-pin marks, leading us to believe that this weapon was malfunctioning. Without more cases fired from the same weapon to examine, it is difficult to conclude whether the warriors had obtained a lot of bad Henry ammunition or whether many of their weapons were in need of a good cleaning.

Rimfire cartridges are not very functional for reloading, and an Indian paid a heavy price for these little cartridges in the 1870s. Despite the difficulty, one cartridge case in the collection might have been reloaded (FS1757). It has two sets of firing-pin marks made by different weapons; each set has penetrated the copper base deeply enough to detonate the primer. DuMont (1975:50, 56) points out the ingenuity of the Indians in reloading rimfire cartridges and their possible use in this battle. The army was also aware of the potential for Indians to reload cartridges, and Adjutant General's Office General Order 13, February 16, 1876, stated: "Great care will therefore be exercised by all officers to prevent Indians from procuring the empty shells thrown away by troops after firing, either in action or at target practice."

Fifteen of the .44-caliber cartridge cases in the collection bear only a single firing-pin mark (table 9), which indicates they were fired from weapons other than the Henry chambered for the .44-caliber rimfire. They were fired in the Colt Model 1871 Open Top Revolver (fig. 50a'), Remington Model 1858 conversion (fig. 50d), Colt Model 1860 conversion (fig. 50b), and a Ballard sporting rifle (fig. 50c) (Flayderman 1980).

There were approximately 97,000 firearms of the .44 Henry rimfire caliber that could have been on the frontier in 1876 (Harmon 1987). It appears that New Haven Arms Company and Winchester Repeating Arms Company had supplied the majority of these with the production of the Henry repeating rifle and the Model 1866 Winchester. The Henry rifle gained its popularity during the Civil War but was replaced shortly after with what Winchester advertised as the "Improved Henry", the Model 1866 Winchester. The Improved Henry was easier to load, lighter in weight, and produced in three variations.

Both weapons were very popular on the frontier during the 1870s and much sought by the Indians, not only for their rapid firing ability, but because they were also very appealing to the eye (Parsons 1955: 69). They were often called "Yellow Boy" or "Yellow Fire Stick" by the Indians. Several of these rifles and carbines were surrendered by members of the tribes that participated in the Battle of the Little Bighorn (War Department 1879). A Henry rifle reportedly has been recovered from the Custer battlefield area (Greene 1979: 53).

Many early accounts of the battle claim that most warriors were armed with either Henry or Winchester repeating rifles and carbines. A statement from *Army and Navy Journal* in 1876 makes light of the heavy use of Winchesters by Indian warriors:

We advise the Winchester Arms Co. to act upon the suggestion offered them by Capt. Nickerson, of Gen. Crook's staff, and prosecute the Indians for infringement of their patent. The Captain testifies with others, that Winchester rifles are plenty among them; the agency and the traders solemnly affirm that they don't furnish them; so it can only be inferred that the Indians manufacture them themselves. If Gov. Winchester could get out a preliminary injunction, restraining the Indians from the use of his rifle, it might be of signal service to our troops in the next engagement [*Army and Navy Journal* 13(50):805].

Ballistic examination of the 202 .44-caliber Henry cases and cartridges show that 93 percent were fired in either the Henry rifle or the Model 1866 Winchester. The remaining 7 percent were fired in handguns and a single-shot Ballard rifle. An analysis of the double-strike firing-pin marks left on these Henry .44-caliber cases and cartridges has identified 108 different Henry rifles and Winchester Model 1866s (table 7). Three guns were used at both battlefields. The same analysis also shows that ten different weapons fired the cases with a single firing-pin mark (table 7). Sitting Bull stated in 1877 that his warriors rained lead from repeating rifles on Custer's troops when they attempted to cross the river and attack his camp (Graham 1953:70, 71). One Bull, a Lakota Sioux and Sitting Bull's nephew, said, "The Indians had rifles with little short cartridges, I didn't use mine" (Everett 1930:7). One Bull may not have used his repeating rifle on that hot Sunday in 1876, but the archaeological evidence certainly confirms that other warriors were using theirs that afternoon.

Caliber .44 Bullets (200-Grain)

Two hundred fifty-six .44-caliber bullets were recovered at the two battlefield sites. They are of the type used in .44-caliber rimfire ammunition, but some of them may have been fired from the early .44/40-caliber center-fire ammunition. These are described separately from their related cartridges and cases because they could have been fired from either type of ammunition. The majority were probably fired from either the Henry or Winchester Model 1866 because of the larger number of the Henry rimfire

Table 10 Caliber .44 Bullets (200-Grains) by Field-Specimen Number

Fired from Henry and Winchester repeating rifles (222 specimens):

Custer Battlefield
14, 20, 30, 31, 35, 44, 46, 61, 179, 254, 270, 312, 313, 315, 319, 333, 357, 416, 449, 470, 517, 547, 574, 583, 631, 705, 706, 734, 781, 801, 915, 946, 981, 1017, 1073, 1083, 1085, 1219, 1227, 1363, 1393, 1394, 1397, 1406, 1591, 1657, 1658, 1682, 1733, 1748, 1773, 1782, 1797, 2579, 4608, 5017, 5026

Reno-Benteen Defense Site
2146, 2256, 2270, 2286, 2332, 2378, 2386, 2388, 2393, 2397, 2398, 2399, 2432, 2467, 2489, 2499, 2512, 2529, 2556, 2595, 2627, 2636, 2639, 2668, 2706, 2716, 2735, 2747, 2757, 2760, 2803, 2858, 2871, 2872, 2884, 2908, 2973, 2976, 2991, 3002, 3027, 3064, 3089, 3090, 3096, 3114, 3130, 3131, 3152, 3154, 3155, 3157, 3159, 3167, 3173, 3176, 3177, 3189, 3199, 3221, 3225, 3239, 3248, 3249, 3257, 3260, 3263, 3270, 3278, 3279, 3280, 3294, 3295, 3298, 3299, 3300, 3318, 3319, 3325, 3339, 3348, 3598, 3600, 3611, 3613, 3621, 3631, 3650, 3652, 3653, 3671, 3698, 3701, 3703, 3705, 3709, 3714, 3719, 3730, 3741, 3743, 3745, 3762, 3806, 3807, 3846, 3848, 3859, 3921, 3949, 3974, 4018, 4026, 4074, 4120, 4124, 4126, 4130, 4135, 4138, 4157, 4164, 4171, 4176, 4177, 4216, 4220, 4282, 4311, 4361, 4375, 4377, 4380, 4617, 4621, 4623, 4630, 4631, 4643, 4647, 4696, 4713, 4730, 4734, 4754, 4757, 4760, 4764, 4777, 4786, 4849, 4863, 4867, 4870, 4874, 4876, 4903, 4912, 4917, 4921, 4927, 4929, 4948, 4970, 5032, 5043

Fired in weapons with six-groove, left-hand-twist rifling (4 specimens):

Reno-Benteen Defense Site
2219, 2389, 3858, 4738

Unidentified rifling marks (29 specimens):

Custer Battlefield
29, 138, 146, 156, 322, 432, 501, 1004, 1460, 1586, 1684, 1685, 5036

Reno-Benteen Defense Site
2426, 2464, 2891, 2983, 3229, 3664, 3828, 3839, 4078, 4134, 4172, 4514, 4620, 4626, 4708, 4744, 5020

No rifling marks, unfired (1 specimen):

Custer Battlefield
18

cases (202) recovered as compared with the number of .44/40 center-fire cases (14). Two hundred twenty-two of the bullets bear rifling marks clear enough to show they were fired from either the Henry rifle or Winchester Models 1866 and 1873 (fig. 51b, c, d). The rifling in these weapons is five groove, right-hand-twist. The Henry had deeper rifling than the early Model 1866s. Some in the serial number range of 17,000 to 22,000 had six-groove, right-hand-twist rifling (Madis 1979:113). We found no bullets that could be identified as having been fired from a Winchester with this rifling. The Model 1873 Winchester also had five-groove, right-hand-twist rifling (Madis 1979:173). There were slight variations in the width and depth of the lands and grooves of the Model 1866s and Model 1873s during their production, with no variation in the rifling of the Henry.

We were able to identify the bullets that had been fired from the Henry or Winchester Model 1866 and Model 1873, but beyond that it was impossible to determine which model because of more than a hundred years of oxidation. Four of the bullets in this group have six-groove, left-hand-twist rifling marks (table 10) distinctive of a Colt revolver. The Colt Single Action Army Revolver Model 1872, a .44-caliber rimfire, has such rifling (Graham, Kopec, and Moore 1979:32).

There are five variations of bases and cannelures in the .44-caliber bullets: single cannelure, *H* cast in base; single cannelure, flat base; two cannelures, *H* cast in base; two cannelures, flat base; and three cannelures, raised base. Twenty-nine of the bullets were mushroomed or flattened on impact and their rifling marks could not be determined. FS583 has bone embedded in its mass. Cannelure distortion, caused by black-powder buildup in the bore, appears on a number of bullets. Repeated firing, twenty or thirty rounds, without cleaning the bore causes buildup to occur. It is not surprising to see this evidence on the Henry and Winchester battle-related bullets, and it is consistent with the cartridge-misfire evidence discussed previously. These two independent lines of evidence tend to support the contention that many of the repeating firearms used by the Indians were not clean or became fouled during the battle.

Winchester .44/40-Caliber

Fourteen cartridge cases of .44/40-caliber (FS108, 209, 643, 646, 1335, 1527, 1621, 1710, 1749, 1763, 1770, 1771, 1776, 1821) were found on the Custer battlefield and seven cases of this caliber were recovered on the Reno-Benteen defense site (FS2240, 2258, 2259, 2267, 4655, 4655, 4983). These brass cases are center-fire and were primed with the Winchester-Milbank primer (fig. 50i) The .44/40 cartridge was first introduced in 1873 along with the lever-action Model 1873 Winchester Repeating Rifle. Approximately 23,000 guns of this model had been shipped from the Winchester warehouse by the end of 1876, and all were .44/40-caliber (Madis 1979:132, 214). The Model 1873 was a great improvement over the Henry and Model 1866 because it had been adapted to handle the heavier center-fire cartridge, which could be reloaded. This model was produced in three variations: rifle, carbine, and musket.

One of the few references to specific weapons used during the battle is to Sitting Bull's being armed with a Winchester Model 1873 carbine and a .45-caliber revolver (Vestal 1952:161). The .44/40 was, and continues to be, a popular cartridge. It has seen wide use, and many different firearms were chambered for the cartridge. It is said the caliber has killed more game, big and small, and more men, good and bad, than any other cartridge manufactured (Barnes 1969:61). The firing-pin and extractor-mark analyses identified at least eight different .44/40-caliber firearms (table 7), with one used at both battle sites.

Colt and Smith and Wesson Schofield .45-Caliber

During the battle, the soldiers used the .45-caliber Colt Single Action Army Revolver Model 1873 or possibly a .45-caliber Smith and Wesson Schofield revolver. Twelve unfired Colt cartridges (fig. 53c) (table 11), eleven fired cases (fig. 53f) (table 11), and twenty-nine hollow-base bullets (fig. 53a) (table 11) were found on the Custer battle-field. Thirteen bullets were deformed by impact, and four have bone fragments embedded in the bullet mass (FS750, 991, 1324a, 4613). Two were found associated with

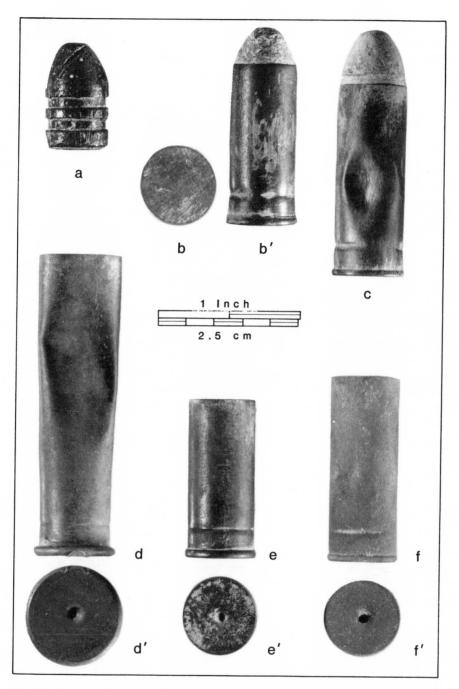

Fig. 53. Army revolver and carbine ammunition. a: A .45 Colt bullet. b, b′: A .45 Schofield cartridge. c: A Colt .45 cartridge. d, d′: A .45/55 carbine case. e, e′: A .45 Schofield case. f, f′: A .45 Colt case.

Table 11   Colt .45 Cartridges, Cases, and Bullets by Field-Specimen Number

Colt cartridges:

Custer Battlefield
197, 283, 314, 410, 444, 692, 856, 1049, 1050, 1396, 2578, 5025

Reno-Benteen Defense Site
2001, 2030, 2300, 2732, 2743, 2765, 2802, 2898, 2899, 3006, 3058, 3147, 3148, 3179, 3180, 3188, 3195, 3750, 3831, 3952, 4095, 4109, 4113, 4116, 4815, 4819, 4861, 4944

Colt cases:

Custer Battlefield
269, 381, 577, 578, 829, 1149, 1379, 1605, 4977, 4978, 4979

Reno-Benteen Defense Site
2094, 2315, 2353, 2616, 2625, 2660, 2798, 2800, 3063, 3099, 3101, 3139, 3146, 3960, 4023, 4035, 4037, 4038, 4148, 4325, 4758, 4830, 4988, 4990, 4991

Colt bullets:

Custer Battlefield
190, 347, 351, 377, 424, 513, 514, 542, 667, 672, 750, 945, 991, 1003, 1027, 1042, 1060, 1303, 1324, 1432, 1434, 1520, 1669, 1736, 1828, 4613, 5033, 5048

Reno-Benteen Defense Site (hollow-base bullets)
2090, 2168, 2216, 2230, 2491, 2531, 2592, 2613, 2695, 2749, 3022, 3028, 3033, 3042, 3076, 3141, 3695, 3717, 3827, 3843, 3860, 3996, 4121, 4175, 4417, 4765, 4933, 4950, 4954, 4955, 4993, 5009

Reno-Benteen Defense Site (solid-base bullets)
2750, 3122, 4387, 4947, 5005, 5008

excavation units; FS1324a was found during excavation at Marker 7 and FS4613 at Marker 128; both contained human bone. One unfired cartridge (fig. 53b) and one spent case (fig. 53e) for the .45-caliber Schofield were recovered (FS872, 147) on Custer battlefield. The Reno-Benteen defense site yielded twenty-eight unfired cartridges (table 11), twenty-five fired cartridge cases (table 11), thirty-one hollow-base bullets (table 11), and six solid-base bullets (table 11). One unfired cartridge (FS4815) had the upper part of the case torn away in order to remove the bullet, and in another cartridge (FS3831) the lead bullet has clear evidence of teeth marks. The marks may have been made in an unsuccessful attempt to remove the bullet. Six bullets were deformed by impact.

Firearm-identification analysis indicated the cases from the Custer battlefield were fired in eleven Colt revolvers. Twenty revolvers are represented by the cases from the Reno-Benteen defense site. The Smith and Wesson Schofield case was fired in a Colt revolver.

Springfield .45/55-Caliber

Thirty unfired cartridges (fig. 54e) of .45/55-caliber were found on the Custer battlefield and sixty at the Reno-Benteen defense site (table 12). These cartridges were used by the army in the Model 1873 Springfield carbine. This was the principal firearm

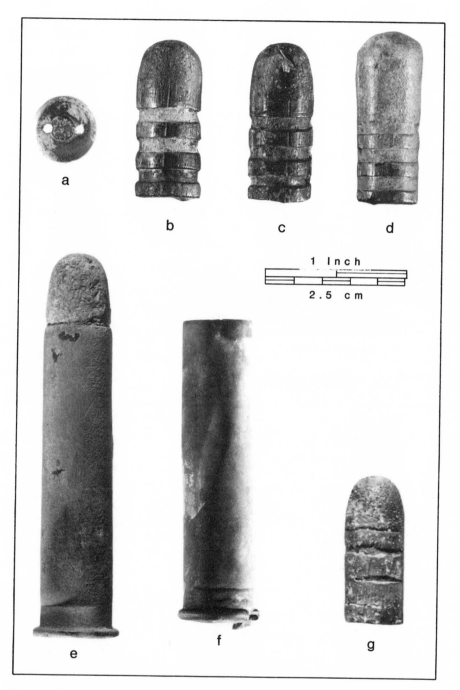

Fig. 54. Army carbine ammunition components. a: A Benét primer cup. b–d: Small, medium, and large base cavity .45/55 bullets. e: A .45/55 carbine cartridge. f: A .45/55 case with an example of extraction failure. g: A .45/55 bullet fired in a Sharps sporting rifle.

Table 12 Springfield Carbine Cartridges, Bullets, and Cartridge Cases by Field-Specimen Number

Unfired .45/55 Cartridges (90 specimens):

Custer Battlefield

228, 288, 349, 520, 569, 572, 584, 628, 629, 673, 691, 695, 729, 752, 919, 923, 942, 944, 1072, 1263, 1590, 1626, 1629, 1649, 1650, 1709, 1715, 1742, 1830, 1831

Reno-Benteen Defense Site

2115, 2316, 2321, 2324, 2482b, 2620, 2621, 2664, 2701, 2704, 2715, 2726, 2789, 2806, 2812, 2830, 2841, 2870, 2897, 2904, 3020, 3021, 3030, 3032, 3051, 3125, 3163b, 3163c, 3218, 3618, 3654, 3830, 3853, 3941, 3942, 3943, 3948, 3988, 4004, 4008, 4059, 4060, 4067, 4114, 4115, 4154, 4202, 4280, 4341, 4386, 4648, 4653, 4660, 4821, 4852, 4853, 4855, 4985, 4986, 5062

Cartridge cases (415 specimens):

Custer Battlefield

2, 72, 74, 80, 92, 99, 133, 135, 136, 148, 150, 175, 196, 199, 200, 226, 232, 238, 239, 240, 241, 242, 243, 244, 253, 264, 272, 273, 282, 309, 326, 334, 403, 447, 523, 533, 539, 560, 561, 562, 563, 626, 637, 643, 687, 700, 707, 712, 771, 870, 923, 948, 1046, 1112, 1271, 1291, 1345, 1377, 1380, 1381, 1390, 1530, 1532, 1535, 1537, 1538, 1539, 1540, 1541, 1548, 1549, 1550, 1551, 1552, 1555, 1582, 1583, 1584, 1603, 1604, 1614, 1651, 1701, 1730, 1764, 1765, 1813, 1819, 2580, 5049

Reno-Benteen Defense Site

2019, 2020, 2023, 2026, 2051, 2052, 2056, 2062, 2066, 2067, 2071, 2076, 2082, 2083, 2084, 2095, 2096, 2097, 2099, 2100, 2101, 2120, 2121, 2197, 2205, 2206, 2208, 2337, 2242, 2243, 2247, 2248, 2261, 2279, 2281, 2283, 2287, 2289, 2290, 2291, 2293, 2294, 2295, 2298, 2303, 2304, 2305, 2307, 2309, 2310, 2311, 2312, 2328, 2329, 2330, 2367, 2369, 2374, 2412, 2433, 2434, 2435, 2437, 2438, 2461, 2462, 2465, 2466, 2468, 2482a, 2482b, 2482c, 2482d, 2482e, 2482f, 2486, 2584, 2585, 2628, 2918, 2920, 2923, 2924, 2925, 2926, 2927, 2928, 2929, 2939, 2940, 2941, 2948, 2994, 2995, 2996, 2997, 2998, 2999, 3000, 3001, 3003, 3004, 3005, 3008, 3009a, 3011, 3012, 3016, 3025, 3050, 3056, 3057, 3137, 3138, 3163a, 3163b, 3163c, 3163d, 3163e, 3163f, 3163g, 3163h, 3163i, 3163j, 3163k, 3190, 3191, 3192, 3193, 3194, 3200, 3202, 3203, 3204, 3205, 3206, 3207, 3208, 3211, 3213, 3214, 3215, 3216, 3217, 3219, 3220, 3222, 3231, 3232, 3233, 3238, 3244, 3247, 3317, 3324, 3328, 3329, 3340, 3341, 3343, 3344, 3346, 3347, 3577, 3607, 3667, 3669, 3672, 3673, 3677, 3681, 3684, 3685, 3686, 3687, 3722, 3724, 3725, 3726, 3742, 3747, 3753, 3824, 3834, 3863, 3864, 3944, 3950, 3971, 3990, 3991, 3992, 3995, 3997, 3998, 4000, 4001, 4002, 4003, 4005, 4006, 4007, 4009, 4014, 4017, 4019, 4021, 4022, 4024, 4025, 4032, 4041, 4042, 4044, 4046, 4047, 4048, 4049, 4050, 4051, 4052, 4053, 4054, 4055, 4056, 4057, 4058, 4063, 4064, 4066, 4068, 4070, 4090, 4093, 4103, 4104, 4147, 4150, 4151, 4152, 4155, 4217, 4225, 4226, 4227, 4230, 4270, 4271, 4283, 4284, 4287, 4288, 4289, 4292a, 4295, 4296, 4306, 4308, 4309, 4312, 4313, 4319, 4320, 4321, 4322, 4362, 4364, 4367, 4403, 4625, 4632, 4636, 4651, 4674, 4683, 4742a, 4742b, 4742c, 4745, 4746, 4752, 4778, 4790, 4794, 4800, 4816, 4818, 4840, 4850, 4851, 4935, 4940, 4941, 4958, 4968, 4982, 4987, 4989, 4992, 4996, 5002, 5061

Large-cavity bullets (55 specimens):

Custer Battlefield

251, 287, 321, 345, 428, 431, 505, 506, 555, 576, 777, 841, 947, 963, 1034, 1045, 1061, 1070, 1147, 1157, 1161, 1203, 1238, 1249, 1340, 1433, 1579, 1689, 5014

Reno-Benteen Defense Site

2137, 2347, 2377, 2481, 2642, 2777, 2783, 3002, 3044, 3115, 3119, 3158, 3210, 3303, 3646, 3987, 4085, 4131, 4382, 4635, 4637, 4686, 4809, 4811, 4904, 4946

Medium-cavity bullets (118 specimens):

Custer Battlefield

16, 38, 51, 71, 78, 100, 101, 102, 143, 231, 237, 262, 281, 324, 384, 411, 443, 472, 527, 532, 570, 586, 588, 606, 615, 632, 641, 649, 654, 723, 744, 779, 791, 795, 807, 813, 831, 834, 839,

Table 12 *continued*

Medium-cavity bullets (118 specimens):

Custer Battlefield

853, 876, 877, 883, 885, 887, 889, 917, 980, 985, 995, 1036, 1079, 1109, 1139, 1140, 1178, 1207, 1266, 1287, 1305, 1353, 1358, 1362, 1373, 1391, 1400, 1404, 1429, 1571, 1580, 1585, 1600, 1606, 1687, 1712, 1716, 1723, 1724, 1738, 1780, 1784, 1789, 1790, 1798, 1832, 1857, 5015, 5046

Reno-Benteen Defense Site

2138, 2169, 2212, 2371, 2492, 2537, 2557, 2850, 2980a, 3274, 3636, 3696, 3712, 3812, 3932, 4089, 4128, 4141, 4173, 4204, 4214, 4302, 4615, 4624, 4673, 4774, 4833, 4943, 5006

Small-cavity bullets (511 specimens):

Custer Battlefield

32, 140, 340, 383, 390, 430, 433, 445, 483, 488, 492, 732, 827, 850, 636, 854, 862, 867, 967, 1074, 1080, 1086, 1087, 1171, 1250, 1361, 1634, 1791, 2571, 2572, 2574, 5023, 5035, 5039, 5040, 5041, 5044, 5045, 5047, 5050

Reno-Benteen Defense Site

2009, 2012, 2013, 2014, 2016, 2024, 2033, 2078, 2091, 2103, 2118, 2119, 2122, 2124, 2125, 2132, 2134, 2136, 2141, 2142, 2143, 2144, 2145, 2147, 2150, 2151, 2158, 2159, 2164, 2165, 2166, 2167, 2170, 2173, 2174, 2176, 2178, 2179, 2182, 2183, 2187, 2188, 2190, 2191, 2193, 2194, 2195, 2191, 2202, 2209, 2210, 2213, 2214, 2215, 2217, 2222, 2225, 2254, 2301, 2318, 2319, 2322, 2325, 2331, 2338, 2339, 2340, 2341, 2345, 2349, 2350, 2352, 2354, 2356, 2360, 2372, 2375, 2379, 2380, 2382, 2384, 2386, 2390, 2394, 2395, 2402, 2403, 2405, 2407, 2408, 2408, 2411, 2413, 2414, 2423, 2424, 2428, 2443, 2443, 2448, 2454, 2455, 2456, 2458, 2460, 2476, 2484, 2488, 2490, 2493, 2498, 2500, 2511, 2517, 2522, 2528, 2532, 2533, 2536, 2539, 2540, 2542, 2548, 2552, 2553, 2555, 2583, 2587, 2588, 2590, 2598, 2618, 2623, 2624, 2629, 2632, 2634, 2638, 2697, 2705, 2709, 2710, 2727, 2730, 2731, 2734, 2736, 2738, 2745, 2748, 2752, 2756, 2759, 2762, 2763, 2764, 2768, 2769, 2770, 2771, 2773, 2790, 2795, 2818, 2826, 2831, 2833, 2834a, 2837, 2856, 2868, 2875, 2882, 2883, 2885, 2886, 2900, 2912, 2933, 2934, 2966, 2982, 2986, 2989, 2990, 2992, 2993, 3028, 3052, 3053, 3066, 3070, 3075, 3085, 3092b, 3093b, 3108, 3110, 3111, 3112, 3116, 3117, 3118, 3120, 3124, 3127, 3128, 3129, 3132, 3133, 3145, 3156, 3160, 3161, 3164, 3165, 3166, 3174, 3182, 3183, 3184, 3185, 3197, 3209, 3212, 3223, 3228, 3233, 3242, 3250, 3265, 3266, 3267, 3269, 3271, 3275, 3277, 3285, 3286, 3292, 3301, 3304, 3305, 3313, 3315, 3326, 3320, 3330, 3331, 3332, 3333, 3334, 3335, 3337, 3338, 3342, 3576, 3579, 3592, 3593, 3595, 3596, 3599, 3601, 3603, 3604, 3609, 3610, 3615, 3616, 3619, 3620, 3624, 3630, 3632, 3633, 3637, 3638, 3639, 3640, 3641, 3643, 3645, 3649, 3655, 3658, 3663, 3665, 3675, 3678, 3690, 3691, 3692, 3694, 3699, 3700, 3706, 3707, 3708, 3711, 3721, 3727, 3746, 3763, 3771, 3813, 3815, 3816, 3819, 3822, 3825, 3823, 3826, 3829, 3835, 3841, 3844, 3850, 3851, 3852, 3855, 3857, 3861, 3865, 3922, 3926, 3927, 3931, 3946, 3954, 3956, 3969, 3970, 3999, 4029, 4030, 4037, 4043, 4045, 4071, 4073, 4075, 4082, 4084, 4101, 4110, 4111, 4117, 4123, 4125, 4127, 4133, 4139, 4140, 4142, 4143, 4144, 4153, 4156, 4158, 4159, 4160, 4161, 4162, 4165, 4166, 4167, 4170, 4178, 4179, 4180, 4203, 4205, 4208, 4209, 4211, 4212, 4263, 4265, 4266, 4268, 4269, 4275, 4293, 4307, 4310, 4317, 4323, 4366, 4372, 4376, 4379, 4385, 4388, 4616, 4618, 4622, 4627, 4628, 4629, 4633, 4634, 4638, 4640, 4641, 4681, 4685, 4689, 4691, 4692, 4707, 4710, 4731, 4736, 4739, 4740, 4741, 4753, 4759, 4762, 4773, 4782, 4789, 4791, 4795, 4801, 4804, 4808, 4822, 4823, 4834, 4841, 4842, 4847, 4848, 4854, 4857, 4859, 4862, 4866, 4871, 4875, 4906, 4907, 4908, 4910, 4913, 4915, 4920, 4923, 4925, 4926, 4928, 4930, 4931, 4932, 4936, 4938, 4939, 4949, 4959, 4960, 4961, 4963, 4964, 4965, 4994, 4995, 5007, 5065

Miscellaneous and deformed bullets (9 specimens):

Custer Battlefield

375, 605, 1177, 1627, 2148

Reno-Benteen Defense Site

2189, 2564, 2838, 3196

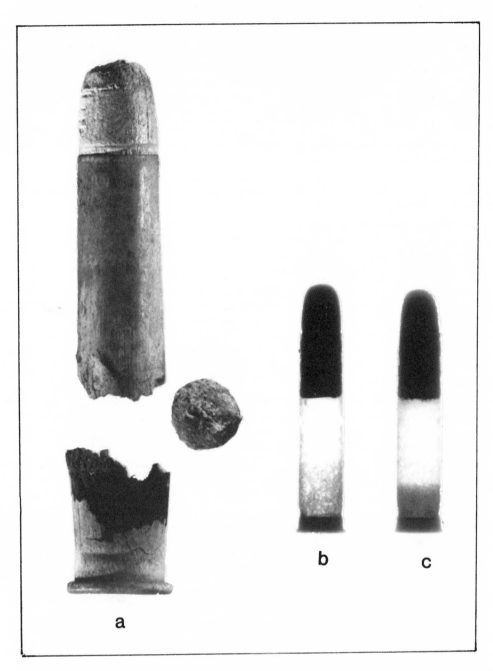

Fig. 55. Army carbine ammunition. a: A .45/55 cartridge and pasteboard wad. b: Radiograph of a .45/55 cartridge with wads in place. c: Radiograph of a .45/55 cartridge with a tube liner.

used by the soldiers at the battle. The .45/55 carbine cartridge does not differ from the .45/70 rifle cartridge, issued to the infantry, except that the case was filled with only fifty-five grains of black powder. In order to keep the smaller powder volume compacted, ordnance personnel developed a wad for the carbine load (fig. 55a). Later experiments used a cardboard tube liner in place of the wad (War Department 1875). Remnants of several liners were noted in the laboratory. All were too disintegrated to preserve. In addition, all unfired rounds were radiographed to determine whether any were rifle rounds. All ninety rounds were identified as carbine by the presence of either the wad (fig. 55b) or tube liner (fig. 55c). Only three rounds exhibited evidence of the tube liner (FS673, 3654, 4852).

One cartridge (FS919) is particularly interesting. The primer end of the case is missing, and the case below the head is crushed and split (fig. 32). The cartridge appears to have been struck by a bullet. It is tempting to speculate that this cartridge was in a soldier's cartridge or thimble belt and was hit by a bullet fired by an Indian attacker. Another cartridge (FS923) also appears to have been struck by a bullet. The mouth and upper third of the case were ripped apart by an external force, probably a bullet, causing the metal to be folded outward. Since the two cartridges were found in close association on the ground, they may have been hit at the same time, perhaps by the same bullet.

In addition to the cartridges, 90 fired cases for the .45/55 Springfield carbine were found on the Custer battlefield and 326 on the Reno-Benteen defense site (table 12). The cases (fig. 53d) and cartridges are Benét internally primed with a wide basal crimp and have no headstamp.

One hundred sixty .45/55 bullets from the Custer battlefield and 528 bullets from the Reno-Benteen defense site were found in three varieties (fig. 54a, b, c). All have three cannelures, but the bases have three different cavity sizes: large, medium, and small (table 12). There are also seven deformed bullets that could not be sorted to a specific cavity variety . These bullets, as well as 81 others from the Custer battlefield and 144 from Reno-Benteen, were deformed on impact. One of the Reno-Benteen bullets (FS3092b), found associated with horse bone, had bone fragments embedded in its mass. All these types are from government-arsenal swagings or from government-contract production (Lewis 1972). Two bullets found in the hospital-swale area of the Reno-Benteen defense site, had been modified; their tips are carved to a point (FS2634, 3160). Both appear to have been carved before firing. The bullets were probably fired from captured Custer carbines by the warriors. Whether the carving was done by one of the Custer command or by a warrior who retrieved the ammunition is not known. However, similar examples of carved bullets are known from nineteenth-century military installations (Scott 1973) and from Civil War−period battlefields (McKee and Mason 1980). The carving or whittling is thought to represent opportunistic recreational activity.

There is one .45-caliber bullet in the group from the Custer battlefield which is a 500-grain specimen (FS2148). This bullet type was not produced by the army until several years after the battle. The bullet is probably associated with postbattle activities, such as the reburials, administration of the national cemetery, hunting, or target shooting. One bullet from the Reno-Benteen defense site (FS2564) has the land-and-groove marks of a Sharps sporting rifle (fig. 54g). The bullet was found embedded on the south

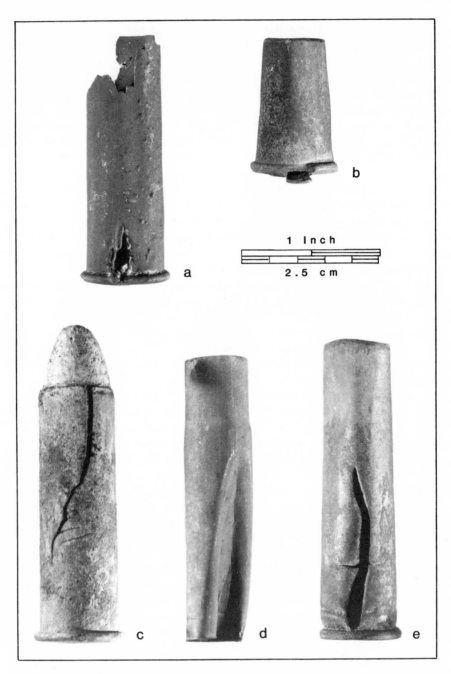

Fig. 56. Large-caliber Indian cartridge cases. a: A .50/70 case with a gouge in the body caused by prying. b: A .56/50 Spencer case with evidence of extraction failure. c: A .50/70 cartridge. d: A .45/55 carbine case fired in a .50/70 that expanded and lost its head in firing. The case was crushed to remove it from the weapon. e: A .45/55 case which has expanded and split when fired in a .50/70.

flank of Sharpshooter Ridge (Wooden Leg Hill). Sergeant John Ryan used a .45-caliber Sharps sporting rifle with a tubular sight to fire at an Indian sharpshooter in the vicinity of this hill. This bullet may represent one of Sergeant Ryan's shots at the warrior.

Five fired cases from the Custer battlefield and eight from Reno-Benteen are distinctly different from the other .45/55 cases. These thirteen were fired in a weapon larger than a .45-caliber. The cases have expanded to approximately caliber .50. Twelve have ruptured (fig. 56e) or split lengthwise (FS378, 566, 1281, 1285, 1732, 2025, 2027, 2060, 2070, 2081, 2260, 2361, 5064) from being fired in the larger diameter chamber. With the exception of FS2081 and FS2361, all were fired in a .50-caliber Sharps. The exceptions were fired in Springfield weapons. FS1336 was fired in a .50-caliber gun, but it did not rupture. However, the head of the case was blown off, and the case was crushed along one side (fig 56d), apparently to extract it from the weapon. All five Custer battlefield expanded cases were found with Indian-associated cartridge cases. They appear to be army cartridges which were fired in larger caliber .50/70 Sharps weapons used by the Indians. This group of cases represents four separate guns. Case FS1732 was fired in the same gun as FS1299.

The Reno-Benteen defense site ruptured cases were found in locations historically associated with Indian positions and with Indian-associated cartridges. Seven separate guns, two Springfields and five Sharps, were identified during the firearm-identification analysis. Only two cases were fired from the same gun (FS2027, 2070), both in a Sharps.

An examination of firing-pin and extractor-marks indicates that at least 70 of the more than 200 Springfield carbines present at the Custer battlefield and 60 of the Reno-Benteen defense site carbines are represented in the archaeological collections (table 7). This means cartridge cases representing about one-third of the Custer battlefield carbines and 17.1 percent of the Reno-Benteen carbines were recovered during the investigations.

Five Benét primers (FS553, 1275, 1311, 1401, 1871) from the Custer battlefield and two (FS2061, 2073) from the Reno-Benteen defense site were also found. These loose primers (fig. 54a) were evidently dislodged from their cartridge cases by the force of the explosion that sent the bullet on its way. These primers are the distinctive cup shape, with two holes in the body designed to transmit the flash of the primer charge to the black-powder propellant. The primers are identical to those illustrated and described by Lewis (1972).

Unidentified .45-Caliber Bullets

There are two .45-caliber bullets from the Custer battlefield that could not be associated with any specific type of firearm. The bullets are flat nosed with three knurled cannelures (FS470, 1703).

Spencers

The Spencer carbine was a military firearm used during the Civil War and the early Indian Wars. It was also produced in civilian models, was widely available, and was a popular weapon. The two calibers of Spencers found were produced for both the military and the commercial markets (Barnes 1969:281; Gluckman 1965:388). Eight cartridge cases from the Custer battlefield representing two different calibers of Spencer rimfire ammunition were found during the inventory.

Two cases represent caliber .56/50 Spencer carbines (FS1257, 1277). Of these, one has a raised-H headstamp (FS1277) denoting Winchester manufacture; the other case is not headstamped (fig. 50j). The remaining six cases (FS6, 1056, 1290, 1295, 1297, 1298) are from caliber .56/56 carbines. Only one is headstamped, and this one is with a *U* (FS1290) denoting Union Metallic Arms Company manufacture. This company began business in 1867 (Logan 1959). One of the nonheadstamped cases (FS1298) was torn on the edge (fig. 56b) by the carbine's extractor when the case was extracted from the weapon. Only one identifiable Spencer bullet (fig. 52a) was recovered during the inventory of the Custer battlefield. It is a .50-caliber variety (FS1200). Three .50-caliber Spencer bullets were found at the Reno-Benteen defense site. One type is a flat-base bullet with a crimping groove high on the shoulder. The two bullets in this type (FS2453, 3297) have impressions of Spencer six-land-and-groove rifling. The third bullet (FS4905) has a raised base with three lubricating cannelures. This bullet also has six lands and grooves. Undoubtedly a number of other .50-caliber bullets were fired in Spencers; however, most Spencers were rifled to arsenal specifications of three lands and grooves. Most U.S. military .50-caliber shoulder weapons of this period were rifled to those same specifications, so it is very difficult to determine weapon type from bullets with three-land-and-groove imprints.

Firing-pin and extractor-mark analysis indicates at least two .56/50 Spencers were present at the battle. At least two .56/56 Spencers were also used (table 7).

Unidentified .50-Caliber Rimfire Case

A single .56/50-caliber rimfire Spencer case (FS644) with an as-yet unidentified block firing-pin imprint was found. The case is the standard Spencer cartridge case with a raised-H headstamp. The rectangular firing-pin imprint has not been identified and associated with a specific firearm type.

Caliber .50/70

The .50/70 cartridge (fig. 56c) was developed for the army's first servicewide adoption of a cartridge weapon. The round was used in various Springfield rifles and carbines from 1866 to 1873. It was also a very popular commercial cartridge, with Sharps, Remington, and other arms manufacturers chambering single-shot firearms for this caliber (Logan 1959). The army also had 33,734 Sharps percussion weapons converted to fire .50/70 cartridges (Sellers 1978:181–82).

Thirty-nine cartridge cases of caliber .50/70 were recovered from the Custer battlefield in 1984 (Scott and Fox 1987). Three additional cases (FS5051, 5054, 5058) were recovered there in 1985 and nine cases (FS2005, 2021, 2550, 2551, 2796, 2880, 3201, 4814a, 4844) were found on the Reno-Benteen defense site. The specimens represent five different primer types (Lewis 1972). The first are U.S. government–issue internally (Benét) primed cases (fig. 57c) (FS222, 1557, 1595, 1610, 1772, 1792,

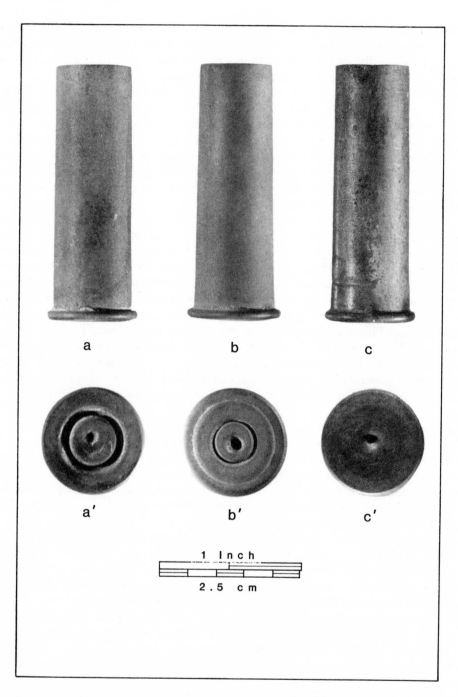

Fig. 57. .50/70 cartridge cases. a, a′ Martin-primed. b, b′: UMC-primed. c, c′: Benét-primed. Note the off-center firing-pin marks, which indicate that these cases were fired in side-hammer firearms.

1809, 2005, 2021, 2796, 2880, 4814a, 5058). In the second group are Springfield Arsenal Martin-primed cases (fig. 57a) (FS59, 1308, 1599, 1602, 1607, 1755, 5051, 5054). Third are the Winchester-Millbank–primed brass cases (FS599, 1067, 1546, 1845), and fourth are the Union Metallic Arms Company–primed (fig. 57b) brass cases (FS73, 94, 185, 229, 311, 348, 647, 769, 1258, 1272, 1273, 1279, 1289c, 1299, 1334, 1337, 1407, 1447, 1556, 1568, 1717, 2550, 2551). Fifth are U.S. government-issue internally (bar) primed cases (FS3201, 4844).

Examination of the extractor marks on each case clearly indicates twenty-eight of the .50/70 cases from the Custer battlefield had been fired in Sharps or Remington guns, and twelve were fired in Springfield rifles, probably the obsolete army Models 1866, 1868, and 1870. Of the Reno-Benteen defense-site cases, three were fired in Sharps or Remington guns and seven in Springfields.

Two cases (FS1407, 1607) from the Custer battlefield and one case (FS2021) from the Reno-Benteen defense site, which were fired in Springfields, show evidence of having been pried from the guns. One case (FS5054) fired in a Sharps on the Custer battlefield also showed evidence of extraction failure (fig. 56a). Copper cartridge cases expand slightly when fired, and occasionally a case expands to such a degree it fails to extract properly. Apparently this was the situation with these four cases. When they did not eject, the person using the gun utilized a sharp object, probably a knife, to remove the spent case. This prying left marks on the edge of the case head. These are clearly discernible during microscopic examination. FS1407 was also gouged and ripped when it was pried from its weapon. The case from the Reno-Benteen defense site (FS2021) had the head blown during firing and the case was crushed in an attempt to extract it from the gun. Firing-pin marks indicate the pried cartridges were all fired in different guns.

Three slightly longer than average .50/70 cases (FS1273, 1334, 1337), all with UMC-type primers, expanded and split when they were fired. Incidentally, all three were fired in the same gun. Union Metallic Arms Company and E. Remington and Sons manufactured some rounds for the .50/70 that were three millimeters longer than the government arsenal–manufactured rounds (Hoyem 1982:50). It is possible that drawing of the extra length case during its manufacture weakened the metal, causing it to split with the stress of being fired.

The firing-pin and extractor-mark analysis of all cases fired in .50/70s, including the thirteen .45/55 ruptured cases, indicate that at least forty-eight .50/70 caliber weapons were used during the battle (table 7). At least thirteen weapons were Springfield .50/70s, and the others were Sharps or Remingtons. Thirty-three of the .50/70s were used on the Custer battlefield, of which six were Springfields. Fifteen different .50/70s were used at the Reno-Benteen defense site; seven were Springfields.

Twenty-five brass .50/70 cartridge cases were found. Twenty-three cases were found on the Custer battlefield and two at the Reno-Benteen defense site. These cases were fired in one Springfield at Reno-Benteen and fifteen different Sharps or Remingtons and two different Springfields on the Custer battlefield.

The collection also contains two unfired rounds of .50/70 UMC-primed ammunition (FS1251, 1671) from the Custer battlefield and one (FS4100) from Reno-Benteen. . The Reno-Benteen defense site also yielded two unfired rounds of Benét-primed ammunition (FS2617a, b) and two rounds of bar-primed (FS2645, 3198).

Table 13 Caliber .50/70 Bullets by Field-Specimen Number and Type

Cadet, two cannelures with hole in base (4 specimens):

Custer Battlefield
43, 55, 1713

Reno-Benteen Defense Site
3062

Dimick experimental, two cannelures with flat base (9 specimens):

Custer Battlefield
105, 1721, 1737, 1807, 1817, 5034

Reno-Benteen Defense Site
3289, 4083, 4860

Experimental with deepened cannelures, three cannelures with small raised base (20 specimens):

Custer Battlefield
226, 276, 463, 663, 838, 1153

Reno-Benteen Defense Site
2376, 2431, 2447, 2449, 2563, 2894, 2896, 3224, 3314, 3622, 3642, 3845, 4281, 4696

Experimental paper patched, three cannelures with large raised base (22 specimens):

Custer Battlefield
149, 434, 1044, 1731, 1806

Reno-Benteen Defense Site
2370, 2392, 2497, 2558, 2594, 2615, 2637, 2952, 2974, 2984, 3175, 3255, 3261, 3273, 3350, 4644, 4916

Experimental with extra tin added, three cannelures with flat base (95 specimens)

Custer Battlefield
75, 76, 344, 826, 913, 1734, 1747, 1787

Reno-Benteen Defense Site
2035, 2172, 2218, 2220, 2336, 2364, 2469, 2470, 2480, 2504, 2509, 2521, 2547, 2561, 2591, 2640, 2648, 2667, 2708, 2746, 2758, 2761, 2776, 2797, 2805, 2893, 2931, 2932, 2946, 3094, 3106, 3109, 3123, 3140, 3151, 3153, 3168, 3170, 3186, 3240, 3241, 3246, 3164, 3272, 3276, 3282, 3316, 3575, 3612, 3627, 3647, 3656, 3697, 3716, 3774, 3817, 3836, 3842, 3847, 3867, 3924, 3945, 4207, 4213, 4215, 4218, 4222, 4223, 4292, 4639, 4656, 4617, 4737, 4743, 4751, 4763, 4785, 4787, 4792, 4805, 4807, 4924, 4937, 4951, 4952, 4966, 4976

Standard issue, three cannelures with small hole in base (91 specimens):

Custer Battlefield
13, 45, 53, 54, 195, 338, 407, 409, 414, 620, 630, 787, 833, 925, 1053, 1059, 1075, 1130, 1394, 1408, 1655, 1746, 1762, 1779, 1816, 5012, 5013

Reno-Benteen Defense Site
2140, 2253, 2348, 2463, 2478, 2508, 2538, 2544, 2589, 2593, 2636, 2643, 2644, 2740, 2742, 2753, 2863, 2901, 2902, 2903, 2907, 2921, 2942, 2978, 3069, 3077, 3178, 3187, 3227, 3253, 3259, 3268, 3296, 3302, 3594, 3597, 3614, 3626, 3648, 3668, 3704, 3720, 3814, 3849, 3856, 3923, 3929, 4013, 4081, 4174, 4181, 4356, 4697, 4771, 4775, 4776, 4788, 4820, 4846, 4909, 4919, 4922, 4975, 5010

Knurled cannelure, three knurled cannelures with small hole in base (9 specimens):

Custer Battlefield
15, 22, 585, 662, 1081, 1236, 1398, 1672, 1801

The .50/70s were one of the largest categories of bullets recovered. There are seven varieties of bullets from .50/70s in the collection. Undoubtedly, the sixty-five bullets from the Custer battlefield and the 229 from the Reno-Benteen defense site represent individual manufacturers' castings, swagings, experiments, or preference in design of bullets. Several types represent the army's experimental attempts to find a more satisfactory bullet during the first years of the wide use of self-contained cartridges. Most bullets (table 13) in the collection are a three-cannelure type, with only minor variations (fig. 52b, c, e, d, g) denoting them as a separate type. One small group has only two cannelures. These bullets represent rounds meant for use in the Cadet Model .50/70 musket and an experimental bullet known as a Dimick. The others are an experimental bullet with the cannelure deepened to hold more lubricant, bullets which had been paper patched, and a bullet that had extra tin added for hardness (Lewis 1972:28). The single most common .50/70 bullet is the one used in most of the standard-issue cartridges up to 1868 (Lewis 1972:28). Another type of bullet is very similar to the standard-issue bullet except that it has a knurled cannelure.

Twenty-five bullets from the Custer battlefield and eighty-three from the Reno-Benteen defense site were deformed to varying degrees as they struck objects. Several bullets have gouges or grooves on their surface that were caused by striking bone. One bullet from the Custer battlefield (fig. 52g) and one from Reno-Benteen had unidentified fragments of bone embedded in them, and two Reno-Benteen bullets contained embedded rock fragments. The majority of bullets had imprints of three-land-and groove rifling. These rifling marks could have been made by any number of military-issue .50-caliber weapons, such as the Springfield, Spencer, Sharps, Remington, or Maynard rifles and carbines. Land-and-groove marks could not be obtained on six specimens, while eight others retained the distinctive six-land-and-groove marks of the Sharps sporting rifle (fig. 52h).

Maynard

One .50-caliber Maynard bullet (FS1735) (fig. 51k) was found on the Custer battlefield. The single-shot percussion Maynard was an obsolete weapon by 1876, but it did see service during the Civil War (Gluckman 1965:342).

Miscellaneous and Unidentified .50-Caliber Bullets

The Reno-Benteen defense site yielded five different varieties of .50-caliber bullets. Thirteen bullets (FS2774, 2861, 2906, 3306, 3628, 3651, 3710, 3820, 3925, 3930, 3933, 4672, 4905) are a three-cannelure, raised-base type. Most of these bullets have a nondistinctive three-land-and-groove impression on them; however, two are more distinctive. One (FS4904) has the Spencer six-land-and-groove pattern. The other (FS2861) has the left-hand-twist, five-land-and-groove pattern of a Remington sporting rifle (fig. 52d). Seven bullets were damaged on impact.

Another type has a single wide cannelure at the base (FS2430, 3226, 3602) and is distinctive of the Smith carbine (fig. 51h). One of the three bullets had been damaged on impact. Five cast bullets (FS2029, 4079, 4112, 4374, 4645) with two wide cannelures and a flat base have the distinctive six-land-and-groove pattern of a Sharps. Four of these five bullets were deformed on impact.

The final two types are each represented by two bullets. One type is a flat-based bullet with a single crimping groove low on the bullet body (FS2406, 2559). One specimen (FS2559) was damaged on impact and has fabric impressions on the base. Both bullets have non-distinctive three-land-and-groove imprints. The other type is flat based with two cannelures (FS3172, 4784). One specimen was damaged on impact and the other (FS4784) has fabric impressions on its base.

Starr

One .54-caliber Starr (FS041) (fig. 51i) bullet was recovered from the Custer battlefield. The single-shot percussion Starr was used in the Civil War and to a limited degree on the frontier during and after the war. It was an obsolete arm by 1876 (Gluckman 1965:354).

Enfield

A single .577-caliber Enfield bullet (FS1781) (fig. 51j) from the Custer battlefield was found. The bullet could have been fired in any number of muzzle-loading weapons of .577-caliber or larger. The bullet, which has cloth-patch impressions on its base, was meant for the British Tower or Enfield rifle-musket. Both guns were imported in large quantities during the Civil War (Gluckman 1965). The bullet diameter also allows it to fit a .58-caliber U.S.-type musket as well. Whether the bullet represents an Enfield in Indian hands, some other trade musket, or an obsolete U.S. musket is uncertain.

Round Balls .44-, .45-, and .50-Caliber

Round balls were usually fired in muzzle-loading firearms, which were considered obsolete by 1876. However, muzzle-loading weapons continued in use across the country for many years because of their wide availability and low price. Indians, as well as others, enjoyed the use of these weapons because where a cartridge of the appropriate caliber could not always be found, powder and ball were easily obtainable, if not from commercial sources, then by disassembling a cartridge for its components. Any lead bullet could be reformed into a usable projectile by hammering or recasting in an appropriately sized mold.

There are fourteen .44- to .45-caliber round balls from the Custer battlefield (FS52, 62, 66, 352, 1016, 1220, 1284, 1324b, 1399, 1645, 1683, 1702, 2586, 5080). Nine balls have a distinctive band around them, which resulted from being fired from a gun with a very tight-fitting bore (FS62, 352, 1016, 1220, 1284, 1399, 1683, 2586). Eight balls were deformed on impact. Rifling marks were indistinct on most of these balls, but three different weapon types could be distinguished. One ball had been fired from a Remington revolver (FS1016), one in a Colt revolver (FS1702), and two (FS66, 1220) in an unidentified gun with very wide lands and grooves.

Four other balls were recovered from the Reno-Benteen defense site (FS2180, 2494,

3291, 3840). One (FS2494) has fabric impressions on one surface. The impressions are not distinct enough to determine whether the mark resulted from a cloth patch or from striking a cloth-covered target. Another ball (FS3291) has unidentified bone embedded in its mass. Two balls were deformed by impact.

There are fifteen .50-caliber balls from the Custer battlefield (FS252, 535, 575, 670, 830, 844, 1063, 1378, 1684, 1744, 1745, 1800, 1818, 5029, 5030). Six balls are somewhat unique; FS1745, 1800, and 1818 have bands around them like those found in the .45-caliber group, FS1744 has been deformed by hammering before being fired, and FS535 and 670 have cloth impressions on one surface. It is possible FS1744 represents a larger ball hammered down to fit the bore of a particular gun. Five balls were slightly deformed on impact.

Twenty-five .50-caliber balls (FS2133, 2160, 2250, 2184, 2429, 2452, 2483, 2530, 2647, 3043, 3061, 3073, 3181, 3256, 3281, 3349, 3635, 3679, 3805, 3936, 4169, 4329, 4619, 4750, 4956) were found at the Reno-Benteen defense site. Thirteen balls in the group were deformed on impact, two balls (FS2452, 3181) have fabric impressions on one surface, and one (FS4619) has a band around it like the .45-caliber balls.

Shot

Nine pieces of shot from shotguns or buck-and-ball loads were found on Custer battlefield. FS475 is a piece of .407-inch diameter iron shot, while the others are lead shot of different sizes. These are #00 shot, FS258; #1 shot, FS975; #4 shot, FS952, 1010, 1133, 1677, 1678; and #6 shot, FS1873.

Three pieces of iron shot were recovered from the Reno-Benteen defense site. They each represent a different shot size; #1 (FS2788), B shot (FS3046), and #3 (FS4967).

Very few references are found regarding Indian warriors armed with shotguns. However, Yellowstone Kelly ran into a band of Prairie Gros Ventres (Big Bellies) armed with Henry rifles and double-barreled shotguns (Kelly 1926:205). We have also examined the stock and locks of a double-barreled percussion shotgun in a private collection; it was found on the Custer battlefield in 1881.

Deformed Bullets, Balls, and Lead Scraps

Within the collection from the Custer battlefield are thirty-seven deformed bullets and balls and fifteen scraps of lead which probably represent fragments of bullets fired during the battle. All are too deformed or fragmentary to identify, but they definitely represent bullets that struck something, causing them to become deformed or to splinter. Soft-lead or unalloyed bullets are known to deform more on impact than alloyed bullets, and that is the case with these bullets. Soft-lead bullets are also known to splinter when they strike bone (DeHaan 1983), and this is clearly exhibited in several of these specimens. Three deformed bullets are somewhat unique. FS389 exhibits impressions of cloth on one surface, and FS699 and FS4406 have fragments of bone embedded in their masses. The origin of the impressions and bone could not be ascertained. Deformed bullets and balls from the Custer battlefield are represented by FS137, 155, 310, 317, 389, 394, 549, 689, 699, 719, 722, 726, 824, 874, 921, 930, 932, 940,

1054, 1062, 1182, 1190, 1196, 1197, 1370, 1405, 1625, 1631, 1643, 1688, 1729, 1827, 1849, 4406, 4409, 4614, and 5024. Lead scraps are represented by FS235, 245, 266, 284, 373, 439, 579, 682, 745, 972, 1026, 1125, 1187, 1617, 1618, and 1833.

Sixteen bullets from the Reno-Benteen defense site are too deformed to identify. They are FS2011, 2123, 2200, 2410, 2425, 2729, 2741, 3031, 3060, 3098, 3574, 3734, 3735, 4034, and 4228. One bullet (FS3574) contained unidentified bone in its mass.

Case Fragments

Two fragments of copper cartridge cases are in the collection: FS871 and 1057. They are not identifiable to caliber or weapon.

Post-Battle Ammunition

Randomly scattered across the Custer battlefield and the Reno-Benteen defense site were 238 cartridges, cases, and bullets which are not associated with the battle. These ammunition components postdate the battle. They represent later hunting activities, incidental shooting activities, salute firing, and battle reenactments. The cartridge-case headstamps and the metal alloys used in manufacturing the components date the artifacts to the post-battle era.

Caliber .22

There are four varieties of .22-caliber cases in the collection. There are three .22 CB cases with an acorn headstamp. There are four .22 short cases, twenty-six .22 long cases, three .22 Remington Special cases, and one .22 Magnum case. There is one .22 long cartridge. Aside from the acorn headstamp, the other cases are stamped with H for Winchester, U for Union Metallic Cartridge Company, US for United States Cartridge Company, P for Peters Cartridge Company, Super X for Western Cartridge Company, and HP and F for Federal Cartridge Company. The collection also contains nineteen .22-caliber bullets.

Caliber .222

There is one .222 Remington cartridge case headstamped REM-UMC for Remington Union Metallic Cartridge Company. Four .222-caliber bullets are also present.

Caliber .243 Winchester

One .243 Winchester case is headstamped R-P for Remington Peters.

Caliber .250/300 Savage

Two .250 Savage cases were found. One is headstamped Super Speed for Winchester Repeating Arms Company and the other is stamped Savage for Savage Arms Company.

Caliber .25/20

Four .25/20 cases headstamped WRACO were recovered. The headstamp denotes Winchester Repeating Arms Company manufacture. Six .25-caliber bullets were also found.

Caliber .30/06

Three commercial .30/06 cases were found. They are headstamped W-W Super (Western Cartridge Company), REM-UMC (Remington Union Metallic Cartridge Company), and R-P (Remington Peters). In addition, six military headstamped blank cases were found near the national cemetery. These cases have military headstamps indicating they were manufactured between 1942 and 1954. Twenty-four copper-jacketed .30/06 bullets were recovered.

Caliber .30/30

Three .30/30 cases were recovered. All are headstamped REM-UMC.

Caliber 30/40 (Krag)

One .30/40 case was recovered. It is also headstamped REM-UMC. Four .30-caliber bullets were recovered. Rifling marks were not distinctive enough to determine whether the bullets were fired in a .30/30- or a .30/40-caliber gun.

Caliber .32 Winchester Center-Fire

One .32-caliber case, headstamped WRACO for Winchester Repeating Arms Company, was found. Four .32-caliber bullets were also recovered.

Caliber .32/40

Two .32/40 cases were found. Both are headstamped WRACO.

Caliber .38 Smith and Wesson

Eight cases for the .38-caliber Smith and Wesson pistol were recovered. Two cases have no headstamps and the others are stamped WRACO.

Caliber .38 Special

One wad-cutter cartridge for the .38 Special was found and is headstamped R-P. Three .38-caliber bullets were found, as were ten .38-caliber semiwad-cutter and wad-cutter bullets.

Caliber .38 Colt

Three cases for the .38 Colt were found. Two are headstamped WRACO, and the other case is stamped with military markings denoting a May 1893 manufacturing date.

Caliber .38/55

One .38/55 case was found and is headstamped Peters for Peters Cartridge Company.

Caliber .38/56

One .38/56 case was recovered, and it is headstamped WRACO.

Caliber .44/40

Five .44/40 cases were found. Three are headstamped WRACO and one is stamped Peters. One copper-jacketed .44/40-caliber bullet was found.

Caliber .45 Auto Rim

One .45 Auto Rim case was found, as were three .45-caliber copper-jacketed bullets.

Caliber .45 Colt

Six .45 Colt cases are in the collection. Two are headstamped UMC, one REM-UMC, and three have no headstamps. The non-headstamped cases are brass with brass primers.

Caliber .45/70

Fifty .45/70 cartridge cases were recovered which postdate the battle. Ten cases are headstamped R-P, two W-W, and four have no headstamps. Three nonheadstamped cases are flat and one is slightly domed. These four cases are copper and could date from the battle period. Their archaeological context suggests they were deposited sometime after the battle. The other cases are headstamped with military markings. One case was produced in May, 1880, two in December 1882, one in January 1883, fifteen in March 1883, one in May 1884, five in June 1884, one in November 1884, one in February 1885, two in March 1886, one April 1886, one in January 1887, and one in May 1888. Two other military cases are headstamped with a contractor's mark of R over B for Rifle Bridgeport.

Shot Shells

Ten shot-shell bases were found. Two are .410 and two are marked Peters and Remington Express, respectively. Two bases are 20-gauge and are marked Winchester Repeater and Winchester Super Speed, respectively. One 16-gauge base is headstamped Winchester Repeater, and three 12-gauge bases are headstamped WRACO New Club, Winchester Repeater, and Winchester Ranger, respectively. Two 10-gauge bases were found. They are headstamped Winchester New Rival and Winchester New Club, respectively.

Deformed Alloyed Bullets

Eight bullets were too deformed to identify to type or caliber. The bullets are heavily alloyed and are of modern configuration. FS1833 is a mass of lead weighing about two pounds. It appears to contain more alloy metal than the battle-related bullets and may represent waste lead from bullet casting done by the National Park Service for its living-history demonstrations.

Firearm Parts

Three screws are the firearm parts recovered during 1985. All three are from army weapons used at the Reno-Benteen defense site. Two screws (FS4659, 4709) are butt-plate screws, and the other (FS4729) is a lock retaining screw. This particular screw has been broken at the threaded end. Only three threads remain. The shaft of the screw is slightly bent. The break at the threads and the bent nature of the screw suggest that it was in place when broken and that some significant external force was applied to cause such a break. Several reports by battle participants mention similar damage.

Major Reno's July 11, 1876 report to the chief of ordnance concerning carbine performance noted that some carbines had been rendered unserviceable after being struck by bullets (DuMont 1974:27). Sergeant Charles Windolph (Hunt and Hunt 1950:104) also mentions that his carbine was hit by an Indian bullet, causing the butt to split. It is conceivable that the broken and bent lock retaining screw was in one of the carbines struck by a bullet.

Seven firearm parts have been recovered archaeologically: the three carbine screws just discussed and four parts recovered in 1984 (Scott and Fox 1987). Four parts found on the Custer battlefield are an ejector-rod button (FS977) for the Colt pistol found on the South Skirmish Line; a Colt-pistol backstrap (FS10), serial number 6048 found near the Calhoun position; an Indian-utilized Model 1858 Remington percussion-revolver loading lever (FS1558) recovered on Greasy Grass Ridge; and a trigger found on the South Skirmish Line. The trigger was erroneously identified as a carbine trigger (Scott and Fox 1987). The trigger has a configuration identical to those found in per-cussion shotguns. The distribution of the parts suggests that each part could represent a different gun.

Knives

Three folding pocketknives and portions of three knife blades were recovered, all at the Reno-Benteen defense site. The knives were identified by knife collector Jerry McCalfin of Wichita, Kansas. The first is a single-blade penknife (FS2221). It is 2½ inches (61 millimeters) long with thin stamped and gilded ferrous metal side plates. The side plates are stamped with "5 Ct. KNIFE" (fig. 58c). The blade is 2¼ inches (52 millimeters) long. This penknife is unmarked but was probably made by the C. W. Holme IXL

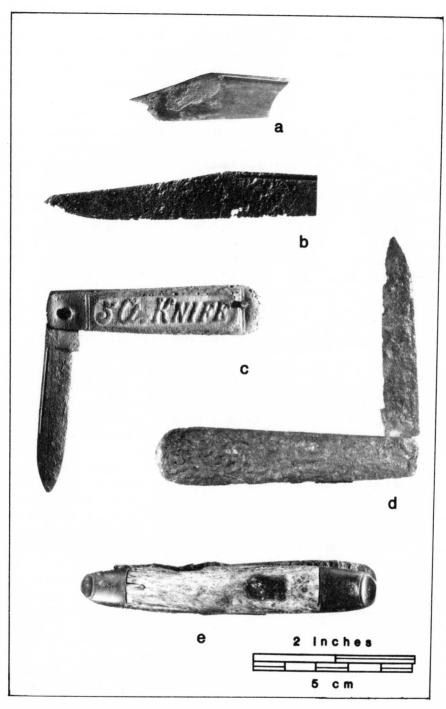

Fig. 58. Pocketknives and blades recovered from the Reno-Benteen defense site. a, b: Clip-point blade fragments. c: Penknife. d: Barlow-style pocketknife. e: wood-handled pocket knife with brass bolsters.

Company. The second pocketknife (FS4098) is 3½ inches (95 millimeters) long with brass bolsters and wooden handles (fig. 58e). One handle is missing and the other has a brass shield-shaped device set into the wood near the hinge end. The iron blade is badly corroded and no measurements were possible. The knife corresponds to the early Case Company style. The third folding pocketknife (FS4201) is an iron-handled barlow-style knife (fig. 58d). It is 3¼ inches (84 millimeters) long. The blade is 2⅜ inches (64 millimeters) long. The knife is identified as an unmarked C. W. Holme type. All three knives date to the third quarter of the nineteenth century, and their context suggests they are battle-related. However, without more reliable dating, this will remain a speculation.

Two of the knife-blade fragments are portions of clip-pointed folding knives. One (FS2510) is 3½ inches (85 millimeters) long and is broken near the rear terminus of the finger slot (fig. 58b). The second blade (FS3142) is a midsection fragment of a similar knife (fig. 58a). The third blade fragment (FS2960) is the point of a butcher knife. The iron blade fragment is 3½ inches (85 millimeters) long and has been painted gold. The blade's shape is similar to that of the famed Russell Green River butcher knife (Hanson 1987). Gold-painted knives often were used for trade purposes (Russell 1967). Similarly shaped and painted blades are known ethnographically to have been set in Sioux gunstock-shaped war clubs. An 1870s dated example of such a club is in the Plains Indian Collections of the Buffalo Bill Historical Center in Cody, Wyoming.

Arrowheads

Other Indian-related arms recovered archaeologically were the iron arrowheads found in 1984 on the Custer battlefield. Eight arrowheads and one tip fragment were recovered. Iron or metal arrowheads were a common trade item from the early 1600s to the early twentieth century and had almost completely supplanted chipped stone projectiles by the mid–nineteenth century (Hanson 1972; Russell 1967). The found arrowheads are of two manufacturing types: mass produced and hand made. Complete descriptions of the arrowheads will be found in Scott and Fox (1987), but a summary is presented below.

The hand-made specimen (FS994) is somewhat crudely formed and appears asymmetrical (fig. 59d). It appears to have been made from a barrel hoop or similar metal stock and was cold-clipped from the stock with a chisel. Another specimen (FS1633) is also asymmetrical, but its oxidized condition precludes a definite assignment to the hand-made category. This artifact could be a poorly finished mass-produced item. Its form does correspond to Hanson's (1972) Type 3 trade point. A three-inch-long (seventy-five millimeter) mass-produced point (FS580) with a T-shaped tang (fig. 59c) conforms to Hanson's (1972) Type 2 point, and another long point (FS727) with a straight tang (fig. 59e) appears to be a Type 1 point (Hanson 1972). Four additional points (FS1015, 1480, 709, 1638) appear to be two varieties of the same type. The difference between the two varieties lies in their dimensions. Both varieties have a straight tang with two barblike protrusions midway on either side of the tang (fig. 59f). The barbs were intended to ensure a more secure attachment of the point to the shaft. Hanson (1972) does not identify this type, but he later (1975) illustrates an identical

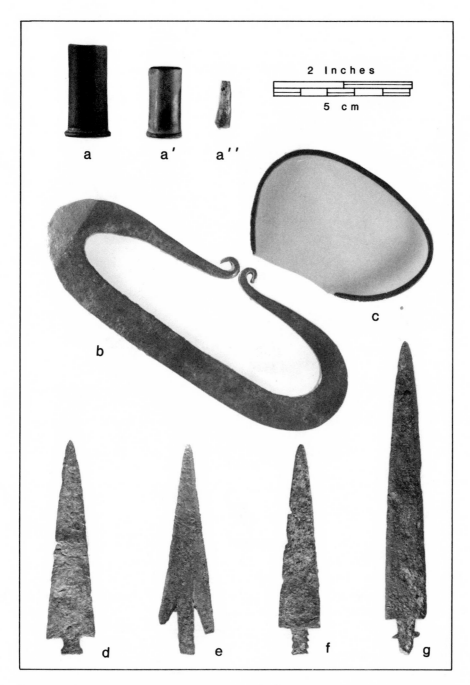

Fig. 59. Indian personal items and arrowheads. a, a', a": An Indian ornament made from cartridge cases and lead. b: A fire steel. c: A brass bracelet. d–g: Types of iron arrowheads.

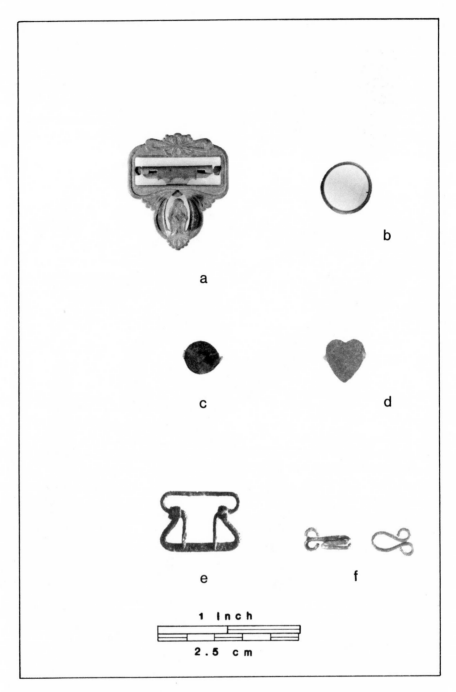

Fig. 60. Army personal items. a: A suspender grip. b: A silver-plated brass finger ring. c, d: Tobacco tags. e: A trouser buckle. f: A hook and eye.

specimen that was found in a human vertebra collected at the Custer battlefield by the reburial party in 1877. The iron tip (FS680) of another arrowhead was also recovered. It appears to be from a mass-produced item, but its small size precludes positive identification.

These arrowheads are typical of those available to Indians during the latter part of the nineteenth century. The arrowheads were not endemic to the Northern Plains or the Sioux or Cheyennes. Use of these arrowhead types is documented by the surgeon general (War Department 1871). The types were reported to have been found in wounds of soldiers and civilians from Texas and Arizona to the Northern Plains.

CLOTHING AND PERSONAL ITEMS

The personal items recovered are predominantly associated with the soldiers. The Custer battlefield yielded a watch chain, a suspender grip, a silver-plated brass wedding band, two tobacco tags, and three five-cent pieces. The personal items from the Reno-Benteen defense site associated with the soldiers are a watch, a five-cent piece, and a tobacco tag.

The Indian-associated personal item are even fewer in number. The Custer battlefield yielded an ornament made from cartridge cases, a fire steel, and a brass tack possibly used for decorating a firearm. Only one Indian-associated item was found at the Reno-Benteen defense site, a brass bracelet.

Finger Rings

Three finger rings were found. A silver-plated brass wedding band (FS992) (fig. 60b) was found still encircling a finger joint in 1984 (Scott and Fox 1987). The ring is a man's size 6½. There is no inscription on the ring. Two modern rings were recovered at the Reno-Benteen defense site. One is a fourteen-carat gold-plated man's wedding band and the other is a silver child's or woman's ring with a setting of turquoise and jet. This ring is a distinctive southwestern Indian tourist-market piece.

Cloth

Several very small fragments of cloth and thread were found adhering to a few buttons (FS1472, 1493, 1516). The thread was cotton and the other fabric was wool, quite probably remnants of uniform cloth. The only sizable piece of cloth recovered was found with the human remains at Marker 128 (Square M85). The cloth (FS4494, 4529, 4568) consists of about seven and a half square inches (eighteen and three-fourths square centimeters) of a white ribbed cotton flannel. The weave is simple over and under, with forty-five threads per inch. Stitching holes occur on two of the pieces. The holes are spaced one-sixteenth of an inch (two millimeters) apart, suggesting a machine stitch. The cloth conforms to the specifications for army white canton-flannel under-drawers. The archaeological specimen perfectly matches existing examples of 1870s army-issue underdrawers.

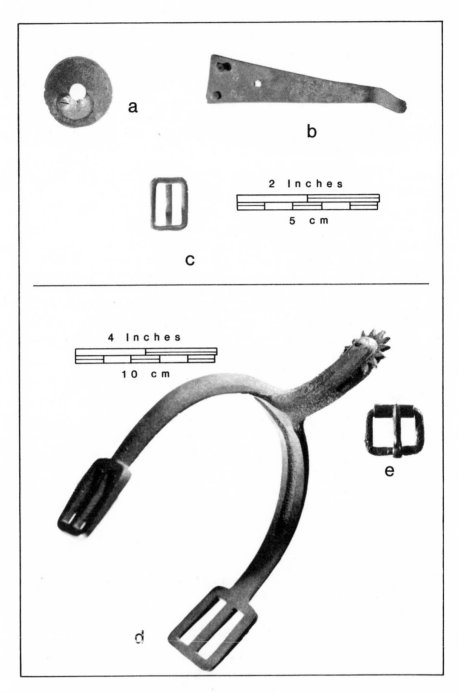

Fig. 61. Army equipment. a: A telescope eyepiece. b: Model 1855 waist-belt adjustment hook. c: A forage-cap chin-strap slide. d: A Model 1859 spur. e: A spur strap buckle.

Trouser Buckle

One trouser buckle (FS4980) was recovered at the Reno-Benteen defense site. The buckle (fig. 61e) is iron. Buckles of this type were known to have been introduced as early as 1875 by the Quartermaster Department, although they may have been in use before that date (Herskovitz 1978:37).

Suspender Grip

A stamped brass suspender grip (FS718) was found on Last Stand Hill. It is stamped with a floral and stippled design (fig. 60a) but is otherwise unmarked. The grip is a private-purchase style and could have been used by an officer, enlisted man, or a civilian. The military did not adopt issue suspenders until 1883 (Herskovitz 1978).

Forage-Cap Chin-Strap Slide

A stamped brass chin-strap slide (FS3143) was recovered at the Reno-Benteen defense site. The slide measures five-eighths of an inch (fifteen millimeters), inside dimension. Slides of that measurement are usually associated with the pattern 1858 forage cap, the pre–Civil War dress cap, the pattern 1872 enlisted man's dress shako, and the pattern 1872 enlisted man's or officer's dress helmet (Herskovitz 1978:44). The association of this artifact with other battle-related remains suggests it was from a forage cap.

Coins

A number of coins were found during the field investigations. Most of them had twentieth-century dates (table 14) and were undoubtedly dropped by visitors or monument staff. Four coins were recovered which dated to the battle era. Three were recovered during the 1985 work. One (FS4099) was found near the L-shaped entrenchment in the H Company position at the Reno-Benteen defense site. This coin is a five-cent piece dated 1876. There is practically no wear on the coin, which is consistent with its loss during the battle.

Table 14   Twentieth-Century Coins

Penny		Dime		Quarter		Half-Dollar	
Date	FS#	Date	FS#	Date	FS#	Date	FS#
1919S	436	1916S	3104	1961D	3144	1933S	2015
1941	1675	1944D	2416	1981	2368		
1959D	2438						
1964D	2809						
1969D	2444						
1972D	2440						
1975D	3135						
1976	2441						

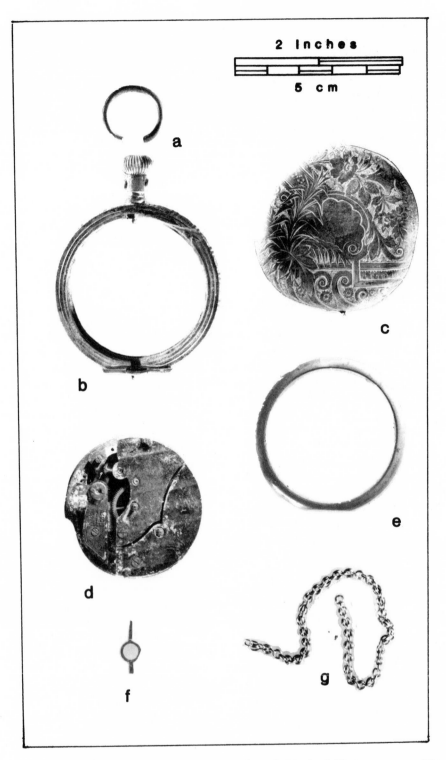

Fig. 62. A watch. a: A fob ring. b: The case. c: The etched back. d: The movement. e: The bezel. f: A regulator hand. g: A fourteen-carat gold watch chain.

Two coins (FS3911a, b), both five-cent pieces, were found during excavation at Marker 201 (Square D85) in the Keogh group. One was were lying on top of the other. Their position relative to the skeletal material that was recovered suggests they may have been in the right trouser pocket of the man whose body lay in that location. The coins are dated 1869 and 1870. The fourth coin (FS676) was found in 1984 (Scott and Fox 1987) on Last Stand Hill. It is a five-cent piece dated 1870.

Watch

Six artifacts are parts of the same object, a pocket watch. The watch came from the Reno-Benteen defense site and is an inexpensive gold-plated, engraved, hunting-case timepiece. The back (FS2733) is engraved with a floral design. Traces of the gold plate are still present in the engraving and on the interior surface. The back (fig. 62c) has been bent and the hinge pin rotated downward and to the right by extreme force, causing the pin to shear.

The back was found in the barricade area slightly to the south of the bottom of the hospital swale. The other watch parts were east of the barricade area. The parts are the case (FS3308) (fig. 62b), bezel (FS3309) (fig. 62e), regulator hand (FS3310) (fig. 62f), fob ring (FS3311) (fig. 62a), and the movement (FS3312) (fig. 61d). The case has the stem intact but bent toward the rear. The hinges and pins for the covers are present. The front-cover hinge is intact and in place, while the internal back-cover hinge pin is twisted and bent and the back-cover pin is bent and sheared as described earlier. The bezel is complete and still retains most of its gold plate. The movement is cylinder escapement, lever set, and stem wound. An intertwined *M W* is stamped on the back and the words *Swiss* and *Switzerland* are stamped into the movement body.

The watch is a type popular in the last half of the nineteenth century (Baille 1929), but it appears to be an inexpensive Swiss copy of a more desirable American pocket watch. The Swiss were known for copying American watches and marketing them under brand names similar to the more expensive American watches. Legislation passed in 1871 required foreign-made watches imported to the United States to bear the name of the country of origin (Shugart and Engle 1984:58–59). This watch postdates 1871, although the precise date of manufacture cannot be ascertained. The context in which it was found suggests it was lost during the battle; however, a later date cannot be ruled out. The bent nature of the back, hinge pins, and winding stem all suggest the watch received rough treatment about the time of its deposition. The blow which scattered the components came from the front, causing the movement to be pushed out the back. That motion sheared away the back cover as well. The cause of the blow and the means of the scattered deposition cannot be determined.

Watch Chain

A length of fourteen-carat gold watch chain (FS5071) was recovered in the excavations at Markers 152 and 153. The chain (fig. 62g) is 5½ inches (142 millimeters) long and is constructed of double-circle fancy links joined by an intermediate curb link. The chain is a type popular during the late nineteenth century.

Tobacco Tags

A round tobacco tag (FS 2040) was recovered along the retreat line from Weir Point. Tobacco tags were developed about 1870 (Campbell 1964:100–104) to identify specific brands of retail plug tobacco as a genuine product. Tags were used by retailers for at least seventy years to identify their products. Two tags (fig. 60c, d), another round style (FS168), and one heart-shaped style (FS756), were found during the 1984 investigations on the Custer battlefield in the Keogh area and on Last Stand Hill, respectively (Scott and Fox 1987). The context in which all three were found suggests a battle-related association, but this is not certain.

Buttons

One hundred twenty-three buttons were recovered during the two seasons of archaeological investigation. Sixty-two are reported in Scott and Fox (1987). The 1985 assemblage is very similar to the 1984 group.

The most distinctive buttons are the military general-service button. These brass line-eagle buttons are represented in three sizes. The smallest (fig. 63b) are one-half inch (twelve millimeters) in diameter. There are three of this size, one (FS1051) from the Custer battlefield (Scott and Fox (1987) and two from the Reno-Benteen defense site (FS3013, 3776). All three are backmarked "Scovill's Co. Extra," a backmark used from 1840 to 1850 by the Scovill Company (Gillio, Levine, and Scott 1980). The medium-size button (FS4087) is five-eighths of an inch (sixteen millimeters) in diameter, has an *I* (for infantry) in the eagle's shield (fig 63c), and is backmarked "Scovill Co. Waterbury." This button was found near the Company H position at the Reno-Benteen defense site. It is possible that an infantry officer from the relief column or a later visitor lost the button. One medium-size button (FS364) was also found on the Custer battlefield (Scott and Fox 1987).

All of the large blouse buttons (fig. 63a) were found on the Custer battlefield. Eleven (FS285, 365, 956, 1020, 1024, 1066, 1218, 1385, 1472, 1493, 1516) were found in 1984 (Scott and Fox 1987) and the other six in 1985. The 1985 finds were all made in association with excavations at the marble markers. These large buttons are three-quarters of an inch (nineteen millimeters) in diameter. Three buttons (FS1218, 1516, 3885) are backmarked "Extra Quality," three (FS 285, 365, 3909) are backmarked "Scovill Mfg. Co. Waterbury," and eight (FS956, 1020, 1024, 1066, 4184, 4193, 4607, 4614a) are backmarked "Waterbury Button Co." The other three buttons are not backmarked.

There are four button types which can be associated with soldiers' trousers. Two types are iron two-piece, four-hole buttons. The larger size (fig. 63g), thirteen-sixteenths of an inch (nineteen millimeters) in diameter, was used to support suspenders and to close flies. Sixteen (FS170, 686, 688, 1005, 1101, 1122c, 1131, 1132, 1216, 1222, 1329, 1374, 1488, 1525, 1526a, 1870) were found on the Custer battlefield in 1984 (Scott and Fox 1987), twelve (FS3573, 3886, 3903, 3904b, 3908, 3910, 4404, 4459, 4460, 4462, 4481, 5082) during the excavations in 1985, and four (FS2317, 4652, 4693, 4837) were found on the Reno-Benteen defense site. A smaller button (fig. 63f) is nine-sixteenths of an inch (fifteen millimeters) in diameter and was used to close the trouser

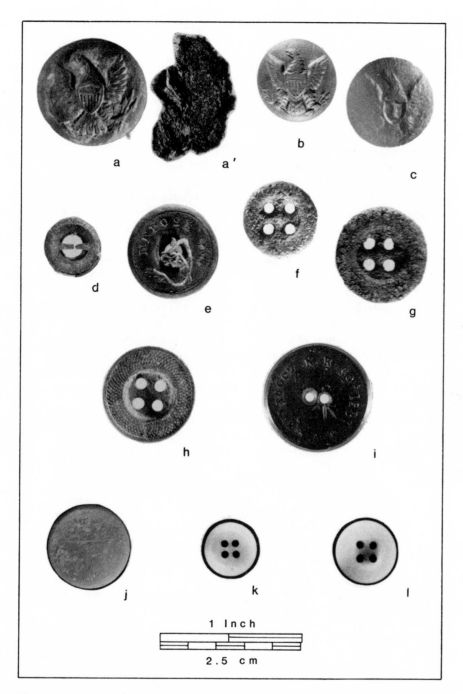

Fig. 63. Buttons. a, a': Large general-service button with blue wool attached. b: A cuff or forage-cap button. c: An infantry "I" button. d: Center-bar pressed button. e: Center-bar button back with thread and "DEPOSE" backmark. f, g: Two four-hole iron trouser buttons. h: A four-holé pressed-metal trouser button. i: A Novelty Rubber Company button. j: A mother-of-pearl button. k, l: White porcelain shirt buttons.

fly. Fifteen (FS27, 306, 720, 735, 751, 1006, 1116, 1122a, 1138, 1312, 1325, 1329, 1389, 1445, 1508) were found on the Custer battlefield in 1984 (Scott and Fox 1987), seventeen (FS3554, 3878, 3883b, 3890, 3895, 3904, 4183, 4198a, 4419, 4420, 4449, 4485, 4602a, 4782, 5072, 5073, 5075) in the excavations at the marble markers, and four (FS2314, 3586, 4016, 4694) were found at the Reno-Benteen defense site.

Four-hole pressed white-metal buttons with a stippled front pattern (fig. 63h) were used on military trousers for attaching suspenders and as closures. These buttons are eleven-sixteenths of an inch (eighteen millimeters) in diameter; nine (FS1221, 1226, 1368, 1402, 1419, 1489, 1497, 1524, 1661) were found on the Custer battlefield in 1984 (Scott and Fox 1987), four (FS4484, 4489, 5076, 5086) in the 1985 excavations, and two (FS4701b, 4755) at the Reno-Benteen defense site. A single two-piece single-bar button (FS5018) (fig. 63d), thirteen-sixteenths of an inch (twenty millimeters) in diameter, was found in 1985 on the Custer battlefield. Two other single-bar buttons (FS685, 760) in two sizes were recovered in 1984 (Scott and Fox 1987). These buttons were used as suspender attachments and as trouser closures.

Two white-porcelain four-hole buttons (fig. 63k, i) commonly used on shirts and underwear were recovered in excavations on the Custer battlefield in 1985. One (FS3893) is seven-sixteenths of an inch (eleven millimeters) in diameter and is similar to two buttons (FS1498, 1526b) found in 1984 (Scott and Fox 1987). A larger button (FS5074) is one-half inch (fourteen millimeters) in diameter. No corresponding size was noted in the 1984 collection, although three slightly smaller buttons (FS1126, 1329a, b) were found (Scott and Fox 1987).

Two other battle-related buttons, a hard-rubber poncho button (FS1126) (fig. 63i) and a mother-of-pearl shank button (FS1210) (fig. 63j), were found in 1984 (Scott and Fox 1987) but have no counterparts in the 1985 collection. The hard-rubber button is backmarked "N.R. Co. Goodyears Pat. 1851." This mark was used by the Novelty Rubber Company from 1855 to 1879 (Gillio, Levine, and Scott 1980). It was used on a variety of outerwear, such as rain slickers and Civil War–issue ponchos.

In addition, five nonbattle-related buttons were found. Three, two overall and one blazer, were found in 1984 (Scott and Fox 1987) on the Custer battlefield. An iron-ball button with an omega shank was found at the Reno-Benteen defense site near the existing road. This button (FS2085) is seven-sixteenths of an inch (eleven millimeters) in diameter and appears to be from a woman's dress. The general style suggests a late nineteenth-century or early twentieth-century context. The face of a modern snap-type button (FS2201) was also found in this area.

Fasteners

Two eyes and three hooks from iron hook-and-eye assemblies were recovered. These hooks and eyes (fig. 60f) were used on military uniforms to fasten collars and blouse shirts. They were also used on overcoats and the 1874 campaign hat. Two hooks (FS2784, 2877) and one eye (FS2689) were found at the Reno-Benteen defense site. One hook (FS4471) and one eye (FS4480) were found in excavations at Marker 128 (Square M) on the Custer battlefield.

The hook-and-eye assembly was not used on the campaign blouse of the period. It was used on older-style blouses and on the campaign hat. The found hooks and eyes probably represent the presence of both older uniform blouses and the campaign hat at the battle.

Boots and Boot Nails

Three boot-nail sizes were found on the Custer battlefield in 1984 (Scott and Fox 1987). They were recovered in thirty-two groups totaling sixty-seven nails. The number of nails in a group ranges from one to sixteen. There are four groups of small nails (FS1128, 1664, 1665, 1693) totaling eight individual nails ranging in size from one-quarter inch (six millimeters) to three-eighths of an inch (ten millimeters). These nails were probably used to hold soles to the uppers. There are twenty-seven nails in thirteen groups (FS159, 986, 987, 988, 990, 1008, 1041, 1441, 1444, 1663, 1666, 1668, 1811) in the medium size. These range in length from seven-sixteenths of an inch (eleven millimeters) to eleven-sixteenths (sixteen millimeters). These nails were also used to hold soles to uppers, although some longer nails could be worn-down heel nails. The largest group of thirteen (FS187, 558, 559, 589, 738, 950, 954,1007, 1093, 1261, 1412, 1647, 1810) contains thirty-four nails ranging in size from three-quarters of an inch (eighteen millimeters) to one and seven-sixteenths inches (thirty-six millimeters). These nails are heel nails. Two other nails (FS198, 1092) were inadvertently lost in the field.

The 1985 investigations recovered six boot nails. Two heel nails (FS2505, 2506) are one and one-quarter inches (thirty millimeters) long, two (FS3798, 4719) are fifteen-sixteenths of an inch (twenty-three millimeters) long, and two sole nails (FS2507, 5037) are nine-sixteenths of an inch (fifteen millimeters) long. Three nails (FS2505, 2506, 2507) were found in close proximity to one another and probably represent one boot. The others were found widely dispersed and undoubtedly represent losses by different individuals. All of the nails, with one exception, were found at the Reno-Benteen defense site. FS5037 was found on the Custer battlefield.

Portions of two Model 1872 cavalry boots were found on the Custer battlefield in 1984. One (FS1129) is a portion of leather bootheel. The heel is comprised of fragments of several leather heel counters. The heel was found in the excavations at Markers 33–34. The boot (FS302) is the lower portion of a right boot. The boot (fig. 64) conforms to the 1872 pattern (Steffen 1978; Brinkerhoff 1976) in its construction. The remains consist of the sole, heel, and a portion of the upper and counter. When excavated, the top, or leg, was entirely missing and appeared as an even cut at the top of the upper. The removal of boot tops by the warriors is noted in Marquis (1931). The warriors used them for such things as making pouches. A photograph of the battlefield taken in 1879 by S. J. Morrow shows a boot nearly identical to FS302 lying on the ground near some horse bones on Last Stand Hill.

Portions of two more boots were recovered in 1985, one from the Reno-Benteen defense site and the·other from the Custer battlefield. The boot fragments (FS3323) from the Reno-Benteen defense site consist of nine pieces of leather from the boot sole and heel counters, one 5/16-inch-diameter (7 millimeters) iron counterwear insert, sixteen 9/16-inch-long (15 millimeters) sole nails, seventeen 1¼-inch-long (30 millimeters) heel nails, and five 3/8-inch-long (9 millimeters) cobbler's tacks.

Fig. 64. A Model 1872 cavalry boot as it was found in the excavations at Marker 200. Note the upper has been cut away.

The other boot was found with the articulated lower right human leg excavated at Marker 128 on the Custer battlefield. The boot (FS4611) consists of the sole and heel and portions of the upper attached at the heel. Several individual fragments of upper leather were also recovered (FS4553, 4609, 4610). The boot appears to be about a modern size 7½, although the leather is dry and may have shrunk to some degree. The archaeological context suggests the boot was complete and on the right foot of a soldier when buried. The upper does not appear to have been cut away as in the case of the boot found at Marker 200 (Scott and Fox 1987).

In total, portions of three boots have been found on the Custer battlefield and one boot at the Reno-Benteen defense site. Boot nails were found in thirty-three different assemblages on the Custer battlefield and four at the Reno-Benteen defense site. Taken as a whole, artifact assemblages representing at least thirty-six boots have been recovered from the Custer battlefield and five from the Reno-Benteen defense site. The seven-to-one recovery ratio between the two sites is not unexpected, considering that the ratio of dead in the hilltop fight to the Custer fight was about one to twelve. Statistically, the recovery ratio is expected and significant, indicating the number of boot remains are a statistically valid sample. The archaeological boot sample and that of the monument museum collection clearly indicate that the footwear of the soldier participants was the regulation cavalry boot.

Brass Bracelet

The bracelet (FS2262) is made of about eight-gauge brass wire flattened on two sides. The ends have a slight taper to them, which is probably a result of hammering to flatten the wire. The bracelet (fig. 59c) was found in association with a number of .44-caliber Henry cartridge cases on a small knoll at the Reno-Benteen defense site. The knoll appears to be an Indian position, and the bracelet was probably lost during the fight by one of the warriors.

Fire Steel

An Indian personal item from the Custer battlefield is a fire steel or strike-a-light (FS77). The steel (fig. 59b) is hand forged and neatly executed. It is made on the pattern of the famous Hudson's Bay fire steel (Engagés 1971). The specimen is three and a half inches long (eighty-seven millimeters), about three-quarters of an inch wide (nineteen millimeters), and three-sixteenths of an inch thick (four millimeters) on the striking surface. One edge has been thinned down during manufacture to a thin profile. The thinned edge probably served as a tool to re-edge a dull flint.

Ornament

The other Custer battlefield Indian personal item is an ornament (FS1248). It is made of two expended cartridges and a cone of lead (fig. 59a). A .50/70-caliber cartridge case had about half its length removed, and a one-eighth-inch (three-millimeter) hole had been drilled through the primer. A cone-shaped piece of lead about three-quarter of an inch long (nineteen millimeters), with a small hole drilled through the cone's apex, was inside the device. A .44/40-caliber cartridge case was forced into the .50/70 case to keep the cone in place. How the ornament was used or where it was suspended is not known.

ACCOUTREMENTS

The quantity of military equipment is relatively small, but it is representative of the types in common use during the 1870s. There is probably a twofold reason for the small quantity. First, the soldiers who fought at the Reno-Benteen defense site were there only a short time and the amount of equipment lost would be small. Second, at the Custer battlefield the Indians stripped the dead and took most of the usable and interesting items. Those who buried the dead also retrieved many items as mementos or to be returned to the families of the deceased (Hutchins 1976).

Spurs

Two spurs were recovered from the Reno-Benteen defense site. One (FS4291) (fig. 61d) is a Model 1859–pattern brass spur with a small iron rowel. Two similar spurs

(FS552, 1783a) were recovered from the Custer battlefield in 1984 (Scott and Fox 1987). The other Reno spur (FS2619) is also brass but is nonregulation. The cast spur has studs instead of slots for attaching the straps. The spur's body and the neck are cast with a design instead of the plain 1859 pattern. The rowel is brass and much larger than the regulation spur. This spur was undoubtedly a private-purchase item, but whether it belonged to an officer, an enlisted man, or a civilian employee is not known.

Spur Buckles (Contributed by Ralph Heinz)

Three ⅞-by-¾-inch (22 by 18 millimeters) iron roller buckles (FS412 from Custer and 3782, 4769 from Reno-Benteen) (fig. 61e) are probably spur-strap buckles. Similar buckles were used on the Civil War (1859 pattern) spurs. Another Custer iron roller buckle (FS1576) was designed for a ¾-inch-wide (19-millimeter) strap. This buckle is slightly wider than the regulation Civil War–era and 1874-issue spur strap. If these are spur buckles, then old-stock straps were used by the troopers in the field, as the regulation spurs of that period had brass buckles on the straps (Steffen 1973).

Carbine Swivel

A carbine swivel and snap hook (FS3854) was found along the retreat line from the river at the Reno-Benteen defense site. The snap-hook spring and lever are missing. A complete swivel and snap hook (FS380) was recovered on the Custer battlefield in 1984. The snap hook was first introduced in service during the Mexican War and continued in use well into the Indian Wars period (Arnold 1974).

Carbine Socket

A poorly preserved carbine socket (FS3287) was found near the Company H position on the Reno-Benteen defense site. A part of the leather socket, the attachment strap, and the buckle were recovered. The socket is the Model 1859 type (Steffen 1978).

Mess Fork

A broken iron mess fork (FS4290a, b) was found at the Reno-Benteen defense site in the area of the June 26 redoubt. The fork is cast iron with a recessed handle. It has three tines, and all three are broken to some degree. The fork has been broken at the neck between the tines and the handle. Army-issue forks of this type and construction are known to date from the Civil War to 1885. A similar fork dated 1876 is known to exist (Crouch 1978).

Cooking Pot

Another mess item recovered is a small fragment of a cooking pot (FS4304). The fragment is two inches (fifty-three millimeters) high with a slightly flared rim and a flat bottom. The specimen most nearly conforms to the common nineteenth-century flat-bottomed, three-legged, eight- to ten-inch-diameter cast-iron pot.

Cups

Two army-issue tin cups were found at the Reno-Benteen defense site. One cup (FS3937), which was found on the retreat line from the river, consists of only two fragments of the wire-reinforced rim and three fragments of the body. The second cup (FS2313) is nearly complete but is crushed flat. It was found near the northern line of entrenchments. The cup appears to be a standard-issue tin cup with the rolled wire-reinforced rim. The body and bottom are soldered and the handle is riveted and soldered in place. There is no evidence of a stamped *US* on the handle, which is a characteristic of mid-1880s cups according to Paul Hedren (personal communication March 2, 1988), but the handle is also broken at that point. Three initials are scratched into the cup bottom. They are 'KKK' in block letters. A review of the names of the battle participants failed to reveal anyone with those initials. The letters may refer to an individual means of identification, a member of Company K, a previous owner, or a political preference.

Telescope

One item of equipment is not issue, but it is one commonly used by the military of the era. It is the eyepiece cover for a telescope (FS2028). The eyepiece cover (fig. 61a) is brass with a depressed area in the center for the glass optic. A movable iron dust cover is mounted to the eyepiece by a small iron screw. The eyepiece compares favorably with complete examples dated from the Civil War and Indian Wars. Most comparative specimens were manufactured in France.

Tent-Pole Ferrule

A tinned iron tent-pole ferrule (FS3126) was found near the Company H position. The ferrule is four inches (ten centimeters) long and one inch (twenty-five millimeters) in diameter. Portions of the wooden tent-pole remain in the ferrule secured by two small tacks. The ferrule conforms exactly to the 1889 tent pole specifications for the shelter half (Office of the Quartermaster General 1889). Similar poles appear to have been in use as early as the Civil War (personal communication, Paul Hedren, May 19, 1986, and Dan Brown, July 8, 1986).

Tent Grommets and Grommet Stiffeners

Two grommets (FS3784, 4701a) and six iron grommet-stiffener rings (FS3761, 3787, 3790, 4096, 4294, 4732) were found at the Reno-Benteen defense site. All could have been used on army-issue shelter tents and other tentage.

Canteen Stopper Ring

A Model 1858 canteen stopper ring was recovered from the Custer battlefield in 1984 (Scott and Fox 1987). The ring is broken near its tip, but it conforms to the Models 1858 and 1874 stopper type (Sylvia and O'Donnel 1983; Todd 1974:216). It was found on the South Skirmish Line.

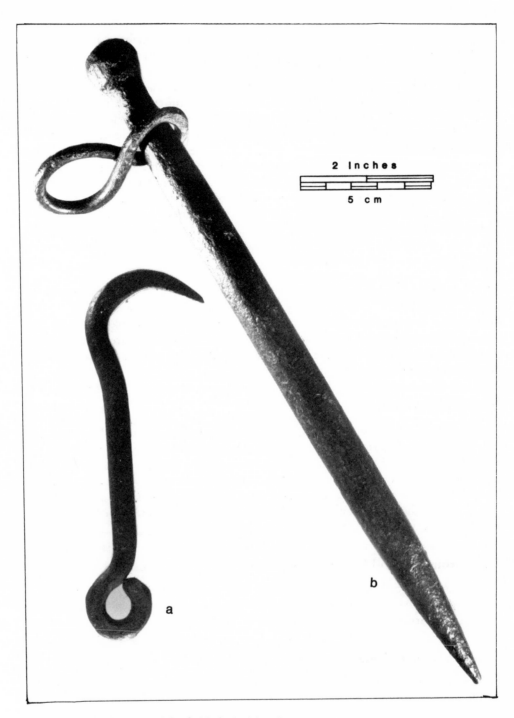

2 Inches

5 cm

a

b

Fig. 65. Horse equipment. a: A hoof pick. b: A picket pin.

Belt Adjustment Hook

A brass adjustment hook (fig. 61b) for the Model 1855 waist belt was recovered in 1984 (Scott and Fox 1987). The hook conforms to the specifications for the Model 1855 waist belt (Dorsey 1984:6; Todd 1974:219).

Leather Fragments

Three groups of leather fragments (FS182, 733, 1135) were found on the Custer battlefield. FS733 is buff leather and may be from a Model 1855 waist belt, but the attribution is speculative. The other fragments are unidentified.

Hoof Pick

A hand-forged iron hoof pick (FS3629) was found at the Reno-Benteen defense site. The pick (fig. 65a) is 5¾ inches (145 millimeters) long, with an eye formed on one end. The pick was made of ⅜-inch (9-millimeter) round stock.

Tack Buckles (*Contributed by Ralph Heinz*)

Fourteen harness buckles were recovered. Four are roller buckles (FS1783b from Custer and FS4091, 4292b.3, 4292b.4 from Reno), one is a D-shaped buckle (FS4292.5 from Reno), and nine are center-bar buckles (FS1409, 1716 from Custer and FS2450, 2676, 4239, 4675, 4701a.2, 4704, 4829 from Reno). The iron roller buckles (fig. 66a) may have been used on packsaddles or perhaps on hand-made cartridge belts. The D-shaped buckle was desgined for a one-inch-wide (two and one-half centimeters) strap and was probably used on the horse nose (feed) bag. The center-bar buckles (fig. 66b) (FS4701a.2, 4704, 4829) are of the size used on bridle cheek pieces, link straps, and the carbine socket. The other center-bar buckles could have been used on either the bridle throat strap, the 1874 curb strap, the 1872 bridle curb strap, or the Civil War–era saddlebags (Ordnance Memorandum No. 18 1874:50; Steffen 1978:59–62). One of these buckles (FS1409) appears to have been nickeled or tinned. Privately purchased officer bridles often had nickeled or tinned hardware to prevent rusting. Ordnance Memorandum No. 9 (1868) recommended that regulation bits be tinned and that all old bits requiring cleaning be tinned as well. This buckle may also represent an experimental variation in regulation finishes for rust prevention.

Tack Rivets (*Contributed by Ralph Heinz*)

Twenty-three copper harness rivets were found at the Reno-Benteen defense site (FS2043, 2149, 2674, 3054, 3796, 4241, 4292b.10–16, 4297.5, 4342, 4346, 4357, 4701a.3–6, 4703, 4972). One rivet is oval headed (FS4241) and may have been used to secure the girth strap to the underside of the saddletree or to secure the bullseye rosette to the 1874 bridle (Ordnance Memorandum No. 18 1874:51). The other rivets could have been used on a variety of equipment, such as the halter, nose bag, girth straps, safes, billets, soldiers' waist belts, belt loops, or holsters.

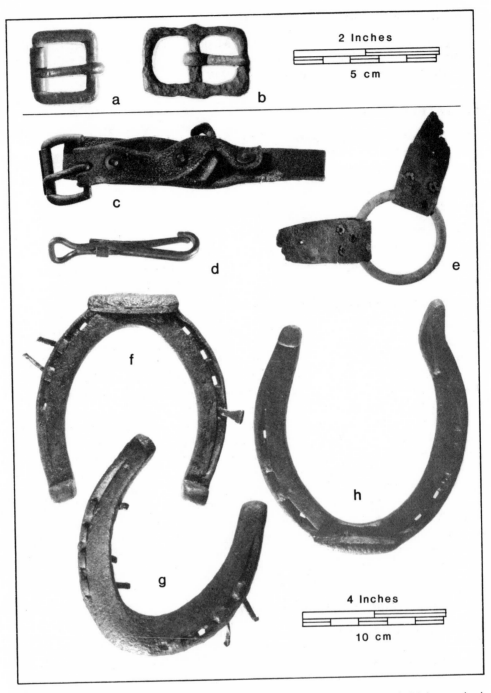

Fig. 66. Horse-related items. a, b Harness buckles. c: Postbattle harness strap. d: Link strap hook. e: Postbattle halter fragment. f–h: Horseshoes.

Another group of rivets, both copper and iron, was associated with FS4136 at Reno. There are three copper rivets and washers and an iron rivet (two and three-eighths inches, or fifty-nine millimeters, long) associated with a halter square. The iron rivet is from a stirrup and passes through the top of the wooden stirrup. One of the copper rivets is of the size used to attach the leather hood to the stirrup. It is generally accepted that Lieutenant Colonel Custer ordered the leather stirrup hoods removed from all Seventh Cavalry stirrups. However, the guidon bearers still would have needed the hooded stirrups because the guidon socket was riveted to the hood of the left stirrup. This rivet may represent one of those stirrups.

One copper rivet (FS248.5) was found at Custer. It is of the size used to fasten reins of the Civil War era to the bit rings. The 1874 regulations called for the reins to be buckled to the bit instead of riveted (Ordnance Memorandum No. 18 1874:52−53).

Saddle and Tack Parts (*Contributed by Ralph Heinz*)

A variety of saddle parts and other items of tack were recovered. Saddletree nails (FS248.3−4) were found at Custer, and a fragment of an iron cantle or pommel plate (FS4231) was recovered at Reno. Two iron skirt rings (FS4292.1, 4690) were found at Reno, as were seven skirt-ring staples (FS2801, 2811, 4292b.6−9, 4706). FS2801 is a brass staple and is significant as these were called for on the Model 1874 saddles. The other staples are iron which were used on the Civil War−era and Model 1872 saddles. Also found at Reno were an iron foot staple (FS4701a.1) and two brass saddle guard plates (FS 3171, 4705). These items meet the specifications for the Civil War−era and Model 1872 saddles.

Military halters are represented by three iron rings (FS4297.1−2, 4300). These halters employed three rings, two halter squares, a halter bolt, and an iron bar buckle. Two halter squares (FS4136.1, 4297.4) were also recovered as was a halter bolt (FS4297.3). Because of their distribution, these Reno-related items suggest that at least three different halters are represented. FS4297 probably represents a relatively complete halter on which the leather has disintegrated.

Six iron rings of the type used in girthing were recovered. One ring (FS1229) with a 1½-inch (37 millimeters) inside diameter is a nonmilitary type that probably represents a civilian piece. It is possible it represents part of an Indian saddle girth. FS3770 is a 2½-inch-inside-diameter (62 millimeters) Model 1874 saddle near-side (left) girth ring. This ring is significant because it indicates that some saddles made to the 1874 specifications (Ordnance Memorandum No. 18 1874:49) were in use at the battle. Another ring (FS4292b.2) is 2 millimeters smaller but probably represents the same thing. Two iron rings (FS3769, 4292b.1) of 2 inches (50 millimeters) and 3½ inches (87 millimeters) inside diameter, respectively may represent rigging rings for packsaddles. The larger ring may also represent an unauthorized company-saddler modification of an army saddle. Civilian cinches utilized a ring this large, and many officers used civilian rigging. Henry·Weibert of Columbus, Montana, found the remains of an army McClellan saddle near the Reno position, and a pair of these large rings was associated with the relic find. This may indicate Custer's saddlers were adapting a proven nonmilitary system to their issue saddles. McClellan saddles of the Civil War era and those meeting the 1872 and 1874 specifications utilized two (in the latter case one) D-rings. One of those rings (FS3113) was found on the south flank of the hospital swale at the Reno-Benteen defense site.

Two link-strap hooks (fig. 66d) (FS587, 4358) (Steffen 1978), one each from Custer and Reno, were recovered. In addition to the Reno link-strap hook, two smaller snap hooks (FS2520, 4206) were found. These two are significant tack items in that they correspond to the size used on the 1874 side lines (hobbles) (Ordnance Memorandum No. 18 1874:54). The presence of at least two side lines indicates that the new-model material had either reached Custer before his departure or that company saddlers were constructing these items in accordance with current specifications.

Two nonmilitary halter or bridle fragments (FS211, 1726) were found at Custer (fig. 66c, e), but they are constructed with copper tube rivets which postdate the battle by some ten years. Another nonmilitary harness item (FS1146) was also found at Custer. This leather strap and harness buckle appears to be made up of parts, perhaps as an expiedent measure. A single nonmilitary steel snap hook (FS3019) was found at Reno. It probably postdates the battle by many years since it is steel and not a cast-iron or stamped piece.

Two items of wagon harness were found at Reno. One (FS2545) is a side-line hook and hasp and the other is a neck chain (FS4292c) which conforms to the 1877 quartermaster specifications for horse and mule harness. It is possible they may have been associated with the pack train or they may have been with one of the later parties to visit the field.

Horseshoes and Horseshoe Nails

Nineteen horseshoes or horseshoe fragments were recovered during the archaeological project. Thirteen were found on the Custer battlefield and the others were from the Reno-Benteen defense site. It is difficult to ascertain, except for one instance, whether the shoes are battle related. Horses were used for many years in the area, and the method of construction and attachment of shoes varies little through time. Nevertheless, manufacturing techniques and the context in which the shoes were found are clues to their origin. All shoe identification and nomenclature follow Rick Morris (personal communication, January 8, 1987), Spivey (1979), and Berge (1980: 237–49). The shoes recovered are all of the light riding- or saddle-horse type.

The shoes were found in four types: a blacksmith- or farrier-made shoe, Burden pattern, Goodenough pattern, and an unidentified late commercially made shoe. The late commercial specimen (FS4981) has applied caulks. This shoe and caulk type was not manufactured until the end of the nineteenth century; thus it postdates the battle. Eleven caulked and fullered shoes were found on the Custer battlefield (Scott and Fox 1987), and two were recovered at the Reno-Benteen defense site. The Custer shoes will be discussed first, then the Reno shoes. The Custer shoes, except FS613, are Burden-pattern shoes. Burden shoes (fig. 66f) were introduced before the Civil War. Burden supplied most of the army's horseshoe needs from the 1860s until World War I. The blacksmith- or farrier-made shoe (FS613) is a right hind shoe with toe and heel caulks. The other Custer shoes are the Burden pattern. FS106 is a fullered front shoe that exhibits extreme toe wear. As a general rule of thumb, army horseshoes were replaced on a monthly basis, so this and other worn shoes may have been near the end of their life expectancy. Another front shoe is FS361, which also has some toe wear. FS526 is a right hind shoe with an added-on toe caulk and one heel caulk. The other heel is on a long lateral branch extension (fig. 66h). This shoe was designed to correct a gait fault. Caulks were generally added to the commercial shoe by the farrier to give the horse better traction. Specific types of caulks were added, depending on the ground conditions and the horse's job. The caulks on these shoes are common for grassland situations. FS675 is nearly identical to FS526 and was probably made by the same farrier for a horse with a nearly identical problem. FS903 is a left front shoe with integral heel and toe caulks. FS943 is a right hind shoe with extreme toe wear, and F1206 is a left hind shoe with robust heel and toe caulks. The shoe does not exhibit much wear and may have been lost when it was fairly new. FS1592 is a front shoe with toe and heel caulks, and it has some toe wear. FS1727 is a front shoe with no distinctive traits, and FS1785 is a front shoe with some toe wear.

Three Reno shoes are of the Burden pattern (FS2775, 3307, 3947) and three are of the Goodenough pattern (FS2862, 3038, 4080). The Goodenough-brand horseshoe was introduced in 1875, and the army immediately bought a large quantity for field trials. One Burden shoe (FS2775) is a front shoe with integral heel caulks. It exhibits extreme toe wear and has seven nails still in place. The second specimen (FS3947) is a left hind shoe that also exhibits moderate toe wear. Six nails are present in the shoe. The third Burden (FS3307) is a front shoe that shows moderate wear overall, with pronounced wear on the toe. The heel was drubbed off by a blacksmith using a hot-cut technique. Two nails are still in place (fig. 66g).

One Goodenough shoe (FS3038) is a right hind shoe with an integral toe caulk. Five nails are still present. The second (FS2862) is a front shoe with extreme toe wear. It has also had the heel drubbed off by hot cutting. Six nails are still present. The final Goodenough shoe (FS4080) has an integral toe caulk and exhibits very little wear. Only one nail is still present.

A small Burden front shoe (FS928) with some toe wear was found on the Custer battlefield (Scott and Fox 1987) and is marked "HA" on the inside. The mark may be a shoe size. One Goodenough shoe (FS2862) from the Reno-Benteen defense site is marked. The mark is illegible because of corrosion.

Horseshoe nails were not a common find during the investigations; however, 115 nails or nail fragments were found. Two head types are represented among the nails. One has a large beveled head and the other has a small beveled head (table 15). These head types probably represent different manufacturing sources. Forty nails are complete and show no evidence of use. These nails (4 from Custer and 36 from Reno) were probably lost from the soldiers' saddlebags during the battle. Soldiers were required to carry extra horseshoes and nails in their saddlebags while on the march. In addition, 5 horseshoe-nail fragments were found in 1984 on the Custer battlefield (Scott and Fox 1987). Twenty-three nail fragments (table 15) were recovered from the Reno-Benteen defense site in 1985, and an additional fragment (FS5038) was found on the Custer battlefield.

The Custer battlefield yielded twelve horseshoes and nineteen horseshoe nails. These artifacts were widely distributed across the battlefield and could easily represent different horses. Two corrective shoes are so nearly alike they were undoubtedly made by the

Table 15   Horseshoe Nails by Field-Specimen Number

Small bevel-headed nails (25 specimens):

   Reno-Benteen Defense Site
2681, 2682, 2772, 2780, 2781, 2782, 2819, 2820, 2821, 2823, 2836, 2967, 2988, 3102, 3940, 4256, 4257, 4258, 4272, 4273, 4363, 4371, 4389, 4642, 4868

Large bevel-headed nails (61 specimens):

   Custer Battlefield
180, 268, 713, 360, 476, 627, 664, 701, 716, 973, 1160, 1209, 1256, 1844

   Reno-Benteen Defense Site
2163, 2659, 2663, 2675, 2677, 2680, 2804, 2817, 2842, 2843, 2844a, 2844b, 2845, 2848, 2849, 2852, 2876, 2945, 2954, 2955, 2956, 2957, 2958, 2972, 2975, 2979, 2985, 3336, 3683, 3729, 3951, 4132, 4658, 4682, 4684, 4698, 4701ca, 4701cb, 4711, 4813, 4824, 4836, 4918, 4969, 4971, 5042

Nail Fragments (29 specimens):

   Custer Battlefield
401, 604, 708, 978, 1676, 5038

   Reno-Benteen Defense Site
2473, 2519, 2717, 2832, 2835, 2869, 2873, 2971, 2977, 3018, 3034, 3035, 3068, 3087, 3149, 3713, 3731, 4802, 4826a, 4838, 4869, 4873, 4957

same farrier for two different horses. At least two horses at the Custer battlefield may have had a gait problem which required these corrective shoes. The six shoes and eighty-four horseshoe nails from the Reno-Benteen defense site exhibit no such distinctions. The majority of the shoes and nails were in the vicinity of the barricade.

The consistency in styles of horseshoes and nails between the two battlefields strongly suggests the artifacts are battle related. With one exception which clearly postdates the battle, all the styles meet the general army specifications for the period, further supporting a battle association.

Picket Pins

Portions of four Model 1859 army-issue picket pins were recovered from the Reno-Benteen defense site. One complete specimen (FS2857) (fig. 64b) was found in the barricade area still in its vertical position. A broken shaft (FS4262) was found near the June 26 redoubt. One complete (FS3768) and one broken (FS4749) figure-eight tether ring were found in the vicinity of the Company H position.

Concha

A nickel-plated brass saddle concha (FS2474) was located on the Reno-Benteen defense site. The copper attachment wires are also nickel plated and soldered to the center of the back of the concha. The concha is one and one-eighth inches (twenty-nine millimeters) in diameter. The method of manufacture suggests the concha is pre-1900, but its archaeological context is not rigorous enough to assign it to the battle period.

Ammunition Box Screws

Some of the square or cut nails are, as will be noted, the appropriate size for use in the construction of ammunition and hardtack boxes. Two-and-one-half-inch flat-head wood screws, were used by the Ordnance Department to attach the box top and bottom to the sides of the ammunition crates. The screws were countersunk and sealed with wax impressed with the arsenal device (Anon. 1979). Seven screws (FS2905, 4390, 4666a, 4666b, 4695, 4700, 4701) that meet the specifications for ammunition-box fasteners were recovered at the Reno-Benteen defense site.

Ammunition-Box Seal

One piece of military equipment unrelated to the battle was recovered from the Custer battlefield. It is a lead bale seal from an ammunition box. The seal has "USA" around the interior of the rim on one side and a disfigured bursting-bomb ordnance device on the other side. Holes for two sealing wires run through the seal. Seals of this type were not introduced to the military until the advent of .30-caliber ammunition at the end of the nineteenth century (Anon. 1979). This seal may be related to the 1926 battle reenactment.

NAILS AND TACKS

A total of 611 cut and wire nails and tacks (table 16) were recovered at the Custer battlefield and the Reno-Benteen defense site. This artifact class represents approximately 12 percent of the total number of artifacts collected during the project. The artifacts also represent disappointment for a volunteer who had expected to find a more interesting object. However, nails have a tale of their own to tell and long have aided archaeologists in interpreting a site's history (Nelson 1968).

Square or cut nails and tacks account for 84 percent of the nail collection, with a size range from 2d to 60d (table 16). The majority of the larger-size cut and wire nails were found on the Custer battlefield. Most of these nails were found along the monument's boundary fence or near old fence lines which defined the original monument boundary. Undoubtedly these nails represent the construction, rebuilding, and demolition of those fences. The cut nails represent the first fences installed at the monument in 1891. These fences were barbed wire with wooden posts and had a wooden cap rail (Rickey 1958:79).

Cut nails were found near some of the markers and probably indicate where early wooden crosses and markers were placed to locate where a soldier had been interred. Cut nails are dominant around the markers, but wire nails were also found. The wire nail had virtually replaced the cut nail by 1890 (Nelson 1968), and their presence can be attributed to the repair of the old markers before their replacement by the marble markers.

Cut nails in the 4d and 5d sizes (table 16) dominated the nail finds at the Reno-Benteen defense site. The concentration of these nail sizes in direct association with army-related artifacts suggests a battle association for the nails. Hardtack ration boxes and ammunition boxes were constructed of wood and nailed and screwed together. No period ration boxes are known to survive, although their construction is known to have

Table 16 Nails and Tacks by Type, Size, and Field-Specimen Number

Cut Nails

2d (17 specimens):

Custer Battlefield
220, 739, 998a, 998b, 998c, 998d, 998e

Reno-Benteen Defense Site
4292a, 4292b, 4292c, 4292d, 4292e, 4292f, 4292g, 4292h, 4292i, 4292j

3d (11 specimens):

Custer Battlefield
163, 1812

Reno-Benteen Defense Site
3800, 4247, 4253, 4292k, 4292l, 4292m, 4318, 4402, 4756

4d (56 specimens):

Custer Battlefield
103, 164, 212, 213, 215, 308, 690, 714, 736, 749, 754

Reno-Benteen Defense Site
2156, 2334, 2651, 2670, 2672, 2679, 2691, 2713, 2722, 2723, 2816, 2914, 2917, 2922, 3169, 3230, 3236, 3237, 3659, 3740, 3758, 3780, 3785, 3973, 3985, 3989, 4238, 4260, 4292n, 4292o, 4292p, 4292q, 4301, 4315, 4331, 4336, 4360, 4715, 4723, 4727, 4798, 4810, 4839, 4843, 4973

5d (99 specimens):

Reno-Benteen Defense Site
2671, 2678, 2685, 2687, 2698, 2720, 2724, 2766, 2839, 2919, 2936, 2947, 3107, 3121, 3235, 3245, 3322, 3581, 3582, 3584, 3588, 3589, 3590, 3591, 3660, 3676, 3728, 3731, 3736, 3737, 3744, 3748, 3749, 3755, 3756a, 3756b, 3759, 3767, 3786, 3795, 3797, 3972, 3975, 3978, 4010, 4012, 4061, 4062, 4065, 4088, 4092, 4094, 4105, 4234, 4240, 4248, 4264, 4277, 4286, 4292r, 4292s, 4292t, 4292u, 4292v, 4292w, 4292x, 4292y, 4292z, 4292aa, 4292bb, 4292cc, 4292dd, 4292ee, 4292ff, 4292gg, 4292hh, 4292ii, 4298, 4332, 4335, 4345, 4349, 4350, 4351, 4352, 4354, 4359, 4649, 4650, 4714, 4716, 4716, 4718, 4720, 4722, 4728, 4803, 4806, 4962

6d (14 specimens):

Custer Battlefield
104a, 104b, 374, 721, 979, 1047, 1152, 1646, 1674, 1697

Reno-Benteen Defense Site
common 2930, 3756c finish 2915, 3986

7d (26 specimens):

Custer Battlefield
104c, 104d, 104e, 118, 567, 755, 1009, 1410, 1413, 1416, 1418, 1422, 1426, 5093

Reno-Benteen Defense Site
3756d, 3764, 3779, 3788, 3789, 3793, 3794, 4292jj, 4292kk, 4292ll, 4292mm, 4292nn

8d (32 specimens):

Custer Battlefield
124, 1001, 1344, 1454

Reno-Benteen Defense Site
2006, 2335, 2754, 2944, 3733, 3738, 3754, 3756, 3778, 3781, 3802, 4292oo, 4292pp, 4292qq, 4392, 4393, 4394, 4395, 4401, 4662, 4663, 4664, 4665, 4666b, 4667, 4668, 4669, 4670

Table 16 *continued*

9d (9 specimens):

Custer Battlefield
113, 114, 116, 158, 737, 1423, 1424, 1425, 1427

10d (3 specimens)

Custer Battlefield
1000, 1420, 1439

12d (1 specimen)

Custer Battlefield
4882b

30d (26 specimens):

Custer Battlefield
009, 191a, 491b, 811, 855, 857, 861, 863, 865, 871, 897, 1286, 1349, 1379, 1437, 1527, 1561a, 1562, 1563, 1573, 1574, 1619, 1620, 1838, 1846, 1853a

40d (17 specimens):

Custer Battlefield
087, 262, 511, 1743, 1840a, 1840b, 1840c, , 1842, 1850, 1851, 1852, 1861, 1863, 1864, 1865, 1866, 1869

50d (9 specimens):

Custer Battlefield
086, 665, 859, 1189, 1282, 1301, 1741, 1847, 1856

60d (2 specimens):

Custer Battlefield
651, 1577

Miscellaneous Cut Nails (20 Specimens)

Custer Battlefield
Saddletree nails - 225, 259, 267, 277, 842, 1854
Cut tacks - 1033, 5093

Reno-Benteen Defense Site
Finish #1 - 2961, Finish 1⅜ - 2751, Finish 1¼ - 4299, Barrel ¾ - 2514, Tack #4 - 4292rr, 4292ss, 4292tt, 4292uu, Tack #10 - 2381, Tack #12 - 4292vv, Tack fragment - 2523, 4292fff

Nail Fragments (173 Specimens)

Custer Battlefield
028, 088, 112, 117, 119, 120, 121, 122, 123, 125, 126, 127, 128, 152, 154, 157, 160, 161, 162, 165, 166, 169, 216, 464, 528c, 611, 702, 710, 711, 762, 869, 893, 993, 1011, 1037, 1122c, 1143, 1158, 1244, 1315, 1376, 1384, 1411, 1421, 1622, 1648, 1659, 1699, 1823, 4461, 4472

Reno-Benteen Defense Site
2031, 2385, 2472, 2526, 2666, 2673, 2711, 2718, 2767, 2810, 2840, 2864, 2879, 2895, 2909, 2911, 2913, 2914, 2915, 2916, 2950, 3014, 3015, 3071, 3082, 3084, 3105, 3162, 3234, 3243, 3583, 3585, 3587, 3591, 3680, 3739, 3752, 3756e, 3757, 3760, 3766, 3777, 3783, 3791, 3792, 3799, 3801, 3953, 3955, 3965, 3977, 3979, 3981, 3982, 3983, 3984, 4011, 4013, 4027, 4086, 4096, 4097, 4219, 4233, 4235, 4236, 4237, 4240, 4242, 4243, 4244, 4245, 4246, 4249, 4250, 4251, 4252, 4254, 4255, 4259, 4261, 4274, 4276, 4278, 4292ww, 4292xx, 4292yy, 4292zz,

Table 16 *continued*

4292aaa, 4292bbb, 4292ccc, 4292ddd, 4303, 4316, 4326, 4327, 4328, 4330, 4333, 4334, 4340, 4343, 4344, 4347, 4348, 4353, 4368, 4369, 4383, 4384, 4391, 4396, 4397, 4398, 4399, 4400, 4702, 4721, 4724, 4726, 4817, 4826b

Wire Nails

3d (1 specimen):

Custer Battlefield
848

4d (4 specimens):

Custer Battlefield
104f, 207, 209, 489, 446b

Reno-Benteen Defense Site
2111, 2155

5d (1 specimen):

Custer Battlefield
415

6d (4 specimens):

Custer Battlefield
104g, 590, 1095

Reno-Benteen Defense Site
2010

7d (27 specimens):

Custer Battlefield
104h, 104i, 104j, 104k, 104l, 104m, 104n, 104o, 104p, 104q, 104r, 104s, 104t, 167, 208, 234, 256, 257, 650, 1038, 1078, 1243, 1341, 1414, 1443, 1696

Reno-Benteen Defense Site
3232

8d (1 specimen):

Reno-Benteen Defense Site
2007

9d (4 specimens):

Custer Battlefield
104u, 104v, 104w, 104x

12d (1 specimen):

Custer Battlefield
194

20d (21 specimens):

Custer Battlefield
192, 193, 203, 205, 206, 1183, 1304, 1342, 1430, 1561b, 1572, 1575, 1802a, 1802b, 1802c, 1802d, 1802e, 1803, 1804, 1805, 1918

Table 16 *continued*

40d (1 specimen):

Custer Battlefield
1802f

50d (2 specimens):

Custer Battlefield
1306, 1565

Miscellaneous Wire Nails (21 Specimens)

Custer Battlefield
1 inch finish - 1257, 1 inch tack - 1653, ¾ inch brad - 1740a, 1740b, 1740c, 1740d, 1740e, 1740f, 1740g, 1740h, 1740i

Reno-Benteen Defense Site
Standard barb 1¼ inch 10 gauge - 2244, Standard barb 2 inch 10 gauge - 2231, Chisel point 1 inch 10 gauge countersunk head - 3688, American felt ⅞ inch - 2127, Thumb tacks - 2865, 3100, 3959, 4761, ⁹⁄₁₆ inch head 1¼ inch square shank tack - 4748, 4856, ½ inch brad - 3759

Wire-Nail Fragments (8 Specimens)

Custer Battlefield
104y, 204, 392, 1077, 1581, 1682

Reno-Benteen Defense Site
2058, 2851b

been lighter than the ammunition box. Period ammunition boxes do survive (Anon. 1979). Examination of construction specifications and extant examples indicated that 4d and 5d nails were used in the construction of ammunition boxes. This suggests many of the Reno-Benteen nails may be associated with ration or ammunition boxes. Many nails from the Reno-Benteen defense site are likely to have been deposited as a result of the breakage or disintergration of these boxes.

A few saddletree nails (table 16) were also recovered, but the small number is not surprising because of their small size and the amount of oxidation they suffered through the last 110 years. The cut brass tacks (table 16) are of the type commonly used by Indians to decorate gunstocks, war clubs, and tomahawks, among other items. This possible association can only be suggested, since the tacks served many other decorative purposes.

TIN CANS (*Contributed by Patrick Phillips*)

Tin cans, like nails, have a tale to tell the archaeologist. Can manufacturing technology changed through time, and those changes are well documented and dated. The various tin-can manufacturing methods have established a range of dates for various features present on a can. This allows archaeologists to date the period of manufacture for almost any can recovered at an archaeological site. The can and can fragments from the 1984 and 1985 investigations were analyzed on the basis of the criteria provided in Fontana et al. (1962) and Rock (1984).

Table 17 Cans from the Custer Battlefield by Field-Specimen Number

FS	Completeness	End Type	End Seal	Side Seal	Size, U.S. Bureau of Standards
001	Y	HIC	STM	LPM	
003	F		DBL		
008	N		STM	DBL	
036	N		DBL	DBL	
039	F		DBL		
040	N		DBL	DBL	
070	F		DBL	DBL	
174	Y	HIT	STM	DBL	
189	Y	HIC	STM	LPM	
201	N		DBL	DBL	NO 3
230	F		DBL	DBL	
274	N		DBL	LPM	
275	F			LPM	
323	Y		DBL	DBL	
358	F				
359	N		DBL	DBL	
399	N		STH	LPM	
400	F				
402	F				
408	N	HIC		LPM	
417	F		DBL	LPM	
454	N		DBL	DBL	
457	Y		DBL	DBL	
477	F				
480	Y			LPH	
510	F				
515	F				
528	N	HIC	STM	LPH	NO 3
534	Y	HIC	STM	LPM	NO 2
536	Y	HIC	STM	LPM	NO 3
537	Y	HIC	STM	LPH	NO 3
538	F		DBL	DBL	
548	Y			LPH	
571	N		DBL	DBL	
572	N	HIC	STM	DBL	NO 3
595	N	HIC	STM	DBL	NO 3
623	N		DBL	LPM	
652	N	HIC	STM	LPM	
653	F		ST?		
661	N		INS	LPM	
681	N		DBL	DBL	
715	F		ST?		
728	N	HIC		LPM	
800	F		ST?		
804	F				
805	F	HIC	ST?		
809	F				
810	Y		DBL	DBL	
836	Y			LPH	
873	F	HIC	ST?		

Table 17 *continued*

FS	Completeness	End Type	End Seal	Side Seal	Size, U.S. Bureau of Standards
875	F		ST?		
879	F	HIC	STM	LPM	
882	F		DBL		
884	Y		DBL	DBL	
886	F	HIC	STM	LPM	
896	N			LPH	
898	N			LPH	
910	Y		DBL	DBL	
941	F				
961	F		DBL		
1096	N		DBL	DBL	
1099	N	HIC		DBL	
1100	F		DBL		
1164	N		ST?	LPM	
1169	Y		DBL	DBL	
1172	N	HIC	STM	DBL	
1176	N	HIC	STM	LPM	
1184	N		DBL	DBL	NO303
1195	N		DBL	LPM	
1217	N		DBL	DBL	
1239	F		DBL	DBL	
1260	N	HIC			
1350	Y			LPH	
1588	N		DBL	DBL	
1636	F		DBL		
1720	Y		DBL	DBL	
1824	N	HIC	STM	DBL	NO 2
1825		HIC	STM	LPH	
1826	Y	HIC	ST?	LPH	
1829	F	HIC			
1857	N	HIC	STM	LPM	NO 10
1858	F		DBL	DBL	
1860	F		ST?		
1868	Y	HIC	STM	LPM	NO 2

Y   = yes
N   = no
F   = fragment
HIC = hole in cap
HIT = hole in top
ST? = stamped, unknown soldering method
STH = stamped, hand soldered
STM = stamped, machine soldered
DBL = modern double seam
INS = insert in body and hand soldered
CRP = crimped seam
LP? = lap seam with unknown soldering style
LPH = hand soldered side seam
LPM = machine soldered lap seam

Cans manufactured during the battle would be hole-in-cap types with stamped ends and simple side-seam overlap. The side seams were hand soldered. Machine soldering was developed in 1876, and cans with machine-soldered seams would not have been present during the battle.

Overall, of the 85 cans and can fragments recovered on Custer battlefield (table 17), 59 (including 15 of the 19 intact cans) are post-1876 manufacture. The Reno-Benteen defense site yielded 128 cans and can fragments (table 18). All 14 intact cans and two fragments are definitely post-1876 manufacture. Unfortunately, the other can and can fragments cannot be definitively classified as pre-1876 manufacture.

In order to make a definitive classification, enough of the can must be present to identify the manufacturing technology employed on the sides and end. Many recovered can fragments do not have any observable manufacturing features. In addition, the soldered side-seam fragments must be large enough to determine the soldering techniques. The majority of fragments in the collection retain no observable datable characteristics. The Reno-Benteen collection contains 112 undatable fragments, while the Custer battlefield collection has only 26 unidentified cans and fragments.

The fact that so many small and undatable fragments came from the Reno-Benteen defense site is suggestive. Given the nature of the battles fought at the two locations, Reno-Benteen is the one at which it is more likely that cans were discarded. This could have occurred during the fight as someone stopped for a meal or during the days following the battle and before the command moved the wounded to the steamboat *Far West*. It is also possible that the oldest can remains would be the least well preserved. Thus the possibility that the small can fragments recovered at Reno-Benteen could be associated with the battle cannot be discounted. Additional provocative evidence of this possibility is the fact that Bray (1958) reported finding can fragments in his excavations at the Reno-Benteen defense site. It is also possible that the small fragments may not be from cans but are deteriorated remnants of tinned ration-box liners, mess plates, or tin cups.

In addition to the expected manufacturing technologies observed among the recovered tin cans, several surprises came to light. One can (FS1099) recovered from the Custer battlefield has a stamped end and a double-seal end. Another example of two different end-sealing methods on the same can are present on cans FS661 from Custer and FS4292 from Reno-Benteen. These cans have a post-1876 machine-soldered stamped end and another end consisting of a hole-in-top with a hand-soldered seal. Several other (FS2631, 2815, 2969, 3689, 4845) Reno-Benteen cans also have the hole-in-top end, but the other end has not been preserved. A possible explanation for the cans with two different end seals is that they may have been recycled cans.

Another unusual technology was an end seal which seemed to consist of a single crimp instead of the double crimp. This seal was present on five can fragments (FS2600, 2603, 2605, 2609, 2611) from Reno-Benteen. The fragments were found near one another and may be from one can or canlike object. This seal type is not mentioned in the literature, although it may represent a transitional form of the double seal.

Five sardine cans (FS480, 548, 836, 1350) were found on the Custer battlefield and do not exhibit any of the modern features. However, sardine-can history is not as well documented as that of the tin can. It appears that the unusual shape of the sardine can

Table 18 Cans from the Reno-Benteen Defense Site by Field-Specimen Number

FS	Completeness	End Type	End Seal	Side Seal	Size, Bureau of Standards
2003	F				
2042	F				
2045	Y		DBL	DBL	8OZ
2054	Y			DBL	
2059	F				
2105	Y	HIT	STM	DBL	
2106	Y		DBL	DBL	
2107	Y		DBL	DBL	
2108	F				
2110	F		ST?		
2112	Y	HIC	STM	LPM	
2113	F				
2128	Y				
2131	Y		DBL	DBL	
2153	Y	HIC	STM	DBL	8OZ
2154	Y	HIC	STM	DBL	
2597	F				
2599	F				
2600	F		CRP		
2601	F				
2602	F				
2603	F		CRP		
2604	F				
2605	F		CRP		
2606	F				
2607	F				
2608	F				
2609	F		CRP		
2611	F		CRP		
2631	F		INS		
2683	N		ST?	LP?	
2684	F				
2686	F				
2690	F				
2692	F				
2694	F		ST?		
2699	F		ST?	LP?	
2700	F	HIC	ST?		
2702	F		ST?		
2703	N	HIC			
2707	F				
2712	F		ST?		
2714	F				
2719	F		ST?		
2725	F				
2728	F				
2737	F		ST?		
2808	F				
2809	F				
2815	F		INS		

Table 18 *Continued*

FS	Completeness	End Type	End Seal	Side Seal	Size, Bureau of Standards
2822	F				
2825	F				
2827	F				
2828	F				
2829	F			LP?	
2851	F				
2853	F				
2853	F				
2854	F				
2935	Y	HIC	STM	LPM	NO3
2937	F				
2938	F				
2951	F				
2951	F				
2953	F				
2959	F				
2965	F		ST?		
2968	F			LP?	
2969	N		INS	LP?	
2970	F				
2973	F				
2980	F		ST?		
3010	F				
3017	F		ST?	LP?	
3029	F		ST?	LP?	
3041	F			LP?	
3045	F	HIC			
3055	F	HIC			
3072	F				
3074	Y	HIC	STM	LSM	303
3078	F				
3079	F				
3080	F			LS?	
3081	F			LS?	
3083	F				
3091	F		ST?	LP?	
3103	F	HIC			
3321	N		LP?		
3345	F				
3580	F				
3605	F				
3625	Y	HIC	STM	LPM	
3644	Y	HIC	STM	LSM	NO3
3689	N		INS	LS?	
3772	F	HIC			
3773	N	HIC	ST?		
3775	F				
3804	Y	HIC	STM	LPM	
3976	F	HIC	ST?		
3980	F		ST?		
3994	F				

Table 18 *continued*

FS	Completeness	End Type	End Seal	Side Seal	Size, Bureau of Standards
4015	F		ST?		
4072	F				
4077	Y	HIC	ST?	LPM	8OZ
4106	F				
4221	F				
4224	F		ST?		
4292	Y	HIT	INS	LPM	
4305	F	HIC			
4324	F				
4355	F				
4657	F				
4677	F				
4678	F				
4679	F			LP?	
4680	F				
4733	F				
4735	F		ST?		
4747	F			LP?	
4793	F				
4812	F				
4825	F		ST?		
4828	F		ST?		
4831	F				
4832	F				
4835	F				
4845	F	HIT	INS		

Y   = yes
N   = no
F   = fragment
HIC = hole in cap
HIT = hole in top
ST? = stamped, unknown soldering method
STH = stamped, hand soldered
STM = stamped, machine soldered
DBL = modern double seam
INS = insert in body and hand soldered
CRP = crimped seam
LP? = lap seam with unknown soldering style
LPH = Hand soldered side seam
LPM = Machine soldered by seam

precluded the application of sophisticated manufacturing technologies until late in the nineteenth century.

In summary, no cans or fragments can be conclusively associated with the Battle of the Little Bighorn. This is especially true of the intact cans recovered. The association of the can fragments recovered from the Reno-Benteen defense site is not as clear. These fragments were found in good association with definite battle-related artifacts and may be either can fragments or pieces of ration-box liners. Unfortunately, without more complete specimens to analyze, this must remain speculation.

MISCELLANEOUS POST-BATTLE MATERIALS

A variety of artifacts were recovered that date to the post-1876 period. These materials reflect the use of the battlefield as a national cemetery and a national monument. The artifacts also reflect the various activities of caretakers and visitors. These activities range from burying the dead, constructing memorials, and building fences to the disposal of domestic trash.

Ceramics

Three pieces of white ironstone china were found in trench 11 in Deep Ravine. These were a part of a deeply buried trash deposit discovered during the trenching operation. The ceramics and a few other items dislodged by the backhoe were collected. The ironstone artifacts consist of a cup foot-ring, body, and rim; a foot-ring fragment of a vessel about sugar-bowl size; and an unidentified body shard. The foot rings on both the bowl and the cup exhibit extreme wear, suggesting extensive use.

One white-china rim fragment from an unidentified bowl was recovered. It has no distinguishing marks.

Glass

Sixty-one pieces of bottle glass and three complete bottles were recovered from the monument. Six different glass colors were noted, representing a variety of bottle types. Most of the glass artifacts are unidentified body fragments.

Thirty-two fragments of brown bottle glass, one base, two finishes, and one complete bottle were found. The brown color is usually associated with alcoholic-beverage containers. The one base fragment is marked "R & Co." This is attributed to Roth and Company, a San Francisco bottler that used this mark from 1879 to about 1888 (Toulouse 1971: 438–39). The finish fragments are tooled finishes for cork bottles. One still has the remnants of the wire cork retainer adhering to the base of the finish. The finishes probably belong to sixteen-ounce beer bottles of the same type as the base. One complete twelve-ounce-crown-cap beer bottle was also recovered. The base of this bottle is marked with the Owens Illinois Glass Company trademark, which was in use from 1929 to 1966 (Toulouse 1971: 403).

One green glass fragment, probably from a relatively recent soda-pop bottle, was found. Four amber glass fragments and three opalized glass fragments were recovered, including the base of a six-ounce oval-panel bottle.

Seven clear glass fragments were found. Also among the clear-glass group are an unidentified finish fragment, two continuous threaded finishes, and the base and body of a sixteen-ounce bottle. Several fragments of an eight-ounce acid bottle with a continuous-thread finish were also recovered. A four-fifths-quart continuous-thread finish bottle was recovered. The base is marked E & J Gallo Winery. A crown-cap twelve-ounce soda-pop bottle is also present, as is a one-quart continuous-thread finish bottle. This bottle has an Owens Illinois base mark dating to 1929–54 (Toulouse 1971: 403). The base marks indicate the bottle was made at plant number 5 in either 1936 or 1946.

This particular bottle was found in trench 11 in Deep Ravine. Its presence suggests that the trash at the ravine headcut was deposited some time between 1930 and 1950.

None of the glass bottles or fragments can be attributed to the Battle of the Little Bighorn. All of the glass appears to be of later production and deposition. Only two clear-glass fragments were found at the Reno-Benteen defense site. The others were found in the trash dumps or randomly scattered on the Custer battlefield. The glass present in the collection appears to be the result of the discard of liquor, soda-pop, and other containers from about 1880 to the present day.

Wood

Several wooden stakes or stake fragments were recovered during the inventory and from the marble marker excavations. Twelve pine stakes made from one-by-four-inch lumber were found on the battlefield. The stakes probably represent the locations of artifact finds. All the stakes were charred to some degree and were displaced. Excavations at Squares A-84, C-85, M-85, and O-85 recovered fragments of stakes which may have been used to mark the grave locations prior to the installation of the marble markers. Square P-85 also yielded wood fragments that were part of the wooden form used to pour the marker's concrete base.

Metal

A variety of metal fragments and objects were found scattered across the two battlefields. They appear to be randomly lost or discarded items. The artifacts consist of a cast-iron stove lid, two wagon-wheel hub fragments, a trace chain, six chain links or fragments, six stays for floral arrangements, twenty-one pieces of metal box bands or barrel hoops, a piece of shielded electrical cable, three pieces of hacksaw blades, two fragments of files, a paint brush, a Ford Model T tire jack, a pair of fencing pliers, and a farrier's horseshoe-nail puller. Additional items are twenty-eight pieces of wire of various sizes; forty-three nuts, bolts, screws, washers, and staples; eight tags with impressed numbers for identifying containers; fifty-four unidentified pieces of scrap iron; and fifty-five miscellaneous items.

These miscellaneous items consist of two fragments of tobacco-package foil liners, six bobby pins, three straight pins, three M-1 flashbulbs, one transistor, two-safety razor blades, six fish hooks and two lead sinkers, two nut picks, a small-chest-size padlock, a bucket bail, a piece of lead pipe, a safety pin, a toy horse and jockey, a shoe heel plate, a pencil ferrule, a gilt pot-metal pendant, a garter hook, a girdle fastener, a kerosene lamp fragment, a grease fitting, a grommet from a paper tag, a coil spring from a seat, a piston ring, a shipping-coffin handle, a boiler handle, a button snap, a spark-plug washer, two chrome flanges, a babbit rod, two S-hooks, a lipstick tube, two spring clips, and an aluminum decorative belt disc. None of the items is associated with the battle. These are the result of later deposition by administrators or visitors to the site.

Chapter 8

Archaeological Geology of Deep Ravine, Custer Battlefield National Monument

by C. Vance Haynes, Jr.

INTRODUCTION

The Custer battlefield is perhaps the only battlefield in the world where the locations of most of the fallen members of one side are marked. In a few cases the name of the individual is known; however, a major unanswered question regarding the battle that took place around Custer battlefield on June 25, 1876, is what happened to twenty-eight men, presumably from Company E, Seventh Cavalry. The remains of these men have never been adequately accounted for in spite of four official attempts to do so: one immediately after the battle, another in 1877, another in 1879, and still another in 1881 (Dustin 1953). Personal accounts on these occasions claim that an unknown number of men, mostly from E Company, were annihilated in a gully heading on the southwest side of Last Stand Hill. Today, this is believed to be what is known as Deep Ravine (fig. 67).

Some accounts say that the gully walls were too steep and high for the men to get out and ended in a cul-de-sac. This was probably what geomorphologists today refer to as a headcut, where a relatively broad, shallow, vegetated drainage becomes entrenched by the erosion of a gully or arroyo, forming a steplike cut in the grassy floor of a swale. When two or more headcuts form along a broad, shallow drainage, it is referred to as a discontinuous gully. Eventually, as the headcuts erode their way upstream (headward) the drainage may become a continuous gully. As further erosion proceeds, gully widening may occur. Both widening and deepening are in part restricted by older and more resistant deposits. Eventually, headward erosion stops and gullies commonly fill with sediments washed from adjacent slopes. The causes for gully cutting and filling are controversial and dependent upon many variables, but changing climate is a major factor.

On the basis of contemporary accounts, it is likely that the troopers who were annihilated in Deep Ravine were trapped in a headcut with nearly vertical walls more than six

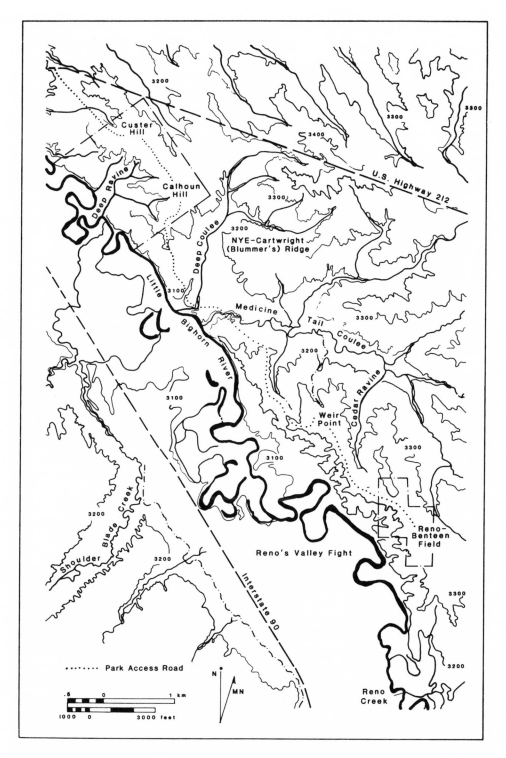

Fig. 67. Map of Custer Battlefield National Monument showing geomorphological features.

feet high. Three days after the battle, surviving members of the command set out to identify as many of the bodies as possible and cover the remains with brush and what-ever earth could be scooped up with the very limited tools at hand (Dustin 1953). The bodies in Deep Ravine were said to be so putrid that members of the burial detail became nauseated. An effort to remove the bodies from the gully was abandoned, and a mass burial was made instead by simply caving off the gully sides. It is not clear from various accounts how completely the remains were buried or how many may have been removed. Several accounts claim that many exposed bones were observed the following year during reburial efforts, but there are conflicting statements as to whether any re-mains were removed. There are also conflicting statements as to just where the presumed concentration of bodies was located in Deep Ravine, and a contemporary sketch map of the ravine shows the location of the bodies with twenty-nine X's scattered along Deep Ravine for more than four hundred meters (1312 feet), including one in a tributary (King 1980).

Furthermore, at least one account mentions the occurrence, a few days before the 1877 reburial detail, of "a severe hail storm" that "devistated the whole valley, washing out several of the bodies which had been buried near a ravine" (Wheeler 1923). So we are left with uncertainty as to where the soldiers fell, whether their bodies were removed and reburied, and whether some may have been flushed down the ravine by a "gully washer."

DESCRIPTION OF DEEP RAVINE

On the basis of 1977 aerial photography (CUBF-HQ-1-2), Deep Ravine is today a fourth-order drainage (Strahler 1957) with a drainage area (catchment) of approxi-mately 739,205 square meters (7,957,513 square feet). The drainage extends north-easterly 1,340 meters (4,397 feet) from the mouth to near the divide on Last Stand Hill. A southeasterly tributary (Calhoun Coulee) branches off at the lower fork, 350 meters (1,148 feet) from the mouth. A prominent bend occurs 550 meters (1,805 feet) above the mouth; a small headcut occurs 120 meters (394 feet) above the bend, and the upper fork occurs 190 meters (624 feet) above the bend (fig. 68). The drainage area above the lower fork is 320,470 square meters (3,449,847 square feet).

The floor of Deep Ravine below the headcut slopes approximately 1 degree (2.1% grade), is relatively flat, 5 to 15 meters (16.4 to 49.2 feet) wide, and confined to grassy sloping banks 3 to 6 meters (9.8 to 19.7 feet) high and sloping 40 to 60 degrees. Above the headcut the ravine is considerably shallower, broader, and without steep banks (fig. 68). The first-order drainages stop approximately 100 meters (328 feet) short of the crest of the ridge extending to Last Stand Hill from Calhoun Hill.

OBJECTIVES

Initial testing to discover the remains of the missing men with metal detectors and a soil auger met with negative results in 1984 (Scott and Fox 1987). It was decided to con-tinue testing in 1985 by excavating a series of backhoe trenches across Deep Ravine at

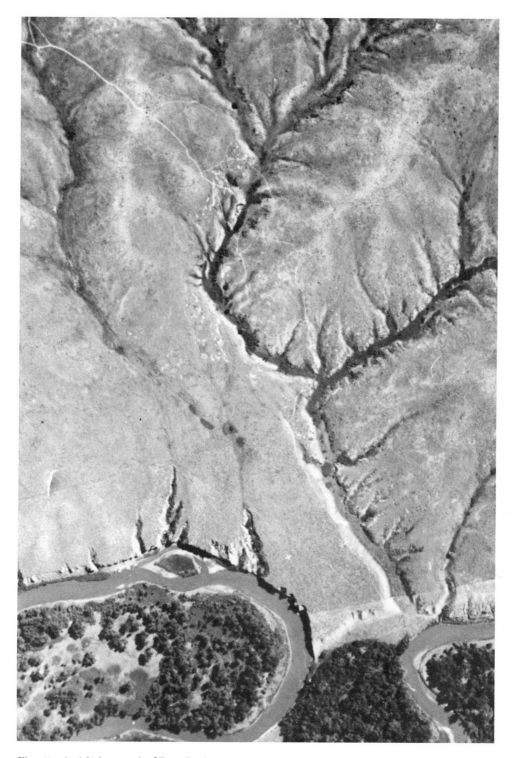

Fig. 68. Aerial photograph of Deep Ravine.

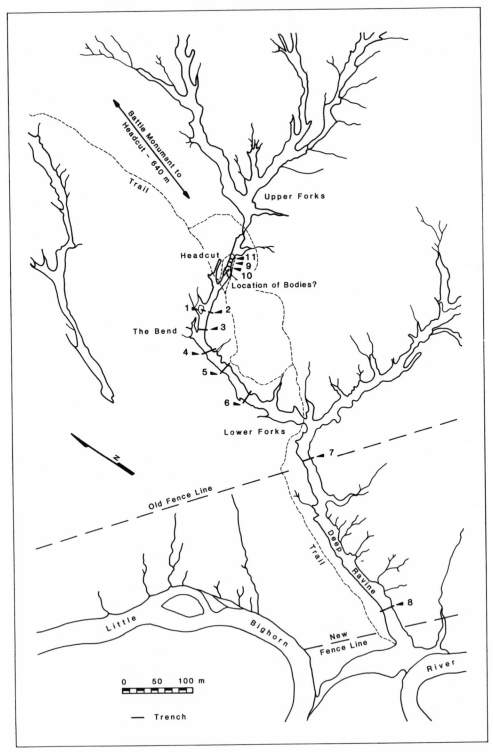

Fig. 69. Map of Deep Ravine showing locations of 1985 backhoe trenches 1 through 11 and hypothesized location of the missing troopers marked by X.

right angles (transverse) to the axis (fig. 69) in order to examine and record the sequence of sediments (stratigraphy) beneath the present floor. By studying the stratigraphy of the trench walls, it would be possible to reconstruct the history of cutting and filling in Deep Ravine from which the layer of sediment most likely to contain the 1876 remains could be identified and prospected.

In addition, knowledge of the stratigraphic succession of a gully such as Deep Ravine is of interest to science in eventually understanding the fundamental causes of erosion and deposition, especially if the geochronology of the layered deposits can be determined from their contained artifacts and/or from radiocarbon dating. If the deposits of Deep Ravine could also be tied into (correlated with) the terraces of the Little Bighorn River, an approach could be made to understanding the sedimentary (alluvial) history of this larger system.

Furthermore, the Custer battlefield provides an unusual opportunity to evaluate the degree of slope-wash erosion that has occurred on grassy slopes under a semiarid climate because the landscape was sprinkled with thousands of cartridge cases in an instant of geologic time: June 25, 1876. The subsequent movement of these cases over the surface and into the subsurface could tell us something of value regarding geologic processes on slopes and in soil (pedogenic) horizons.

BACKHOE TRENCHING

With these objectives in mind, but with the missing troopers having first priority, we decided to place the initial backhoe trench 30 meters (98 feet) below the small, 1 meter (3.28 feet) high, headcut located where the current upper foot trail crosses Deep Ravine. This area between the present upper and lower trail crossings (X on fig. 69) is what Sergeant Daniel Knipe of Co. E referred to in 1910 as the location of the cul-de-sac (headcut) that trapped 20 or so troopers (Hammer 1976:95–96). Metal detecting in 1984 produced false anomalies in the area that were thought to be the results of salts resulting from the evaporation of shallow groundwater, but, as was learned later, these may have come from metal-bearing trash dumped into the ravine in the 1930s. No significant metal finds were made downstream, suggesting that the remains, which must have included some metal objects, had not been flushed down the draw. Or, if they had been, they were now too deeply buried for detection.

As soon as the backhoe got into the first priority area, it sank into soft ground that became wetter with every motion. After an hour or so of work, we extracted the backhoe and began a series of trenches on firm ground farther downstream. Backhoe trench 85–1 (BHT85–1), placed against the right bank (looking downstream) 80 meters (262 feet) below the headcut (fig. 69), revealed up to 25 centimeters (9.8 inches) of pale gray clayey fine sand (unit F, table 19) over yellowish brown clayey, silty fine sand of unit C containing lenses of coarser sand and fine pebble gravel (fig. 70). The water table at approximately 0.8 meters (2.62 feet) made any deeper excavation pointless. Neither unit F nor unit C contained any battle-related evidence, but four thin (2–5 millimeter, .08–0.2-inch) black, organic layers occur at the base of unit F. Each is similar to a layer on the present surface produced by the range fire of August 1983.

A radiocarbon analysis of 1.38 ± 0.03% Modern (AA-1904) on the surface layer of

Table 19   Description of Stratigraphic Units of Deep Ravine Exposed by Backhoe Trenching

Unit	Description	Thickness*
F_2	Sand—Light yellowish brown (2.5Y6/4, 4.4) to olive (5Y6/3, 4/3) soft, clayey, very fine to fine sand to silty sand some places containing thin (2–8 mm) carbonaceous streaks, the most pronounced being at the basal contact.	0.6
G_2	Gravel—Gray, loose, clayey, sandy gravel of well sorted (selected) rounded cobbles with dispersed fragments of rotten wood in lower third.	0.9
G_1	Gravel—Orange to yellowish brown, loose, wet, sandy, clayey gravel and historic trash of glass, crockery, wood, and rusted iron.	0.4
F_1	Sand—Same as F_2	
E_2	Sand & silt—Light yellowish brown (2.5Y6/4, 4/4), soft to firm, inter-bedded 2–10 cm bands of clayey fine sand, silty sand, clayey silt, and olive (5Y5/3, 4/3) silty clay, and lenses up to 5 cm thick of silty, sandy fine angular pebble gravel. Thin (2–8 mm) discontinuous carbonaceous streak along basal contact.	1.6+
E_1	Sand & silt$_3$—same as E_2; nodules up to 1 cm diameter occur 20 to 80 cm below the surface in places.	
A	Sand—Tan, friable, current bedded medium sand	2.2+
K	Mudstone—Bedrock of brownish gray (2.5Y6/2, 4/2) conchoidal mudstone or claystone, crumbly in places, with interbedded layers of yellow clay. This is probably the Cretaceous Fort Union Formation.	3.6+

*Maximum observed thickness in meters.

charcoal and $1.72 \pm 0.0\%$ Modern (AA-1903) on the basal charcoal layer of unit F_2 proves that the burned vegetation grew within the Nuclear Age. Therefore, the 1983 fire is probably represented by both values because the fire would have burned dead vegetation and litter from previous years, and charcoal from various years would be mixed in varying proportions. These results demonstrate that the multiple black layers in unit F_2 do not represent separate fires but slope-washing events instead. After a range fire, charred plant remains (charcoal) littering the surface are washed down slopes by rainstorms. Each layer could represent a different rainstorm, in which case four rainstorms were intense enough to wash clean the adjacent slopes, but each produced insufficient discharge (stream power) to erode the floor of Deep Ravine. Instead, the slope-washed sediment was deposited along the floor, thereby causing it to aggrade.

Backhoe trench 85–2 (BHT85–2) was placed in line with trench 1 and started from the opposite (left) bank. It revealed a yellowish-brown loesslike fine sand, unit D, in the bank wall and overlying unit C (fig. 70). Unit F_2, inset against these, is the same as and continuous with that in trench 1. There are fewer carbonaceous layers, and a small channel filled with pebbly sand (unit F_2) occurs between units F_2 and C, indicating local discharge adequate to cut a small channel.

All backhoe trenches downstream of 1 and 2 were cut clear across the floor of Deep Ravine from one side to the other. BHT85–3 exposed another alluvial sand deposit, unit F_1, between F_2 and C. It contains another thin black carbonaceous layer at the base, which could represent a range fire known to have occurred in 1908 (J. Court, personal communication). Unit D at the northwest end of trench 3 forms a small ridge approxi-

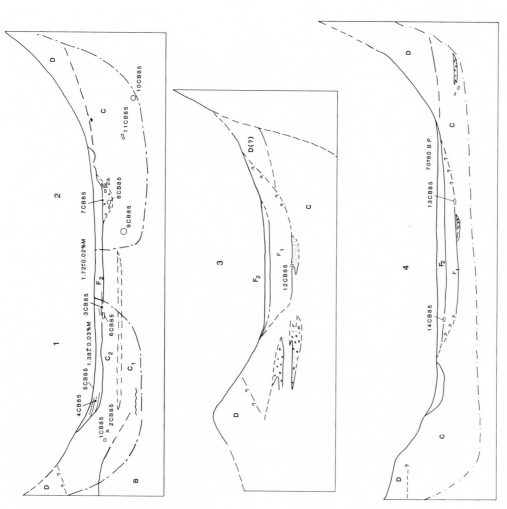

Fig. 70. Stratigraphic cross sections of Deep Ravine backhoe trenches 1–11.

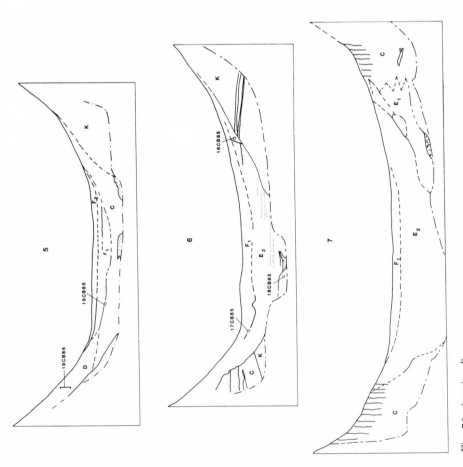

Fig. 70. (*continued*)

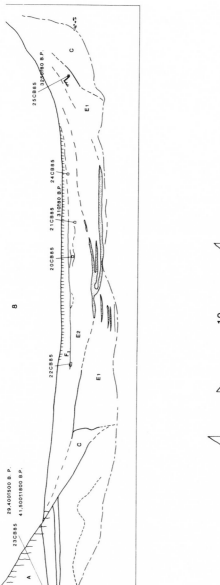

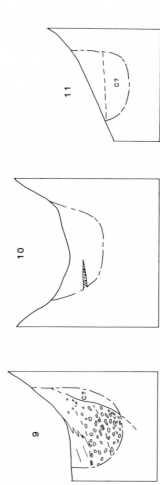

Fig. 70. (*continued*)

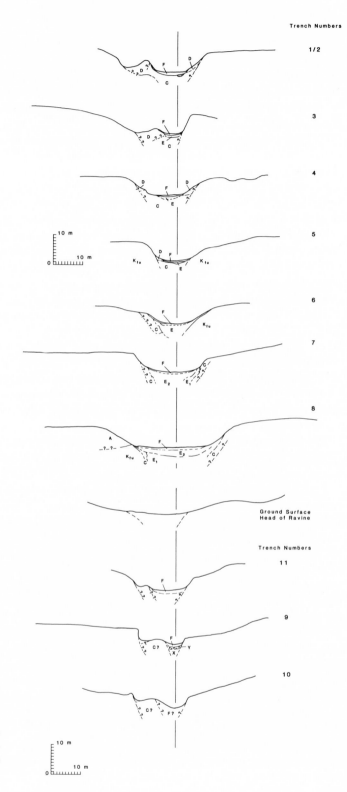

Fig. 71. Transverse profiles of Deep Ravine based on backhoe trenches and electronic leveling.

mately paralleling the ravine but joining the right bank a few meters upstream. The contact between D and C is obscure but appears to dip anomalously away from the center of the ravine (fig. 70). The ridge could be the result of slumping of the right bank as could a similar ridge or knoll at the same end of trench 1 (fig. 71).

Trenches 4 and 5 exposed similar stratigraphy downstream except that bedrock shale, the Cretaceous Fort Union Formation, was encountered at both ends of trench 5 (fig. 70). Trench 4 exposed the same thin, black carbonaceous layer at the base of unit F_1 as seen in trench 3. A radiocarbon analysis provided a date of 70 ± 80 B.P. (AA-2020). Therefore, the carbon is most likely a result of the 1908 fire because no other rangefires are known in the historic record. Farther downstream trench 6 showed another deposit, unit E_2 (fig. 70) indicating that a buried headcut may lie between it and trench 5. Trenches 7 and 8 farther downstream also exposed unit E, which could be subdivided into upper (E_2) and lower (E_1) members. Several dark, discontinuous carbonaceous bands occur at the top of unit E_2 in trench 8. One provided charcoal for a radiocarbon date of 310 ± 70 B.P. (AA-1906), providing a prehistoric age for the alluvium. A charcoal sample from the upper half of unit E_1 produced another prehistoric radiocarbon date of 3250 ± 80 B.P. (AA-1909). The south end exposed unit A, a moderately well sorted, current-bedded fluvial sand perched on a bedrock bench. Unit A is probably a late Pleistocene strath (channel) deposit of the Little Bighorn River because trench 8 is only 50 meters (164 feet) from the mouth of Deep Ravine at the bluffs forming the right bank of the river (fig. 69).

Charcoal flecks at the base of unit A produced two radiocarbon dates, $29,400 \pm 500$ (AA-1907) and $41,500 \pm 1800$ B.P. (AA-2009) years ago and possibly twenty thousand years earlier, depending on whether the younger value is contaminated or the older value redeposited.

From the excavation of backhoe trenches 1 through 8 and the radiocarbon dates, it is clear that the unit E is prehistoric which precludes the deep burial of the missing troopers in unit E, even though a buried headcut lies between trenches 5 and 6.

Unit F_2, being post-1983 in age, is not a candidate for having buried 1876 battle-related skeletons. If the upper charcoal layer in unit F represents the 1908 fire, it indicates that several episodes of slope wash aggradation have occurred in Deep Ravine since the 1876 battle. Unit F, being 40 to 80 centimeters (16 to 32 inches) thick, could effectively bury 28 scattered human skeletons and associated metal artifacts deep enough to escape detection by the archaeological survey. The lack of cartridge cases slope-washed into unit F is probably explained by (1) the paucity of such items on the adjacent slopes, (2) bioturbation (animal burrowing and soil turnover) that has taken items below the surface, and (3) the gentle nature of unconfined runoff of rainwater such that fine-grained charcoal, plant remains, and sediments are washed downslope while cartridge cases are dense and heavy enough to remain behind as lag. The sediment of unit F could, in part, derive from the erosion of a headcut. If such erosion had cut into the burial site, human bones and artifacts could be expected to occur downstream along the basal contact of unit F_1. In spite of the fact that no such clues have been seen in unit F in the trench exposures, it appears to be the unit most likely to cover battlefield remains below trenches 1 and 2.

After completing trenches 1 through 8 without encountering any evidence of historic remains, we decided to try to trench the floor of Deep Ravine just below the modern headcut and above the place where we first wanted to trench. The ravine, being too narrow for maneuvering on the floor, was reached by placing the backhoe on top of the terrace on the south side. From here, trench 9 exposed approximately 2 meters (6.6 feet) of stratigraphy before the limit of the backhoe's arm was reached (fig. 70). It revealed 0.6 meter (1.97 feet) of silt or fine sand, presumably unit F_2, over 1 meter (3.28 feet) of stream-rounded cobbles, over 0.2 meter (0.66 feet) of historic trash dating to the 1930s. The trash, including glass, crockery, cast-iron pipe, and rotten wood and the river cobbles (unit G) are inset against unit C, which forms the south bank of Deep Ravine. The cobbles were undoubtedly put there as riprap to prevent further erosion of what must have been a headcut because trench 10, placed 5 meters (16.4 feet) upstream, showed only natural strata, unit C, between trench 9 and the modern headcut. Similar riprap in a short tributary of Deep Ravine that leads to the marker stones of Deep Ravine Trail appears in a photograph taken by Charles Kuhlman in 1937 (fig. 73). Trench 11, placed 8 meters (26.3 feet) below 9, exposed only unit C because the backhoe could not reach the presumed extension of unit G downstream.

RADIOCARBON SAMPLING

The stratigraphic position of selected charcoal and organic samples, collected for radio-carbon dating from units A, C, E, and F, are shown in figure 72. These were selected on the basis of stratigraphic position and suitability for reliable dating. Fifteen additional samples were collected, some of which could be dated for improved confidence in the geochronology, provided they prove suitable and adequate funds become available (table 20). Sample 1CB85, a stem fragment from a weedlike plant found exposed on the fresh face of trench 1, could be redeposited from the surface litter by the backhoe bucket. If so, it is unfortunate because it is the only sample from unit C. No suitable radiocarbon samples were found in unit D. Units E & F, on the other hand, provided most of the samples. Charcoal from the base of unit A, as expected, proved to be late Pleistocene in age.

CONCLUSIONS AND RECOMMENDATIONS

The historic deposits revealed by trench 9 fill a gully that is at least 2 meters (6.6 feet) deep measured from the present floor of Deep Ravine. To this can be added another 2.3 meters (7.55 feet) for the height of the south back above the floor to give a total depth of at least 4.3 meters (14.11 feet) for the steep south wall as it must have been prior to the filling with trash and riprap.

The north wall today, although 2.7 meters (8.86 feet) higher, is not as steep in its lower part as the south wall because of what appears to be a slump (fig. 71) that is not apparent in the 1937 Kuhlman photograph (fig. 73). This slumping of unit C along the north wall has more than doubled the width of the ravine. From these indications it is possible, if not probable, that this part of Deep Ravine in 1876 was at least 4.3 meters (14.11 feet) deep and 7 meters (22.97 feet) wide with a headcut height of perhaps 3 meters (9.84 feet), thus forming the cul-de-sac described by several witnesses

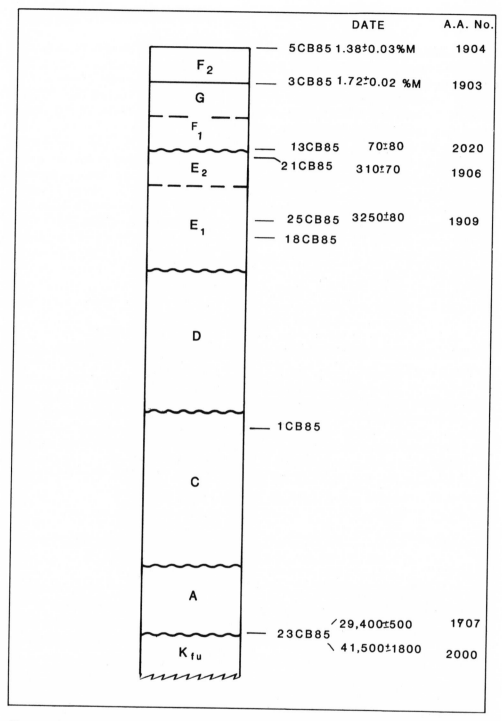

Fig. 72. Stratigraphic column of sediments in Deep Ravine showing the relative positions of selected radiocarbon samples.

Table 20   Radiocarbon and Sediment Samples Collected from Stratigraphic Units
at Custer Battlefield National Monument

1CB85 *	charred(?) twig, N. end of BHT 85-1, E. wall. May have been redeposited by backhoe. Unit C(?).
2CB85	bone(?) fragment at same locality as 1CB85. Appears to be a fragment of a calcareous concretion from bedrock—discarded. Unit C.
3CB85 *	dark brown to black carbonaceous organic band 24 cm below surface and in W. wall of BHT 85-1, S. end. Basal unit F_2.
4CB85	same as 3CB85 but 12 cm below surface in E. wall, N. side. Unit $_2$.
5CB85	same as 3CB85 but at the surface and presumably from the range fire of August 1983.
6CB85	same as 3CB85 but 28 cm below surface in W. wall, S. end. Basal unit F_2.
7CB85	same as 3CB85 but 20 cm below surface in E. wall, BHT 85-2, N. end. Basal unit F_2.
8CB85	olive gray pebbly, clayey, sand in small channel in E. wall, BHT 85-2. Unit F_{2a}.
9CB85	olive gray, clayey sand or sandy clay in E wall, BHT 85-2. Unit C.
10CB85	gray clayey silt or fine sand in E. wall, BHT 85-2. Unit C.
11CB85	large root segment in unit C, E. wall, BHT 85-2.
12CB85	dark gray to black carbonaceous organic band at base of unit F_1, E. wall, BHT 85-3, center.
13CB85	same as 12CB85 and at base of unit F_1, NE wall, BHT 85-4, SE of center.
14CB85	same as 12CB85 and at base of unit F_2, NE wall, BHT 85-4, NW of center.
15CB85	same as 12CB85 and at base of unit F_1, N wall, BHT 85-5, W. of center.
16CB85	gray fine sand or volcanic ash, in unit E_2, N. wall, BHT 85-6, E. end.
17CB85	same as 12CB85 and at base of F_1, N. wall BHT 85-6, W. end.
18CB85 *	charcoal(?) flecks in silty, sandy clay in lower unit C(?), N. wall BHT 85-6, W. of center.
19CB85	tan clayey, loesslike fine sand, unit D, N. wall BHT 85-5, W. end.
20CB85 *	charcoal flecks on disconformity near top of unit E_2 W. wall BHT 85-8, N. end.
21CB85 *	charcoal lump in upper unit E_2 W. wall BHT 85-8, N. end.
22CB85	thin, dark gray to black carbonaceous band at base of unit F_1, W. wall BHT 85-8, S. of Center.
23CB85 *	charcoal flecks at base of unit A, S. end of BHT 85-8.
24CB85 *	charcoal lump 30 cm below surface and near top of unit E^2, W. wall BHT 85-8, N. of center.
25CB85 *	dark grey to black irregular carbonaceous mass in unit E_1, W. wall BHT 85-8, N. end.
26CB85 *	dark gray to black, 1 cm thick lens (old burn) 52 cm below surface of 3.8 m terrace of the Little Big Horn River in first cut 140 m below (W. of) mouth of Deep Ravine.

*Selected first-priority samples for radiocarbon dating.

in 1876. However, the characteristic of headcuts is that they migrate upstream by headward erosion during intense storms. At least one such storm is known to have occurred a year after the battle and to have exposed several skeletons (Wheeler 1923; Forsyth 1878). Unit F indicates that other storms have moved sediment, some since 1908 and some since 1983. We can assume, therefore, that the headcut was farther downstream in 1876. This plus the location of the bodies, estimated by Sergeant Knipe to be 2,000 feet from the monument (Hammer 1976), is compatible with our earlier selection of

a

b

Fig. 73. Repeat photographs of the headcut area of Deep Ravine: a: A photograph by Charles Kuhlman 1937 (courtesy Custer Battlefield National Monument), b: The same area rephotographed in 1987.

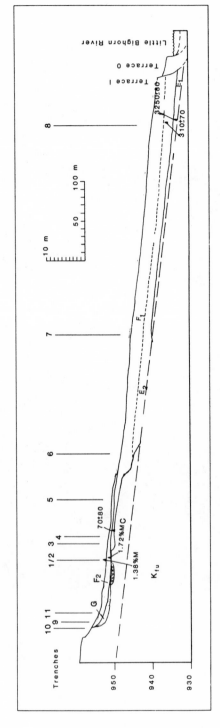

Fig. 74. Longitudinal profile of Deep Ravine from near the modern headcut to the Little Bighorn River with stratigraphy extrapolated between 1985 backhoe trenches. Hypothesized location of missing troopers noted by X's.

the first-priority location, which is 640 meters (2,100 feet) from the monument. The trail of marble markers leads to the tributary with the riprap mentioned earlier. This may have been a relatively easy descent in 1876. If the troopers turned upstream or were driven upstream, they would, in 20 or 30 meters (66 to 98 feet), come to the headcut, with no way out but the way they entered. With the enemy in hot pursuit, they were probably trapped and annihilated as described by He Dog (Hammer 1976).

The bodies, some said to have lain in a pile, plus the earth, reportedly caved from the banks by the burial details, could conceivably have created a low check dam in the floor of Deep Ravine. This would have promoted sedimentation and partial filling of the ravine immediately above the obstruction and may have resulted in partial filling of the headcut to produce a depositional unit (X) between units F_1 and F_2. This possibility could not be tested in 1985 because we could not get the backhoe into the critical reach between trenches 1 and 11. A hypothetical unit X in this reach is shown on figure 74 with the possible location of human remains shown by the X's. Renewed cutting in the 1930s appears to have been effectively checked by the emplacement of trash and riprap in the headcut, but apparently no human remains were exhumed. At least none were reported.

The slumping referred to earlier, postdating Kuhlman's 1937 photograph (fig. 73), would, upon "melting down" from rain, contribute to aggradation of unit F_2 downstream. It is likely, therefore, that the lower part of unit F_2 above trenches 1 and 2 predates the 1983 fire. This process may have occurred after the battle and before the 1908 fire, thus making possible alluvial deposition before unit F_1 and after unit E_2 that can be included in unit X.

Another possibility for burial of the missing troopers is in basal F_1; however, the total absence of any artifacts or bone in this unit in any of the six trenches that exposed it does not lend much support for this hypothesis. On the other hand, the mode of aggradation revealed by the radiocarbon dates and the charcoal bands in unit F_2 is one of incremental accumulation of slope-wash sediments, with little or no erosion of the valley floor. Under such circumstances, there may have been no significant redeposition of bones and artifacts as unit F_1 was deposited. Therefore, the base of unit F_1 cannot be ruled out as a possible stratigraphic position for the sought-after remains.

While the area between trenches 1 and 11 remains untested, all of our circumstantial evidence gathered to date points to the area between 30 and 60 meters (98 to 197 feet) below the present headcut as the most likely area for the burial of the missing troopers. This allows for 10 meters (32.8 feet), more or less, of headward migration of the 1876 headcut. This is the reach that shows the most evidence of slumping, which is probably caused by the shallow water table's fluidizing the base of the banks. Such action at the burial site after the 1876 battle would likely aid burial and allow the denser metal items to sink farther into the muck of unit X.

To test the area between trenches 1 and 11, a reasonable plan would be to hand-excavate 1-meter-wide (3.28 feet) transverse trenches every 5 meters (16.4 feet), starting 30 meters (98 feet) below trench 11 and working upstream on the assumption that some of the buried remains were spread downstream by occasional rain storms before being buried by unit F. Five such trenches would be required to cover the area. If no positive evidence were found after completion of the third trench, I would be inclined to start over with the trenching at 5-meter (16.4 feet) spacing 10 meters (32.8 feet) above trench 1.

Before any of the trenching could be done, the local water table would have to be lowered by pumping from a well strategically placed above (up the hydraulic gradient from) the area to be trenched. The water from the well would have to be discharged well below the work area, and a monitoring well should be placed at the lower end of the work area.

Chapter 9

Human Osteological Remains from the Battle of the Little Bighorn

By Clyde Collins Snow and John Fitzpatrick

INTRODUCTION

When Lieutenant Colonel George Armstrong Custer led his men to their death on the Little Bighorn on that bright June afternoon in 1876, he left a legacy shrouded in mystery. Part of that legacy is written in the bones of the troopers which still lie in the silent earth of the battlefield. As those who study them have come to learn, bones make good witnesses—although they speak softly, they never lie and they never forget. Each bone has its own tale to tell about the past life and death of the person whose living flesh once clothed it. Like people, some bones impart their secrets more readily than others; some are laconic; others are positively garrulous. Thus, given a fairly complete skeleton, the physical anthropologist can often derive a surprisingly complete life history, or osteobiography, of the long-departed decedent. This is because bones, which appear as dry and inert objects in the laboratory, form part of a very dynamic tissue system in the living body and many significant events in the biological history of the individual leave some evidence in the skeleton. Thus a study of the skeleton reveals not only the individual's age, sex, race, and physique, but also the more subtly recorded evidence of old disease and injuries, growth and hormonal disturbances, nutritional stresses, and other biological vissicitudes encountered in the long, or sometimes short, journey to the grave. Because they are so few in number, the bones examined here can only add a footnote to the voluminous archaeological and historical record of the Battle of the Little Bighorn. Nonetheless, since they provide the only testimony we will ever have from the troopers themselves, they deserve to be heard.

THE CASUALTIES

In all, 268 soldiers and civilians are known to have lost their lives in the Battle of the Little Bighorn. This amounts to about 40 percent of the 675 men of the Seventh Cav-

Table 21 Distribution of the Little Bighorn Casualties by Rank

	Valley-Hilltop	Custer	Total
Officers	3	13	16 (6.0%)
Enlisted	49	193	242 (90.3%)
Crow Scouts	3	0	3 (1.1%)
Civilian	3	4	7 (2.6%)
Total	58 (21.6%)	210 (78.4%)	268 (100%)

Table 22 Custer-Fight Casualties by Regimental Unit and Rank

	Co. C	Co. E	Co. F	Co. I	Co. L	Hdq.	Civ.	Total
Officers	3	2	1	2	2	3	—	13 (4.9%)
Enlisted	37	36	34	37	44	5	—	193 (72%)
Total	40	38	35	39	46	8	4	210
(%)	19.0	18.1	16.7	18.6	21.9	3.8	1.9	100.0%

alry who made up the expedition led by Custer. The casualties can be divided into three subgroups:

1. *Valley Fight*: Men lost in Major Reno's ill-fated attack on the Indian village and his subsequent retreat across the river to join Captain Benteen.

2. *Hilltop Fight*: Casualties sustained during the two-day siege of the position on the bluffs defended by the combined Reno and Benteen commands.

3. *Custer Fight*: Men of the five companies of the Seventh Cavalry under the direct command of Custer.

Fifty-eight men were killed in the valley and hilltop fights. This figure includes six wounded who survived long enough to be evacuated and were buried away from the battlefield. Except for some whose bodies were never found, the remaining fifty-two were buried close to the places where they fell. The skeletons of several, including those of three officers and civilian scout Lonesome Charley Reynolds, were later recovered and buried elsewhere. Thus the bones of about fifty Little Bighorn casualties must lie somewhere close to these positions. The distribution of these casualties by military status is shown in table 21. Since the bones described here were recovered from the Custer site about three miles away, the men buried at the valley and hilltop positions can be ruled out as possible decedents.

The 210 men who lost their lives in the Custer fight were members of five Seventh Cavalry companies (C, E, F, I, and L), Custer's small headquarters staff, and four civilians (table 22). Among the civilian casualties were two relatives of Custer: his youngest brother, Boston Custer, and his eighteen-year-old nephew, Harry Armstrong Reed. Thus, along with another brother, Captain Tom Custer, who was commanding C Company, and a brother-in-law, Lieutenant James Calhoun, five members of the Custer family died in the battle. The other two civilians were Mark Kellogg, a newspaper correspondent, and the mixed-blood interpreter Mitch Boyer.

DISPOSAL OF THE DEAD

On June 27, about forty-eight hours after Custer was last seen alive, a reconnaissance patrol from the column commanded by General Terry discovered the bodies of the Seventh Cavalry troopers killed in the Custer fight. Most of the dead had been stripped of uniforms, and many had been subjected to postmortem mutilations ranging from scalping to dismemberment. Over the next two days, Terry's troopers, aided by survivors of the Reno-Benteen command, buried the bodies. Each man was buried at or close to the spot where he fell. As the burial details lacked proper tools and were pressed by the possibility that the hostiles were still in the area, the bodies were hastily covered. The graves were marked with crude wooden stakes (Godfrey 1892).

According to several accounts, the bodies of about twenty-five to thirty troopers of Company E, the Grey Horse Troop, were found at the bottom of a narrow defile, now called Deep Ravine, where they had been trapped and killed. Because they were badly decomposed when discovered, they could not be carried out of the ravine for individual burial. Instead, earth from the sides of the ravine was pushed down over them (King 1980).

A number of bodies were identified on the basis of physical features or, in the case of those who had not been completely stripped, by personal effects. To some extent, the probability of identification was no doubt influenced by rank and length of service of the victim; officers and higher-ranking enlisted men were better known and hence more likely to be recognized by their surviving comrades than recently recruited privates. When such identifications were made, the name of the victim was written on a slip of paper and placed with the body, usually inside a cartridge case (Hammer 1976:110).

The reliability of these identifications is difficult to assess. To a large extent, clues to facial recognition include habits of expression which are lost in the cadaveric face, an observation which accounts for the frequent misidentification of the dead by close relatives. In the case of Custer's men, wounds and postmortem disfigurement, along with the bloating and decomposition resulting from several days of summer exposure, would add to the difficulty of identification and increase the probability of error. That this was so is indicated by the fact that one of the surviving troopers of the hilltop fight was unable to find his brother, Private George W. Hammon of F Company, among the scattered bodies of the Last Stand Hill casualties (statement by John Hammon on file, Custer Battlefield National Monument). The bodies of three officers (Lieutenants Harrington, Porter, and Sturgis) could not be located. Considering the difficulties of the situation, it seems likely that they were buried, like the majority of the other troopers, as unidentified bodies.

In June 1877, about a year after the battle, a detachment of Seventh Cavalry troopers was sent to the battlefield to recover the remains of Lieutenant Colonel Custer and those of his officers whose graves could be located (Graham 1953:365–88). They found that many of the graves had been eroded by wind and rain and that some of the markers had been scattered. Judging from the prevailing climate and the conditions of burial, it is safe to assume that by then the remains were more or less completely skeletonized.

In all, ten skeletons, including one presumed to be that of Custer, were exhumed from the Custer battlefield. At the request of his family, the bones identified as those of

Second Lieutenant J. J. Crittenden were reburied in a deeper grave close to the site of his original interment. The bones identified as Custer's were buried at West Point; the other eight skeletons were returned to their families for private burial.

That same year, the bodies of the two civilian kinsmen of Custer, Boston Custer and Autie Reed, were exhumed and reburied in Michigan. A final exhumation took place in 1932 when Crittenden's skeleton was again taken up and formally reinterred in the national cemetery at the entrance of the monument grounds.

During the years immediately after the battle, visitors to the site described further scattering of markers and exposure of the graves (King 1980). To remedy this, a detachment was sent to the site in 1881. Exposed human bones were collected and placed in a common grave located on the top of Last Stand Hill where the granite marker commemorating the dead now stands. With the exception of Crittenden's, all of the graves that could still be located were also exhumed and their contents transferred to the common grave. The bones of the many horses which still littered the field were also collected and placed in a separate burial pit close to that reserved for the human remains. Nine years later the original graves were provided with more permanent stone markers (King 1980).

In subsequent years, visitors and custodians of the site have occasionally found isolated bones in the area. Some of these items were probably reburied or carried away as grisly souvenirs, while others have found their way into the small collection of artifacts and bones in the museum on the monument grounds.

If the records are correct, 198 human skeletons would have remained on the battlefield after the bones of the 10 officers and 2 civilians were removed. This tally would include 193 enlisted men, the 3 missing officers (Harrington, Porter, and Sturgis) and 2 civilians (Kellogg and Boyer). However, the accuracy of this count, as well as the reliability of the identification of the dead, might well be questioned by experts.

The count of 198 bodies still on the field might be an overestimate, since several Indian participants told stories of scattered troopers who broke out of the encirclement but were pursued and eventually cut down a considerable distance from the battlefield. That at least one of these stories might have been true is indicated by the 1928 discovery of a skeleton in North Medicine Tail Coulee about two miles from the main battleground. A metal arrowhead was embedded in one of the cervical vertebrae, and numerous expended cartridge cases were found among the bones. The remains were collected and buried in the national cemetery in a grave marked "Unknown." A few years earlier, a boot still encasing some human foot bones was discovered near the same place. The initials *J.D.* were still legible inside the boot. Two troopers among the Custer fight casualties bore these initials: Privates John Darris and John Duggan of E and L companies, respectively. It is also possible that some of the wounded, left for dead by the Indians, may have revived long enough to wander away from the battlefield to die elsewhere.

Whether the exhumed skeletons were actually those of the officers and civilians under whose names they were buried also seems questionable. As already mentioned, because of the condition of the corpses, it is possible that some were incorrectly identified after the battle. To this uncertainty must be added the difficulties the exhumation team apparently encountered in locating the graves. Some hint of the problem is provided by the fact that, after removing the skeleton from the grave first thought to be Custer's, it was discovered that the rotting uniform blouse found with the bones contained the name of a Seventh Cavalry corporal. Baffled, the searchers then opened a second grave near the first. It was found to contain only a skull, rib cage and a femur. For one reason or another—possibly only because there was no evidence to the contrary—the searchers were satisfied that these bones were those of Custer. At least some of the witnesses of the exhumation appear to have some doubts, and Connell (1984:344) quotes one as saying, "It was a disconcerting discovery to find that even the General could not be satisfactorily identified." However, it appears that any such misgivings were put aside and the bones from this second grave were eventually buried at West Point as those of Custer.

The suspicion that the West Point bones are not Custer's deepens when the description of the exhumation is compared with accounts of Custer's burial after the battle. According to Sergeant John Ryan of M Company, who personally supervised Custer's interment, special care was given to his burial. In contrast to most of the other dead, whose bones were barely covered, the grave prepared for Custer was dug to a depth of about eighteen inches. It was also made wide enough to hold the body of his brother Tom, and the two bodies were laid side by side. The general had been shot twice; one bullet had entered the left temple and the second struck him in the chest. There was also a wound in his right forearm, which could have been caused either by a third bullet or an exiting fragment of the bullet that caused the chest wound. He had not been scalped or dismembered. Tom Custer had been scalped, his skull completely crushed; his body bristled with arrows, and his abdomen was cut open. Before the grave was closed with earth, the bodies were covered with blankets and some canvas tent sheets. Finally, an Indian travois found in the abandoned village was laid over the grave and weighted down with rocks (Hardorf 1983). While far from Pharaonic, such an interment should have been sufficient to protect the bodies from the elements and animal scavengers, which combined to expose the shallower graves of the lesser dead. One would expect, therefore, that the exhumation team would have found two complete sets of remains instead of a single partial skeleton. It also seems strange that they apparently found no remnants of the blankets and canvas sheets used to cover the bodies.

If the exhumation crews had problems in finding the well-marked double grave of the Custer brothers, they may have also had difficulties in correctly locating the less-elaborate burials of the other officers and the two civilians whose remains they were sent to collect. Thus there exists the possibility, at least, that one or more unknown troopers may be perpetually doomed to the commission of that most cardinal of military sins: impersonating an officer. If so, it also follows that the bones of one or more of the officers or of Custer's civilian kinsman may now either lie commingled with those of the enlisted men in the common grave under the granite monument or in a solitary grave overlooked by the reburial party when they transferred the skeletons to the common grave in 1881.

The question also arises as to whether any of the skeletal remains could be those of Indian dead. Here the record is much clearer. All contemporary accounts agree that by the time the Custer-fight bodies were discovered, the Indians had removed their dead from the battlefield. Therefore, the osteological remains described in this report can be confidently treated as representing those of Seventh Cavalry troopers.

ANTHROPOLOGICAL VARIABLES

Anthropological information on the Custer casualties is largely limited to data in their army records (Hammer 1976; Carroll 1986). It includes race, age, and stature. In addition, some physical and medical data are available on a few men. For example, First Lieutenant Algernon E. Smith, attached to E Company, had difficulty raising his left arm as a consequence of a Civil War shoulder wound, and Captain Myles Keogh, who commanded I Company, had broken his right ankle in 1868; injuries such as these would be apparent on the bones and, along with skeletally derived estimates of ante-mortem stature and age, might be useful in narrowing the list of possible decedents for a given skeleton. Thus the recovery of scattered shards of a glass eye among the cranial fragments of the skeleton of a twenty-two-year-old would at least suggest that the decedent might be Lieutenant Crittenden whose body was found on the field shot full of arrows, one of which had shattered his glass left eye.

Aside from its potential utility in identification, the limited amount of anthropological data we have on these men is of interest in its own right. They are, after all, a fairly typical sample of U.S. Cavalry troopers of the Indian-fighting army, who, along with the Indian, the mountain man, the cowboy, the outlaw, the lawman, and other subspecies of the Westerner, form the cast of the longest-running morality play in American history: *The Winning of the West*.

Nativity

About 42 percent of the men killed in the Custer fight were of foreign birth (table 23). They consisted of eighty-five enlisted men; two officers, Captain Myles Keogh (Ireland) and First Lieutenant W. W. Cooke (Canada); and the civilian newspaper correspondent, Mark Kellogg (Canada). Most of the foreign-born were from Ireland (twenty-eight), followed by Germans (twenty-seven) and Britons (sixteen); the rest represented a scattering from six countries: Canada (six), Denmark (three), Switzerland (three), France (one), Greece (one) and Russia (one). One man, Regimental Sergeant-Major William Sharrow, was born at sea. The casualty list would have also included an Italian, Trumpeter Giovanni Martini, had not Custer dispatched him with a message to Major Ben-

Table 23   Custer-Fight Casualties by Nativity and Rank

Rank	Foreign-Born						Native-Born		Total	
	Ger	Ire	Brt	Other	Total					
					N	%	N	%	N	%
Officers	0	1	0	1	2	(2)	11	(9)	13	(6.2)
Sergeants	2	5	2	2	11	(12)	6	(5)	17	(8.1)
Corporals	2	1	0	1	4	(5)	12	(10)	16	(7.6)
Other*	2	1	1	2	6	(7)	12	(10)	18	(8.6)
Privates	21	20	13	10	64	(73)	78	(64)	142	(67.6)
Civilians	0	0	0	1	1	(1)	3	(2)	4	(1.9)
Total	27	28	16	17	88	(100)	122	(100)	210	(100.0)

*Other includes military specialty occupations, such as trumpeters, farriers, and saddlers.

teen shortly before the battle. The low representation of men from eastern European and Mediterranean countries reflects a period when immigration to the United States was still predominantly from northern Europe.

The majority (58 percent) of the Custer casualties were born in the United States. They included 108 enlisted men, 11 officers, and 3 civilians. Represented among the dead were men from twenty-three of the thirty-seven states that had been admitted to the Union by the time of the battle, the District of Columbia, and New Mexico Territory. Most numerous were New Yorkers and Pennsylvanians, with 27 and 22 men, respectively; there were also 16 men from Ohio and 15 from Massachusetts. Together, men from these four states made up about 65 percent of the U.S.-born casualties. All of the Civil War Union states were represented except Vermont and Minnesota, but only 4 men came from those of the former Confederacy (1 trooper each from Virginia, North Carolina, Georgia, and Texas). Thus the Seventh Cavalry still retained a distinctly Yankee flavor more than a decade after Appomattox. Most were also easterners; only 6, or 4.9 percent, were from states or territories west of the Mississippi.

Race

Only four nonwhites are listed as army casualties in the Battle of the Little Bighorn. Three were Indian scouts: Bloody Knife, Bob-tailed Bull, and Little Brave. The fourth was the black interpreter Isiah Dorman. All four were killed under the command of Major Reno during the valley fight.

So far as can be determined from existing records, all of the Custer-fight casualties were white with the exception of Mitch Boyer, an interpreter; his father was French, his mother a Santee Sioux. His bones might be expected to show some morphological traits characteristic of a Caucasoid-Mongoloid hybrid.

Age

At the time of the Battle of the Little Bighorn, the minimum age for enlistment in the United States Army was twenty-one. However, in a period when births records were likely to consist of nothing more than a note in the family Bible or church baptismal records, any teenager old enough to shave stood a good chance of passing himself off as twenty-one. It is also unlikely that recruitment officers of an army plagued by high desertion rates were apt to be overscrupulous in rejecting underage volunteers.

At least two troopers are known to have been younger than the minimum age (Hammer 1976). One was Private Thomas Downing of Company I, who was actually twenty years old at the time of death but was carried on the rosters as twenty-four. The other, Private Willis Wright of C Company, was listed as twenty-two years old but had only reached his seventeenth birthday on June 7, less than three weeks before his death. It seems probable that in addition to Wright and Downing there were at least a few other underage troopers in the command, but the exact number will probably never be known. At the time of the battle, the standard term of enlistment was five years. Since there would be no point in carrying an age deception beyond the first enlistment, it is likely that most of the underage troopers were among those officially listed as twenty-one to twenty-six years of age. Since such errors are more likely to affect the mean than

Table 24   Age Distribution of Custer-Fight Casualties by Rank

Rank	N	Min	1st Quartile	Median	3rd Quartile	Max
Officers	13	22		30.3		36
Enlisted						
Sergeants	17	26	28.0	30.3	31.1	36
Corporals	16	24	25.4	26.2	28.0	31
Other ranks*	18	21	25.5	28.2	31.0	45
Private	142	17	25.1	27.1	30.6	42
Civilian	4	18				33
Total	210	17	25.4	27.5	31.0	45

*Includes military specialty ranks: trumpeters, farriers, saddlers, and blacksmiths.

the median, the latter statistic is used in table 24, which summarizes the age data for the Custer-fight casualties.

The total command ranged in age from seventeen-year-old Private Wright to Farrier Benjamin Brandon of F Company, who was forty-five years old. Eldest among the officers were Captain Myles Keogh of I Company and Lieutenant Colonel Custer, both of whom were thirty-six years of age. The median age for officers and sergeants was about thirty, that of corporals, specialty rankers, and privates about two to four years younger. As a group, the Custer troopers were fairly homogeneous in terms of age: about half of them were between twenty-five and thirty-one years old at the time of death. Although the exact number of these troopers who were Civil War veterans is not known, about one-third were over thirty years of age and hence were old enough to have seen action in that war.

Stature

Army records of the enlisted men who died in the Custer fight (Hammer 1976) include stature as recorded at the time of their enlistment. Statistics derived from these data are given in table 25. The average height of all of these men was 67.07 inches, with a total range from 60 to 73 inches—almost 2 inches shorter than U.S. Army soldiers measured ninety years later (White and Churchill 1966). This difference is a manifestation of the general increase in stature observed in the U.S. population during the past half-century (table 26). It is also interesting to note that the troopers averaged about a half-inch shorter than Union soldiers of the Civil War. As most of the Civil War veterans were infantrymen, it is possible that the difference is due to a tendency to assign shorter and lighter men to the cavalry. There was no statistically significant difference in the stature of foreign-born (most of whom were from northern Europe) and native-born Americans (student's $t = 1.202$, $p > .05$, 191 df).

There appears to be a gradient in stature with rank: privates were slightly shorter than corporals, who, in turn, were shorter than sergeants by more than an inch. The difference in height between corporals and sergeants is statistically significant (student's $t = 1.841$, $p < .05$, 31df). This trend suggests that larger men had an advantage in promotion in an army, in which sheer physical ability to impose one man's will on another was still an important factor in leadership.

Unfortunately, the Army did not routinely record the stature of officers during this period. The heights of only four (Custer, Cooke, Keogh, and Yates) are known, and all four were much taller than the average enlisted man. Custer, in a letter of recommending him for appointment to West Point, is described as being about five feet, ten inches in height; as he was seventeen years old at this time, it is likely that he stood at least an inch or so taller in adulthood. Judging from photographs showing them together, his brother Tom was approximately the same height. Assuming them to be about five feet, eleven inches at the time of the battle, the mean height of these five officers would have been seventy-one and eight-tenths inches, or nearly five inches taller than the average enlisted man. However, since biographers are not apt to mention their subjects' height unless they were exceptionally tall or short, it seems improbable that the available records are representative of all of the thirteen officers killed in the Custer fight. On the other hand, it is possible that they were, in fact, somewhat taller than the average enlisted man, since officers were generally from families of higher socioeconomic status. Many anthropometric studies have shown that the offspring of such families are, on the average, taller than those from the more disadvantaged classes because of better childhood nutrition. It is known, for example, that male college students of the 1860s (who, in those days, were more apt to be from affluent families) averaged about an inch taller than the general U.S. male population of that period (Allen 1869). Even today, anthropometric surveys of U.S. military populations consistently show higher statural means for officers than for enlisted men (Hertzberg 1950; Churchill 1970; Webb Associates 1978).

Table 25   Stature (in Inches) of Custer-Fight Casualties

Category	N	Mean	S.D.	Range
Officers	5	71.75	—	71–73
Sergeants	17	68.18	1.78	66–73
Corporals	16	67.09	1.61	65–71
Privates	142	66.98	1.94	60–73
All enlisted men	193	67.07	1.90	60–73
Native-born	108	66.93	1.92	60–73
Foreign-born	85	67.26	1.86	63–73

Table 26   Stature (in Inches) of U.S. Army Enlisted Men, 1839–1966

Series	Mean	Source
Recruits, 1839–55	67.4	Coolidge, 1856
Recruits, 1853–55	67.0	Tripler, 1866
Recruits, Civil War	67.4	Baxter, 1875
Custer 1876	67.1	Present work
World War I draftees	67.5	Davenport & Love, 1921
World War II	68.1	Off. Surg. Gen., n.d.
U.S. Soldiers, 1966	68.7	White & Churchill, 1971

Table 27 Human Osteological Remains from the Custer Battlefield

Bone	Collections			Assemblages																				Total	%Total
	MUS	S83	S84	A84	G84	H84	I84	J84	K84	M84	A85	B85	C85	D85	F85	G85	J85	K85	M85	N85	O85	P85	R85		
Cranium	1	1	0	1	1	1	1	1	1	0	0	1	1	1	0	0	0	0	1	0	1	1	1	14	3.4
Mandible	0	0	0	1	0	0	1	0	0	0	0	0	0	1	0	0	0	0	1	0	0	0	0	3	0.7
Hyoid	0	0	0	1	0	0	0	0	0	0	0	0	0	0	0	0	0	0	1	0	0	0	0	2	0.5
Dentition	0	0	8	1	0	1	1	1	1	0	1	1	0	3	0	1	0	1	12	0	1	5	0	36	8.8
Vertebra	0	0	1	2	3	0	0	0	0	1	1	0	0	0	0	0	0	0	24	0	0	1	0	34	8.3
Sacrum	0	0	0	0	0	0	0	0	0	0	0	0	0	0	0	0	0	0	1	0	0	0	0	1	0.2
Coccyx	0	0	1	1	0	0	0	0	0	0	0	0	0	1	0	0	0	1	1	0	0	0	0	5	1.2
Sternum	0	0	0	0	1	1	0	0	0	0	0	0	0	0	0	0	0	0	1	0	0	0	0	3	0.7
Ribs	0	0	0	0	0	5	0	0	0	0	0	0	1	0	0	0	0	0	23	0	2	0	0	31	7.5
Clavicle	0	0	0	0	0	0	0	0	0	0	0	0	0	0	0	0	0	0	2	0	0	0	0	2	0.5
Scapula	0	0	0	0	0	1	0	0	0	0	0	0	0	2	0	0	0	0	2	0	0	0	0	5	1.2
Humerus	0	0	0	0	0	2	0	0	0	0	0	0	0	1	0	0	0	0	2	0	0	0	0	5	1.2
Radius	1	0	0	0	0	1	0	0	0	1	0	1	0	1	0	0	0	0	2	0	1	0	0	7	1.7
Ulna	1	0	0	0	0	2	0	0	1	1	0	0	0	1	0	0	0	0	2	0	1	0	0	9	2.2
Hand	5	1	2	2	0	7	1	0	3	27	10	3	1	32	1	3	2	1	33	0	27	1	5	167	40.6
Os Coxa	0	0	0	0	0	0	0	0	0	0	0	0	0	0	0	0	0	0	2	0	0	0	0	2	0.5
Femur	0	0	0	0	0	0	0	0	0	0	1	0	0	0	0	0	0	0	2	0	0	0	0	3	0.7
Patella	0	0	2	0	0	1	0	0	1	0	0	0	0	0	0	0	0	0	0	1	0	0	0	5	1.2
Tibia	1	0	0	0	0	0	0	0	0	0	0	0	0	0	0	0	0	0	2	0	0	0	0	3	0.7
Fibula	0	0	0	0	0	0	0	0	1	0	0	0	0	0	0	0	0	0	2	0	0	0	0	3	0.7
Foot	4	1	2	8	0	8	0	0	8	4	1	0	2	0	10	0	1	2	25	0	3	0	0	71	17.3
Total	13	3	13	33	4	33	4	1	16	34	14	6	5	44	11	4	3	5	141	1	34	10	5	411	
% Total	3.2	0.7	3.2	8.0	1.0	8.0	1.0	0.2	3.9	8.3	3.4	1.5	1.2	10.7	2.7	1.0	0.7	1.2	34.3	0.2	8.3	2.4	1.2		100.0
# Individ.	4	3	1	1	1	1	1	1	1	1	1	1	1	1	1	1	1	1	1	1	1	1	1	34	

EXAMINATION PROCEDURES

The osteological and dental remains described in this study consist of twenty-three separate sets or recovery units. A recovery unit is composed of all of the items found in a
given archeological operation such as a surface survey or the excavation of a particular
trench or square. The total series of recovery units can be further subdivided into two
types: collections and assemblages. This distinction is helpful in arriving at an estimate of the number of individuals whose bones are represented in the total series of recovery units.

A collection consists of a set of bones recovered from a wide area and which, therefore, can usually be assumed to represent the remains of different individuals. For
example, while the bones still present on the battlefield may have been extensively scattered by wind, water, or animal scavengers, it is still statistically improbable that an
isolated rib and a single foot bone found several hundred yards apart might belong to
the same skeleton. Thus, as used here, the term *assemblage* refers to a set of bones found
in sufficiently close spatial context to permit the assumption that they belong to a single
skeleton, provided, of course, that there is no morphological evidence to the contrary.
Since *assemblage* implies plurality, it should be pointed out that, as defined here, an
assemblage could consist of a single bone or fragment of bone.

The bones submitted for examination were first cleaned of adherent soil by dry-
brushing them or, in a few stubborn cases, by soaking them for a few hours in warm
water and allowing them to air-dry. As nearly all were in remarkably sound condition,
they did not require the application of special preservatives. After they were clean and
dry, they were labeled with a field-specimen number relating them to their recovery
unit. Each bone or sizable bone fragment was then examined to determine species. Only
those which could be definitely diagnosed as human are treated in this study; nonhuman
remains were retained for other studies (see chapter 10). When fragments could be
identified as coming from the same bone, they were reunited with the aid of an acetone-
soluble glue.

Next, the bones from each recovery unit were examined to determine, when possible,
anthropological-status variables, such as age, race, stature, and physique. The maximum length of intact long bones was measured on an osteometric board, and from these
measurements antemortem stature was estimated, using the equations for U.S. white
males developed by Trotter and Gleser (1958). The bones were then X-rayed, with the
exception of those of the museum collection (see below). Any signs of old disease or
injuries, such as healed fractures, discerned in the visual and radiographic examinations
were recorded. Finally, the bones were reviewed for evidence of perimortem wounds,
postmortem mutilation, or damage by animal scavengers.

RECOVERY ANALYSIS

In all, twenty-three recovery units containing a total of 375 bones or bone fragments
and 36 teeth were examined. The recovery units consist of three collections and twenty
assemblages. The first collection (MUS) comprises a small series of items presently
stored in the monument museum. They are bones accumulated from the battlefield over

many years and from various sources. Some were found by park visitors and others by the staff in the course of maintenance or construction work conducted in the area. Although 37 human bones are present in the series, most were eliminated from this study because the museum records showed that they were found outside the immediate area of the Custer fight. The 13 bones that the records indicate came from the Custer fight represent the remains of four individuals.

The other two series, S83 and S84, are bones collected in the course of surface searches of the Custer battleground conducted in 1983 and 1984. As these bones were found in widely separate locations, they can be safely assumed to represent different individuals. Thus three individuals are represented in S83 and seven in S84.

The twenty assemblages consist of bones recovered by archaeological excavation conducted in the immediate area of individual marble markers. Although generally few in number, in no case did the bones recovered from these individual sites display any morphological inconsistencies suggestive of commingling, and therefore each is considered as a separate assemblage representing the remains of a single trooper.

Table 27 shows the anatomical distribution of the bones and bone fragments represented in the twenty-three recovery units. In compiling this table, any bone, whether complete or represented only by a fragment of sufficient size to offer some useful anthropological data about the individual, was scored as *1*. Since the bones of the adult human cranium are more or less firmly united into a single unit, it was classified as a single bone in this inventory.

Counting the cranium as a single unit, an adult human skeleton consists of about 181 bones, and the 210 skeletons of the Custer fight casualties would comprise an array of nearly 38,010 bones. The 375 bones recovered from the battlefield make up slightly less than 1 percent of the total number of bones that were originally present at the site. Since we estimate that they are from 34 skeletons, about 16 percent of the 210 dead men are represented in the entire series.

The overall distribution of bones within the collection is obviously a reflection of the effectiveness of the 1881 burial party in recovering the remains for transfer to the mass grave. Larger bones, such as crania, innominates, and the long bones of the arms and legs, are underrepresented. In contrast, smaller and hence more easily overlooked items, such as teeth, ribs, vertebrae and bones of the hand and feet, comprise more than 80 percent of the total collection. Only two assemblages fall out of this pattern. The first, H84, consists of thirty-three bones but six of these are major bones of the upper extremity. Also, although it is extensively fragmented, nearly the entire cranial vault is present. Yet, except for eight foot bones and a patella, none of the lower extremity elements were found. The second exception, M85, is even more striking. This skeleton is complete except for the cranium, one rib and a few small bones of the hands and feet. It is obviously a burial that was completely overlooked by the 1881 reburial party.

MUSEUM COLLECTION

In the course of the examination, it was found that some of the bones listed in the museum accession records as human were in fact animal bones. Also, in several cases, bones correctly diagnosed as human were incorrectly identified anatomically (e.g. bones of the hand recorded as foot bones and vice versa). When these mistakes were rectified, the collection was reduced to thirty-seven human bones and a single tooth. Examination of the bones and the available records shows that the collection can be subdivided into fifteen assemblages, each representing a separate individual. Four of these assemblages were found at the Custer site and five at the Reno-Benteen site; of the remaining seven, two were found in other areas, and the records of five contain no indication of where they were found. Only the four assemblages recovered from the Custer-fight assemblages are described here. The museum catalog number of each item is given in parentheses.

1. This is a hamate bone (#8106) from the right wrist found about four feet from the marker of George Custer on Last Stand Hill in 1956. It is that of an adult male. No signs of pathology or trauma are noted.

Summary: Hamate from right wrist of adult male.

2. This assemblage consists of four foot bones and a cranial fragment which are described as having been found near the grave marker of 1st Lieutenant W. W. Cooke. The date of the find is not given in the museum records. The cranial fragment (#8140) is from the left parietal bone and measures twenty-six by forty-nine millimeters. Its margins display the abrupt fracture lines indicative of perimortem blunt-force trauma. The foot bones include a right medial cuneiform (#8141), right navicular (#8143), left fifth metatarsal (#8142), and proximal phalanx (#8139). Based on size and morphology, they are diagnosed as those of an adult male. There are no signs of pathology or perimortem trauma.

Summary: Cranial fragment and several bones from the right and left feet of an adult male. Cranial fracture suggests blunt-force trauma inflicted at or about time of death.

3. This assemblage consists of four hand bones and a left tibia found "near drain on Custer Hill" in 1941.

The tibia (#8263) is missing its proximal end, but whether this loss occurred at the time of death or some years later cannot be definitely determined. Although this damage precludes exact measurement, a maximum length of about 360 millimeters can be closely estimated. This would correspond to an antemortem stature of approximately sixty-six to sixty-seven inches. The epiphyses are closed, indicating an age of twenty-plus years at the time of death. Judging from the general condition of the bone and the lack of signs of incipient osteoarthritis, an upper age limit of about thirty-five years seems reasonable.

The four hand bones of this assemblage are noted as having been found in a boot—an unlikely circumstance. They are adult in size and morphology and display no pathologies or signs of perimortem trauma. The series consists of a right triquetrium (#8173a), left capitate (#8173b), proximal phalanx (#8173c), and intermediate phalanx (#8173d).

Summary: Left tibia and four bones of the left and right hands. Adult male between eighteen and thirty-five years old at the time of death.

4. This assemblage consists of a right radius (#8265) and ulna (#8266) found in 1942 near the grave marker of Mark Kellogg, the civilian newspaper correspondent. All epiphyses are closed. From their maximum lengths (radius = 233 millimeters,

ulna = 251 millimeters), antemortem stature can be estimated at sixty-seven ± three and four-tenths inches. Kellogg's stature is unknown. Kellogg is known to have broken an arm or wrist through a fall a year or two before his death (Warren Barnard, personal communication 1985). However, the extent of the injury and the exact location of the fracture site are not known. These bones display no evidence of old injury.

Summary: Right forearm bones of adult male between eighteen and thirty-five years of age at the time of death. No evidence of perimortem trauma.

SURFACE FINDS, 1983

This material consists of bones collected during the 1983 surface survey of the Custer battlefield. All of the bones and bone fragments display the bleaching and weathering characteristic of surface exposure. Four items are nonhuman bone fragments and seven are fragments too small to classify. The three human bones include a forty-one- by forty-nine-millimeter cranial-vault fragment, one finger phalanx, and one toe phalanx. Considering the area over which these items were collected, it seems doubtful that the human bones are from the same individual. No antemortem pathologies or anomalies are present.

The cranial-vault fragment displays a short segment of patent sutural border; its remaining margins display linear fractures consistent with blunt-force injury inflicted at or around the time of death.

Summary: Surface collection which includes a human cranial fragment and two phalanges; each bone represents a separate individual. The cranial fragment is from an eighteen to thirty-five-year-old male who suffered blunt-force trauma to the head about the time of death. The phalanges are adult.

SURFACE FINDS, 1984

This collection consists of scattered surface finds collected throughout the battlefield during the 1984 season. Aside from nine nonhuman bones and seven unidentified fragments, it includes the following human remains: a midcervical vertebra, a left scaphoid, an intermediate hand phalanx, two right patellae, a right fourth metatarsal, and a proximal toe phalanx. None of the bones displays signs of disease or trauma, and several show signs of prolonged surface weathering. The superior annular epiphysis of the vertebra is in a very late stage of closure, indicating an age of less than about twenty-five years. These bones most likely represent the remains of seven individuals.

Summary: Seven human postcranial bones with no signs of disease or trauma. They most likely represent isolated bones from as many individuals. The cervical vertebra is from an adult male who was about eighteen to twenty-five years old at the time of death.

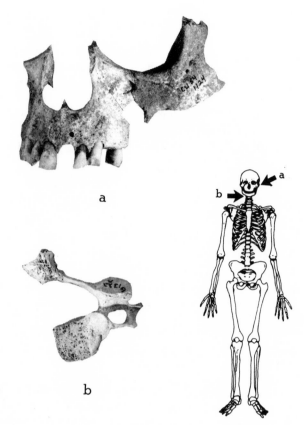

Fig. 75. a: Facial bones from Markers
33–34. b: Obliquely severed cervical
vertebra from Marker 7.

1984 EXCAVATION UNIT ASSEMBLAGES

Trench A84 (Markers 33 and 34)

This assemblage consists of three cranial fragments, one cervical vertebra (probably C3
or C4), the fused caudalmost coccygeal vertebrae, a right greater multangular, a left
fifth metacarpal, and fourteen unidentified bone fragments. The bones are in sound
condition and show no signs of weathering suggestive of surface exposure.

One of the cranial fragments is from the left parietal and it includes a fifty-five-
millimeter segment of the partially closed coronal sutural margin. The other borders of
this fragment display the linear, abrupt fracture margins consistent with perimortem
blunt-force trauma.

The remaining cranial fragments comprise the anterior portion of the maxilla and
most of the left zygoma (fig. 75a). The anterior dentition, including the premolars, is
present except for the left central incisor, which has been lost postmortem, and the left
first premolar, which had been lost or extracted prior to death. The left lateral incisor
and canine are heavily worn in the pattern typically seen in pipe smokers. Fracture

margins are indicative of massive blunt-force damage inflicted at or about the time of death.

The cervical vertebra exhibits slight osteophytic lipping. Its dorsal spine and a portion of its lamina are missing, but whether this represents perimortem trauma or damage sustained some months or years after death cannot be definitely determined.

The nasal aperture is rather wide (twenty-five millimeters) and the nasal sill does not display the raised margins characteristic of Caucasoids. The zygomatic bone is robust and angular. These findings suggest the possibility of some Mongoloid admixture. On the other hand, the incisors do not display the shoveling often observed in Mongoloids.

Summary: The dental wear and early osteophytosis of the cervical vertebra suggests an age of about thirty-five to forty-five years at the time of death. Perimortem injury consists of massive blunt-force trauma to the head. The configuration of the facial bones suggests some Mongoloid (e.g., American Indian) racial admixture. The arched dental wear pattern confined to the left anterior teeth indicates that he was a habitual pipe smoker.

Square G84 (Marker 7)

This assemblage consists of fourteen cranial fragments, eight maxillary teeth, part of a midcervical vertebra, a nearly intact lumbar vertebra, a portion of the sternal body, and two unidentified fragments. The bones are in sound condition and display no signs of weathering from surface exposure. There are no significant anomalies or antemortem pathologies.

The largest cranial fragment measures twenty-four by thirty-three millimeters. One of its margins is a short segment of sutural border still patent at the time of death. Its other margins, as well as those of several other vault fragments, display the sharply defined borders typical of fractures produced by blunt-force injuries inflicted at or about the time of death.

The cervical vertebral fragment, judging from its size and morphology, is most likely C4 or C5. The right side of the bone is missing, having been separated from the specimen by a single oblique cut extending transversely and inferiorly across the vertebral body and arch—a finding clearly indicative of decapitation (fig. 75b). The two lumbar vertebrae are intact except for minor erosional damage. The annular and process epiphyses of all three of these vertebrae are closed; osteoarthritic or osteophytic changes are absent.

The twenty-five- by fifty-one-millimeter sternal body fragment is from the right margin of the bone and includes parts of two segments which had united prior to death.

Summary: While the vertebral epiphyses were closed, there are no signs of osteoarthritic or osteophytic changes; cranial sutures were apparently still patent at the time of death. These findings suggest an age at death of about eighteen to thirty-five years. Evidence of perimortem trauma includes extensive comminuted craniofacial fractures indicative of massive blunt-force injury and the cleanly transected cervical vertebra caused by a single decapitating blow inflicted with a sharp-edged instrument, such as a hatchet or ax.

Square H84 (Markers 9 and 10)

Next to M85, this is the most complete skeleton yet recovered from the Custer site. The cranium is represented by thirty-one fragments, which together comprise about one-third of the surface area of the cranial vault. The trunk skeleton consists of one cervical and two lumbar vertebrae, the sternum and five ribs. From the upper extremity are two fragments of the right scapula, both humeri, the left ulna and radius, and several bones from the hands. Lower extremities are missing except for a right patella and some bones of the right foot. The bones are in sound condition and display no signs of weathering indicative of prolonged surface exposure. Except for minor erosion, they are intact except for the single thoracic vertebra, which is represented only by its neural arch, and the ribs; this damage appears to have occurred after skeletonization and is typical of that caused by earth pressure in long-buried bones.

The long bones are stout with relatively large condyles and well-developed muscle attachments typical of a large male of robust physique. Antemortem stature, derived from humeral length, is seventy and four-tenths ± one and six-tenths inches, which is well above the average of the Seventh Cavalry troopers.

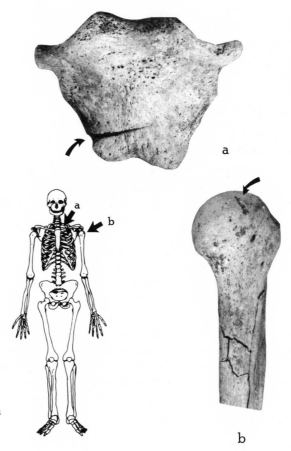

Fig. 76. Human bone from Markers 9–10. a: Sternum with cut marks. b: Humerus with cut marks.

Several cranial fragments present sutural lines which were still patent at the time of death. All postcranial epiphyses were completely closed. Incipient osteophytic lipping is present on the two lumbar vertebrae recovered and there are some slight osteoarthritic changes in the margins of the proximal joints of the ulnae. These features suggest an age at death of about thirty to forty years.

The cranial-vault fragments comprise portions of the frontal, both parietals, the occipital squamous and squamous portion of the left temporal bone. All display curvilinear fracture margins indicative of massive blunt-force trauma inflicted at or around the time of death. The available fragments are insufficient to determine the direction and number of blows.

In the sternum, there is a deep cut mark on the anterior surface of the manubrium (fig. 76a). It extends transversely from a point on the right border about ten millimeters above the inferior angle to a point just to the left of the midline. It is deepest and widest laterally and narrows progressively as it passes across the surface.

On the head of the left humerus, there is a vertically oriented cut mark twelve millimeters in length; it is located on the anterior aspect of the articular surface and begins seven millimeters from the joint margin (fig 76b). The left humerus also displays a comminuted fracture of the medial surface of the upper third of the shaft.

Summary: The remains are those of a male with a robust physique who was between thirty and forty years of age at death. Antemortem stature is estimated at about five feet, ten and one-half, inches which would have made him about three inches taller than the average trooper killed in the Custer fight. Evidence of perimortem trauma includes massive comminuted cranial fractures and a stellate fracture of the upper third of the left humerus. There are also cut marks of the manubrium and left humeral head produced by a sharply edged instrument, such as a knife, hatchet, or metal arrow point.

Square I84 (Marker 2)

This assemblage consists of thirteen cranial and two mandibular fragments, the root and small portion of the crown of a mandibular incisor, a hand proximal phalanx and six unidentified fragments. The bones are in sound condition and show no signs of surface weathering. There are no anomalies or antemortem pathologies.

The largest cranial fragment is a thirty-six- by forty-seven-millimeter piece of the right parietal. It exhibits a thirty-two-millimeter segment of the coronal sutural margin which was still patent at death; two smaller cranial vault fragments include short segments of closed suture. These findings suggest that at least some of the principal vault sutures had begun to close at the time of death. The mandibular fragments consist of the head of the right condyle and a forty-two- by thirty-three-millimeter fragment of the right ramus which includes a short segment of the superior margin of the coronoid process. The tooth root has been transversely fractured at the dentinoenamel junction. The fracture lines of the cranial and mandibular fragments are consistent with massive blunt-force trauma inflicted at or around the time of death.

Summary: This small assemblage represents the remains of an individual who was between twenty-five and forty years of age at the time of death. Perimortem trauma consists of massive blunt-force injury to the head.

Square J84 (Markers 52 and 53)

This is a large fragment (seventy by forty-three millimeters) of the petrous portion of the left temporal bone. It is in sound condition and displays no signs of surface weathering. It is intact except for the posterior-superior portion of the mastoid process and adjacent structures which have been separated by an obliquely directed fracture most likely caused by a heavy, edged instrument.

Summary: Petrous portion of adult left temporal bone. The planar fracture surface of the mastoid is characteristic of a blow struck with an edged instrument, such as a hatchet or ax.

Square K84 (Marker 200)

This assemblage includes one small cranial fragment, maxillary right first premolar, left ulna, right fibula, right patella, and several hand and foot bones. The bones are in sound condition. The lateral surface of the proximal end of the ulna is eroded from surface exposure; its distal epiphysis is missing but was only partially fused at the time of death. The fibular epiphyses are closed. The only evidence of perimortem trauma is the small cranial fragment with fracture margins indicative of blunt-force injury.

Summary: The bones are those of a young male between eighteen and twenty-two years of age at the time of death. Antemortem stature, estimated from fibula length (379 millimeters), was between sixty-six and seventy-one inches with a midpoint estimate of sixty-eight and two-tenths inches. The single cranial fragment has fracture margins indicative of perimortem blunt-force trauma.

Monument Hill Excavation (M84–Marker 105)

This assemblage consists of a single thoracic vertebra, left ulna, left radius, most of the bones of the left hand and a few from the right, a left calcaneus, two left metatarsals, and a distal phalanx from a toe. The bones are in excellent condition and display no signs of surface weathering.

The thoracic vertebra, T10, bears a small cut mark on the superior border of the centrum (fig. 77a). It is located on the right border nineteen millimeters posterior to the anterior midpoint of the centrum. It is about three-tenths of a millimeter in width and seven millimeters in length and penetrates the bone to a depth of about four millimeters. Such a wound would most likely be caused by a sharply edged instrument, such as a knife or metal arrowhead.

From long-bone lengths, antemortem stature is estimated at about sixty-three ± one and seven-tenths inches.

The epiphyses of the vertebra, long bones, and those of the hands and feet are closed and show no signs of recent union. No osteoarthritic changes are noted, although there is some slight osteophytic lipping of the vertebral centrum. These observations are consistent with an age at death of about thirty to forty years.

There is a poorly healed fracture of the base of the fourth left metatarsal with extensive osteosclerotic remodeling of the plantar surface of the bone (fig. 77b). The adjacent

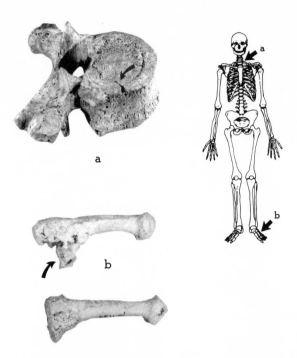

Fig. 77. Human bone from Marker 105. a: Thoracic vertebra with possible arrow wound. b: Metatarsals exhibiting a poorly healed fracture.

bone, the third metatarsal, shows some remodeling of the joint surfaces of the base correlated with the fourth metatarsal fracture.

Summary: This assemblage is from the skeleton of an individual whose most likely age at death was between thirty and forty years. Antemortem stature, estimated from the length of the radius, was between sixty and sixty-seven inches but most likely close to sixty-three and a half inches. There is evidence of an old fracture of the left foot involving the base of the left fourth metatarsal and adjacent bones. Perimortem trauma is present in the form of a cut mark on the superior margin of the centrum of the tenth thoracic vertebra; this injury could have been caused by either a knife or a metal arrowhead.

1985 EXCAVATION UNIT ASSEMBLAGES

Square A85 (Markers 201 and 202)

This assemblage consists of a mandibular left canine tooth, a fragment of the neural arch of the lower cervical vertebra, several bones of the hand, an intact left femur, and a foot phalanx. The bones display no signs of surface weathering and are in good condition. The metacarpal and femoral epiphyses are closed. Antemortem stature, derived from femoral length, is sixty-seven and a half ± one and three-tenths inches.

The posterior aspect of the greater trochanter of the femur bears a series of five closely spaced parallel cut marks which extend downward into the bone from the superior margin of the trochanter. They are oriented along the coronal plane of the bone. The posterior aspect of the femoral head also bears a similarly oriented cut, which has detached a circular flake of bone. These were inadvertently introduced during excavation. There is a series of three transverse cut marks on the distal end of the bone (fig. 78a). One of these is situated on the lateral border approximately seven centimeters above the distal end of the bone; a second extends obliquely across the epicondylar surface and the third is located on the posterior aspect of the lateral condyle.

Summary: These are the bones of an adult male who was most likely between twenty and thirty-five years of age at death. Antemortem stature is estimated at sixty-seven and a half inches, which is close to the average height of the Seventh Cavalry troopers. Cut marks on the distal end of the left femur indicate postmortem mutilation and, possibly dismemberment.

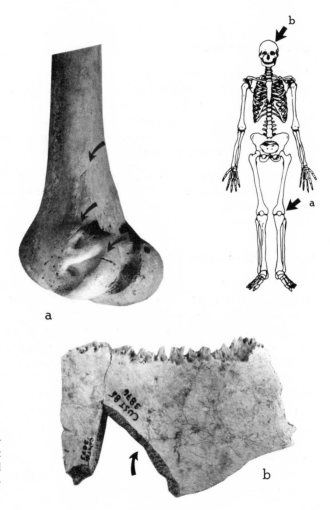

Fig. 78. Human bone from Markers 201–202 and 194–195. a: Cut mark on the end of a femur. b: Skull fracture caused by massive blunt-force trauma.

Square B85 (Markers 194 and 195)

This assemblage consists of two fragments of the left parietal bone, a left maxillary third molar, a left radius, a right second metacarpal, a right trapezium and trapezoid, and one unidentified fragment. The bones are in sound condition and show no signs of surface weathering. All are consistent with belonging to a single individual. The cranial sutures were patent at the time of death, and the root apex of the molar is closed. The radial and metacarpal epiphyses are fused. Antemortem stature is estimated at sixty-five and eight-tenths ± three and thirty-four hundredths inches. The two cranial fragments, when united, show a deep Gothic V-shaped fracture caused by massive perimortem blunt-force trauma (fig. 78b).

Summary: Young adult, probably about twenty to thirty years of age at death and standing about five feet six inches in stature. Evidence of massive perimortem blunt-force trauma to the cranium is present.

Square C85 (Marker 178)

This assemblage consists of a sixteen- by twenty-one-millimeter fragment of cranial vault, a left first rib, a fragmented left capitate, a left medial cuneiform bone and a toe phalanx, and three unidentified fragments. Although it is small, the fracture lines of the cranial fragment are consistent with blunt-force trauma. The cuneiform is badly eroded and shows signs of prolonged surface exposure. Epiphyses are closed on the rib and base of the proximal phalanx of the toe.

Summary: These bones are from an adult between twenty and forty years of age at death. The cranial fragment bears fracture margins indicative of perimortem blunt-force trauma.

Square D85 (Marker 199)

These remains consist of numerous fragments of the cranium, mandible and three teeth, a coccyx, some scapular epiphyses, and the complete right arm skeleton as well as a few of the smaller bones of the left hand (fig. 79a). The bones are well preserved and show no signs of surface exposure. Aside from the cranial and mandibular fractures suggestive of perimortem blunt-force trauma, the bones display no signs of violence.

The large cranial-vault fragment includes a segment of patent suture line. The root apices of the teeth (a mandibular right first molar and the right central and lateral mandibular incisors) are closed. The superior annular ring of the coccyx is partially closed. The scapulae are represented only by unfused epiphyses. The proximal humeral epiphyses are missing and had not fused at the time of death; the distal epiphyses are closed. The proximal epiphysis is closed, the distal open. The distal metacarpal epiphyses of the right hand are unfused. All of these findings are consistent with an age esitmate of about seventeen ± two years with a high probablity that the subject's actual age was on the lower side of this range.

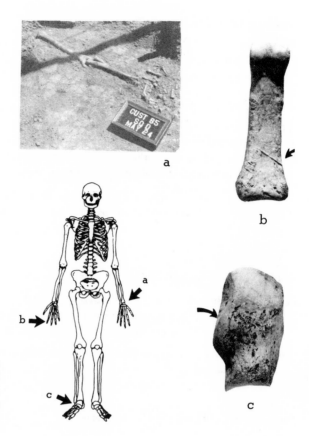

Fig. 79. Human bone from Markers 199 and 152–155. a: The right arm and hand of the young soldier in place. b: Cut marks on a phalanx. c: Cut marks on a talus.

Summary: This skeleton is that of a young male between fifteen and nineteen years of age at the time of death. The massive cranial fragmentation is consistent with blunt-force trauma.

Square F85 (Markers 152 and 155)

This assemblage consists of one proximal hand phalanx, a talus, cuboid, four metatarsals, four foot phalanges (three proximal, one terminal), and a sesamoid of the foot. Of the foot bones in which side can be determined, all but one—a fifth left metatarsal—are from the right. All epiphyses are closed. Although the bones show no signs of surface weathering, there is a considerable amount of erosion of the metatarsal extremities.

The volar surface of the hand phalanx displays a series of four parallel cut marks extending obliquely across the proximal end of the shaft (fig. 79b). There are two deep longitudinal cut marks on the plantar surface of the head of the talus (fig. 79c). The plantar surface of the cuboid also bears a shallow cut mark running in the same general direction. The base of one of the proximal toe phalanges appears to have been severed.

Summary: These bones are those of an adult male. The hand phalanx and three of the foot bones bear cut marks suggestive of postmortem mutilation. It is possible that those on the foot were inflicted during an attempt to remove the subject's boot.

Square G85 (Marker 135)

This assemblage consists of a fragment of the crown of a premolar tooth, a right capitate, and two terminal hand phalanges with closed proximal epiphyses. The right dorsosuperior angle of the capitate is missing; the surface of this defect is planar, but whether it represents an incised perimortem injury or postmortem erosion cannot be determined with certainty.

Summary: Adult hand bones and premolar tooth fragment. Possible cut mark on right capitate.

Square J85 (Marker 257)

This find consists of three badly eroded fragments of adult bones: a right capitate, right metacarpal shaft, and a portion of the left cuboid. None display signs of disease or perimortem trauma. They are anatomically consistent with the bones of a single skeleton.

Summary: Three fragmentary hand and foot bones of an adult with no signs of disease or perimortem violence.

Square K85 (Markers 112 and 113)

This group of bones consists of a small portion of tooth crown, the first segment of the coccyx, a terminal phalanx of the hand, and both phalanges of the first toe of an adult individual. There are no signs of perimortem disease or trauma. Mild osteoarthritic lipping of the joint margins suggests an age of more than thirty-five years at death.

Summary: Small bones consistent with those of a single skeleton. Age estimated at about thirty-five to forty-five years at death. No signs of perimortem trauma or disease.

Square M85 ("Mike"; Marker 128)

This assemblage comprises the most complete set of human remains so far recovered from the battlefield site. The only major element missing from this skeleton is the cranium, which is represented by only three small fragments; one of these is from the cranial vault and the other two are from the facial skeleton. Although it is badly fragmented, a complete mandible is present. The entire postcranial skeleton is present except for the hyoid, one rib, both patellae, and some of the smaller bones of the hands and feet; of the twenty-five foot bones recovered, all are from the right foot except one: the left first metatarsal. As there is no duplication of skeletal elements or any inconsistencies in size or morphology, the assemblage obviously represents the skeleton of one individual.

The distal (sternal) portions of the left ribs display some bleaching, weathering fractures, and cortical erosion indicative of several weeks to several months of surface exposure. Similar changes are noted in the left tibia, fibula, and the single bone recovered from the left foot. This pattern of exposure suggests that the burial was partially exposed to the elements during a period while the rib cage was still partially articulated and that exposure was largely limited to the left side of the body. Since it appears that both legs were disarticulated at the hip joint shortly after death (see below), the heavier weathering and bleaching of the left leg bones suggests that some attempt was made to reassemble the mutilated body parts in their correct anatomical relationship in the initial interment in 1876. At some time after this first burial—and probably during the first year or two after the battle—the grave was eroded and the bones of the left side were partly exposed. The exposed bones must have attracted the attention of one of the army burial details that returned to the battlefield in 1877 and 1879 to tend the graves, and the bones were gathered up and reburied. In this second interment, no attempt was made to lay out the disarticulated bones in anatomical order, which accounts for their anatomical disarray when discovered in 1985. Perhaps the cranium was also lost during the second burial. For one reason or another, this skeleton was apparently overlooked in the transfer of the skeletons to the mass grave in 1881.

Pelvic morphology is strongly male. Racial traits are Caucasoid and include the nonshoveled upper central incisor, strongly projecting chin, relatively narrow mandibular ramus, moderately bowed long bones, and low (80.0) crural index.

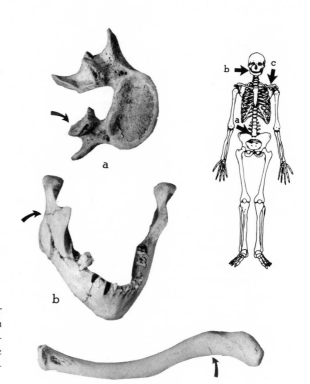

Fig. 80. Human bone from Marker 128. a: Congenital anaomaly of the fifth lumbar vertebrae. b: The mandible exhibiting evidence of massive blunt force trauma. c: Cut mark on the inferior surface of the clavicle.

Based on pubic symphysial morphology, age at death is estimated at about twenty-one ± two years. All postcranial epiphyses are closed except those at the medial end of the clavicles, which had not yet begun to fuse at the time of death. In the sacrum, the S1-S2 segment is unclosed while the S2-S3 and S3-S4 segments are in a late (stage 3) phase of closure. These latter findings suggest an upper age limit of twenty-two years. Therefore, the final age estimate for this skeleton is nineteen to twenty-two years.

Antemortem stature, calculated from the combined lengths of the femur and tibia, is sixty-six and eight-tenths ± one and eighteen-hundredths inches. Physique was stocky with well-developed musculature. Posterior glenoid beveling is more pronounced in the right scapula than the left, indicating that this individual was right-handed.

The first mandibular molars were lost or extracted a few months or years prior to death. The only major skeletal anomaly is the congenital absence of the right lamina and inferior articular facet of the fifth lumbar vertebra (fig. 80a). This defect might have caused some lower back pain, which was particularly uncomfortable to a cavalry-man. The mandible displays strong gonial eversion, suggesting well-developed masseter musculature—possibly a functional response to a diet requiring much heavy chewing. Both femurs display prominent abductor tubercles and some phalangelike cresting of the medial supracondylar lines immediately above the tubercles; such findings indicate the well-developed *m. adductor magnus* characteristic of horsemen. Radiographs of the left femur reveal a medullary bony lesion with thickened septa and cystic portions; there is a narrow zone of transition with portions of the lesion having sclerotic rim.

The bones display several signs of perimortem trauma:

1. *Skull*: The cranial vault is represented by a single twenty-four- by forty-milli-meter fragment of the inferior angle of the right parietal bone which displays fissure (linear) fractures. The only elements of the facial skeleton are an intact right nasal bone, a seventeen- by nineteen-millimeter fragment of the frontal process of the right maxilla (which articulates with the nasal bone), and the maxillary right central incisor.

The mandible, as recovered, consisted of six fragments, including the right second molar. When reconstructed, it is complete except for the tip of the left coronoid process and three teeth from the right side of the jaw: the canine, second premolar, and third molar, all of which were lost postmortem (as noted above, both second molars were lost antemortem). The mandibular fractures consist of a vertical break passing downward from the socket of the right premolar through the mental foramen and a more complex fracture of the ramus which separates the angle, coronoid process, and condyle. The teeth remaining in the jaw have been fractured transversely at the alveolar level, leaving only their roots intact (fig. 80b).

These findings, taken together, indicate massive blunt-force trauma to the skull inflicted at or about the time of death.

2. *Left Clavicle*: There is a cut mark of the inferior surface of the bone (fig. 80c). It is oriented at a right angle to the long axis of the bone. It was most likely to have been caused by a sharply edged instrument, such as a metal-tipped arrowhead or a knife.

3. *Thorax*: Perimortem trauma to the thoracic bones consists of several rib fractures caused by bullets or bullet fragments. They are:

a. A cresenteric fracture about ten millimeters wide and three deep on the inferior margin of the right eighth rib. It is located at the midpoint of the rib, approximately thirteen centimeters from its distal end (fig. 81a).

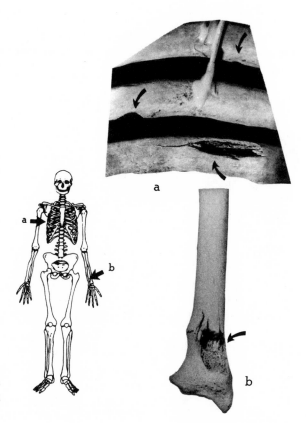

Fig. 81. Marker 128 wounds. a: Evidence of gunshot trauma to the ribs. b: A bullet embedded in the radius.

This appears to be an entrance wound, with the bullet striking the right side and passing medially and anteriorly to exit the anterior chest wall without striking a rib in exiting, possibly because it exited at a level below the inferior margin of the rib cage.

b. A six- by thirty-five-millimeter fracture defect of the visceral surface of the right ninth rib which exposes the underlying cortical bone. Overlying this site on the external surface are two, parallel fractures about fifty millimeters in length. This injury is located slightly distal to the angle of the rib and about sixteen centimeters from its distal end (fig. 81a).

It seems probable that this injury was caused by a fragment of the bullet which caused the entrance wound of the right eighth rib described above. This fragment appears to have struck the internal surface of the rib at a grazing angle, causing the elongate fracture of the cortex without completely penetrating the bone. However, radiographs of this lesion do not reveal any embedded metal particles.

c. On the right seventh rib there is a thirty-millimeter fracture defect of the external upper margin located about five centimeters from the distal end of the bone. Like the injury described above, it may also have been caused by a fragment from the bullet which entered the right side at the level of the eighth rib (fig. 81a).

d. On the left tenth rib there is a semicircular fracture defect of the inferior margin, about thirteen centimeters from the distal end of the bone. The internal cortical bone is depressed in an outward direction, and there is some comminution of the external surface surrounding this defect.

This injury is an exit wound from a bullet entering the right abdomen, passing posteriorly and medially to the left to exit at the level of the tenth rib, striking the inferior margin of that bone as it left the body.

4. *Left Radius*: This bone displays the most dramatic evidence of perimortem trauma observed in this skeleton: a bullet (or perhaps a bullet fragment) still embedded in the distal end. This projectile entered the lateral margin of the bone about three and a half centimeters above the styloid process. It passed transversely and slightly upward to lodge near the medial border (fig. 81b).

5. *Femurs*: Both the right and left bones display injuries caused by a heavy-bladed edged instrument, such as a hatchet or ax (fig. 82a,b). There are three such chop marks on the right femur. The most proximal is located on the anteriomedial border of the femoral head; it consists of a nineteen- by eleven-millimeter ovoid depressed area with its long axis parallel to the margin of the head. The second, a thirty-two-millimeter linear chop mark, extends diagonally across the anterior surface of the base of the femoral neck just medial to the intertrochanteric line; it is five millimeters wide and three deep superiorly and becomes progressively narrower and shallower as it passes distally. The third injury is located on the anteriomedial aspect of the shaft about thirteen and a half centimeters distal to the femoral head. It is twenty-five by twelve millimeters in greatest dimensions, with its long axis at about forty-five and a half degrees to the longitudinal axis of the bone, and penetrates the cortex to a depth of about five millimeters.

In the left femur, the head and upper portion of the neck was separated from the shaft of the bone by two chop marks. The most proximal left a twenty-two- by ten-millimeter ovoid depression on the medial aspect of the neck just below the margin of the femoral head. The second lies diagonally across the anterior aspect of the neck just medial to the intertrochanteric line. The third is a seventeen- by seven-millimeter diagonal cut across the anteriomedial aspect of the shaft about nineteen and two-tenths centimeters distal to the femoral head.

Summary: This skeleton is that of a young white male between nineteen and twenty-two years of age. His grave apparently became exposed, with the consequent bleaching of some of the bones of the left side and loss of others. It appears that his body was then reburied at another site, or perhaps the original grave was simply recovered. The only major bone missing is the cranium, which, except for three fragments, is missing entirely. It is possible that it was dragged away by animals during the period of exposure or somehow was lost or mistakenly placed in another grave during reburial.

Antemortem stature is estimated at about sixty-six and eight-tenths ± one and eighteen hundredths inches. He was of stocky physique with well-developed musculature and was right-handed. His bones display no old fractures. Radiographs reveal a medullary lesion of unknown etiology in the subtrochanteric region of the left femur.

The ribs display evidence of two gunshot wounds. One entered the right side at the level of the eighth rib, nicking its inferior margin. It then passed forward and to the

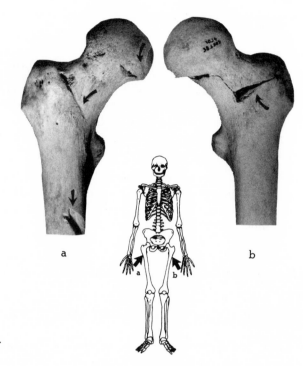

Fig. 82. Marker 128 multilation marks.
a–b: Cut marks on both femurs.

left; some of its fragments also damaged the right seventh and ninth ribs. The other bullet appears to have entered the upper right quadrant of the abdomen, passing to the left and posteriorly to exit at the level of the lower margin of the left tenth rib, damaging it in passing.

He was also wounded in the left forearm just above the wrist. The evidence for this is an irregular body of lead about one and a half centimeters in greatest diameter embedded in the anterior surface of the radius. It may have been caused by a third bullet or by an exiting fragment from one of the two which passed through the chest.

The cutmark on the lower surface of the lateral end of the left clavicle indicates a wound caused either by a metal-tipped arrow or a stab wound in the left shoulder.

The cranial fragments and mandible display evidence of massive blunt-force trauma inflicted by repeated blows to the head with a heavy instrument, such as a rifle butt, war club, or perhaps a large stone. Finally, the legs were dismembered at the hip joint with a heavy-bladed weapon, such as an ax or hatchet.

Square N85 (Markers 86 and 87)

This consists of an anomalous adult right patella. The anomaly consists of a defect of the upper portion of the right border. It may represent a congenital defect (bipartite patella) or, perhaps, the result of an old injury.

Summary: Anomalous right patella of an adult.

Square O85 (Marker 78)

The assemblage consists of nine cranial fragments, a mandibular right canine tooth, the distal one-third of a left ulna, a nearly complete left hand skeleton, a few right hand bones, and three small bones of the foot. The bones are in good condition except for the right hamate, which is somewhat demineralized and shows signs of erosion. Signs of perimortem trauma include the cranial fragmentation and the complete ulnar fracture. Radiographs of the ulna show two pinpoint metallic densities, which probably represent bullet fragments (fig. 83). The epiphyses are closed. The bones appear to be those of a young (eighteen to thirty years) adult male.

Summary: Bone of a young adult male somewhere between eighteen and thirty years of age at the time of death. Metal fragments embedded in the shattered ulnar fragment indicate a gunshot wound in the forearm. The cranial fragmentation suggests perimortem blunt-force trauma.

Square P85 (Markers 67 and 68)

The assemblage consists of six cranial fragments, five teeth, a fragmented lumbar vertebra, two ribs, and a hand phalanx. One of the cranial fragments is a fifty-eight- by forty-four-millimeter portion of the occipital bone that includes part of the posterior margin of the foramen magum; its superior margin is a transverse fracture line produced by massive blunt-force trauma. A second cranial fragment consists of the nasal

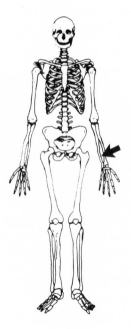

Fig. 83. Marker 178 radiograph of a distal ulna showing lead fragments from a gunshot wound.

bones, which are still articulated. Three of the cranial fragments are from the maxilla and two include the alveolar portion, which bears the following teeth from the right side of the jaw: lateral incisor, canine, first premolar, second and third molars. The teeth display slight attrition but no signs of dental disease except for moderate alveolar resorbtion. The vertebral fragments consist of the anterior body and arch of a midlumbar vertebra; the central margins display slight osteophytotic lipping, which suggests an age in the late thirties or early forties. The more complete of these two vertebrae shows some loss of height of the posterior portion of the centrum consistent with an old healed compression fracture.

One of the two ribs is the right first; the second is the left twelveth. The latter displays a ten-millimeter semicircular defect of its superior margin located seventeen millimeters distal to the head. This defect most probably was caused by a bullet or bullet fragment.

Summary: These bones are most likely from an individual between thirty-five and forty-five years of age at the time of death who had suffered an old compression fracture of one of the lumbar vertebrae. The small defect in the twelfth left rib may represent a bullet wound. The cranial fragmentation is suggestive of massive blunt-force inflicted at or about the time of death.

Square R85 (Marker 42)

This find consists of four adult hand bones: a left pisiform, a proximal phalanx of the right little finger, two intermediate phalanges, and a single terminal phalanx. The base of the larger of the two intermediate phalanges appears to have been transversely severed in a blow upward, although, because of weathering, postmortem erosion cannot be ruled out with certainty.

Summary: Adult hand bones. Possible perimortem severing of the base of one of the intermediate phalanges.

DISCUSSION

The human remains from the Custer battlefield consist of 375 human bones (some of which are fragmentary) and 36 teeth, a total of 411 items. We estimate that the remains of thirty-four individuals are represented in this collection. However, the 141 bones and teeth from one of these (M85) comprise 34.3 percent of the entire collection. In other words, thirty-three of the individuals are represented by only 270 bones and teeth, or an average of eight and two-tenths specimens per person. Furthermore, the bones present in the collection tend to be those, such as ribs, vertebra, and hand or foot bones, which, unless they display some unusual signs of trauma or disease, are not apt to tell us much about their former owners. For this reason, the amount of osteobiographical detail that can be extracted from the study of the Custer-fight remains is apt to be rather sketchy. Considering the wealth of anatomical and pathological knowledge that the 210 skeletons offered in 1881, when, still more or less intact, they were gathered up and

Table 28 Summary of Principal Findings

#	Assmb.	Bones	Teeth	Age	Stature	Perimortem Trauma			Remarks
						GSW	BFT	CUT	
1	MUS-1	1	0	adult		no	no	no	Cranial fracture
2	MUS-2	5	0	18–35		no	yes	no	
3	MUS-3	5	0	18–35	65.7	no	no	no	
4	MUS-4	2	0	18–35	65.8	no	no	no	
5	282A	1	0	18–35		no	yes	no	Cranial fracture
6	282B	1	0	adult		no	no	no	
7	282C	1	0	adult		no	no	no	
8	CUS84a	1	0	18–25		no	no	no	
9	CUS84b	1	0	adult		no	no	no	
10	CUS84c	1	0	adult		no	no	no	
11	CUS84d	1	0	adult		no	no	no	
12	CUS84e	1	0	adult		no	no	no	
13	CUS84f	1	0	18–40		no	no	no	
14	CUS84g	1	0	adult		no	no	no	
15	A84	5	8	35–45		no	yes	no	Cranial fractures
16	G84	4	0	18–35		no	yes	yes	Cranial fractures, Decapitation at C4
17	H84	32	1	30–40	70.4	no	yes	yes	Cranial and L Humerus fractures. Cutmarks on sternum and L Humerus
18	I84	3	1	25–40		no	yes	no	Cranial fractures

19	J84	1	0	adult		no	no	yes	Shearing blow to L. Temporal
20	K84	15	1	18–22	68.2	no	yes	no	Cranial fractures
21	M84	34	0	30–40	63.5	no	no	yes	Cutmark on thoracic vertebra (T10)
22	A85	13	1	20–35	67.5	no	no	yes	Postmortem mutilation; cutmarks on Left Femur
23	B85	5	1	20–30	65.8	no	yes	no	Cranial fractures
24	C85	5	0	20–40		no	yes	no	Cranial fractures
25	D85	41	3	15–19	67.5	no	yes	no	Cranial fractures
26	F85	11	0	20–45		no	no	yes	Postmortem mutilation; cutmarks on hand and foot bones
27	G85	3	1	adult		no	no	yes	Cutmark of right capitate
28	J85	3	0	adult		no	no	no	
29	K85	4	1	35–45		no	no	no	
30	M85	129	12	19–22	66.8	yes	yes	yes	Cranial fractures. Gunshot wounds of chest and L radius. Cutmarks on L Clavicle. Postmortem mutilation: Cutmarks on both femora
31	N85	1	0	adult		no	no	no	
32	O85	33	1	18–30		yes	yes	no	Cranial fracture. Gunshot fracture of L ulna
33	P85	5	5	35–45		yes	yes	no	Cranial fracture. Gunshot fracture of L 12th rib
34	R85	5	0	adult		no	no	no	

GSW = Gun shot wound
BFT = Blunt force trauma
CUT = Cut marks

reburied in the common grave, one cannot help but regret that the reburial detachment did not include a team of medicolegal experts detailed to describe carefully each skeleton as it was exhumed. Even though the forensic science specialties were in their infancy in those days, such a systematic study undoubtedly could have answered many questions about the battle which still perplex the Custer scholars of today.

Nonetheless, the few bones and teeth of Custer's men that have come down to us do have some tales to tell. The information derived from the present study is summarized in this section. Some of the principal findings are presented in table 28.

Age and Death

Estimates of age for the majority of the individuals represented by these assemblages are understandably broad. For example, those represented by only a few small bones could only be characterized as adult on the basis of the size and morphology of the elements available for examination. In some cases, the span could be narrowed somewhat, based on the presence or absence of generalized aging features, such as evidence of cranial suture closure, osteoarthritic lipping of the joint margins, vertebral osteophytosis, or dental attrition. In most populations, these age-related changes usually become manifest in the middle thirties or early forties. Therefore, when signs of the changes were absent, we felt justified in placing the upper boundary of the age estimate at about thirty-five to forty-five years. In the assemblages where some signs of these changes were observed, they were invariably in their earliest or incipient stages, and for this reason an age range of about thirty-five to forty-five years seemed reasonable. It should be noted that in no individual were such changes present in their more advanced stages so that the findings are generally consistent with the available age statistics of Custer's troopers which indicate that all were less than forty-five years old.

Four assemblages (Cus-84a, K84, D85, G85, M85) offered more specific age information in the form of maturational criteria, such as epiphyseal closure and pubic symphyseal morphology. Since such criteria are associated with the later stages of adolescence and early adulthood, all five of these were men in their late teens or early twenties. The youngest, D85, was certainly no older than nineteen and may have been as young as fifteen years at the time of his death. At the other extreme, three individuals (A84, K85, P85) appear to have been in the thirty-five to forty-five age range at the time of death.

Racial Traits

The best skeletal clues to race are found in the skull and dentition. Because no complete skulls and only a few teeth were found, race could not be diagnosed with confidence in any of the assemblages. However, with one exception, none displayed any obvious non-Caucasoid features.

The exception was A84, which consists of a large portion of the lower facial skeleton of an individual judged to be in the thirty-five- to forty-five-year age range. This fragment displays several traits characteristic of Mongoloids, such as the relatively broad nasal aperture, low nasal sills, and large zygomatic (cheek) bones. On the other hand, the so-called shovel-shaped incisors—practically a Mongoloid racial hallmark—are not present. These findings suggest that this individual may have been of mixed white-Indian ancestry. It is tempting to associate this specimen with Custer's interpreter, Mitch Boyer, whose father was French and whose mother was a Santee Sioux. However, there is a controversy as to the fate of Boyer's body (see the discussion of Boyer in chapter 5).

Antemortem Stature

Nine of the assemblages contained at least one long bone, thus permitting the estimation of antemortem stature. These estimates ranged between 63.5 and 70.4 inches, with a mean value of 66.8 ± standard deviation of 1.83 inches. This is just slightly lower than the mean of 67.1 inches derived from the statural records of the Custer troopers. This difference is not statistically significant.

Antemortem Pathologies

The bones available for the study present few signs of antemortem disease or injuries. Healed fractures are limited to two cases: M84, which has healed fractures of the base of the right third and fourth metatarsals, and the lumbar vertebra of P85, which displays signs of an old compression fracture. The apparent infrequency of fractures is somewhat surprising in bones of active-duty cavalrymen, who frequently must have been exposed to falls.

Evidence of systematic disease is also sparse. Absent are signs of the two infectious diseases, syphillis and tuberculosis, which are frequently seen in pre–twentieth-century skeletal collections. One reason for this is that both diseases tend to involve bone late in the course and would not be expected to manifest themselves in the relatively young age group represented by these bones. Dental disorders appear limited to tooth loss either to extraction or periapical abscess. No caries were present in the thirty-six teeth examined. The bones and teeth display none of the changes often observed in individuals who have suffered from chronic nutritional stress. The only congenital condition affecting the bones is the arch defect of the fifth lumbar vertebra of M85, the nearly complete skeleton. This same skeleton has a medullary lesion of unknown etiology in the subtrochanteric region of the left femur.

Perimortem Trauma

The evidence of perimortem trauma observed in these skeletal remains is of three kinds. First, and most frequent, is that of blunt-force trauma. This is predominantly manifested as extensive fragmentation of the cranial vault and facial skeleton and, in a few cases, the postcranial bones. A second and less frequently observed form consists of incised fractures or cut marks resulting from stabbing, slicing, or chopping wounds inflicted by edged weapons, such as knives, hatchets, axes, or metal arrowheads. Finally, and rarest of all among these bones, is evidence of bullet wounds.

A difficulty in interpreting the evidence of all three classes of observed injuries—blunt-force trauma, incised factures, and bullet wounds—lies in determining whether they occurred immediately prior to death or sometime after death; that is, whether they are antemortem or postmortem. For this reason, we have cautiously described them as perimortem, a term implying that the observed injury occurred around the time of death. Generally, an injury to the bone which has occurred a week or two prior to death will display some signs of healing (callus formation) or, in some cases, an inflammatory response (periostitis, ostitis, or osteomyelitis) when the wound has become infected.

Injuries to bone which do not display such reaction can generally be assumed to have occurred very close to the time of death, at most a few hours or days. In cases where the wound is severe enough to be obviously fatal—for example, a through-and-through gunshot wound of the cranium—it is generally safe to assume that it occurred immediately prior to death and indeed was the likely cause of death of the victim. On the other hand, one cannot entirely rule out the possibility that it was inflicted shortly after death.

Blunt-Force Trauma

As noted above, the most frequently observed injury takes the form of blunt-force trauma of the skull. In all, fourteen assemblages contain some portion of the cranium or mandible. In each case, the skull bones display evidence of massive comminuted fractures. The cranial fragments in thirteen of the fourteen cases display the abrupt splitting margins characteristic of perimortem fractures and not the more irregular borders typically observed in breaks sustained after the bones have become dry through skeletonization. Of course, it is possible that some of the fragmentation may be the result of bullet wounds. However, if this were so, we might expect the margins of at least a few of the fragments to display the characteristic beveling of bullet entrance or exit wounds, but none are present. Therefore, the impression is that the majority of these skulls were fractured by heavy blows inflicted at or around the time of death.

Incised Wounds

Eight of the assemblages contain bones bearing evidence of trauma by edged instruments. These lesions take two forms: linear, finely incised cut marks, such as are produced by sharp, thin-bladed weapons; and shearing or chopping fractures resulting from blows struck by heavy, thick-bladed weapons. The former type might have been caused either by metal arrowheads or by knives. One individual, H84, bears two such wounds, one on the head of the left humerus and the other on the sternum. Such a cut mark is also present on the underside of the left clavicle of M85. A third is in the form of a small Gothic V-shaped incision on both of the tenth thoracic vertebrae of M84. In all three of these cases, the wounds are single, isolated lesions occurring in the upper torso (shoulder or chest). It seems slightly more probable that they were inflicted during active combat. The right capitate of a fourth individual; G85, bears a transverse cut mark on its palmar surface.

One of the assemblages containing bones with finely incised cut marks differ from those described above in that there are multiple, more or less parallel, and evenly spaced cut marks on the same bone. The individual, F85, bears two sets of serial marks. The first set is on the palmar surface of a proximal phalanx of the hand; on this bone, four parallel incisions extend obliquely across the proximal end of the bone. The second set of cut marks in F85 involve two bones of the right foot: on the talus, there are two parallel transverse incisions on the plantar surface, and a single cut, similarly oriented, is present on the plantar surface of the cuboid. In addition, the three proximal toe phalanges present in this assemblage are missing their bases, which appear to have been severed. Because they are multiple and tend to be parallel, it is safe to say that these wounds were inflicted by knives and not by arrows. Furthermore, such regularity would not be possible to produce in a struggling victim; they must have been inflicted postmortem. The cut marks on the palm and the foot sole of F85 may have been done in an effort to strip the victim of his gauntlets and boots.

Three assemblages present evidence of wounds inflicted by heavy edged weapons, such as axes or hatchets. The first is J84, which is represented by only a fragment of the petrous and mastoidal portion of the left temporal bone of the skull. This fragment bears a flat planar fracture surface extending obliquely through the mastoid. In the second individual (G84), the upper portion of the body and neural arch of the fourth cervical vertebra has been cleanly sheared away. The fracture surface is smooth and continuous, indicating that the decapitation was accomplished with a single blow. As some cranial fragments are present in this assemblage, it appears that the burial party was able to locate the head for interment with the rest of the body. The final individual in this series is M85, each of whose femora display the set of three chopping blows to the head, trochanter, and shaft. The symmetry of these wounds denotes a systematic process of postmortem mutilation and possible dismemberment.

Gunshot Wounds

Bones of three assemblages display evidence of gunshot wounds. The first of these is M85, who appears to have suffered at least two wounds in the upper body. The first bullet entered from the right near the posterior auxiliary line at the level of the eighth interspace, leaving a small entrance wound on the inferior margin of the eighth rib. The second bullet apparently entered the upper right abdomen to exit at the level of the left tenth interspace. A third wound is in the left forearm, where a bullet fragment is embedded in the anterior surface of the distal end of the radius. Whether this wound was caused by an exiting fragment of one of the bullets causing the chest wounds or by a third bullet cannot be definitely determined.

The second individual with evidence of a gunshot wound is O85. The affected bone is the right ulna, the distal third of which displays comminuted fractures. X-rays of this specimen reveal metallic particles embedded close to the fracture margins. The third case is P85, in whom the left twelfth rib bears a semicircular fracture defect of the margin, indicating the passage of a bullet into the lower thorax.

The human remains from the Custer battle, while scanty, nonetheless offer some information on the manner in which death was inflicted. First, it is likely that the vast majority of the troopers initially suffered projectile wounds, either from metal-tipped arrows or, probably in the vast majority of cases, bullets. As in most armed conflicts of the period, it is likely that most of these wounds, unless to the head, heart, or major vessels, were not instantly lethal and the victims would have survived from a few minutes to a few hours without medical treatment. In fact, a fair proportion of such wounds might have been survivable had they been rendered the minimal medical attention available under field conditions during this period. The nearly complete skeleton from Square M85 is probably typical in this respsect. This trooper suffered one and possibly two gunshot wounds in the chest. While the wounds were likely to have been critical, he might have been expected to survive for a short time unless one of the bullets or bullet fragments penetrated the heart or aorta. He was also wounded in the left radius by either a separate bullet or an exiting fragment from the chest. If, as is likely, he received these wounds during the relatively short firefight (estimated by most authorities at no more than thirty minutes to an hour), they would certainly have been sufficient to prevent him from taking any further part in the battle. On the other hand, it is possible that he was still alive at the time effective resistance ended. At this time, like many of the other wounded, he would have been dispatched by means of heavy blows to the head, as is attested by the extensive fractures of the mandible and shearing fractures of the mandibular dentition. Finally, the body was dismembered, which, in this particular case, appears to have consisted of separation of the legs at the hip joint by means of a heavy edged instrument, such as an ax or hatchet.

Certain students of the Custer battle have proposed the theory that a sizable number of the troopers killed themselves when they saw that further resistance was useless (Spencer 1983, Marquis 1976). This mass-suicide theory has been used to account for the brevity of the battle by troops which in many other Plains Indian warfare fights had given a good account of themselves despite overwhelming numerical odds. If such were the case, one would expect to find a high frequency of close-range gunshot wounds in the head, the most common site of suicide wounds. Unfortunately, the osteological remains available in this study include no complete skulls. However, as pointed out above, none of the cranial fragments available for study shows any clear-cut signs of gunshot trauma. Although, because of the paucity of the materials, the absence of evidence of gunshot wounds in the head is not sufficient of itself to rule out the suicide theory, it certainly offers it no support.

To summarize, the available osteological evidence suggests a general pattern of wounding, final killing—often by blunt-force trauma of the head—followed in many cases by postmortem mutilation. This picture is consistent with the description of the bodies given in contemporary accounts and with general recollections of many of the Indian participants.

CONCLUSIONS

1. The human osteological remains from the Custer battle include bones from 34 of the 210 troopers who died in the battle. Most of the 411 bones and teeth in the total collection represent the smaller and less significant bones overlooked in the exhumation of the skeletons from their original graves for transfer to the mass grave in 1881. An exception is the nearly complete skeleton from Square M85, which was obviously overlooked by the reburial party.

2. Although the scantiness of the remains precluded precise age estimates for most of the thirty-four individuals, at least four could be diagnosed as being under twenty-five years of age at the time of death. Of these younger individuals, one was between fifteen and nineteen years old and hence definitely under the official enlistment age of twenty-one. It is possible that at least some of the other skeletons in this group were also under twenty-one. Although the sample size is small, this finding at least suggests that there may have been a considerably larger number of underage troopers in the command than the historical records reflect.

3. The bones and teeth available for study display little evidence of disease, healed injuries, or signs of nutritional deprivation. In other words, the troopers appear to have been physically fit and possibly in better general health than their civilian compatriots of the period.

4. Perimortem trauma includes evidence of massive blunt-force trauma to the head in fourteen cases. This trauma was probably inflicted as a means of dispatching the wounded. In eight cases, there were incised wounds produced by sharply edged weapons, such as metal arrowheads or knives, or chop marks resulting from ax or hatchet blows. Some were apparently inflicted in the course of postmortem mutilation and dismemberment of the dead. They include one decapitation by means of a transverse shearing fracture of the fourth cervical vertebra. Three cases display osteological evidence of gunshot wounds. In one of these, two bullets apparently struck the victim in the right side of the upper torso and a large bullet or bullet fragment is embedded in the left radius just above the wrist. A second individual has a bullet wound shattering the lower left ulna. The third gunshot victim was struck in the left side of the lower thorax at the level of the eleventh rib.

5. No evidence of bullet entrance or exit wounds were present in the cranial bones available for study, nor did X-rays of these fragments reveal any embedded bullet particles commonly found in such wounds. Although this finding is not sufficient to refute the theory that a large number of troopers committed suicide, it provides no evidence to support the theory.

6. The available osteological evidence supports a scenario of the events as consisting of a brief firefight followed by the close-range dispatch of the wounded. It appears probable that the majority of the troopers were still alive but more or less helplessly wounded when resistance ceased and that many were finished off with massive crushing blows to the head. After death, many were mutilated and dismembered.

7. Familiarity with the problems of visually identifying the dead in mass-disaster situations and consideration of the condition of the bodies when they were found leads

the authors to question the validity of some of the identifications made by the original burial crews. The positive identification of skeletal remains of the eleven officers and two civilians exhumed from the site for reburial elsewhere is also questionable. This is particularly true in the case of George Custer's exhumation, where the description of the grave and its contents are at odds with the account of the original burial.

Chapter 10

Nonhuman Vertebrate Faunal Remains from Custer Battlefield National Monument

By John R. Bozell

INTRODUCTION

This chapter provides a brief consideration of nonhuman vertebrate faunal remains recovered during controlled surface and subsurface investigations carried out at Custer Battlefield National Monument during the 1984 and 1985 field seasons. The project was developed in response to a unique opportunity to examine the present battlefield surface as a result of a fire which destroyed 90 percent of the vegetation within the monument. The project was sponsored by the National Park Service and the Custer Battlefield Historical and Museum Association.

The study was carried out in accordance with National Park Service purchase orders dated November 1984 and July 1985. The Park Service requested that species and element identifications be completed, as well as pertinent analysis and preparation of a report describing the methods and results of the work. Beyond sample description, specific objectives of the project included provision of comments regarding origin of remains, identification of cultural or natural modifications, and identification of present and future research potentials for fauna recovered from the monument.

It is not precisely known how many of the cavalry horses died during the battle; however, it is assumed a majority of the mounts perished with the Seventh Cavalry. Most of these remains were buried about the turn of the century in a mass grave, although some scattered horse bones were either left undetected on the battlefield or have been exposed as a result of erosion. Other events responsible for the composition of the present assemblage include cattle-ranching activities in the area after the battle and the natural death of various local wild mammals and birds, either before or after the battle. More specific lines of evidence regarding these processes will be presented in the results and concluding sections of the report.

Table 29 Frequency and Weight Information for Nonhuman Vertebrate Remains
Recovered from Custer Battlefield National Monument, Montana, 1984 Season

Field-Specimen Number	Total Number (Burned)	Total Weight-Grams (Burned)
2	1	<1
3	4	1
8	13(2)	1277(617)
13	1(1)	4(4)
25	6(6)	344(344)
32	1(1)	9(9)
42	16(16)	1797(1797)
43	10(10)	430(430)
44	8(8)	577(577)
47	1(1)	128(128)
48	1(1)	218(218)
335	1	2
353	2	35
355	1	1
427	1(1)	36(36)
440	1	13
484	8(8)	62(62)
522	1	23
524	1	20
529	4(4)	625(625)
531	1(1)	95(95)
608	35	10
617	1(1)	121(121)
619	1(1)	65(65)
621	5	396
624	3	52
635	1(1)	27(27)

METHODOLOGY

The collection was submitted to the author packaged by individual provenience bags labeled with field-specimen numbers.

Material from each provenience bag was independently counted and weighed, with the charred portion also tabulated. Potentially identifiable specimens were separated from the unidentifiable debris during preliminary frequency and weight tabulation. Several specimens were in poor condition, displaying various degrees of surficial cracking and abrasion. These elements were stabilized for identification by gluing together loose pieces. No additional chemical treatment was implemented.

A specimen was considered identifiable if it could be allocated to the family level or below and the element, side, and portion determined. Identifications were completed primarily through comparison with vertebrate collections curated by the Nebraska State Historical Society and the author. Several specimens required verification through examination of more extensive collections maintained by the Midwest Archeological Cen-

Table 29 *continued*

Field-Specimen Number	Total Number (Burned)	Total Weight-Grams (Burned)
642	23(11)	870(238)
668	2(2)	218(218)
669	4(4)	181(181)
683	1	1
730	1	4
783	1	38
851	1(1)	11(11)
905	1	124
907	4	19
1041	1	<1
1055	1	<1
1065	4	3
1142	1	51
1163	6(5)	236(221)
1180	1(1)	550(550)
1208	1(1)	63(63)
1230	1	2
1237	2(2)	8(8)
1253	1	1
1255	1(1)	258(258)
1351	1(1)	281(281)
1352	1(1)	337(337)
1360	1	1
1567	10(10)	57(57)
1587	1	311
Total	201(103)	9993(7578)

ter. None of the available collections contains a complete horse skeleton; therefore, consultation of pertinent osteological manuals was deemed necessary for some of the equid remains (Sisson and Grossman 1953; Brown and Gustafson 1979). Additionally, identification of osteologically similar taxa, particularly anetlope/deer and cattle/bison, was accomplished through a combination of visual inspections of the comparative collections and consultation of published diagnostic criteria (Lawrence 1968; Olsen 1960).

Each identification was recorded on index cards which contained the following information categories: field-specimen number, taxon, element, side/portion, and comment. The comment entry was reserved for recording evidence of a variety of traits, such as charring, animal gnawing, butcher marks, and pathology, as well as general age category (fetal/neonate, immature, etc.).

Minimum number of individuals (MNI) estimates were figured for each identified taxon as a means of further characterizing the relative proportion of various animals scattered across the surface of the monument. MNI calculations were completed using the standard method of determining the element, side, and portion that occurs in the greatest frequency for a given taxon (Chaplin 1971:69–75).

All sorting, identification, and tabulation, as well as preparation of the report, were completed by the author.

ANALYSIS OF THE 1984 SAMPLE

The total 1984 nonhuman vertebrate collection is comprised of 201 specimens weighing 9.9 kilograms. (21.95 pounds). The sample is almost entirely mammal, a single bird element being the only exception. Bone debris was collected from fifty-two surface provenience units. The sample size from each location ranges between 1 and 35 specimens with a mean of 3.87. By weight, more than 75 percent of the sample exhibits some degree of burning or charring, likely a result of the fire which burned off a large portion of the grass within the monument. Frequency, weight, and field-specimen number information is provided in table 29.

The identified portion of the sample includes eighty-eight specimens. While this figure is only 43.8 percent of the total sample by count, it reflects more than 90 percent by weight. Essentially the entire collection is identifiable with the exception of more than a hundred very small, heavily fragmented bone splinters, many of which likely are derived from larger identified pieces.

Table 30 Summary of Identified Nonhuman Vertebrate Remains
Recovered from Custer Battlefield National Monument, Montana, 1984 Season

Taxon	Number	(MNI)*	% of total	(MNI)
Tetraonidae (grouse/prairie chicken)	1	(1)	1.14	(7.69)
Sylvilagus sp. (cottontail)	1	(1)	1.14	(7.69)
Lepus townsendii (white-tailed jackrabbit)	4	(1)	4.55	(7.69)
Equus caballus (horse)	21	(2)**	23.86	(15.38)
Odocoileus sp. (deer)	5	(1)	5.68	(7.69)
Antilocapra americana (pronghorn)	4	(1)	4.55	(7.69)
Odocoileus/Antilocapra (deer or pronghorn)	1	(1)	1.14	(7.69)
Bos taurus (cattle)	50	(4)***	56.82	(30.77)
cf. *Bison bison* (bison)	1	(1)	1.14	(7.69)
Total	88	(13)	100.02	(100.0)

*Minimum number of individuals
**MNI based on two left articulated tarsal units and right distal tibiae.
***MNI based on three adult left metatarsals and fetal/neonatal remains.

Identified Remains

The eighty-eight identified elements represent nine taxonomic groupings identified to the family level or below (table 30). The identified portion is dominated by horse and cattle remains which contribute 23.86 percent and 56.82 percent, respectively, of the combined total.

In general, the identified sample can be characterized as being in a good to excellent state of preservation. However, fifteen elements are heavily eroded on the outer surfaces, a characteristic diagnostic of exposure to sunlight, moisture, and temperature changes. In addition, nineteen elements exhibit evidence of gnawing, largely by carnivores and, to a lesser degree, rodents.

Additional taxon-specific comments organized by family are presented below. All element identifications are presented in table 31.

Tetraonidae (Grouse/Prairie Chicken)

A single element was allocated to this avian family. The element is fragmented, precluding definitive specific identification. However, based on the rather small size and known ranges (Johnsgard 1975), the specimen is probably *Pedioecetes phasianellus* (sharp-tailed grouse). Another possibility is *Tympanuchus cupido* (prairie chicken); however, the Monument is situated nearly two hundred miles west of the documented range (Johnsgard 1975:54).

Leporidae (Rabbit)

Two species of leporids were recovered from the battlefield surface. One *Sylvilagus* (cottontail) element could represent either *S. nuttalli* (mountain cottontail) or *S. auduboni* (desert cottontail) based on range maps (Burt and Grossenheider 1976:208–10). The remainder of the sample is comprised of large elements clearly within the size range of jackrabbit, of which *Lepus townsendii* (white-tailed) is the only representative native to southeastern Montana (Burt and Grossenheider 1976:204–6). One *Lepus* element is charred.

Equidae (Horse)

Twenty-one *Equus caballus* (horse) bones were identified from the sample and probably hold the most significance for the present study of material recovered during 1984 investigations. Based on standard MNI estimates, at least two individuals are represented. It should be kept in mind that the horse remains were both eroding from the so-called horse cemetery and scattered at various locations on the battlefield and in all probability reflect more than two animals. Two articulating tarsal sections were recovered, as were other remains.

Heavy surficial erosion is more common on horse bones than those from any other taxon. More than 40 percent of the equid remains display this characteristic, suggesting long-term exposure to natural elements. While all horse bones exhibit erosion or flaking to some degree, some are very well preserved, indicating burial within a relatively short

Table 31 Taxonomic and Element Identifications for Nonhuman Vertebrate Remains Recovered from Custer Battlefield National Monument, Montana, 1984 Season

Field-Specimen Number	Taxon	Element	Side/Portion	Comment
3	*Bos taurus*	cranium	complete occipital parietal, temporal, and frontal	heavily eroded; immature
		maxilla	right posterior (PM4/-M3/)	
		molar 2/ (?)	right complete	fragmented
25		femur	left complete	epiphyses unfused; charred
		metacarpal, 1st phalanges, and 2nd phalanges	right articulating unit	carnivore gnawed on proximal metacarpal and distal 2nd phalanges; charred; metacarpal epiphysis unfused
32		fibular tarsal	right proximal epiphysis	unfused; charred
42	*Odocoileus* sp.	humerus, ulna, and radius	left articulating unit	ulna carnivore gnawed; radius distal epiphysis unfused; all charred
	Bos taurus	non-specific lumbar vertebra	complete	articular surfaces unfused; charred
		humerus	left complete	charred
		fused radius-ulna	left complete	charred
		ulnar carpal	left complete	charred
		metacarpal	left complete	charred
		2nd phalange	unsided complete	charred
		lumbar vertebra (1–6)	left lateral articulating unit	carnivore gnawed on most processes, all charred and sawn through saggital plane
44	cf. *Bison bison*	radius	left posterial diaphysis	heavily eroded; charred
	Bos taurus	tibia, metatarsal	left articulating unit	fetal/neonatal; charred
		tibia, metatarsal	right articulating unit	carnivore gnawed; epiphyses unfused; charred
		fibular tarsal	right complete	epiphysis unfused; charred

No.	Species	Element	Portion	Comments
47		metatarsal	left proximal	heavily eroded; immature; charred
48	*Equus caballus*	metacarpal	left complete	charred
353		central + 4th tarsal, 2nd + 3rd tarsal	left articulating unit	
355	*Odocoileus/ Antilocapra*	ilium	right posterior	heavily eroded
427	*Equus caballus*	humerus	right distal medial	heavily eroded; charred
484	*Antilocapra americana*	humerus, ulna, radius	left articulating unit	charred
522	*Bos taurus*	non-specific rib	unsided shaft segment	sawn on both ends
524	cf. *Odocoileus* sp.	femur	right anterior diaphysis	pathological bone growth on lateral surface; carnivore gnawed
529	*Equus caballus*	metatarsal	left complete	epiphysis of fibular tarsal unfused; charred
531	*Bos taurus*	fibular tarsal, tibia tarsal, 2nd + 3rd tarsal	left articulating unit	distal epiphysis unfused; charred
		metacarpal	right complete	immature; carnivore gnawed; charred; cut marks on shaft
		tibia	left diaphysis segment	carnivore gnawed on proximal surface; charred
619	*Antilocapra americana*	tibia	left complete	
621	*Bos taurus*	metatarsal	left complete	
		2nd phalange (2)	unsided complete	
		3rd phalange	unsided complete	
		3rd phalange	unsided complete	
		distal sesamoid	unsided complete	
624		1st phalange	unsided complete	epiphysis unfused; charred
635	*Equus caballus*	radius	right proximal medial	charred
642		radius	right distal	heavily eroded
		metacarpal	right distal	heavily eroded; charred
		tibia	left proximal posterior	heavily eroded; charred
		tibia	right distal	heavily eroded
		fibular tarsal	right complete	heavily eroded
		1st phalange	unsided distal	heavily eroded
		2nd phalange	unsided complete	heavily eroded

Table 31 *continued*

Field-Specimen Number	Taxon	Element	Side/Portion	Comment
668	*Bos taurus*	2nd phalange	unsided complete	charred
		metatarsal, 2nd + 3rd tarsal	left articulating unit	rodent gnawed and cut marks on anterior surface; epiphysis unfused; charred
669		femur	left distal	epiphysis unfused
		tibia	left proximal	epiphysis unfused; charred; sawn along transverse plane
783	*Equus caballus*	acetabulum	left superior	
851	*Bos taurus*	intermediate carpal	left complete	charred
905	*Equus caballus*	ilium	right anterior	
907	*Bos taurus*	premaxilla	right complete	
1055	Tetraonidae	carpometacarpus	right proximal	
1065	*Lepus townsendii*	humerus	right distal	charred
		fibular tarsal	left complete	
		fibular tarsal	right complete	
		central + 4th tarsal	left complete	
1142	*Bos taurus*	ulna	right complete	carnivore gnawed on proximal surface; proximal epiphysis unfused
1163		os coxae	right/left complete	immature; carnivore gnawed; charred
1180	*Equus caballus*	scapula	right complete	charred
1208	*Bos taurus*	scapula	right distal blade fragment	charred
1253	*Sylvilagus* sp.	mandible	right anterior	
1255	*Bos taurus*	radius	right complete	heavily eroded; distal epiphysis unfused; charred
1351	*Equus caballus*	tibia	right distal posterior and diaphysis	heavily eroded; charred
1352		metatarsal	left complete	heavily eroded; charred
1567	*Odocoileus* sp.	metacarpal	left complete	heavily eroded; epiphysis unfused; charred
1587	*Bos taurus*	tibia	right proximal	

period of time, probably following the battle, or possibly a more recent twentieth-century origin.

Additional characteristics recorded for the horse sample include: charring (two), carnivore gnawing (one), unfused epiphysis (one), and pathological bone growth (one). The unfused epiphysis appears to represent a young adult individual and not a colt. The pathology does not appear to be the result of an injury received during the battle but, rather, is comprised of calcium deposits and a lesion on the anterior shaft of a metatarsal. This trait is believed to be quite typical for both active cavalry and Indian horses (personal commentary Dr. E. O. Dickinson, Veterinary Diagnostic Center, UNL).

Cervidae (Deer and Allies)

Five *Odocoileus* elements were collected, and three of these make up an articulating forelimb unit. The sample is much too limited to attempt more specific identification of the material as either *O. virginianus* (white-tailed deer) or *O. hemionus* (mule deer). Both have present and historic ranges throughout southern Montana (Jones et al. 1983: 320–27).

Characteristics of the deer sample include: charring (two), carnivore gnawing (one), heavy erosion (one), and immature elements (two).

Antilocapridae (Antilocaprids)

Antilocapra americana (pronghorn antelope) is the only representative of this family with a distribution in North America and is relatively common across many regions of eastern Montana (Burt and Grossenheider 1976: 222–223). Only four pronghorn elements were recovered, and three of these form an articulating forelimb unit. All four elements are charred, and one displays evidence of gnawing by carnivores.

One additional ilium fragment was collected and appears to be a pronghorn, although the possibility of deer could not be eliminated because of the eroded nature of the specimen.

Bovidae (Bovids)

The bovid sample is dominated by *Bos taurus* (cattle), which constitutes 56.82 percent of the combined 1984 identified portion. Fifty elements were recovered which represent at least four animals and probably more, based on available MNI estimations.

The cattle sample is very well preserved, with significant erosion recorded for only three fragments, indicating relatively recent origins. Charring (thirty-eight) and gnawing by rodents or carnivores (sixteen) is fairly common. Evidence of butchering was noted on ten elements, including a complete lumbar vertebra series sawn through the sagittal plane, as well as saw marks on rib shafts and a tibia diaphysis and smaller cut marks on tibia and metatarsal diaphyses. Microscopic examination indicates cut marks were produced by a knife as opposed to a saw or cleaver (Walker and Long 1977). Butchering marks probably reflect both initial carcass dismemberment as well as division of smaller meat cuts, such as spare ribs or soup and stew portions. Twenty-two bones are from immature individuals. No systematic steps were taken to order these remains by age group; however, the sample appears to reflect a wide age structure, including mature, young adult, juvenile, and fetal/neonatal.

One bovid element is considerably larger and less well preserved than the cattle remains and is tentatively identified as *Bison bison* (bison). The bone is charred.

ANALYSIS OF THE 1985 SAMPLE

The 1985 sample is limited to 101 specimens weighing one and one-tenth kilograms. All materials are mammalian and were recovered from twenty surface or subsurface provenience units. The sample size from each provenience ranged from one to twenty-seven bones, with a mean of four and nine-tenths. In contrast to the frequently charred 1984 materials, none of the 1985 pieces display this characteristic. Frequency and weight information is inventoried by catalog number in table 32.

IDENTIFIED REMAINS

The identified portion of the sample includes twenty-eight specimens representing four taxa (table 33). In general, the identified sample is in a good to excellent state of pres-

Table 32 Frequency and Weight Information for Nonhuman Vertebrate Remains Recovered from Custer Battlefield National Monument, Montana, 1985 Season

Field-Specimen Number	Number	Weight (grams)
2614	4	287
2775	5	7
2834B	3	3
2892	3	92
2962A	1	85
2963	3	39
2965B	8	5
2973B	1	4
2980B	27	63
3067	1	59
3092A	3	34
3093A	1	1
4814B	4	4
4827	7	26
4891	1	21
4892	1	67
4898A	1	19
4898B	1	70
4974	1	194
5094	25	6
Total	101	1086

Table 33 Summary of Identified Nonhuman Vertebrate Remains
Recovered from Custer Battlefield National Monument, Montana, 1985 Season

Taxon	Number (MNI)*	% of Total	(MNI)*
Sylvilagus sp. (cottontail)	9 (1)	32.1	(20)
Thomomys talpoides (northern pocket gopher)	4 (1)	14.3	(20)
Equus caballus (horse or mule)	10 (1)	35.7	(20)
Bos taurus (cattle)	5 (2)	17.9	(40)
Total	28 (5)	100.0	(100.0)

*Minimum number of individuals

Table 34 Taxonomic and Element Identifications for Nonhuman Vertebrate Remains
from Custer Battlefield National Monument, Montana, 1985 Season

Field-Specimen Number	Taxon	Element	Side/Portion	Comment
2614	*Bos taurus*	metacarpal	right complete	
		carpal 2 + 3	right complete	one articulating unit
		carpal 4	right complete	
		radial carpal	right complete	
2892	*Equus caballus*	ischium	left complete	
2962A		1st phalange	left complete	
2963		ulna	right proximal	heavily eroded
2980B		non-specific cervical	articular process	
		rib	left medial	
3067		2nd phalange	left complete	heavily eroded
4891		tarsal 4	right complete	heavily eroded
4892		2nd phalange	left complete	heavily eroded
4898A		intermediate carpal	left complete	heavily eroded; carnivore gnawing
4898B		patella	left complete	heavily eroded
4974	*Bos taurus*	metacarpal	right complete	distal epiphysis unfused
5094	*Sylvilagus* sp.	tibia	left proximal	
		tibia	left distal	
		fibular tarsal	left complete	
		tarsal 4 + 5	left complete	
		metatarsal II	left complete	one articulating unit
		metatarsal III	left complete	
		metatarsal IV	left complete	
		1st phalange	left complete	
		1st phalange	left complete	
	Thomomys talpoides	maxilla	anterior	
		mandible	left anterior	
		mandible	right anterior	
		tibia	right complete	

ervation; however, six bones display heavy erosion. Taxon specific comments are provided below, and all element identifications are inventoried in table 34.

Sylvilagus sp. (Cottontail)

Nine cottontail elements representing one animal were recovered from a single provenience unit. The sample represents a single left rear leg articulating unit. The remains could represent either *S. nuttalli* (mountain cottontail) or *S. auduboni* (desert cottontail), based on range maps (Burt and Grossenheider 1976: 208–10). A single *Sylvilagus* element was recovered from the surface during the 1984 season. All recovered rabbit specimens are believed to be present as the result of natural causes. The remains were recovered during the test excavation at Square E in the Calhoun position. Only non-human bone was found at this location.

Thomomys talpoides (Northern Pocket Gopher)

Four pocket-gopher elements, representing one individual, were recovered from the same provenience as the cottontail materials. Pocket gophers are a common resident of the area, and these remains are believed to be of recent origin.

Equus caballus (Horse or Mule)

Ten elements from eight provenience units were identified as horse or mule. A variety of body parts is represented, including: vertebra (one), rib (one), ulna (one), carpal (one), first phalange (one), second phalange (two), pelvis (one), patella (one), and tarsal (one). Six bones are heavily eroded and one has been subjected to gnawing by a canid-sized carnivore. No battle-related injuries were observed. An MNI of one was calculated for the horse sample; however, the spatial distribtuion of remains would suggest at least two different individuals are represented. One group (FS4891, 4892, 4898A, 4898B), probably representing one individual, was found in the excavation at Square P on Last Stand Hill. The other group (FS2892, 2962A, 2963, 2980B, 3067) are all from individual locations in the barricade and hospital areas of the Reno-Benteen defense site. These remains could represent several different individuals. Several unidentified elements found in the same area and in association with battle-related artifacts could be *Equus*. These unidentified elements are FS2775, associated with a horseshoe; FS2834b, associated with a .45/55 bullet; FS3093, also associated with a .45/55 bullet; and FS4814, which was associated with a .45/55 cartridge case. Several of the horse bones are relatively small, suggesting they may be either pack mules or Indian ponies as opposed to cavalry mounts. The location of the horse bones at Last Stand Hill and the Reno-Benteen defense site barricade area plausibly argues for an army association.

Bos taurus (Cattle)

Five cow bones were recovered from two provenience units and represent two individuals, based on right complete metacarpals. Four of the elements form a partial proximal metacarpal-carpal articulating unit. As with the 1984 materials, it is assumed the cattle remains are related to ranching activities probably associated with the surrounding Crow Indian Reservation (Rickey 1958:4).

DISCUSSION

The final section of this report offers comments which may be useful in evaluating the overall significance of the vertebrate sample.

Origin of the Sample

Processes relating to the origin of the assemblage can be grouped into three generalized categories: natural deaths, cattle ranching, and the battle.

Much of the fauna is assumed to be present as a result of natural causes. This is particularly applicable to the grouse/ prairie chicken, cottontail, jackrabbit, deer, and antelope remains, which are common residents of the area (Rickey 1958:4). All of these forms may have died within the battlefield area as a result of disease, old age, or predation by other animals. Most bones of these taxa are fairly well preserved in relation to the horse sample, indicating recent deaths perhaps during the past several years.

All of the cattle bone is probably related to ranching operations, and much of it may be directly associated with the surrounding Crow Indian Reservation. Rickey (1958:4) states: "Following the destruction of the buffalo herds, great numbers of long horn cattle were grazed here." However, Rickey also notes that the battlefield was fenced in 1891, which suggests that cattle grazing within the monument was not on a large-scale basis but probably was limited to occasional strays wandering through downed fences. The presence of a fairly high percentage of butchered remains may, on the other hand, suggest that cattle were being slaughtered and processed within the monument by army personnel superintending the national cemetery.

The horse remains are assumed to be present as a result of the battle; however, the precise historical location and number of horses killed, as well as definition of Indian or cavalry horses, is difficult to determine. Several eyewitness accounts and other information may shed some light on the nature of the present horse sample. There are several accounts which testify to the fact that some cavalry horses were driven off by the Indians.

According to the Hunkpapa leader, Gall, "the warriors directed a special fire against the troopers [of I and L] who held the horses while the others fought." When a holder fell, the Indians moved in and drove the horses away. This "made it impossible for the soldiers to escape." Some Cheyennes who watched from a point southeast of the battle ridge also acknowledged that this happened. Kate Bighead saw "lots of Indians running toward the end of the ridge, and the soldier horses there were running away" [Greene 1979:37].

This account refers to action which took place in the Deep Coulee vicinity east of the battlefield proper. To the west, where Custer and Companies I and F were killed (Last Stand Hill), it appears as if most of the horses also died. Greene (1979) provides some pertinent information:

As the gray horse company was being wiped out, the troopers remaining on Custer's hill faced dangerous odds, too. The warriors edged closer, still arching their arrows to strike the men and animals without revealing their own positions. With the dead horses the soldiers hastily improvised barricades against bullets fired by Indians situated 200 yards directly west of the ridge [Greene 1979:42].

After the engagement, the remains of dead horses scattered across the battlefield were left in place, while the human remains were hastily buried in shallow graves (Rickey 1958:36). Approximately one year later, in the spring and summer of 1877, a reburial and recovery expedition was organized. Photographs taken in 1879 depict the horses fully decomposed and subject to dismemberment and scattering by scavengers (see photograph in Greene 1979:50). It was about 1881 or possibly later in the nineteenth century that horse skeletal debris was collected and massed in a trench northwest of the memorial shaft erected in 1881. It is obvious that not all the skeletal remains were collected, however, given the material noted by Greene (1979) and recovered during the 1984–85 project.

Greene (1979) also provides a map of the battlefield showing the location of the battle debris collected during National Park Service and private operations before 1973. The figures shows scattered horse remains were picked up on Last Stand Hill, the Calhoun position, the Deep Ravine area, the Keogh area, Nye-Cartwright Ridge, and the Reno-Benteen defense site.

The spatial distribution of the archaeologically recovered horse remains corresponds to the distribution of battle-related artifacts. The horse bones found on the Custer battlefield, with one exception, were in direct association with other battle-related artifacts and in areas historically noted as combat sites. The distribution of archaeological horse bone is similar to those casually collected bones noted by Greene (1979). The Calhoun position is represented by two eroded and charred leg and foot bones (FS1351, 1352). The Keogh area is represented by two widely separated leg and foot bones (FS3533, 427). The distance between the elements (nearly 250 meters) suggests at least two different animals are represented. One horse pelvic fragment (FS905) was found near the mouth of Deep Ravine not far from a horseshoe (FS943). The horses killed on Last Stand Hill are represented by one individual found in the excavations at Square P85 (FS4891, 4892, 4898a,b). Other horse remains were found in the barricade and hospital area of the Reno-Benteen defense site as was discussed earlier.

Horses that died in Indian positions may be represented by FS642, found near the knoll northeast of Last Stand Hill; FS783, found one hundred meters west of the South Skirmish Line; and FS1180, which was found about three hundred meters northwest of the South Skirmish Line. Whether these remains represent Indian ponies killed during the battle or errent cavalry mounts cannot be definitively stated at this time. The wide separation of the units does suggest that three different horses are represented.

The only horse remains not associated with battle remains are FS529. This group of bones, representing at least one left leg, was found eroding out of the so-called horse cemetery. It is assumed these remains were among those deposited here during the battlefield cleanup.

The bone elements recovered archaeologically suggest that a minimum of three individual horses should be represented if the spatial distribution is not considered. Taking spatial distribution into account, at least nine different horses are likely to be represented. At least eight would be represented on the Custer battlefield and at least one at the Reno-Benteen defense site. In all probability, more horses actually are represented, but definitive data to support this conclusion are not available.

References Cited

Allen, Nathan
  1869 Physical Culture in Amherst College. Vital Statistics 74.

Allen, William A.
  1903 *Adventures with Indians and Game*. Chicago: A. W. Bowen.

Altman, P. L., and D. S. Dittmer (eds.)
  1963 Growth including reproduction and morphological development. *TDR # AMRL-TDR-63-2*. Wright-Patterson Air Force Base, Ohio: Biomedical Laboratory, Areospace Medical Division, Air Force Systems Command.

Anderson, Adrienne
  1968 The Archeology of Massed-produced Footwear. *Historical Archeology* 2:56–65.

Anonymous
  1979 Ammunition Boxes. *Haversack* 1(4).

Arnold, Ralph E.
  1974 U.S. Cavalry Carbine Slings. *Gun Report* 19(9):16–22.

Baillie, G. H.
  1929 *Watches: Their History, Decoration, and Mechanisms*. London: Methuen and Co.

Balducci, E.
  1903 *Archeological Zoology Italy* 1:375.

Barnes, Frank C.
  1969 *Cartridges of the World*. Chicago: Follett Publishing Co.

Baxter, J. H.
  1875 Statistics—medical and anthropological of the Provost-Marshal-General's Bureau derived from records of the examination for military service in the armies of the United States during the late War of Rebellion over a million recruits, drafted men, substitutes, and enrolled men. Washington, D.C.: Government Printing Office.

Berge, Dale L.
  1980 Simpson Springs Station Historical Archaeology in Western Utah. *Cultural Resource Series 6*, Bureau of Land Management, Salt Lake City, Utah.

Bray, Robert T.
  1958 A Report of Archeological Investigations at the Reno-Benteen Site, Custer Battlefield National Monument. MS on file in Midwest Archeological Center, Lincoln, Nebr.

Brinkerhoff, Sidney B.

1972   Metal Uniform Insignia of the Frontier U.S. Army, 1846–1902. *Museum Monograph* 3, Arizona Historical Society.

1976   Boots and Shoes of the Frontier Soldier, 1865–1893. *Museum Monograph* 7, Arizona Historical Society.

Brininstool, E. A.

1952   *Troopers with Custer: Historic Incidents of the Battle of the Little Bighorn.* Harrisburg Pa.: Stackpole.

Brown, Christopher L., and Carl E. Gustafson

1979   A Key to postcranial skeletal remains of the cattle/bison, elk, and horse. *Reports of Investigations* No. 57. Washington State University Laboratory of Anthropology.

Bozell, John R.

1985   Non-Human Vertebrate Faunal Remains Recovered During 1984 Surface Collections at the Custer Battlefield National Monument, Montana. MS on file in Midwest Archeological Center, Lincoln, Nebr.

Burt, William H., and Richard P. Grossenheider

1976   *A Field Guide to the Mammals.* Boston: Houghton Mifflin.

Campbell, Hannah

1964   *Why Did They Name It?* New York: Fleet Publishing Co.

Carroll, John (ed.)

1974   *The Benteen-Goldin Letters on Custer and His Last Battle.* New York: Liveright.

1982   *Custer's Chief of Scouts: The Reminiscences of Charles A. Varnum.* Lincoln: University of Nebraska Press.

1987   *They Rode with Custer.* Bryan, Tex.: J. M. Carroll.

Chaplin, Raymond E.

1971   *The Study of Animal Bones from Archeological Sites.* New York: Seminar Press.

Chappell, Gordon

1972   The Search for the Well-dressed Soldier 1865–1890. *Museum Monograph* No. 5, Arizona Historical Society.

Carrington, Henry B.

1973   *The Indian Question.* New York: Sol Lewis.

Chief of Ordnance

1873   Report of the Secretary of War. House Executive Documents, 43d Congress, 1st session, Part 2, Washington, D.C.

Churchill, E.

1970   Anthropometry of U.S. Army aviators—1970. *Technical Report 75-52-CE.* Natick, Mass.: U.S. Army Laboratories.

Connell, Evan S.

1984   *Son of the Morning Star: Custer and the Little Bighorn.* San Francisco: North Star Press.

Coolidge, Richard H.

1856   Statistical Report on Sickness and Mortality of the Army of the United States Compiled from the Records of the Surgeons General's Office Embracing a Period of Sixteen Years from January 1839 to January 1855. Washington, D.C.: Office of the Surgeon General.

Crouch, Daniel J.

1978   Archaeological Investigations of the Kiowa and Comache Indian Agency and Commissaries 34-Cm-232. Lawton, Okla.: Contributions of the Museum of the Great Plains, Number 7.

Davenport, C. B., and A. G. Love

1921   Army anthropometry. Washington, D.C.: Government Printing Office.

De Haan, John D.

1983   Homicide with a Black Powder Handgun. *Journal of Forensic Sciences* 28(2):468–81.

Dorion, Robert B. J.

1983   Photographic Superimposition. *Journal of Forensic Sciences* 28(3):724–34.

Dorsey, R. Stephen

1983   *American Military Belts and Related Equipment.* Union City, Tenn.: Pioneer Press.

Downey, Fairfax
1971 *Indian Fighting Army*. Fort Collins, Colo.: Old Army Press.
DuMont, John S.
1974 *Custer Battle Guns*. Fort Collins, Colo.: Old Army Press.
Dustin, Fred
1936 *The Custer Fight*. Hollywood, Calif.: privately published.
1953 Some Aftermath of the Little Bighorn Fight in 1876: The Burial of the Dead. In W. A. Graham. *The Custer Myth*, pp. 362–72 New York: Bonanza Books.
Dutton, C. E.
1877 Report to Chief of Ordnance, 14 January 1877. Record Group 156, National Archives, Washington, D.C.
Dyer, Gwynne
1985 *War*. New York: Crown Publishers.
Engagés
1971 Trade Fire Steels. *Museum of the Fur Trade Quarterly* 7(4):2–4.
Everett, John P.
1930 Bullets, Boots, and Saddles. *Sunshine Magazine* 11(1):1–10.
Flayderman, Norm
1980 *Flayderman's Guide to Antique American Firearms and Their Values*. Northfield, Ill.: DBI Books.
Fontana, Bernard L., and J. Cameron Greenleaf
1962 Johnny Ward's Ranch, A Study in Historic Archaeology. *Kiva* 28(1–2).
Forsyth, G. A.
1878 Report to Lieut. Gen. P. H. Sheridan. In W. A. Graham (ed.) *The Custer Myth*. New York: Bonanza Books.
Fox, Richard A., Jr.
1983 1983 Archeological Investigations at Custer Battlefield National Monument. MS on file at Custer Battlefield National Monument, Crow Agency.
1984 Suggestions for Archaeological Investigations at Custer Battlefield National Monument. MS on file Custer Battlefield National Monument, Crow Agency.
Gibbon, John
1877 Last Summer's Expedition Against the Sioux. *American Catholic Quarterly Review* 2(1): 271–304.
1899 Hunting Sitting Bull. *American Catholic Quarterly Review* 11(3):619–639.
Gillio, David, Frances Levine, and Douglas Scott
1980 Some Common Artifacts Found at Historical Sites. *Cultural Resources Report* 31, Southwestern Region, U.S. Forest Service, Albuquerque, N. Mex.
Gluckman, Arcadi
1956 *United States Martial Pistols and Revolvers*. New York: Bonanza Books.
1965 *Identifying Old U.S. Muskets, Rifles, and Carbines*. New York: Bonanza Books.
Godfrey, E. S.
1892 Custer's Last Battle. *Century Illustrated Monthly Magazine*. Reprint. San Francisco: General Headquarters, U.S. Army, 1932.
Goldin, Theodore W.
1928 Finding the Bodies of the Slain. *Winners of the West* 6(1).
Gould, Richard A.
1983 The Archaeolgy of War: Wrecks of the Spanish Armada of 1588 and the Battle of Britain, 1940. In Richard A. Gould (ed.), *Shipwreck Anthropology*. Albuquerque: University of New Mexico Press.
Graham, Ron, John A. Kopec, and C. Kenneth Moore
1976 *A Study of the Colt Single Action Army Revolver*. Dallas, Tex.: Taylor Publishing.
Graham, W. A.
1953 *The Custer Myth: A Source Book of Custeriana*. New York: Bonanza Books.
Gray, John S.
1976 *Centennial Campaign: The Sioux War of 1876*. Fort Collins, Colo.: Old Army Press.

Greene, Jerome A.
    1979   *Evidence and the Custer Enigma: A Reconstruction of Indian-Military History*. Reno, Nev.: Outbooks.
Gregory, T., and J. G. Rogerson
    1984   Metal-detecting in Archeological Excavation. *Antiquity* 58(224):179–84.
Hackley, F. W., W. H. Woodin, and Eugene L. Scranton
    1967   *History of Modern U.S. Military Small Arms Ammunition*. New York: Macmillan.
Hammer, Kenneth
    1976   *Men with Custer*. Fort Collins, Colo.: Old Army Press.
Hans, Frederick M.
    1907   *The Great Sioux Nation*. Chicago: M. A. Donahue and Co.
Hanson, Charles E. Jr.
    1987   Butcher Knives. *Museum of the Fur Trade Quarterly* 23(3):1–5.
Hanson, James
    1972   Upper Missouri Arrow Points. *Museum of the Fur Trade Quarterly* 8(4):2–8.
    1975   *Metal Weapons, Tools, and Ornaments of the Teton Dakota Indians*. Lincoln: University of Nebraska Press.
Hardorff, R. Dutch
    1984   Burials, Exhumations and Reinterments: A View from Custer Hill. In *Custer and His Times*, Book 2. New York: Little Bighorn Associates.
    1985   *Markers, Artifacts, and Indian Testimony: Preliminary Findings on the Custer Battle*. Short Hills, N.J.: W. D. Horn.
Harmon, Dick
    1987   Henry .44-Caliber. In *Archeaeological Insights to the Custer Battle* by Douglas D. Scott and Richard A. Fox Jr. Norman: University of Oklahoma Press.
Harris, C. E.
    1980   Sherlock Holmes Would Be Impressed. *American Rifleman* 128(5):36–39, 82.
Hatcher, Julian, Frank J. Jury, and Jac Weller
    1977   *Firearms Investigation, Identification, and Evidence*. Harrisburg, Pa.: Stackpole Books.
Hedren, Paul L.
    1973   Carbine Extraction Failure at the Little Big Horn: A New Examination. *Military Collector and Historian* 25(2):66–68.
Herskovitz, Robert M.
    1978   Fort Bowie Material Culture. *Anthropological Papers of the University of Arizona* 31.
Hertzberg, H. T. E.
    1954   Anthropometry of Flying Personnel. *Technical Report 52–321*. Wright Patterson Air Force Base, Ohio: Wright Air Development Center.
Heski, Thomas M.
    1978   *Icastinyaka Cikala Hanzi, the Little Shadow Catcher*. Seattle: Superior.
Hoyem, George A.
    1981   *Historical Development of Small Arms Ammunition*. Vol 1. Tacoma, Wash.: Armory Publications.
    1982   *Historical Development of Small Arms Ammunition*. Vol. 2. Tacoma, Wash.: Armory Publications.
Hutchins, James S.
    1956   The Cavalry Campaign Outfit at the Little Bighorn. *Military Collector and Historian* 10(4):91–101.
    1958   7th Cavalry 1876. *Military Collector and Historian*. 12(4):108–10.
    1976   *Boots and Saddles at the Little Bighorn*. Fort Collins, Colo.: Old Army Press.
Johnsgard, Paul A.
    1975   *North American Game Birds of Upland and Shoreline*. Lincoln: University of Nebraska Press.
Jones, J. Know, David M. Armstrong, Robert S. Hoffman, and Clyde Jones
    1983   *Mammals of the Northern Great Plains*. Lincoln: University of Nebraska Press.
Kelly, Luther S.
    1926   *Memoirs of Luther S. Kelly*. edited by M. M. Quaife. New Haven, Conn.: Yale University Press.

King, W. Kent
1980   Tombstones for Bluecoats: New Insights into the Custer Mystery. Marion Station, Calif.: Privately published by the author.
Kinzer, James B.
1983   The Invention of the Extractor: The Successful Winchester Repeating Rifle. *Gun Report* 28(8).
Klenaris, N. S., and Tadao Furue
1980   Photographic Superimposition in Dental Identification. Is a Picture Worth a Thousand Words? *Journal of Forensic Sciences* 25(4):859–65.
Krogman, Wilton Marion
1962   *The Human Skeleton in Forensic Medicine*. Springfield, Ill.: Charles C. Thomas.
Kuhlman, Charles
1951   *Legend into History*. Harrisburg, Pa.: Stackpole Books.
Lawrence, Barbara
1968   Post-cranial Skeletal Characters of Deer, Pronghorn, and Sheep-Goat with Notes on Bos and Bison. *Reports of the Awatovi Expedition*, No. 4. Harvard University Peabody Museum.
Lewis, Berkeley R.
1956   Small Arms and Ammunition in the United States Service, 1776–1865. *Smithsonian Miscellaneous Collections* 129. Washington, D.C.: Smithsonian Institution.
1972   Small Arms Ammunition at the International Exposition Philadelphia, 1876. *Smithsonian Studies In History and Technology* 11. Washington, D.C.: Smithsonian Institution.
Lewis, Kenneth E.
1984   *The American Frontier: An Archeological Study of Settlement Pattern and Process*. New York: Academic Press.
Logan, Herschal C.
1959   *Cartridges*. New York: Bonanza Books.
Madis, George
1979   *The Winchester Book*. Brownsboro, Tex.: Art and Reference House.
Magnussen, Daniel O.
1974   *Peter Thompson's Narrative of the Little Bighorn Campaign 1876*. Glendale, Calif.: Arthur H. Clark.
Mallery, Garrick
1893   Picture Writing of the American Indians. *Tenth Annual Report of the Bureau of Ethnology*. Washington, D.C.: Smithsonian Institution.
Marcot, Roy M.
1983   *Spencer Repeating Firearms*. Irvine, Calif.: Northwood Heritage Press.
Marquis, Thomas B.
1931   *Wooden Leg; A Warrior Who Fought Custer*. Lincoln: University of Nebraska Press.
1976   *Keep the Last Bullet for Yourself*. Algonac, Mich.: Reference Publications.
McClernand, Edward J.
1927   With the Indians and Buffalo in Montana. *Cavalry Journal* 36:7–54.
McDougall, Thomas M.
1909   Letter to Edward Godfrey May 18, 1909. On file manuscript room New York Public Library.
McDowell, R. Bruce
1984   *Development of the Henry Cartridge*. Metuchen, N.J.: A.M.B.
McKee, W. Reid, and M. E. Mason Jr.
1980   *Civil War Projectiles II: Small Arms and Field Artillery*. Orange, Va.: Moss Publications.
McLeod, K. David
1985   Metal Detecting and Archaeology: An Example from EbLf- 12. *Manitoba Archaeological Quarterly* 9(2):20–31.
Michaelis, O. E.
1876   Report to Chief of Ordnance 3 October 1876. Record Group 156, National Archives, Washington, D.C.
Miles, Nelson A.
1897   *Personal Recollections and Observations*. New York: Werner.

Morris, Gruig
   1979   Sampling in the Excavation of Urban Sites: The Cure at Hv'anaco Pumpa. In James W. Muller
           (ed.), *Sampling Archeology*. Tuscon: University of Arizona Press.
Neal, Robert J., and Roy G. Jinks
   1966   *Smith and Wesson 1857–1945*. New York: A. S. Barnes.
Neihardt, John G.
   1961   *Black Elk Speaks*. Lincoln: University of Nebraska Press.
Nelson, Lee H.
   1968   Nail Chronology as an Aid to Dating Old Buildings. *History News* 24(11).
Nichols, Ronald H. (ed.)
   1983   Reno Court of Inquiry. Costa Mesa, Calif.: Privately printed.
Noel Hume, Ivor
   1969   *Historical Archaeology*. New York: Alfred Knopf.
Office of the Surgeon General
   n.d.   Height and weight data for men inducted into the Army and for rejected men. *Report no.
           1-BM*. Washington, D.C.: Office of the Surgeon General, Medical Statistic Division.
Olsen, Stanley J.
   1960   Post-cranial Skeletal Characters of *Bison* and *Bos*. *Papers of the Peabody Museum of Archeology and
           Ethnology* 35(4), Harvard University.
Palmer, Robert G.
   1975   White Handled Revolvers. *By Valor at Arms* 2(1):28–33.
Parsons, John E.
   1955   *The First Winchester*. New York: William Morrow.
Powell, Peter J.
   1969   *Sweet Medicine*. Norman: University of Oklahoma Press.
Quartermaster
   1877   U.S. Army Wagon Harness (Horse and Mule). Washington, D.C.: Government Printing
           Office.
Reedstrom, Ernest L.
   1977   *Bugles, Banners, and War Bonnets*. New York: Bonanza Books.
Rickey, Don, Jr.
   1958   Administrative History of Custer Battlefield National Monument Crow Agency Montana. MS
           on file in Custer Battlefield National Monument, Crow Agency.
   1967   *History of Custer Battlefield*. Billings, Mont.: Custer Battlefield Historical and Museum
           Association.
Reno, Marcus
   1876   *Army-Navy Journal* 5(26):1–2.
Rock, James T.
   1984   Cans in the Countryside. *Historical Archeology* 18(2):97–110.
Russell, Carl P.
   1967   *Firearms, Traps, and Tools of the Mountain Men*. New York: Alfred A. Knopf.
Scott, Douglas D.
   1972   The Nordenskiold Campsite: A Test in Historical Archeology. *The Kiva* 37(3):128–40.
   1973   The Archaeology of Fort Larned National Historic Site, Kansas. Unpublished master's thesis,
           Department of Anthropology, University of Colorado, Boulder.
   1977   Historical Fact Versus Archaeological Reality. Unpublished Ph.D. dissertation, Department of
           Anthropology, University of Colorado, Boulder.
   1984   Archeological Research Design for Custer Battlefield National Monument. MS on file in Mid-
           west Archeological Center, Lincoln, Nebr.
   1985   Archeological Research Design for Custer Battlefield National Monument. MS on file in Mid-
           west Archeological Center, Lincoln, Nebr.
Scott, Douglas D., and Richard A. Fox Jr.
   1987   *Archaeological Insights into the Custer Battle: A Preliminary Assessment*. Norman: University of
           Oklahoma Press.

Sellers, Frank
  1978   *Sharps Firearms*. North Hollywood, Calif.: Beinfield Publishing Co.
Shugart, Cooksey, and Tom Engle
  1984   *American Pocket Watches*. Cleveland, Tenn.: Overstreet Publications.
Sisson, Septimus, and James D. Grossman
  1953   *The Anatomy of Domestic Animals*. Philadelphia: W. B. Saunders.
South, Stanley
  1977   *Method and Theory in Historical Archeology*. New York: Academic Press.
Spencer, Jerry D.
  1983   George Armstrong Custer and the Battle of the Little Bighorn: Homicide or Mass Suicide?
          Journal of Forensic Sciences 28(3):756–61.
Spivey, Towana (ed.)
  1979   A Historical Guide to Wagon Hardware and Blacksmith Supplies. *Contributions of the Museum
          of the Great Plains* 9, Lawton, Okla.
Stands in Timber, John, and Margot Liberty
  1972   *Cheyenne Memories*. Lincoln: University of Nebraska Press.
Steffen, Randy
  1973   *United States Military Saddles, 1812–1943*. Norman: University of Oklahoma Press.
  1978   *The Horse Soldier, 1776–1943:* Volume 2, *The Frontier, The Mexican War, the Civil War, the
          Indian Wars, 1851–1880*. Norman: University of Oklahoma Press.
Stewart, Edgar I.
  1955   *Custer's Luck*. Norman: University of Oklahoma Press.
  1972   The Custer Battle and Widows Weeds. *Montana Magazine* Winter.
Strahler, A. N.
  1957   Quantitative Analysis of Watershed Geomorphology. *American Geophysical Union Transactions*
          38:914.
Sylvia, Stephen W. and Michael O'Donnell
  1983   *Civil War Canteens*. Orange, Va.: Moss Publications.
Taunton, Francis B.
  1980   A Scene of Sickening, Ghastly Horror: The Custer Battlefield—27th and 28th June 1876. In
          Barry C. Johnson, ed., *Ho, for the Great West*, pp 107–32. London: Eatome.
  1986   *Custer's Field: "A Scene of Sickening Horror."* London: Johnson-Taunton Military Press.
Todd, Frederick P.
  1974   *American Military Equipage, 1851–1872*. Providence, R.I.: Company of Military Historians.
Toulouse, Julian H.
  1971   *Bottle Makers and Their Marks*. New York: Thomas Nelson.
Tripler, Charles S.
  1866   Manual for the Examination of Recruits. Washington D.C.: Government Printing Office.
Trotter, M., and G. C. Gleser
  1958   A Re-evaluation of Estimation of Stature Based on Measurements of Stature Taken During Life
          and of Long Bones After Death. *American Journal of Physical Anthropology* 16:79–123.
Utley, Robert
  1969   *Custer Battlefield National Monument, Montana*. Washington, D.C.: Office of Publications, Na-
          tional Park Service.
  1972   *The Reno Court of Inquiry: The Chicago Times Account*. Fort Collins, Colo.: Old Army Press.
  1980   *Custer and the Great Controversy*. Pasadena, Calif.: Westernlore Press.
Vestal, Stanley
  1932   *Sitting Bull, Champion of the Sioux: A Biography*. Norman: University of Oklahoma Press.
Wagner, Glendolin Damon
  1973   *Old Neutriment*. New York: Sol Lewis.
Walker, Phillip L., and Jeffery C. Long
  1977   An Experimental Study of the Morphological Characteristics of Tool Marks. *American Antiquity*
          42(4):605–10.

War Department
    1871   *A Report of Surgical Cases Treated in the Army of the United States from 1865 to 1871.* Cicrular
            3, Washington, D.C.: Surgeon General's Office.
    1874   Cavalry Equipment, 1874. Ordnance Memoranda, No. 18, Washington, D.C.
    1875   Comparison of "Lined" with "Wad" Carbine Cartridges.
            Ordnance Notes, No. 43, Washington, D.C.
    1879   Ordnance Notes, No. 115. Washington, D.C.
Webb Associates
    1978   Anthropometric Source Book, Volume II: A Handbook of anthropometric data. *NASA Reference
            Publication 1924.* Houston, Tex.: National Aeronautics and Space Administration, Scientific and
            Technical Office
Weibert, Henry
    1986   *Sixty-six Years in Custer's Shadow.* Billings, Mont.: Privately published by the author.
Wheeler, H. W.
    1923   *Buffalo Days.* Indianapolis, Ind.: Bobbs-Merrill.
White, R. M., and E. Churchill
    1971   The Body Size of Soldiers: U.S. Army Anthropometry—1966. *Technical Report 72-51-CE,*
            Natick, Mass.: U.S. Army Natick Laboratories.
Whittaker, Frederick A.
    1876   *Life of Maj. Gen. George A. Custer.* New York: Lippincott.
Williamson, Harold F.
    1952   *Winchester: The Gun That Won the West.* New York: A. S. Barnes.

Index

DATE			